INTRODUCTION TO AI AND MACHINE LEARNING

INTRODUCTION TO AI AND MACHINE LEARNING

Dr. Munesh Chandra Trivedi
Mr. Ankit Srivastava

KHANNA BOOK PUBLISHING CO. (P) LTD.
Publisher of Engineering and Computer Books
4C/4344, Ansari Road, Darya Ganj, New Delhi-110002
Phone : 011-23244447-48 **Mobile:** +91-9910909320
E-mail : contact@khannabooks.com
Website : www.khannabooks.com

Dear Readers,

To prevent the piracy, this book is secured with HIGH SECURITY HOLOGRAM on the front title cover. In case you don't find the hologram on the front cover title, please write us to at contact@khannabooks.com or whatsapp us at +91-99109 09320 and avail special gift voucher for yourself.

Specimen of Hologram on front Cover title:

Moreover, there is a SPECIAL DISCOUNT COUPON for you with EVERY HOLOGRAM.

How to avail this SPECIAL DISCOUNT:

Step 1: Scratch the hologram
Step 2: Under the scratch area, your "coupon code" is available
Step 3: Logon to www.khannabooks.com
Step 4: Use your "coupon code" in the shopping cart and get your copy at a special discount
Step 5: Enjoy your reading!

Thanks,
Khanna Publishing House

Price: ₹ 495.00

ISBN: 978-93-5538-688-5

Introduction to AI and Machine Learning
by Dr. Munesh Chandra Trivedi,
Ankit Srivastava

First Edition: 2025

To view complete list of books, please scan the QR Code:

Published by:
Khanna Book Publishing Co. (P) Ltd.
CIN: U22110DL1998PTC095547

Visit us at: www.khannabooks.com
Write us at: contact@khannabooks.com

Printed in Bharat.

Preface

Welcome to "Introduction to AI and Machine Learning." This book is designed to serve as a comprehensive guide for anyone interested in diving into the fascinating and rapidly evolving fields of artificial intelligence (AI) and machine learning (ML). Whether you are a student, educator, professional, or enthusiast, this book aims to provide you with a solid foundation and practical knowledge in these areas.

The journey of AI and ML began decades ago, and today, these technologies are at the forefront of innovation, transforming industries and everyday life. From healthcare and finance to marketing and technology, AI and ML are driving advancements that were once the realm of science fiction. This book seeks to demystify these technologies, making them accessible and understandable, even for those with no prior background in the field.

Our goal is to equip you with the fundamental concepts and tools needed to understand and implement AI and ML solutions. Through detailed explanations, real-world applications, and hands-on exercises, you will gain a deep understanding of how these technologies work and how they can be applied to solve complex problems. Python, one of the most popular programming languages for AI and ML, will be our primary tool for practical exercises and coding examples.

In addition to technical knowledge, this book also addresses the ethical considerations and societal impacts of AI and ML. As these technologies continue to evolve, it is crucial to think critically about their implications and ensure they are developed and used responsibly.

We also look ahead to the future of AI and ML, exploring emerging trends and potential developments that promise to shape the world in the coming years. By understanding the current state and future direction of these fields, you will be better prepared to navigate and contribute to this exciting landscape.

We hope this book inspires you to explore the possibilities of AI and ML and provides you with the skills and confidence to embark on your own journey in these transformative fields.

—Author

Contents

Contents

1

Artificial Intelligence

HOW DO WE DEFINE ARTIFICIAL INTELLIGENCE [AI?]

AI is a technique that facilitates a machine to perform all cognitive functions such as perceiving, learning and reasoning that are otherwise performed by humans.

"The Science and Engineering of making intelligent machines, especially intelligent Computer programs is Artificial intelligence" –JOHN MC CARTHY [Father of AI]

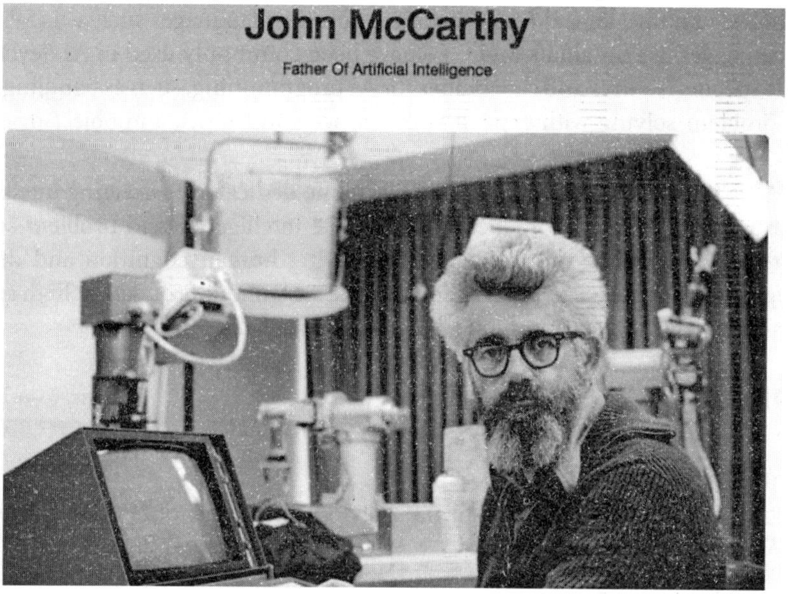

The yardstick to achieve true AI still seems decades away. Computers execute certain tasks way better than humans e.g.: Sorting, computing, memorizing, indexing, finding patterns etc. While identifying of emotions, recognising faces, communication and conversation are unbeatable human skills. This is where AI will play a crucial role to enable machines achieving equalling human capabilities.

WHAT IS AI?

AI is a field of study that focuses on enabling machines to solve complex problems using approaches inspired by human intelligence. By incorporating human-like characteristics and implementing them in computer algorithms, AI aims to replicate intelligent behavior. The level of flexibility and efficiency in AI methods can vary depending on specific requirements, which determines the extent to which the machine's behavior appears genuinely intelligent.

Artificial intelligence (AI) encompasses the development of machines and computer programs that exhibit intelligent behavior. This intelligence is aimed at mimicking human-like capabilities and problem-solving approaches. One important aspect of AI is the ability to pass the Turing test, which means that a computer's responses are indistinguishable from human responses.

From the perspective of intelligence, AI focuses on creating machines that can reason, learn, and make decisions similar to humans. This involves incorporating knowledge and expertise in specific domains to enable effective problem-solving. By leveraging relevant information and constraints, AI systems can tackle complex tasks and provide intelligent solutions.

In the business realm, AI is regarded as a set of powerful tools and methodologies for addressing various business challenges. It offers innovative approaches and technologies that can enhance decision-making processes, automate tasks, optimize operations, and improve overall efficiency and productivity.

From a programming standpoint, AI involves the study of symbolic programming, problem-solving techniques, and search algorithms. Unlike traditional numerical processing, AI programs manipulate symbols and utilize logical reasoning. Programming languages such as LISP, PROLOG, and object-oriented languages like Smalltalk and C++ have been commonly used in AI development. These languages provide specific features and capabilities for AI programming, such as handling heterogeneous lists, declarative problem-solving with explicit search space constraints, and object-oriented modeling and inheritance.

In essence, AI is the science and engineering discipline dedicated to creating intelligent machines and computer programs. It strives to replicate human-like intelligence and problem-solving abilities, aiming to understand and utilize the principles underlying human cognition and decision-making processes. Through AI, computers can process and analyze vast amounts of data at high speeds, enabling advanced problem-solving and decision support across various fields.

HISTORY OF AI

In 1950's

The modern-day AI got impetus since 50s of the previous centuries, once Alan Turning introduced "Turning Test" for assessment of intelligence.

In 1955

John McCarthy known as the founder of Artificial Intelligence introduced the term 'Artificial Intelligence'. McCarthy along with Alan Turing, Allen Newell, Herbert A. Simon, and Marvin Minsky too has the greatest contribution to present day machine intelligence. Alan suggested that if humans use accessible information, as well as reason, to solve problems to make decisions – then why can't it be done with the help of machines?

In 1970's

70's saw an upsurge of computer era. These machines were much quicker, affordable and stowed more information. They had an amazing character to think abstract, could self-recognize and accomplished natural language processing.

In 1980's

These were the years that saw flow of funds for research and algorithmic tools. The learning skills were enhanced and computers improved with deeper user experience.

In 2000's

Many unsuccessful attempts, Alas! The technology was successfully established by years 2000.The milestones were realised, that needed to be accomplished. AI could somehow manage to thrive despite lack of government funds and public appreciation.

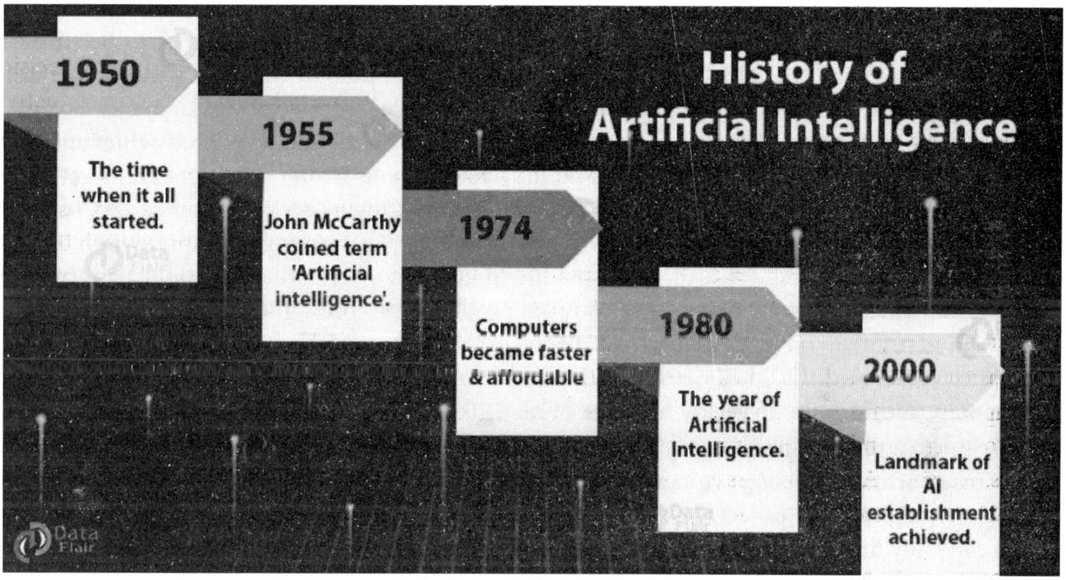

Fig. 1.1. Image Source: www.data-flair.com

WEAK AND STRONG AI

Weak AI: Weak AI, also known as narrow AI or applied AI, refers to AI systems that are designed to perform specific tasks or functions within a limited domain. These systems are focused on solving specific problems and do not possess general intelligence or consciousness. Weak AI is designed to simulate human-like intelligence in a particular area, but it is not capable of surpassing human capabilities or understanding beyond its programmed scope. Examples of weak AI include virtual assistants like Siri or Alexa, recommendation systems, and image recognition algorithms. It focuses on developing AI systems that are designed to perform specific tasks and simulate certain aspects of human intelligence without actually possessing true consciousness or general intelligence. Advocates of weak AI acknowledge that while computers can be programmed to exhibit intelligent behavior in specific domains, they do not possess true understanding or consciousness like humans. Weak AI views AI systems as powerful tools that can augment human capabilities and perform tasks more efficiently than humans in certain areas. Weak AI systems are designed to solve well-defined problems within a limited scope. These systems are trained or programmed to perform specific tasks, such as language translation, image recognition, or playing chess. While they may exhibit impressive performance in their specialized domain, they lack the broader cognitive abilities and awareness associated with human intelligence. A common example of weak AI is a chess program that can play chess at a high level but lacks the general intelligence and understanding that humans possess. Despite their impressive performance in specific tasks, weak AI systems are not considered truly "intelligent" or capable of independent thinking.

In summary, weak AI recognizes the limitations of current AI technologies and focuses on developing specialized systems that can mimic human intelligence in narrow domains, but without achieving true consciousness or general intelligence. Weak AI systems are valuable tools for solving specific problems and augmenting human capabilities but fall short of exhibiting human-like understanding or true cognitive abilities.

Strong AI: Strong AI, also known as artificial general intelligence (AGI) or human-level AI, refers to AI systems that exhibit intelligence and cognitive abilities at a level that is equal to or surpasses human intelligence. Strong AI aims to replicate the full range of human cognitive abilities, including understanding, reasoning, learning, and adapting to new situations across various domains. Strong AI would be capable of performing any intellectual task that a human can do. However, achieving strong AI remains an ongoing research challenge, and no fully autonomous strong AI system exists yet. strong AI holds the promise of developing machines that can exhibit human-level intelligence and reasoning capabilities. Advocates of strong AI argue that by appropriately programming a computer with the right algorithms and cognitive architectures, it is possible to create a system that possesses true cognitive abilities and can effectively reason and solve complex problems. According to the proponents of strong AI, a well-programmed computer is not just a tool or a mimicry of human intelligence, but it can genuinely possess a mind. They believe that such AI systems can understand, learn, make decisions, and exhibit consciousness similar to that of humans.

John Searle, a philosopher of mind, coined the term "strong AI" to describe the hypothesis that certain forms of artificial intelligence can genuinely understand and have mental states. Searle is known for his thought experiment called the "Chinese Room" argument, which challenges the claim that a computer can truly understand language or possess true intelligence.

It's important to note that the terms "weak" and "strong" do not imply the quality or effectiveness of AI systems. Weak AI systems can be highly sophisticated and perform specific tasks with great accuracy, while strong AI represents a more ambitious goal of creating human-level intelligence in machines. The distinction between weak and strong AI helps us understand the current capabilities of AI systems and highlights the ongoing pursuit of achieving higher levels of artificial intelligence.

Importance of AI

Artificial intelligence (AI) holds significant importance in various aspects of modern society and continues to shape our world in numerous ways. Here are some key reasons why AI is important:

1. **Healthcare:**
   (*i*) **Medical diagnosis:** AI algorithms are trained on large datasets of medical images to detect patterns and abnormalities that may indicate diseases. They can assist radiologists in interpreting X-rays, MRIs, and other medical images, leading to faster and more accurate diagnoses.

(*ii*) **Drug discovery:** AI is used to analyze vast amounts of biomedical data, including genetic information, molecular structures, and clinical trial results. By identifying patterns and relationships, AI can accelerate the process of discovering new drugs and treatments.

(*iii*) **Personalized medicine:** AI algorithms analyze patient data, including medical records, genomic information, and lifestyle factors, to provide tailored treatment plans. AI can predict individual patient outcomes and recommend personalized interventions.

2. **Finance:**

(*i*) **Fraud detection:** AI systems analyze large volumes of financial data in real-time to identify patterns and anomalies that indicate fraudulent activities. By continuously monitoring transactions, AI can detect suspicious behavior and trigger alerts for further investigation.

(*ii*) **Risk assessment:** AI models analyze historical financial data, market trends, and other relevant factors to assess creditworthiness, determine insurance premiums, and evaluate investment risks. This helps financial institutions make informed decisions and manage risks.

(*iii*) **Algorithmic trading:** AI algorithms analyze market data, news feeds, and historical patterns to make high-speed trading decisions. By leveraging complex algorithms and predictive models, AI can optimize trading strategies and improve investment returns.

3. **Manufacturing:**

(*i*) **Quality control:** AI-powered systems use computer vision and machine learning to inspect products on the assembly line for defects or inconsistencies. They can detect imperfections that may be missed by human inspectors, ensuring high-quality standards.

(*ii*) **Predictive maintenance:** AI algorithms analyze sensor data from machinery and equipment to predict potential failures or maintenance needs. By detecting early signs of malfunction, AI helps optimize maintenance schedules, reduce downtime, and prevent costly breakdowns.

(*iii*) **Supply chain optimization:** AI analyzes complex supply chain data, including inventory levels, production schedules, and customer demand patterns. By optimizing these factors, AI enables efficient inventory management, streamlined logistics, and improved customer satisfaction.

4. **Retail and E-commerce:**

(*i*) **Customer personalization:** AI algorithms analyze customer data, including browsing history, purchase behavior, and demographics, to provide personalized product recommendations and targeted marketing campaigns. This enhances the customer experience and increases sales.

(*ii*) **Inventory management:** AI systems analyze sales data, market trends, and external factors to optimize inventory levels. By accurately predicting demand, AI helps retailers prevent stockouts, reduce excess inventory, and minimize costs.

(*iii*) **Chatbots and virtual assistants:** AI-powered chatbots use natural language processing (NLP) to understand and respond to customer queries and provide assistance in real-time. They can help customers with product inquiries, support requests, and order tracking, improving customer service and reducing the workload on human agents.

5. **Transportation and Logistics:**

(*i*) **Autonomous vehicles:** AI enables self-driving cars, trucks, and drones by combining sensors, computer vision, and machine learning. AI algorithms process real-time data to perceive the environment, make driving decisions, and navigate safely without human intervention.

(*ii*) **Route optimization:** AI algorithms analyze historical and real-time traffic data, weather conditions, and delivery constraints to optimize transportation routes. This improves fuel efficiency, reduces delivery times, and minimizes transportation costs.

(*iii*) **Demand forecasting:** AI models analyze historical sales data, market trends, and external factors to predict future demand for transportation and logistics services. Accurate demand forecasting helps optimize resource allocation and planning.

6. **Cybersecurity:**

(*i*) **Threat detection:** AI systems use machine learning algorithms to analyze network traffic, identify patterns, and detect anomalies that may indicate cyber threats. By continuously monitoring network activities, AI helps identify and mitigate potential security breaches.

(*ii*) **Anomaly detection:** AI algorithms analyze user behavior, system logs, and access patterns to detect abnormal activities that may indicate insider threats or unauthorized access. AI can alert security teams and trigger appropriate actions to prevent data breaches.

(*iii*) **Data encryption and protection:** AI research is focused on developing advanced encryption algorithms and privacy-preserving techniques to secure sensitive data. AI can also assist in monitoring and analyzing security vulnerabilities in software systems, enhancing overall cybersecurity measures.

These explanations highlight the specific applications of AI in each area and the benefits they bring to industries and society as a whole. AI is transforming these domains by automating tasks, improving decision-making, enhancing efficiency, and enabling new possibilities for innovation. Overall, the importance of AI lies in its ability to augment human capabilities, automate tasks, drive innovation, and provide solutions to complex problems across diverse domains, leading to significant societal and economic benefits.

What are an AI Techniques

AI techniques refer to the various methods and approaches used in the field of artificial intelligence to enable machines to exhibit intelligent behavior, perform tasks, and solve problems. These techniques are designed to mimic or simulate certain aspects of human intelligence and enable machines to reason, learn, perceive, and make decisions.

Intelligence relies on knowledge, but knowledge itself possesses certain characteristics that may not be desirable in the context of artificial intelligence. These characteristics include:

Voluminous: Knowledge can be extensive and vast, making it challenging to manage and process effectively.

Difficult to Characterize: Knowledge may be complex and difficult to accurately represent and describe in a comprehensive manner.

Constantly Changing: Knowledge is not static; it evolves and updates over time as new information becomes available or circumstances change.

Organized for Application: Unlike raw data, knowledge is organized and structured in a way that aligns with its intended application or domain.

To address these challenges, AI techniques leverage knowledge that is represented in a specific manner, allowing for the following advantages:

Generalizations and Grouping: The knowledge representation captures generalizations, identifying common properties and grouping similar situations together rather than treating them separately.

Understandable by Humans: The knowledge can be understood and provided by human experts or domain specialists who have expertise in the specific domain. The representation is designed to be comprehensible to humans while being acceptable for the AI program.

Easy Modification: The represented knowledge can be easily modified and updated to correct errors or incorporate changes in real-world conditions, ensuring the AI system remains adaptable and up-to-date.

Utility despite Incompleteness or Inaccuracy: The knowledge representation can still be valuable and useful even if it is incomplete or not entirely accurate. It can provide valuable insights and help narrow down the range of possibilities to be considered.

By leveraging AI techniques that harness and manipulate knowledge in these ways, the limitations associated with voluminous, dynamic, and complex knowledge can be addressed, making it a valuable resource for intelligent systems

AI techniques can be broadly categorized into two main categories: symbolic AI and computational intelligence.

Symbolic AI: Symbolic AI, also known as knowledge-based AI, focuses on developing systems that rely on explicit knowledge representation and logical reasoning. It involves the use of symbols, rules, and logic to represent and manipulate knowledge. Symbolic AI techniques include expert systems, rule-based systems, knowledge graphs, and ontologies. These systems excel at representing explicit domain knowledge and performing logical inference and deduction.

Expert Systems: Expert systems are computer programs that emulate the decision-making ability of a human expert in a specific domain. They encode expert knowledge in the form of rules or if-then statements to provide intelligent recommendations or solutions to complex problems. Expert systems are built using a knowledge base, which contains factual information and a set of rules derived from experts in a specific domain. The inference engine of an expert system applies these rules to the given input data or user queries to generate intelligent responses or recommendations. Expert systems are widely used in fields such as medicine, finance, and engineering for tasks like diagnosis, decision support, and troubleshooting.

Rule-Based Systems: Rule-based systems use a set of predefined rules to make inferences or decisions. These rules typically take the form of logical statements, such as "if condition A is true, then action B should be taken." Rule-based systems are widely used in areas such as diagnostics, monitoring, and decision support systems. Rule-based systems rely on a collection of rules that describe relationships between conditions and actions. Each rule consists of an antecedent (conditions) and a consequent (actions). When the conditions of a rule are satisfied, the corresponding actions are executed. Rule-based systems are effective in capturing domain expertise and providing transparent decision-making processes.

Knowledge Graphs: Knowledge graphs represent knowledge as a network of interconnected entities and their relationships. They provide a structured way to organize and represent domain knowledge, allowing for efficient knowledge retrieval and reasoning. Knowledge graphs represent knowledge as entities (nodes) connected by relationships (edges). They provide a graph-based structure to capture and organize complex knowledge. Knowledge graphs enable efficient querying, reasoning, and discovery of new insights by traversing the graph structure. They are used in various applications like recommendation systems, semantic search, and knowledge representation.

Ontologies: Ontologies define a common vocabulary and a set of rules for representing and organizing knowledge within a specific domain. They capture the hierarchical relationships and semantic meanings of concepts, facilitating knowledge sharing and interoperability among different systems. Ontologies are formal representations of knowledge in a specific domain. They define the concepts, relationships, and constraints within the domain. Ontologies enable shared understanding and semantic interoperability between different systems. They are commonly used in areas such as semantic web, information integration, and intelligent search.

Natural Language Processing (NLP): NLP techniques enable computers to understand and process human language. They involve tasks such as text parsing, sentiment analysis, named entity recognition, and question answering systems. NLP plays a crucial role in extracting knowledge from unstructured textual data. NLP techniques enable computers to understand and process human language. They involve tasks such as parsing, semantic analysis, sentiment analysis, and language generation. NLP techniques utilize techniques like machine learning, deep learning, and linguistic rule-based approaches to extract meaning from text or speech data.

Automated Reasoning: Automated reasoning techniques aim to derive new knowledge or conclusions from existing knowledge using logical inference and deduction. They employ logical reasoning algorithms to analyze and manipulate symbolic representations to solve complex problems. Automated reasoning focuses on developing algorithms and techniques for logical inference and deduction. It aims to derive new knowledge or conclusions from existing knowledge using logical rules and deduction mechanisms. Automated reasoning is used in theorem proving, logical programming, and problem-solving tasks that require logical reasoning.

Semantic Web: The Semantic Web is an extension of the World Wide Web that focuses on enriching web content with machine-readable metadata. It enables computers to understand and reason about the meaning of information, allowing for more intelligent information retrieval and integration. The Semantic Web is an extension of the World Wide Web that adds semantic meaning to web content. It employs standardized languages and protocols (such as RDF, OWL, and SPARQL) to represent, query, and reason about data on the web. The Semantic Web enables machines to understand the context and semantics of information, leading to more intelligent web services and knowledge integration.

These symbolic AI techniques provide a foundation for representing and processing explicit knowledge in a structured manner. They excel in domains where explicit rules and logical reasoning are prevalent, enabling intelligent systems to make informed decisions and provide expert-level recommendations.

Computational Intelligence: Computational intelligence, on the other hand, is inspired by natural systems and aims to develop computational approaches that can mimic or simulate intelligent behavior. It encompasses various techniques that mimic biological or cognitive processes, such as evolutionary computation, artificial neural networks, and fuzzy logic systems.

Evolutionary Computation: Evolutionary computation techniques, such as genetic algorithms, genetic programming, and evolutionary strategies, are inspired by the process of natural evolution. They involve generating and evolving a population of candidate solutions to solve optimization or search problems.

Artificial Neural Networks: Artificial neural networks (ANNs) are computational models inspired by the structure and functioning of biological neural networks. ANNs consist of interconnected nodes (neurons) organized in layers, and they are capable of learning patterns and making predictions or classifications based on training data.

Fuzzy Logic Systems: Fuzzy logic is a mathematical framework that allows for reasoning and decision-making under uncertainty. Fuzzy logic systems capture and manipulate imprecise or uncertain information by assigning degrees of membership to fuzzy sets. They are useful in handling vague or ambiguous data and making approximate or qualitative decisions.

These two categories of AI techniques, symbolic AI and computational intelligence, offer different approaches to problem-solving and knowledge representation. Symbolic AI emphasizes explicit knowledge representation and logical reasoning, while computational intelligence focuses on emulating intelligent behavior through computational models inspired by natural systems. Both approaches have their strengths and are applicable in various domains and problem types.

PROBLEM, PROBLEM SPACES AND SEARCH

To develop a system that can effectively solve a problem, the following steps are typically involved:

1. **Precisely Define the Problem:** Clearly articulate the problem, including its specific requirements, constraints, and desired outcome. This step involves understanding the problem domain, identifying the key variables and parameters, and defining the criteria for an acceptable solution.
2. **Thoroughly Analyze the Problem:** Conduct a comprehensive analysis of the problem to gain insights into its characteristics, complexities, and potential challenges. Identify any relevant patterns, dependencies, or factors that may influence the choice of solution methods. This analysis helps in selecting appropriate techniques and approaches to tackle the problem effectively.
3. **Acquire and Represent Background Knowledge:** Gather the necessary background knowledge and information that is relevant to the problem at hand. This knowledge may include domain-specific expertise, existing theories or models, empirical data, or insights from previous problem-solving experiences. Represent this knowledge in a structured and usable format that can be utilized by the system during the solution process.
4. **Select Problem-Solving Techniques:** Based on the problem analysis and available knowledge, choose the most suitable problem-solving techniques or algorithms to address the problem. This selection involves considering factors such as the problem complexity, available resources, time constraints, and the desired characteristics of the solution. It may involve choosing from a range of AI techniques, such as symbolic AI, computational intelligence, or machine learning, depending on the nature of the problem and available resources.

By following these steps, a systematic approach can be taken to develop a problem-solving system that incorporates precise problem definition, thorough analysis, relevant background knowledge, and appropriate techniques. This helps increase the chances of finding effective solutions to complex problems and achieving the desired outcomes.

Defining the Problem as state Search

Defining the problem as a state search involves formulating a problem in terms of an initial state, a goal state, and a set of possible actions or transitions that can be applied to move from one state to another. The objective is to find a sequence of actions that leads from the initial state to the goal state, effectively navigating the search space. Defining the problem as a state search is an approach used in artificial intelligence to solve problems by modeling them as a search through different states. Let's explore this concept in more detail:

Problem Representation

- Identify the problem you want to solve and define it precisely, including the initial state, goal state, and possible actions or operators that can be applied to transition between states.
- The problem should be decomposed into a set of discrete states that can be explored during the search process.
- States represent different configurations or arrangements that the problem can take.

State Space

- The state space is the set of all possible states that can be reached from the initial state by applying valid actions.
- Each state represents a specific configuration of the problem.
- The state space can be visualized as a graph, with states as nodes and transitions between states as edges.

Search Algorithms

- Select an appropriate search algorithm to traverse the state space and find a path from the initial state to the goal state.
- Different search algorithms have different strategies for exploring the state space, such as breadth-first search (BFS), depth-first search (DFS), A* search, and others.
- The choice of search algorithm depends on factors such as the size of the state space, memory constraints, optimality requirements, and computational resources available.

Heuristics

- Heuristics are domain-specific techniques or rules that guide the search process by providing additional information about the problem.
- Heuristics can be used to estimate the desirability of states, prioritize exploration, or guide the selection of actions.
- A good heuristic can significantly improve the efficiency and effectiveness of the search algorithm.

Search Process

- Start the search from the initial state and apply actions or operators to generate successor states.
- Use the selected search algorithm to determine the order in which states are explored.
- Maintain a data structure, such as a queue or a stack, to keep track of the states yet to be explored.

Continue the search until the goal state is reached or a termination condition is met.

By defining the problem as a state search, you can leverage search algorithms and heuristics to systematically explore the state space and find a solution. This approach is particularly useful for solving problems that can be modeled as a sequence of states and actions, such as route planning, puzzle solving, scheduling, and many other domains.

Here's an example to illustrate the concept

Problem 1. Finding the shortest path from point A to point B on a map.

Define the Problem

- **Initial state:** The starting point A on the map.
- **Goal state:** The destination point B on the map.
- **Actions:** Possible movements from one point to another, such as moving along roads or paths.

Analyze the Problem

- Consider the characteristics of the map, such as the layout, the presence of obstacles or barriers, and the connectivity between different points.
- Identify any constraints or additional requirements, such as avoiding certain areas or considering specific costs associated with different actions.

Represent the Problem as a State Search

- Represent the map as a set of interconnected nodes, where each node corresponds to a location on the map.
- Define the initial state as the starting point A and the goal state as the destination point B.
- Define the actions or transitions as moving from one node (location) to another along valid paths.

Select a Search Algorithm

- Choose an appropriate search algorithm to navigate the state space and find the optimal or satisfactory path from the initial state to the goal state.
- Examples of search algorithms include breadth-first search (BFS), depth-first search (DFS), A* search, or Dijkstra's algorithm.

Execute the Search

- Apply the chosen search algorithm to explore the state space, considering the available actions and transitions.
- Generate a sequence of actions that lead from the initial state to the goal state, taking into account any constraints or requirements.

By defining the problem as a state search and applying appropriate search algorithms, it becomes possible to find optimal or satisfactory solutions for various problems, including route planning, puzzle solving, and resource allocation, among others.

Example: The water jug problem: There are two jugs called four and three; four holds a maximum of four gallons and three a maximum of three gallons. How can we get 2 gallons in the jug four. The state space is a set of ordered pairs giving the number of gallons in the pair of jugs at any time ie (four, three) where four = 0, 1, 2, 3, 4 and three = 0, 1, 2, 3. The start state is (0,0) and the goal state is (2,n) where n is a don't care but is limited to three holding from 0 to 3 gallons. The major production rules for solving this problem are shown below:

To solve the water jug problem where Jug Four has a maximum capacity of four gallons and Jug Three has a maximum capacity of three gallons, with the goal of measuring 2 gallons in Jug Four, we can follow the steps below:

Step 1: Define the problem:

- **Jug Four capacity:** 4 gallons
- **Jug Three capacity:** 3 gallons
- **Target amount:** 2 gallons in Jug Four
- **Initial state:** (0, 0) (both jugs are initially empty)
- **Goal state:** (2, n) (Jug Four contains 2 gallons, n can be any value from 0 to 3 in Jug Three)

Step 2: Actions/Operators:

- **Fill Jug Four:** Fill Jug Four to its maximum capacity of 4 gallons.
- **Fill Jug Three:** Fill Jug Three to its maximum capacity of 3 gallons.
- **Empty Jug Four:** Empty the contents of Jug Four.
- **Empty Jug Three:** Empty the contents of Jug Three.
- **Pour water from Jug Four to Jug Three:** Pour water from Jug Four into Jug Three until either Jug Three is full or Jug Four is empty.

- **Pour water from Jug Three to Jug Four:** Pour water from Jug Three into Jug Four until either Jug Four is full or Jug Three is empty.

Step 3: Solution with each step:

- **Start with the initial state:** (0, 0)
- **Fill Jug Four:** (4, 0)
- **Pour water from Jug Four to Jug Three until Jug Three is full:** (1, 3)
- **Empty Jug Three:** (1, 0)
- **Pour water from Jug Four to Jug Three until Jug Three is full:** (0, 1)
- **Fill Jug Four:** (4, 1)
- **Pour water from Jug Four to Jug Three until Jug Three is full:** (2, 3)
- **Empty Jug Three:** (2, 0)

Now, Jug Four contains 2 gallons, which is the goal state. The solution steps are as follows:

- Fill Jug Four
- Pour water from Jug Four to Jug Three until Jug Three is full
- Empty Jug Three
- Pour water from Jug Four to Jug Three until Jug Three is full
- Empty Jug Three

Step	State	Action
1	(0, 0)	Initial state
2	(4, 0)	Fill Jug Four
3	(1, 3)	Pour from Jug Four to Jug Three
4	(1, 0)	Empty Jug Three
5	(0, 1)	Pour from Jug Four to Jug Three
6	(4, 1)	Fill Jug Four
7	(2, 3)	Pour from Jug Four to Jug Three
8	(2, 0)	Empty Jug Three

The table shows each step in the solution process, the state of the jugs after each step, and the action performed at that step. Starting from the initial state (0, 0), the actions are executed sequentially until the goal state (2, n) is reached, where n can be any value from 0 to 3 in Jug Three.

Production System

A production system is a type of knowledge representation and problem-solving architecture used in artificial intelligence. It is based on the concept of production rules, which are a set of conditional statements that define actions to be taken in response to certain conditions. A production system consists of a rule base, working memory, and an inference engine. The rule base contains a collection of production rules that encode knowledge about the problem domain. Each rule consists of two parts: a condition (also known as the left-hand side or LHS) and an action (also known as the right-hand side or RHS). The condition specifies a set of conditions or patterns that must match the current state of the system, and the action defines the operations or tasks to be performed if the conditions are satisfied.

The working memory represents the current state of the system or the problem-solving environment. It contains facts or data that can be matched against the conditions in the production rules. The inference engine is responsible for selecting and executing the appropriate production rules based on the current state of the working memory.

The operation of a production system involves a cycle of matching rules against the working memory, selecting applicable rules, executing the actions of those rules, and updating the working memory based on the results of the actions. This cycle continues until a predefined goal or termination condition is met.

Production systems are particularly suited for expert systems, where knowledge is encoded in the form of rules, and the system can make inferences and provide expert-like advice or solutions. They are also used in various other AI applications, including problem-solving, planning, decision-making, and natural language processing. Overall, production systems provide a flexible and modular approach to knowledge representation and problem-solving, allowing for easy modification and extension of the rule base to accommodate new knowledge or problem domains.

Example: An example of a simple production system for a diagnostic expert system:

Rule Base:

1. IF symptom1 = "fever" AND symptom2 = "cough" THEN diagnosis = "common cold"
2. IF symptom1 = "headache" AND symptom2 = "nausea" THEN diagnosis = "migraine"
3. IF symptom1 = "rash" AND symptom2 = "itching" THEN diagnosis = "allergic reaction"
4. IF symptom1 = "fatigue" AND symptom2 = "weight gain" THEN diagnosis = "hypothyroidism"
5. IF symptom1 = "abdominal pain" AND symptom2 = "diarrhea" THEN diagnosis = "gastroenteritis"

Working Memory:

- symptom1 = "fever"
- symptom2 = "cough"

Inference Engine:

1. Match the working memory against the conditions in the rule base.
   - Rule 1 matches the conditions since symptom1 is "fever" and symptom2 is "cough".
2. Execute the action of the matching rule.
   - Set the diagnosis as "common cold".
3. Update the working memory with the results of the action.
   - diagnosis = "common cold"

The production system concludes that the patient's symptoms of fever and cough are indicative of a common cold based on the rule matching and action execution. This is just a simplified example, and in real-world scenarios, a production system can contain a larger rule base with more complex conditions and actions.

The cycle of matching, selecting, executing, and updating continues as new symptoms are provided or additional rules are added to the rule base. The production system allows for efficient problem-solving by using a set of rules to guide the inference process and generate appropriate diagnoses or solutions based on the given inputs.

Control strategies: Control strategies refer to the mechanisms or techniques used to govern the execution and control flow of the system. They determine how rules are selected, applied, and prioritized within the system. Control Strategy decides which rule to apply next during the process of searching for a solution to a problem. Requirements for a good Control Strategy

It should cause motion: In water jug problem, if we apply a simple control strategy of starting each time from the top of rule list and choose the first applicable one, then we will never move towards solution

It should explore the solution space in a systematic manner: If we choose another control strategy, say, choose a rule randomly from the applicable rules then definitely it causes motion and eventually will lead to a solution. But one may arrive to same state several times. This is because control strategy is not systematic.

The breadth-first search algorithm can be applied to solve the water jug problem:

1. **Initialize the search:**
   - Start with the initial state (0, 0) representing both jugs being empty.
   - Create an empty queue to store the states to be explored.
   - Add the initial state to the queue.
2. **Perform the breadth-first search:**
   - **While the queue is not empty:**
     - ❑ Remove the first state from the queue.
     - ❑ Check if the current state matches the goal state (2, n), where n is any value from 0 to 3 for the three-gallon jug.
       - ▪ If it matches, the solution is found. Terminate the search and return the path to the goal state.
     - ❑ Generate all possible next states from the current state by applying the allowed actions:
       - ▪ Fill the four-gallon jug.
       - ▪ Fill the three-gallon jug.
       - ▪ Empty the four-gallon jug.
       - ▪ Empty the three-gallon jug.
       - ▪ Pour water from the four-gallon jug to the three-gallon jug.
       - ▪ Pour water from the three-gallon jug to the four-gallon jug.
     - ❑ Add the generated states to the end of the queue.
3. **Repeat step 2 until a solution is found or the queue becomes empty.**

Here's an example of the breadth-first search process for the water jug problem:

1. **Start:** (0, 0)
2. **Queue:** [(0, 0)]
3. **Remove state from the queue:** (0, 0)
4. **Generate possible next states:**
   (*a*) **Fill four-gallon jug:** (4, 0)
   (*b*) **Fill three-gallon jug:** (0, 3)
   (*c*) **Empty four-gallon jug:** (0, 0)
   (*d*) **Empty three-gallon jug:** (0, 0)
   (*e*) **Pour from four-gallon jug to three-gallon jug:** (1, 3)
   (*f*) **Pour from three-gallon jug to four-gallon jug:** (3, 0)
5. **Add generated states to the queue:** [(4, 0), (0, 3), (0, 0), (0, 0), (1, 3), (3, 0)]
6. Repeat steps 3-5 until the solution is found or the queue is empty.

The breadth-first search algorithm explores all possible states in a breadth-first manner, systematically searching through the state space until the goal state is reached. This ensures that the shortest path to the solution is found. In the case of the water jug problem, the algorithm will find the solution state (2, n) by considering all possible actions and states in a breadth-first manner.

Node Diagram for Water Jug Problem

```
              (0, 0)
               / \
          (4, 0) (0, 3)
           / \    / \
     (1, 3) (4, 3) (0, 0) (0, 3)
        |      |      |
     (1, 0) (4, 2) (0, 2)
        |      |      |
     (0, 1) (4, 1) (0, 1)
           |      |
        (1, 1) (4, 0)
           |
         (2, 1)
```

Explanation:

- Each node represents a state of the jugs, denoted as (four, three), where 'four' represents the gallons in the four-gallon jug and 'three' represents the gallons in the three-gallon jug.
- The initial state is (0, 0) where both jugs are empty.
- The goal state is (2, n), where 'n' can be any value from 0 to 3 for the three-gallon jug.
- The arrows represent the possible actions or transitions between states, which involve pouring water from one jug to another or refilling a jug.
- The BFS algorithm explores the search space level by level, starting from the initial state and expanding all possible successor states before moving to the next level.

Please note that the diagram shows a portion of the search space, and the BFS algorithm would continue exploring other states until it finds the goal state or exhausts all possibilities.

VARIOUS TYPES OF PROBLEMS AND THEIR SOLUTIONS

Missionaries and Carnivals Problem

Definition: In Missionaries and Carnivals Problem, initially there are some missionaries and some carnivals will be at a side of a river. They want to cross the river. But there is only one boat available to cross the river. The capacity of the boat is 2 and no one missionary or no Carnivals can cross the river together. So for solving the problem and to find out the solution on different states is called the Missionaries and Carnival Problem.

Procedure: Let us take an example. Initially a boatman, Grass, Tiger and Goat is present at the left bank of the river and want to cross it. The only boat available is one capable of carrying 2 objects of portions at a time. The condition of safe crossing is that at no time the tiger present with goat, the goat present with the grass at the either side of the river. How they will cross the river?

The objective of the solution is to find the sequence of their transfer from one bank of the river to the other using the boat sailing through the river satisfying these constraints.

Let us use different representations for each of the missionaries and Carnivals as follows.

B: Boat

T: Tiger

G: Goat

Gr: Grass

Step 1: According to the question, this step will be (B, T, G, Gr) as all the Missionaries and the Carnivals are at one side of the bank of the river. Different states from this state can be implemented as

(B, T, G, Gr) Left → (B, T, O, O)X [Condition failed]
(B, T, G, Gr) Left → (B, O, G, O)
(B, T, G, Gr) Left → (B, O, O, Gr)X[Condition failed]
(Right)

`The states (B, T, O, O) and (B, O, O, Gr) will not be countable because at a time the Boatman and the Tiger or the Boatman and grass cannot go. (According to the question).

Step 2: Now consider the current state of step-1 i.e. the state (B, O, G, O). The state is the right side of the river. So on the left side the state may be (B, T, O, Gr)

i.e., (B, O, G, O) → (B, T, O, Gr)
(Right) (Left)

Step 3: Now proceed according to the left and right sides of the river such that the condition of the problem must be satisfied.

(B, T, O, Gr) (Left) → (B, T, G, O)
(B, T, O, Gr) (Left) → (B, O, G, Gr)
(Right)

Step 4: First, consider the first current state on the right side of step 3 i.e.

(B, T, G, O) (Right) → (B, O, O, Gr)X [Condition failed]
(B, T, G, O) (Right) → (B, T, O, Gr)X [Repeatation]
(B, T, G, O) (Right) → (B, O, G, Gr)
(Left)

Now consider the second current state on the right side of step-3 i.e.,

(B, O, G, Gr) (Right) → (B, T, O, O)X [Condition failed]

(B, O, G, Gr) (Right) → (B, T, G, O)

(B, O, G, Gr) (Right) → (B, T, O, Gr)X [Repeatation] (Left)

Step 5: Now first consider the first current state of step 4 i.e.

(B, O, G, Gr) (Left) → (B, T, G, O)X [Repeatation]

(B, O, G, Gr) (Left) → (B, T, O, Gr) (Right)

Now consider the 2nd state of Step-4, i.e.,

(B, T, G, O) (Left) → (B, T, O, Gr)

(B, T, G, O) (Left) → (B, O, G, Gr)X [Repeatation] (Right)

Step 6: Consider the current state of Step-5

(B, T, O, Gr) (Right) ⟶ (B, O, G, O) (Left)

Step 7: From Step-6, the state will be

(B, O, G, O) (Left) ⟶ (B, T, G, Gr) (Right)

Hence the final state will be (B, T, G, Gr) which are on the right side of the river.

Comments:

- This problem requires a lot of space for its state implementation.
- it takes a lot of time to search the goal node.
- The production rules at each level of state are very strict.

Chess Problem

Definition: It is a normal chess game. In a chess problem, the start is the initial configuration of chessboard. The final state is the any board configuration, which is a winning position for any player.

There may be multiple final positions and each board configuration can be thought of as representing a state of the game. Whenever any player moves any piece, it leads to different state of game.

Procedure:

1	2	3
4	5	6
7	8	9

Fig. 1.2. A 3×3 chess board

The above figure shows a 3×3 chessboard with each square labeled with integers 1 to 9. We simply enumerate the alternative moves rather than developing a general move operator because of the reduced size of the problem. Using a predicate called move in predicate calculus, whose parameters are the starting and ending squares, we have described the legal moves on the board. For example, move (1, 8) takes the knight from the upper left-hand corner to the middle of the bottom row. While playing Chess, a knight can move two squares either horizontally or vertically followed by one square in an orthogonal direction as long as it does not move off the board.

The all possible moves of figure are as follows.

Move (1, 8)	Move (6, 1)
Move (1, 6)	Move (6, 7)
Move (2, 9)	Move (7, 2)
Move (2, 7)	Move (7, 6)
Move (3, 4)	Move (8, 3)
Move (3, 8)	Move (8, 1)
Move (4, 1)	Move (9, 2)
Move (4, 3)	Move (9, 4)

The above predicates of the Chess Problem form the knowledge base for this problem. An unification algorithm is used to access the knowledge base.

Suppose we need to find the positions to which the knight can move from a particular location, square 2. The goal move (z, x) unifies with two different predicates in the knowledge base, with the substitutions {7/x} and {9/x}. Given the goal move (2, 3), the responsible is failure, because no move (2, 3) exists in the knowledge base.

Comments:

- In this game a lots of production rules are applied for each move of the square on the chessboard.
- A lots of searching are required in this game.
- Implementation of algorithm in the knowledge base is very important.

8-Queen Problem

Definition: "We have 8 queens and an 8x8 Chess board having alternate black and white squares. The queens are placed on the chessboard. Any queen can attack any other queen placed on same row, or column or diagonal. We have to find the proper placement of queens on the Chess board in such a way that no queen attacks other queen".

		Q					
				Q			
	Q						
							Q
Q							
						Q	
			Q				
					Q		

Procedure: Figure A possible board configuration of 8 queen problem

In figure , the possible board configuration for 8-queen problem has been shown. The board has alternative black and white positions on it. The different positions on the board hold the queens. The production rule for this game is you cannot put the same queens in a same row or same column or in same diagonal. After shifting a single queen from its position on the board, the user have to shift other queens according to the production rule. Starting from the first row on the board the queen of their corresponding row and column are to be moved from their original positions to another position. Finally the player has to be ensured that no rows or columns or diagonals of on the table is same.

Comments:

- This problem requires a lot of space to store the board.
- It requires a lot of searching to reach at the goal state.
- The time factor for each queen's move is very lengthy.
- The problem is very strict towards the production rules.

8-Puzzle Problem

Definition: "It has set off a 3×3 board having 9 block spaces out of which 8 blocks having tiles bearing number from 1 to 8. One space is left blank. The tile adjacent to blank space can move into it. We have to arrange the tiles in a sequence for getting the goal state".

Procedure: The 8-puzzle problem belongs to the category of "sliding block puzzle" type of problem. The 8-puzzle is a square tray in which eight square tiles are placed. The remaining ninth square is uncovered. Each tile in the tray has a number on it. A tile that is adjacent to blank space can be slide into that space. The game consists of a starting position and a specified goal position. The goal is to transform the starting position into the goal position by sliding the tiles around. The control mechanisms for an 8-puzzle solver must keep track of the order in which operations are performed, so that the operations can be undone one at a time if necessary. The objective of the puzzles is to find a sequence of tile movements that leads from a starting configuration to a goal configuration such as two situations given below.

Figure (Starting State) (Goal State)

The state of 8-puzzle is the different permutation of tiles within the frame. The operations are the permissible moves up, down, left, right. Here at each step of the problem a function f(x) will be defined

1	2	3
4	5	6
	7	8

1	2	3
4	5	6
7	8	–

which is the combination of g(x) and h(x). i.e.,

$$f(x) = g(x) + h(x)$$

Where,

g (x): how many steps in the problem you have already done or the current state from the initial state.

h(x): Number of ways through which you can reach at the goal state from the current state or h(x) is the heuristic estimator that compares the current state with the goal state note down how many states are displaced from the initial or the current state. After calculating the f (x) value at each step finally take the smallest f (x) value at every step and choose that as the next current state to get the goal state.

Let us take an example.

Figure (Initial State) (Goal State)

1	2	3
4	5	6

1	2	3
4	8	5

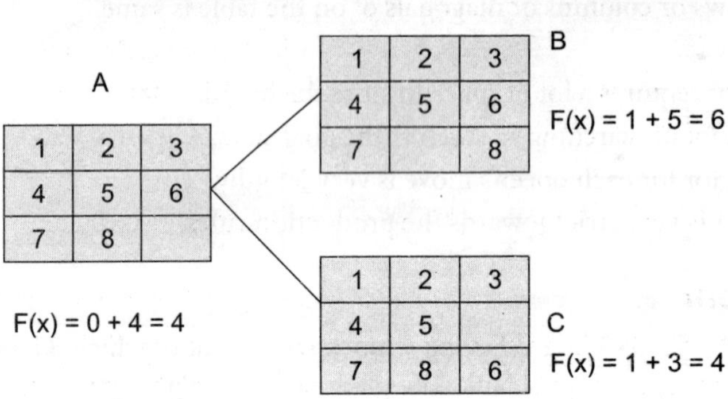

Step 1: f(x) is the step required to reach at the goal state from the initial state. So in the tray either 6 or 8 can change their portions to fill the empty position. So there will be two possible current states namely B and C. The f(x) value of B is 6 and that of C is 4. As 4 is the minimum, so take C as the current state to the next state.

Step 2: In this step, from the tray C three states can be drawn. The empty position will contain either 5 or 3 or 6. So for three different values three different states can be obtained. Then calculate each of their f (x) and take the minimum one. Here the state F has the minimum value i.e. 4 and hence take that as the next current state.

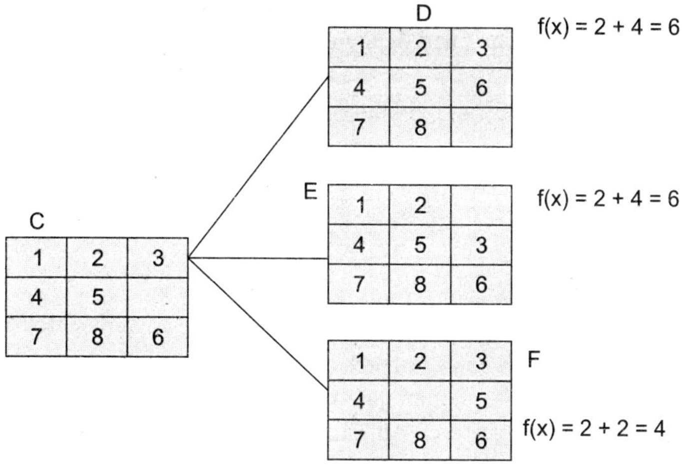

Step 3: The tray F can have 4 different states as the empty positions can be filled with b4 values i.e., 2, 4, 5, 8.

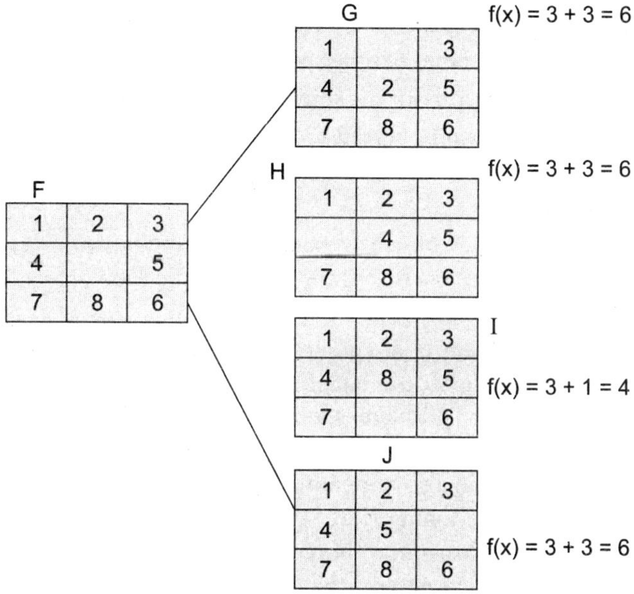

Step 4: In the Step-3 the tray I has the smallest f(n) value. The tray I can be implemented in 3 different states because the empty position can be filled by the members like 7, 8, 6.

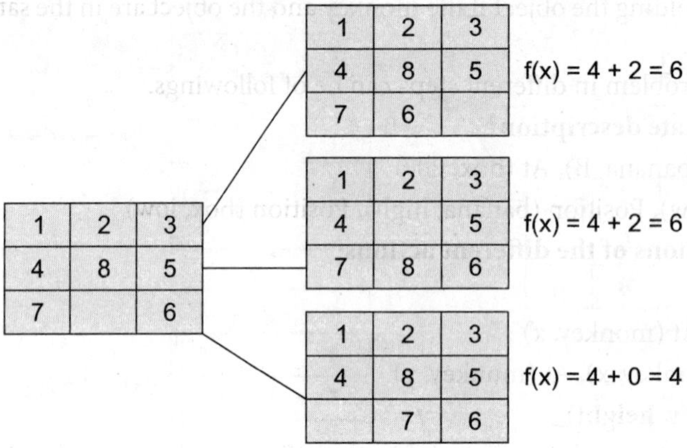

Hence, we reached at the goal state after few changes of tiles in different positions of the trays.

Comments:

- This problem requires a lot of space for saving the different trays.
- Time complexity is more than that of other problems.
- The user has to be very careful about the shifting of tiles in the trays.
- Very complex puzzle games can be solved by this technique.

Monkey Banana Problem

Definition: "A monkey is in a room. A bunch of bananas is hanging from the ceiling. The monkey cannot reach the bananas directly. There is a box in the corner of the room. How can the monkey get the bananas?"

Procedure: The solution of the problem is of course that the monkey must push the box under the bananas, then stand on the box and grab the bananas. But the solution procedure requires a lot of planning algorithms. The purpose of the problem is to raise the question: Are monkeys intelligent? Both humans and monkeys have the ability to use mental maps to remember things like where to go to find shelter or how to avoid danger. They can also remember where to go to gather food and water, as well as how to communicate with each other. Monkeys have the ability not only to remember how to hunt and gather but they also have the ability to learn new things, as is the case with the monkey and the bananas. Even though that monkey may never have entered that room before or had only a box for a tool to gather the food available, that monkey can learn that it needs to move the box across the floor, position it below the bananas and climb the box to reach for them. Some people believe that this is part instinct, part learned behaviour. It is most probably both.

Initially, the monkey is at location 'A', the banana is at location 'B' and the box is at location 'C'. The monkey and box have height "low"; but if the monkey climbs onto the box will have height "High", the same as the bananas.

The action available to the monkey include:

"GO" from one place to another.

"PUSH" an object from one place to another.

"Climb" onto an object.

"Grasp" an object.

Grasping results in holding the object if the monkey and the object are in the same place at the same height.

The solution of the problem in different steps can be of followings.

1. **What is the initial state description?**

   At (monkey, A), At (banana, B), At (box, C)

   Position (monkey, low), Position (banana, high), Position (box, low)

2. **What are the definitions of the different actions?**

   (*a*) **Go (x, y)**

   Precondition: At (monkey, x)

   Effects: ¬At (monkey, x), At (monkey, y)

   (*b*) **Push (object, x, y, height)**

   Pre-condition: At (monkey, x), At (object, x), Position (monkey, height), Position (object, height) **Effects:** ¬ (monkey, x), ¬At (object, x), At (monkey, y), At(object, y)

   (*c*) **Climb up (object, y)**

   Precondition: At (monkey, x), At (object, x), Position (monkey, low), Position (object, low)

   Effects: ¬Position (monkey, low), Position (monkey, high), On (monkey, object)

   (*d*) **Climb down (object)**

   Preconditions: Position (monkey, high), On (monkey, object)

   Effects: ¬Position (monkey, high), ¬ On (monkey, object) Position: (monkey, low)

   (*e*) **Grasp (object, x, height)**

   Preconditions: At (monkey, x), At (object, x), Position (monkey, height), Position (object, height)

   Effect: Hold (object)

   (*f*) **UnGrasp (object, x, height)**

   Preconditions: Hold (object), At (monkey, x), At (object, x),

   Position (monkey, height), Position (object, height)

   Effects: ¬Hold (object)

So the solution to the planning problem may be of following

- GO (A, C)
- PUSH (Box, C, B, Low)
- Climb Up (Box, B)
- Grasp (banana, B, High)
- Climb down (Box)
- Push (Box, B, C, Low)

Comments:

- One major application of the monkey banana problem is the toy problem of computer science.
- One of the specialized purposes of the problem is to raise the question: Are monkeys intelligent?
- ▪This problem is very useful in logic programming and planning.

Tower of Hanoi Problem

Definition: "We are given a tower of eight discs (initially) four in the applet below, initially stacked in increasing size on one of three pegs. The objective is to transfer the entire tower to one of the other pegs (the right most one in the applet below), moving only one disc at a time and never a larger one onto a smaller".

Procedure: The tower of Hanoi puzzle was invented by the French mathematician Eduardo Lucas in 1883. The puzzle is well known to students of computer science since it appears in virtually any introductory text on data structure and algorithms.

- Only one disc can be moved at a time.
- Each move consist of taking the upper disc from one of the rods and sliding it onto another rod, on top of the other discs that may already be present on that rod.
- No disc may be placed on the top of a smaller disk

There is a legend about a Vietnamese temple which contains a large room with three times. Worn posts in it surrounded by 64 golden disks. The priests of Hanoi, acting out of command of an ancient prophecy, have been moving these disks, in accordance with the rules of the puzzle, since that time. The puzzle is therefore also known as the tower of Brahma puzzle. According to the legend, when the last move of the puzzle is completed, the world will end.

There are many variations on this legend. For instance, in some tellings, the temple is a monastery and the priests are monks. The temple or monastery may be said to be in different parts of the world including Hanoi, Vietnam and may be associated with any religion. The flag tower of Hanoi may have served as the inspiration for the name.

The puzzle can be played with any number of disks, although many toy versions have around seven to nine of them. The game seems impossible to many novices yet is solvable with a simple algorithm. The following solution is a very simple method to solve the tower of Hanoi problem.

- Alternative moves between the smallest piece and a non- smallest piece. When moving the smallest piece, always move it in the same direction (to the right if starting number of pieces is even, to the left if starting number of pieces is odd).
- If there is no tower in the chosen direction, move the pieces to the opposite end, but then continue to move in the correct direction, for example if you started with three pieces, you would move the smallest piece to the opposite end, then continue in the left direction after that.
- When the turn is to move the non-smallest piece, there is only one legal move.

Doing this should complete the puzzle using the least amount of moves to do so. Finally, the user will reach at the goal. Also various types of solutions may be possible to solve the tower of Hanoi problem like recursive procedure, non-recursive procedure and binary solution procedure.

Another simple solution to the problem is given below.

For an even number of disks

- Make the legal move between pegs A and B.
- Make the legal moves between pages A and C.
- Make the legal move between pages B and C.

For an even number of disks

- Make the legal move between pegs A and C.
- Make the legal move between pegs A and B.

- Make the legal move between pegs B and C.
- Repeat until complete.

A recursive solution for tower of Hanoi problem is as follows

A key to solving this problem is to recognize that it can be solve by breaking the problem down into the collection of smaller problems and further breaking those problems down into even smaller problems until a solution is reached.

The following procedure demonstrates this approach

- Label the pegs A, B, C - these levels may move at different steps.
- Let n be the total number of disks.
- Number of disks from 1 (smallest, topmost) to n (largest, bottommost).

To move n disks from peg A to peg C.

(*a*) Move n-1 disks from A to B. This leaves disk #n alone on peg A.

(*b*) Move disk #n from A to C.

(*c*) Move n-1 disks from B to C so they sit on disk #n.

To carry out steps a and c, apply the same algorithm again for n-1. The entire procedure is a finite number of steps, since at most point the algorithm will be required for n = 1. This step, moving a single disc from peg A to peg B, is trivial.

Comments:

- The tower of Hanoi is frequently used in psychological research on problem solving.
- This problem is frequently used in neuro-psychological diagnosis and treatment of executive functions.
- The tower of Hanoi is also used as backup rotation scheme when performing computer data backups where multiple tabs/medias are involved.
- This problem is very popular for teaching recursive algorithm to beginning programming students.
- A pictorial version of this puzzle is programmed into emacs editor, accessed by typing M - X Hanoi.
- The tower of Hanoi is also used as a test by neuro-psychologists trying to evaluate frontal lobe deficits.

SEARCHING

Problem-solving in the field of artificial intelligence can be described as a structured exploration of potential actions aimed at achieving a predetermined objective or solution. Within AI, the utilization of search algorithms for problem-solving is a prevalent technique. As we move into the future of AI, its influence on technologies like robotics and pathfinding is anticipated to be substantial. Moreover, its applications extend to areas such as travel planning. This chapter delves into various AI search algorithms employed across diverse domains. Let's delve into the conceptual aspects of visualizing these algorithms.

A search algorithm receives a problem as input and generates a solution in the form of a sequence of actions. Once the solution is obtained, the suggested actions can be executed, which constitutes the execution phase. Agents formulate a search procedure to tackle problems once the goal and problem have been defined. The problem itself can be broken down into five key components:

(*a*) **Initial State:** The starting point from which the agent commences its journey.

(*b*) **Goal State:** The ultimate destination that needs to be reached.

(*c*) **Current State:** The agent's current position after embarking from the initial state.

(*d*) **Successor Function:** This function defines potential actions and their corresponding outcomes.

(*e*) **Path Cost:** A function that assigns a numerical cost to each potential path.

In essence, this encapsulates the process of problem-solving using search algorithms within the realm of artificial intelligence.

Types of Searching

There are several types of searching algorithms used in the field of artificial intelligence for problem-solving. These algorithms vary in terms of their approach, efficiency, and suitability for different types of problems.

- Uninformed
- Informed

Uninformed Search Algorithms

Uninformed search algorithms operate without utilizing any specific knowledge about the problem domain. They employ a brute force approach, often referred to as brute force algorithms. These algorithms lack awareness of the distance to the goal node; their focus is solely on navigating the search space and distinguishing between leaf nodes and goal nodes. Uninformed search algorithms examine each node without any prior insights, earning them the label of "blind search" algorithms.

Uninformed search algorithms are of mainly three types:

- Breadth-first search (BFS)
- Depth-first search (DFS)
- Uniform cost search

Breadth First Search (BFS)

Breadth first search is a general technique of traversing a graph. Breadth first search may use more memory but will always find the shortest path first. In this type of search the state space is represented in form of a tree. The solution is obtained by traversing through the tree. The nodes of the tree represent the start value or starting state, various intermediate states and the final state. In this search a queue data structure is used and it is level by level traversal. Breadth first search expands nodes in order of their distance from the root. It is a path finding algorithm that is capable of always finding the solution if one exists. The solution which is found is always the optional solution. This task is completed in a very memory intensive manner. Each node in the search tree is expanded in a breadth wise at each level.

Concept:

Step 1: Traverse the root node

Step 2: Traverse all neighbours of root node.

Step 3: Traverse all neighbours of neighbours of the root node.

Step 4: This process will continue until we are getting the goal node.

Algorithm:

Step 1: Place the root node inside the queue.

Step 2: If the queue is empty then stops and return failure.

Step 3: If the FRONT node of the queue is a goal node then stop and return success.

Step 4: Remove the FRONT node from the queue. Process it and find all its neighbours that are in ready state then place them inside the queue in any order.

Step 5: Go to Step 3.

Step 6: Exit.

Implementation:

Let us implement the above algorithm of BFS by taking the following suitable example.

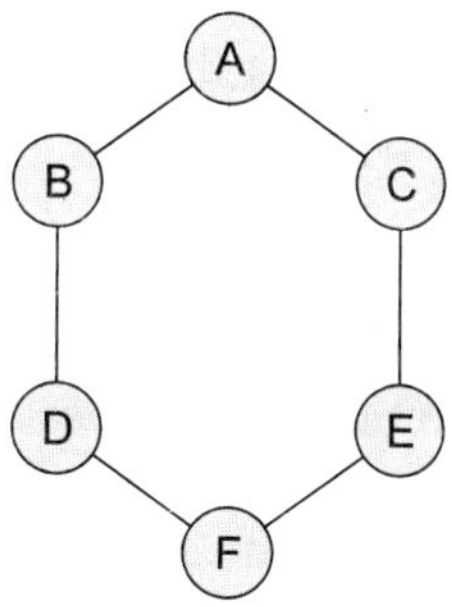

Consider the graph in which let us take A as the starting node and F as the goal node (*)

Step 1: Place the root node inside the queue i.e. A

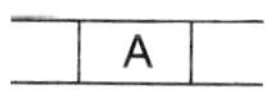

Step 2: Now the queue is not empty and also the FRONT node i.e. A is not our goal node. So move to step 3.

Step 3: So remove the FRONT node from the queue i.e. A and find the neighbour of A i.e. B and C

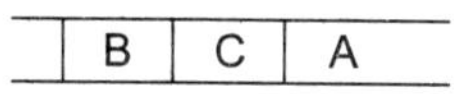

Step 4: Now b is the FRONT node of the queue .So process B and finds the neighbours of B i.e. D.

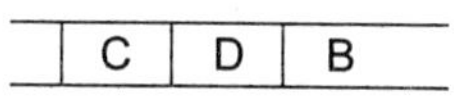

Step 5: Now find out the neighbours of C i.e. E

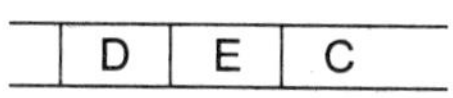

Step 6: Next find out the neighbours of D as D is the FRONT node of the queue

Step 7: Now E is the front node of the queue. So the neighbour of E is F which is our goal node.

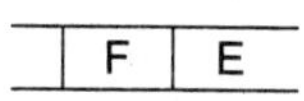

Step 8: Finally F is our goal node which is the FRONT of the queue. So exit

	F	

Advantages

- In this procedure at any way it will find the goal.
- It does not follow a single unfruitful path for a long time.
- It finds the minimal solution in case of multiple paths.

Disadvantages

- BFS consumes large memory space.
- Its time complexity is more.
- It has long pathways, when all paths to a destination are on approximately the same search depth

Depth First Search (DFS)

DFS is also an important type of uniform search. DFS visits all the vertices in the graph. This type of algorithm always chooses to go deeper into the graph. After DFS visited all the reachable vertices from a particular sources vertices it chooses one of the remaining undiscovered vertices and continues the search. DFS reminds the space limitation of breath first search by always generating next a child of the deepest unexpanded nodded. The data structure stack or last in first out (LIFO) is used for DFS. One interesting property of DFS is that, the discover and finish time of each vertex from a parenthesis structure. If we use one open parenthesis when a vertex is finished then the result is properly nested set of parenthesis.

Concept

Step 1: Traverse the root node.
Step 2: Traverse any neighbour of the root node.
Step 3: Traverse any neighbour of neighbour of the root node.
Step 4: This process will continue until we are getting the goal node.

Algorithm

Step 1: PUSH the starting node into the stack.
Step 2: If the stack is empty then stop and return failure.
Step 3: If the top node of the stack is the goal node, then stop and return success.
Step 4: Else POP the top node from the stack and process it. Find all its neighbours that are in ready state and PUSH them into the stack in any order.
Step 5: Go to step 3.
Step 6: Exit.

Implementation

Let us take an example for implementing the above DFS algorithm.

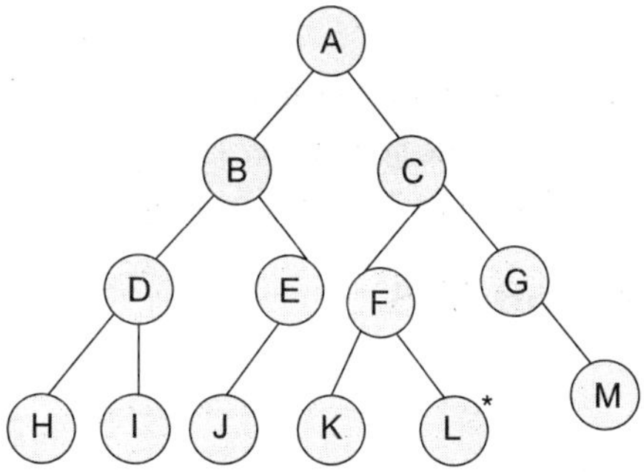

Fig. 1.3. Example of DFS

Consider A as the root node and L as the goal node in the graph figure

Step 1: PUSH the starting node into the stack i.e.

A	

Step 2: Now the stack is not empty and A is not our goal node. Hence move to next step.

Step 3: POP the top node from the stack i.e. A and find the neighbours of A i.e. B and C.

B	C	

A

Step 4: Now C is top node of the stack. Find its neighbours i.e. F and G.

B	F	G	

C

Step 5: Now G is the top node of the stack. Find its neighbour i.e. M

B	F	M	

G

Step 6: Now M is the top node and find its neighbour, but there is no neighbours of M in the graph so POP it from the stack.

B	F	

M

Step 7: Now F is the top node and its neighbours are K and L. so PUSH them on to the stack.

B	K		

L F

Step 8: Now L is the top node of the stack, which is our goal node.

B	K	

L

Also you can traverse the graph starting from the root A and then insert in the order C and B into the stack. Check your answer.

Advantages

- DFS consumes very less memory space.
- It will reach at the goal node in a less time period than BFS if it traverses in a right path.
- It may find a solution without examining much of search because we may get the desired solution in the very first go.

Disadvantages

- It is possible that may states keep reoccurring.
- There is no guarantee of finding the goal node.
- Sometimes the states may also enter into infinite loops.

Difference between BFS and DFS

BFS

- It uses the data structure queue.
- BFS is complete because it finds the solution if one exists.
- BFS takes more space i.e. equivalent to o(b 0) where b is the maximum breath exist in a search tree and d is the maximum depth exit in a search tree.
- In case of several goals, it finds the best one

DFS

- It uses the data structure stack.
- It is not complete because it may take infinite loop to reach at the goal node.
- The space complexity is O(d).
- In case of several goals, it will terminate the solution in any order.

Uniform Cost Search

Uniform Cost Search is an uninformed search algorithm used to find the shortest path in a graph with weighted edges. Unlike breadth-first search, which explores nodes level by level, Uniform Cost Search explores nodes based on their path costs. It aims to find the path with the lowest cumulative cost from the initial state to the goal state.

Key characteristics of Uniform Cost Search

1. **Priority Queue:** Uniform Cost Search employs a priority queue (often implemented using a min-heap) to keep track of nodes to be expanded. Nodes are ordered based on their path costs.
2. **Exploration:** At each step, the algorithm selects and expands the node with the lowest cumulative cost in the priority queue.
3. **Path Cost:** The path cost is calculated by summing up the costs of all edges along the path from the initial state to the current node.
4. **Optimality:** Uniform Cost Search guarantees optimality, meaning it finds the shortest path if the edge costs are non-negative.
5. **Termination:** The algorithm terminates when the goal state is reached or when the priority queue becomes empty.

Uniform Cost Search is particularly useful for finding the shortest path in graphs with different edge costs. It ensures that the path chosen has the minimum total cost among all possible paths explored. However, its performance can degrade if there are large variations in edge costs, as it may explore many paths before finding the optimal one.

In summary, Uniform Cost Search is an uninformed search algorithm that explores paths based on their cumulative costs. It prioritizes nodes with lower costs, making it effective for finding the shortest path in graphs with variable edge costs.

Example: Let's consider an example of using Uniform Cost Search to find the shortest path in a graph with weighted edges. Imagine we have the following graph:

```
A --(4)-- B --(5)-- D
|         |         |
(2)      (3)       (6)
|         |         |
C --(1)-- E --(8)—F
```

In this graph, each letter represents a node, and the numbers in parentheses represent the edge costs. We want to find the shortest path from node A to node F using Uniform Cost Search.

Starting from node A, the search proceeds as follows:

1. Expand node A with a path cost of 0.
2. Expand node C with a path cost of 2.
3. Expand node B with a path cost of 4.
4. Expand node E with a path cost of 7.
5. Expand node D with a path cost of 9.
6. Expand node F with a path cost of 15.

The algorithm terminates when it reaches the goal node F. The final path from A to F is A → B → D → F, with a total path cost of 15.

Uniform Cost Search selects nodes based on their cumulative path costs, ensuring that the shortest path is found. In this example, it explored nodes in the order A → C → B → E → D → F, following the path with the lowest cumulative cost at each step.

Informed Search Algorithms

A heuristic is a technique employed to enhance the efficiency of a search algorithm. Certain heuristics aid in guiding the search process without compromising on the potential for completeness, while others may require a trade-off. A heuristic entails domain-specific knowledge that reduces the anticipated effort required for searching. It is a strategy that may work on some occasions, but not necessarily always. Heuristic search algorithms utilize problem-related information to assist in directing the search path through the search space. These algorithms employ specific functions that estimate the cost from the current state to the goal state, assuming that such a function is efficient.

A heuristic function is a mapping from descriptions of problem states to a measure of desirability, often represented as a numerical value. The primary objective of a heuristic function is to guide the search process towards the most promising directions by suggesting which paths to explore first when faced with multiple options.

In general, heuristics integrate domain knowledge to enhance efficiency compared to blind search methods. Within the realm of artificial intelligence, the term "heuristic" carries both a broad meaning and a more specialized technical meaning. Broadly, "heuristic" signifies any advice or approach that is effective but not guaranteed to succeed in every scenario. For instance, when dealing with the traveling salesman problem (TSP), a heuristic is employed to determine the nearest neighbor. A heuristic acts as a method to provide a more informed estimate about the best choice to make at each decision point, surpassing what random guessing could achieve. This technique proves valuable in solving complex problems that might otherwise be unsolvable within a reasonable time frame, as certain solutions can take an infinitely long time to compute.

Heuristic Search

Heuristic search is a problem-solving technique that aims to find an optimal or near-optimal solution by using heuristics, which are approximate methods or rules of thumb. Unlike exhaustive search algorithms that examine every possible solution, heuristic search algorithms make informed decisions about which paths to explore based on heuristic information.

Heuristic search algorithms typically operate in a search space, where each state represents a possible solution to the problem. The algorithms evaluate the states and use heuristic functions to estimate the desirability or cost of reaching the goal state from a particular state. The heuristic functions provide guidance and help prioritize the search, directing the algorithm towards more promising paths that are likely to lead to better solutions.

The nearest neighbor heuristic is a simple and intuitive approach used to approximate solutions for optimization problems, particularly the Traveling Salesman Problem (TSP). Let's explain it in more detail:

Problem: The Traveling Salesman Problem (TSP) involves finding the shortest possible route that visits a set of cities exactly once and returns to the starting city.

Nearest Neighbor Heuristic:

1. Start with an arbitrary city as the current city.
2. Find the nearest unvisited city from the current city.
3. Move to the nearest unvisited city.
4. Mark the current city as visited.
5. Repeat steps 2-4 until all cities are visited.
6. Return to the starting city to complete the tour.

The nearest neighbor heuristic selects the next city based on its proximity to the current city, assuming that visiting nearby cities will likely lead to a shorter overall route. This approach is guided by local information without considering the global optimization criterion.

Example: Let's consider a simple example with four cities (A, B, C, D) and their pairwise distances:

- **A:** Distance to B = 5, Distance to C = 2, Distance to D = 4
- **B:** Distance to A = 5, Distance to C = 6, Distance to D = 3
- **C:** Distance to A = 2, Distance to B = 6, Distance to D = 1
- **D:** Distance to A = 4, Distance to B = 3, Distance to C = 1

Starting from city A, we follow the nearest neighbor heuristic:

1. A → C (Distance = 2)
2. C → D (Distance = 1)
3. D → B (Distance = 3)
4. B → A (Distance = 5)

The resulting tour is A → C → D → B → A with a total distance of 11 units.

The nearest neighbor heuristic provides a relatively quick solution but does not guarantee the optimal solution for the TSP. It can be efficient for large problem instances but may result in suboptimal solutions, particularly when the distances do not follow the triangle inequality property. Nonetheless, the nearest neighbor heuristic serves as a useful initial approximation or as a baseline for more sophisticated algorithms to improve upon.

There are various heuristic search algorithms, including:

- **Greedy Best-First Search:** This algorithm selects the most promising state based on a heuristic evaluation function and expands it first. It prioritizes states that appear to be closest to the goal. This algorithm selects the most promising state based on a heuristic evaluation function. It prioritizes states that appear to be closest to the goal.

  It expands the state that has the lowest heuristic value, without considering the actual cost of reaching that state. Greedy Best-First Search is efficient but may not always find the optimal solution. It can be misled by heuristic information and get stuck in suboptimal paths.
- **A* Search:** A* combines the cost of reaching a state from the initial state (known as the "g" value) with an estimated cost to the goal state (known as the "h" value). It evaluates the sum of the "g" and "h" values and selects the state with the lowest total cost. A* is known for its optimality and completeness under certain conditions. A* combines the cost of reaching a state from the initial state (known as the "g" value) with an estimated cost to the goal state (known as the "h" value). It evaluates the sum of the "g" and "h" values for each state and selects the state with the lowest total cost. A* is known for its optimality and completeness under certain conditions. It guarantees finding the optimal solution if the heuristic is admissible and the search space is finite.
- **Iterative Deepening A*:** It is a combination of depth-first search and A*. It performs a depth-first search with increasing depth limits and uses A* search with limited depth to guide the exploration. IDA* is a combination of depth-first search and A* search.

  It performs a depth-first search with increasing depth limits and uses A* search with limited depth to guide the exploration. IDA* is memory-efficient as it avoids storing the entire search tree. However, it may revisit states multiple times.
- **Hill Climbing:** This algorithm starts from an initial state and iteratively moves to the neighboring states that lead to better solutions based on the heuristic evaluation. It "climbs" towards higher-valued states but may get stuck in local optima. Hill Climbing starts from an initial state and iteratively moves to neighboring states that lead to better solutions based on the heuristic evaluation. It "climbs" towards higher-valued states, aiming to reach the highest point in the search space.However, Hill Climbing can get stuck in local optima, as it makes moves based on immediate improvements without considering the global picture.

Algorithm

Step 1: Evaluate the starting state. If it is a goal state then stop and return success.

Step 2: Else, continue with the starting state as considering it as a current state.

Step 3: Continue Step-4 until a solution is found i.e. until there are no new states left to be applied in the current state.

Step 4:

(*a*) Select a state that has not been yet applied to the current state and apply it to produce a new state.

(*b*) Procedure to evaluate a new state.

(*i*) If the current state is a goal state, then stop and return success.

(*ii*) If it is better than the current state, then make it current state and proceed further.

(*iii*) If it is not better than the current state, then continue in the loop until a solution is found.

Step 5: Exit.

Advantages

- Hill climbing technique is useful in job shop scheduling, automatic programming, circuit designing, and vehicle routing and portfolio management.
- It is also helpful to solve pure optimization problems where the objective is to find the best state according to the objective function.
- It requires much less conditions than other search techniques.

Disadvantages

The question that remains on hill climbing search is whether this hill is the highest hill possible. Unfortunately without further extensive exploration, this question cannot be answered. This technique works but as it uses local information that's why it can be fooled. The algorithm doesn't maintain a search tree, so the current node data structure need only record the state and its objective function value. It assumes that local improvement will lead to global improvement.

There are some reasons by which hill climbing often gets suck which are stated below.

Local Maxima

A local maxima is a state that is better than each of its neighbouring states, but not better than some other states further away. Generally this state is lower than the global maximum. At this point, one cannot decide easily to move in which direction! This difficulties can be extracted by the process of backtracking i.e. backtrack to any of one earlier node position and try to go on a different event direction. To implement this strategy, maintaining in a list of path almost taken and go back to one of them. If the path was taken that leads to a dead end, then go back to one of them.

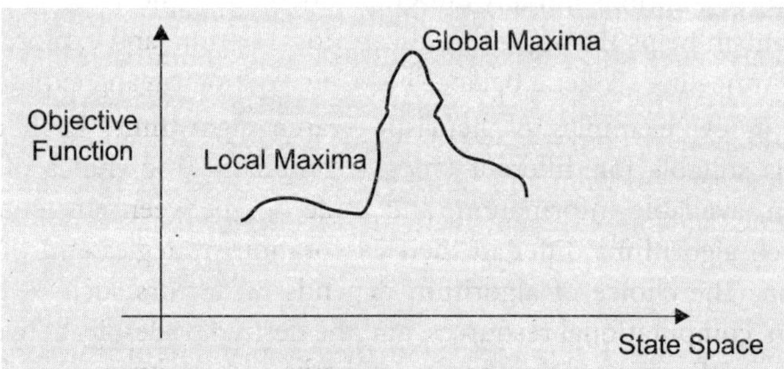

Fig. 1.4. Local Maxima

Ridges

It is a special type of local maxima. It is a simply an area of search space. Ridges result in a sequence of local maxima that is very difficult to implement ridge itself has a slope which is difficult to traverse.

In this type of situation apply two or more rules before doing the test. This will correspond to move in several directions at once.

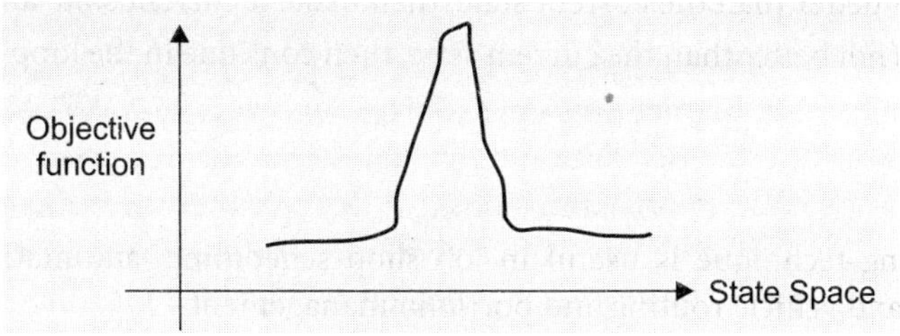

Fig. 1.5. Ridges

Plateau

It is a flat area of search space in which the neighbouring have same value. So it is very difficult to calculate the best direction. So to get out of this situation, make a big jump in any direction, which will help to move in a new direction this is the best way to handle the problem like plateau.

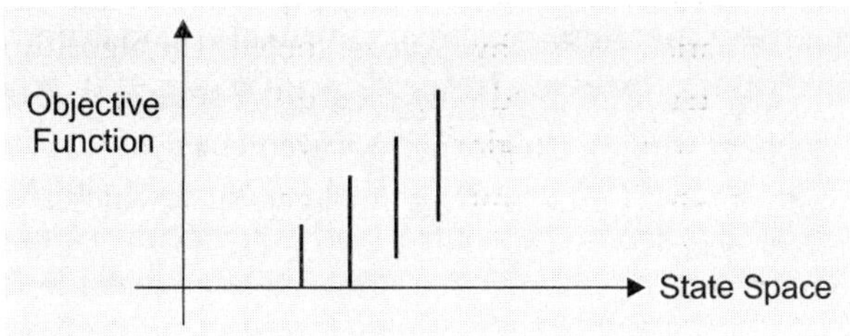

Fig. 1.6. Platcau

- **Simulated Annealing:** Simulated annealing is inspired by the annealing process in metallurgy. It allows the algorithm to accept worse solutions initially but gradually reduces the acceptance probability over time. It helps to escape local optima and explore a wider solution space. Simulated Annealing is inspired by the annealing process in metallurgy. It allows the algorithm to accept worse solutions initially but gradually reduces the acceptance probability over time. This mechanism helps the algorithm escape local optima and explore a wider solution space. Simulated Annealing strikes a balance between exploration and exploitation.

These are just a few examples of heuristic search algorithms. Each algorithm has its own characteristics and is suitable for different types of problems. The choice of algorithm depends on the problem domain, available information, and trade-offs between efficiency and solution quality. These heuristic search algorithms differ in their exploration strategies and the way they incorporate heuristic information. The choice of algorithm depends on factors such as problem characteristics, available information, computational resources, and the desired trade-offs between solution quality and computational efficiency. Each algorithm has its strengths and weaknesses, and the selection should be based on the specific problem at hand.

KNOWLEDGE

Knowledge refers to the accumulation of facts, inference rules, and other information that serves a specific purpose. It goes beyond raw data and information by incorporating relationships, correlations, and dependencies.

The key elements of knowledge include

- a collection of data,
- a set of beliefs or hypotheses,
- meaningful information.

Data and knowledge are distinct concepts. Data refers to raw materials or information, while knowledge comprises specific inference rules and factual information. Knowledge also differs from beliefs and hypotheses. Beliefs are meaningful expressions that can be either true or false, while hypotheses are justified beliefs that are not confirmed as true. Hypotheses are supported by evidence but can still be false. Therefore, knowledge can be described as validated and justified information.

Knowledge Based Systems

Knowledge-based systems are designed to exhibit intelligent behavior by utilizing the expert knowledge that has been encoded within them. This knowledge is stored in a dedicated knowledge base, which serves as a repository of facts, rules, heuristics, and procedures that are essential for problem-solving and decision-making.

The power of knowledge-based systems lies in their ability to access and apply this expert knowledge in real-time. The knowledge base contains a wealth of information and expertise that has been acquired from domain experts or through extensive research and analysis. It represents a comprehensive understanding of a specific problem domain, including its underlying principles, relationships, and best practices.

By separating the knowledge from the control and inferencing components, knowledge-based systems can achieve flexibility and modularity. The knowledge base can be easily updated, expanded, or modified without affecting the overall system structure. This allows for continuous improvement and adaptation to changing circumstances or new discoveries.

During the operation of a knowledge-based system, the control and inferencing components interact with the knowledge base to retrieve relevant knowledge and apply it to the current problem or task at hand. The system can reason, make inferences, and generate solutions based on the accumulated knowledge, enabling it to exhibit intelligent behavior and provide valuable insights and recommendations.

In summary, the knowledge base serves as the foundation of a knowledge-based system, providing the necessary expertise and guidance for intelligent decision-making. It encapsulates the domain-specific knowledge and enables the system to leverage this knowledge effectively, leading to more informed and effective problem-solving capabilities.

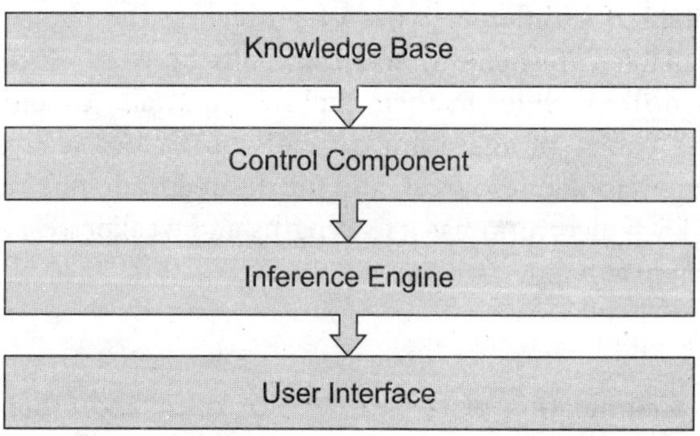

In this representation, the knowledge base is shown as a separate entity that stores the encoded knowledge in the form of facts, rules, heuristics, and procedures. The control component is responsible for coordinating the overall functioning of the system, including managing the interaction with the user interface.

The inference engine is a crucial component that accesses the knowledge base and performs logical reasoning, inference, and decision-making based on the available knowledge. It applies appropriate rules and heuristics to derive conclusions or generate solutions to specific problems.

The user interface allows users to interact with the knowledge-based system, input queries or problem statements, and receive outputs or recommendations generated by the system.

Any choice of representation will depend on the type of problem to be solved and the inference methods available. Knowledge may be vague, contradictory or incomplete. Thus, knowledge is information about objects, concepts and relationships that are assumed to exist in a particular area of interest.

Type of Knowledge

Knowledge can be categorized into various types based on its nature, representation, and usage. Here are some commonly recognized types of knowledge:

1. **Explicit Knowledge:** Explicit knowledge refers to knowledge that is formal, codified, and easily communicated or documented. It can be expressed in the form of facts, procedures, rules, or formulas. Explicit knowledge is typically easy to transfer and share among individuals or within knowledge-based systems. Explicit knowledge can be documented in various forms, including textbooks, manuals, databases, or knowledge bases.
   - **Facts:** These are objective statements or pieces of information that can be easily expressed or documented. Examples include the population of a country, the chemical formula of a substance, or historical events and dates.
   - **Rules:** These are statements that define relationships, conditions, or actions to be taken. Examples include traffic rules, logical rules in computer programming, or guidelines for a specific process or procedure.
   - **Procedures:** These are step-by-step instructions or processes that outline how to perform a task or achieve a specific outcome. Examples include a recipe for cooking a meal, an algorithm for solving a mathematical problem, or guidelines for assembling a piece of furniture.

     Example: In a customer support system, explicit knowledge can include facts about the product, rules for troubleshooting common issues, and procedures for handling customer complaints.
2. **Tacit Knowledge:** Tacit knowledge is the opposite of explicit knowledge. It is personal, experiential, and deeply rooted in an individual's insights, intuitions, and skills. Tacit knowledge is difficult to articulate or codify, making it challenging to transfer or communicate explicitly. It often involves practical know-how, expertise, or context-specific understanding.
   - Tacit knowledge is difficult to express or articulate explicitly. It is often gained through personal experience, practice, and intuition. Examples include skills, expertise, insights, and understanding that are deeply ingrained and difficult to teach or transfer to others. For instance, a seasoned chef's ability to create delicious flavors, a musician's sense of timing and rhythm, or an experienced salesperson's intuition for understanding customer needs.
   - It involves subjective insights, perceptions, and expertise that are not easily transferable to others.

Example: A highly skilled surgeon possesses tacit knowledge in performing complex surgical procedures. This knowledge is built through years of practice, observation, and hands-on experience.

3. **Procedural Knowledge:** Procedural knowledge refers to knowledge about how to perform specific tasks or procedures. It involves knowing the steps, methods, or techniques required to accomplish a particular goal. Procedural knowledge is often captured in the form of standard operating procedures, guidelines, or instructions.
   - Procedural knowledge refers to knowing how to do something. It involves the ability to execute a series of steps or actions to accomplish a specific task or achieve a desired outcome.
   - It focuses on the practical application of knowledge rather than just the theoretical understanding.

   Example: Driving a car, playing a musical instrument, and operating complex machinery all require procedural knowledge.
4. **Declarative Knowledge:** Declarative knowledge is factual or descriptive knowledge about something. It represents knowledge about concepts, objects, relationships, or properties. Declarative knowledge can be explicit or tacit and is often organized in the form of statements or propositions.
   - Declarative knowledge represents factual information and understanding about concepts, principles, or relationships. It involves knowing that something is true or comprehending the nature of certain concepts.
   - It involves knowing that something is true or understanding the nature of certain concepts.

   Example: Knowing the chemical formula of water (H_2O), understanding the concept of supply and demand in economics, and recognizing historical events and dates.
5. **Domain Knowledge:** Domain knowledge is knowledge specific to a particular subject area or domain. It encompasses the understanding of key concepts, principles, terminology, and problem-solving approaches within that domain. Domain knowledge is crucial for expertise and effective decision-making within a specific field or industry.
   - Domain knowledge refers to expertise and specialized knowledge within a specific field or domain. It includes understanding the concepts, principles, and practices relevant to that field. Examples include knowledge of laws and regulations in the legal domain, understanding financial markets and investment strategies in finance, or familiarity with medical diagnoses and treatments in the healthcare domain.
   - It encompasses the specific knowledge, concepts, and skills required to understand and solve problems within a specific domain.

   Example: A software engineer's domain knowledge includes programming languages, software development methodologies, and best practices in software engineering.
6. **Heuristic Knowledge:** Heuristic knowledge involves rules of thumb, strategies, or guidelines that guide problem-solving or decision-making processes. Heuristics are practical, experience-based approaches that help in finding solutions or making reasonable judgments in complex or uncertain situations.
   - Heuristic knowledge involves rules of thumb, strategies, or guidelines that help in problem-solving and decision-making. It is based on past experience, intuition, and practical insights. Examples include using trial and error to solve a puzzle, applying common strategies in problem-solving, or relying on intuition and past successes to make business decisions.

- It is based on past experience and intuition, providing shortcuts or approximate solutions to complex problems.

  Example: In a business setting, sales professionals may rely on heuristic knowledge to identify potential customers based on their behavior, appearance, or engagement level.

7. **Meta-Knowledge:** Meta-knowledge refers to knowledge about knowledge itself. It involves understanding the structure, organization, and utilization of knowledge. Meta-knowledge helps in managing, updating, and evaluating knowledge resources, as well as in adapting knowledge-based systems to different contexts or requirements.
   - Meta-knowledge refers to knowledge about knowledge itself. It involves understanding how to acquire, organize, evaluate, and apply knowledge effectively.

     Example: Knowing different search strategies and techniques to find relevant information online, understanding how to critically evaluate sources for credibility, and being aware of different approaches to organizing knowledge in a database or knowledge base.

These are just some examples of the types of knowledge that exist. In practice, knowledge can be diverse and multifaceted, depending on the specific context and application domain.

Knowledge Acquisition

Knowledge acquisition refers to the process of gathering and collecting knowledge from various sources in order to expand the capabilities of a system or improve its performance. It involves adding new knowledge to a knowledge base and refining or improving existing knowledge. The acquired knowledge can include facts, rules, concepts, procedures, heuristics, formulas, relationships, statistics, and other useful information. Knowledge acquisition can be a goal-oriented process aimed at creating and refining knowledge to enhance system capabilities. It can involve extracting knowledge from experts in the relevant domain, consulting textbooks, technical papers, database reports, journals, and other sources of information. The process of knowledge acquisition is continuous and spans the entire lifespan of a system.

Machine learning is an example of knowledge acquisition, where computer programs autonomously create or refine knowledge based on data. The acquired knowledge needs to be integrated with existing knowledge in a meaningful way, ensuring accuracy, non-redundancy, consistency, and completeness.

Knowledge acquisition supports activities such as entering knowledge into a knowledge base and maintaining the knowledge base. Knowledge engineers play a crucial role in developing and refining knowledge. They work closely with experts to elicit knowledge, integrate knowledge from various sources, create and edit code, operate interactive tools, and build the knowledge base. Overall, knowledge acquisition is a dynamic process that involves acquiring, refining, and integrating knowledge to enhance the capabilities and performance of systems.

There are several methods and approaches to knowledge acquisition, including:

1. **Expert Interviews:** Expert interviews involve direct interaction with domain experts to gather their knowledge and insights. The interviews can be structured, semi-structured, or unstructured, depending on the desired depth and specificity of the acquired knowledge. Experts are asked targeted questions, and their responses are documented and analyzed to extract relevant knowledge.
2. **Observation:** Knowledge acquisition through observation involves directly observing experts or individuals in their natural environment while they perform tasks or activities related to the

domain. Observations can be conducted through shadowing, video recording, or other means. This method allows for capturing tacit knowledge and understanding real-world practices.

3. **Documentation Analysis:** Documentation analysis involves studying existing written materials such as textbooks, research papers, technical reports, manuals, and other relevant documents. By carefully reviewing and analyzing the content, valuable knowledge can be extracted. Key concepts, facts, and relationships are identified and incorporated into the knowledge base.
4. **Knowledge Elicitation Techniques:** Employing various techniques such as brainstorming sessions, focus groups, surveys, or questionnaires to elicit knowledge from experts or a group of stakeholders.
5. **Machine Learning and Data Mining:** Leveraging computational methods and algorithms to extract knowledge from large datasets, often through pattern recognition and statistical analysis. Machine learning algorithms and techniques can automatically acquire knowledge from data. By training models on large datasets, machines can learn patterns, relationships, and rules that represent valuable knowledge. Machine learning approaches include supervised learning, unsupervised learning, and reinforcement learning, which can be applied to various domains and data types.

   Data mining techniques are used to extract knowledge from large datasets. Through data analysis and machine learning algorithms, patterns, correlations, and insights can be discovered. Data mining can be applied to structured data sources, such as databases, as well as unstructured sources, such as text documents and social media posts.
6. **Knowledge Transfer:** Transferring knowledge from one individual or system to another through training, mentorship, or the transfer of explicit knowledge documents. Knowledge transfer refers to the process of sharing knowledge from one individual or entity to another. It involves capturing, packaging, and disseminating knowledge in a way that enables others to understand and apply it effectively. Knowledge transfer is crucial for organizations to leverage existing knowledge, promote learning and innovation, and ensure the continuity of expertise within the organization.
7. **Ontology Development:** Creating formal representations of knowledge structures, relationships, and concepts within a specific domain to facilitate knowledge acquisition and understanding. Ontology engineering involves creating formal representations of knowledge in a specific domain. Ontologies capture concepts, relationships, and properties within a structured framework. By defining ontologies, knowledge engineers can organize and categorize knowledge, enabling more effective knowledge acquisition and reasoning within knowledge-based systems.
8. **Knowledge Engineering:** Applying systematic methods and tools to capture, model, and represent knowledge in a structured and usable format, such as using knowledge representation languages or frameworks. Knowledge engineering is a discipline that focuses on the design, development, and implementation of knowledge-based systems. It involves capturing, organizing, and representing knowledge in a way that can be utilized by intelligent systems, such as expert systems, decision support systems, and artificial intelligence applications. The role of a knowledge engineer is to bridge the gap between domain experts and computer systems by eliciting, formalizing, and encoding expert knowledge into a knowledge base.
9. **Collaborative Knowledge Creation:** Engaging a community or a group of individuals to collectively contribute and refine knowledge through collaborative platforms, wikis, or social

knowledge-sharing platforms. Collaborative knowledge creation refers to the process of collectively generating knowledge and insights through the collaboration and interaction of multiple individuals or groups. It involves leveraging the collective intelligence, expertise, and perspectives of diverse participants to create new knowledge that exceeds the capabilities of any individual.

10. **Crowdsourcing:** Harnessing the collective intelligence of a large group of people to acquire and generate knowledge, often through open calls for contributions or problem-solving challenges. Crowdsourcing involves leveraging the collective intelligence and knowledge of a large group of people, often through online platforms. By posing questions or tasks to the crowd, valuable insights and knowledge can be gathered. Crowdsourcing enables the aggregation of diverse perspectives and expertise, increasing the breadth and depth of acquired knowledge.

Knowledge Representation

Knowledge representation is a crucial aspect of developing artificial intelligence systems. It serves as a bridge between the information obtained from the external world and the higher-level cognitive processes of an AI system. Without proper representation, it would be difficult to identify and understand the thinking processes involved.

The field of knowledge representation has been evolving for several decades, addressing the challenge of representing domain-specific knowledge in flexible and adaptable ways. Rather than hard-coding knowledge into a system, which makes it rigid and difficult to update, more flexible approaches have emerged in recent years.

The need for knowledge representation arises from the fundamental requirement of intelligent systems to possess knowledge. Humans acquire knowledge through various means and store it in memory using specific representation techniques. In other words, knowledge representation is a critical component necessary for enabling a computer to exhibit intelligent behavior.

Knowledge representation in AI refers to the techniques and notations used to structure and organize data. Various approaches have been developed, including semantic networks, frames, logic, production rules, and conceptual graphs. These techniques provide a structured and formalized way to represent knowledge in a format that can be processed and reasoned upon by AI systems.

Semantic networks represent knowledge using nodes and edges, where nodes represent concepts or entities, and edges represent relationships between them. Frames provide a structured way to represent objects, their attributes, and relationships. Logic-based representation uses formal logical languages to express knowledge and reason about it. Production rules capture knowledge in the form of if-then rules, allowing for rule-based reasoning. Conceptual graphs combine elements of graphs and logic to represent knowledge.

These knowledge representation techniques enable AI systems to store, organize, and reason about knowledge in a meaningful way. By using appropriate representation techniques, AI systems can leverage existing knowledge and make intelligent decisions and inferences based on the available information.

It is worth noting that different knowledge representation techniques have their strengths and weaknesses, and their suitability depends on the specific requirements of the AI application and the nature of the knowledge being represented.

Properties for Knowledge Representation

Knowledge representation in AI systems should possess certain properties to be effective and facilitate efficient reasoning and decision-making. Here are some important properties for knowledge representation:

In order to achieve representational adequacy, a knowledge representation system should possess the following characteristics:

1. **Expressiveness:** The representation should be able to capture a wide range of knowledge and express complex concepts, relationships, and dependencies. It should provide a rich vocabulary and syntax to represent diverse types of information.
2. **Inferential Adequacy:** The representation should support reasoning and inference. It should allow for drawing logical conclusions, making inferences, and answering queries based on the available knowledge.
3. **Efficiency:** The representation should be efficient in terms of storage and retrieval. It should enable fast and effective processing of knowledge, allowing AI systems to perform tasks in a timely manner.
4. **Scalability:** The representation should be scalable, capable of handling large and growing knowledge bases. It should be able to accommodate new knowledge without significantly impacting performance.
5. **Modularity:** The representation should be modular, allowing for the decomposition of knowledge into smaller, manageable units. Modularity facilitates easy maintenance, updating, and integration of knowledge.
6. **Consistency:** The representation should ensure consistency and coherence of knowledge. It should avoid contradictions or conflicts within the knowledge base, promoting reliable and accurate reasoning.
7. **Extensibility:** The representation should be extensible, allowing for the addition of new knowledge and the incorporation of domain-specific information. It should support incremental updates and expansion of the knowledge base.
8. **Interpretability:** The representation should be interpretable by humans, enabling domain experts to understand and validate the knowledge encoded. It should use a notation or language that is understandable and meaningful to the intended users.
9. **Contextuality:** The representation should capture the contextual information associated with knowledge. It should consider the situational context, temporal aspects, and other relevant factors that influence the meaning and interpretation of knowledge.
10. **Reusability:** The representation should promote knowledge reuse by allowing the sharing and transfer of knowledge across different domains or applications. It should enable the leveraging of existing knowledge to solve new problems.

These properties contribute to the effectiveness and usability of knowledge representation in AI systems. By adhering to these properties, knowledge representation facilitates efficient knowledge management, reasoning, and decision-making processes.

Requirements for Knowledge Representation System

Representational adequacy refers to the ability of a knowledge representation system to accurately and comprehensively capture and represent the knowledge of a specific domain or problem space.

Representational accuracy refers to the extent to which a knowledge representation system faithfully represents the underlying concepts, relationships, and constraints of the domain it is intended to model. It is crucial for the system to accurately capture the essential characteristics and semantics of the real-world entities and their interactions.

An accurately represented knowledge base ensures that the system's reasoning and decision-making processes align with the actual domain knowledge. It enables the system to make reliable inferences, draw meaningful conclusions, and provide accurate responses or recommendations.

Inferential adequacy refers to the ability of a knowledge representation system to support effective reasoning and inference processes. Inferential adequacy refers to the capability of a knowledge representation system or artificial intelligence model to effectively reason and draw logical conclusions based on the knowledge it possesses. It involves the ability to use the available information, apply appropriate rules and principles, and derive accurate inferences and predictions.

By achieving inferential adequacy, a knowledge representation system or AI model can effectively utilize the stored knowledge to reason, solve problems, and make informed decisions. It enhances the system's ability to draw meaningful conclusions and predictions, leading to more robust and reliable AI applications.

Inferential efficiency refers to the ability of a knowledge representation system to perform reasoning and inference tasks in a timely and resource-efficient manner. It focuses on the speed and computational efficiency of the system's inferential processes. Inferential efficiency in artificial intelligence refers to the ability of a knowledge representation system or AI model to perform reasoning and inference tasks quickly and with minimal computational resources. It involves optimizing the speed and efficiency of the system's reasoning mechanism, data processing, and resource utilization to achieve timely and effective results.

By improving inferential efficiency, AI systems can deliver faster and more responsive results, enabling real-time decision-making and enhancing user experiences. It also allows for scalability, making it feasible to handle large-scale data and complex inference tasks in various domains.

Acquisitional efficiency refers to the ability of a knowledge representation system to acquire new knowledge and integrate it into the existing knowledge base in an efficient manner. It focuses on the effectiveness and efficiency of the system's knowledge acquisition processes. Acquisitional efficiency in artificial intelligence pertains to the system's ability to efficiently acquire new knowledge or information. It involves the process of learning from data or experience and incorporating it into the existing knowledge base or model. An acquisitionally efficient system can rapidly and accurately learn from new data, adapt to changing circumstances, and generalize knowledge to new situations.

Efficient acquisition of knowledge is crucial for AI systems to stay up-to-date, adapt to changing circumstances, and continuously improve their performance. By employing these techniques, AI systems can efficiently learn from data, acquire new knowledge, and enhance their capabilities.

Different Types of Knowledge

In the context of artificial intelligence, knowledge can be classified into different types based on its nature, representation, and usage. Here are some common types of knowledge:

Declarative Knowledge: Declarative knowledge refers to factual information, statements, or propositions about the world. It represents what is known or believed to be true and can be expressed as statements such as "The sky is blue" or "Water boils at 100 degrees Celsius." Declarative knowledge is often represented using symbolic representations like logic or semantic networks.

It is the passive knowledge of the world's facts conveyed in sentences. It provides any phenomenon's basic information, facts, and concepts. It simply refers to the depiction of facts or claims. This is a comprehensive account of the circumstances. For instance, an organization's facts can include its buildings, locations, department counts, personnel counts, etc. The facts could be either static or changing. Unlike dynamic facts, which vary over time, static facts remain constant over time. For instance, a company's name and address are unchanging. However, some new departments might be added.

Procedural Knowledge: Procedural knowledge involves knowledge about how to perform certain tasks or activities. It represents knowledge of procedures, algorithms, rules, or steps required to accomplish specific goals. Procedural knowledge is typically expressed as a series of instructions or steps to be followed. For example, knowing how to ride a bicycle or how to solve a mathematical problem involves procedural knowledge.

The knowledge that has been gathered about carrying out a specific task is known as procedural knowledge. Examples of procedural knowledge include the steps required to solve an algebraic equation. It also does away with the restrictions of declarative knowledge, i.e., that declarative knowledge can only describe the organization; it cannot describe how the workers operate there or how the goods are created. However, procedural knowledge uses production rules and dynamic attributes to define every aspect of the organization.

For example, If: All the employees are very hardworking

They are very punctual

They have productive ideas.

Then: Large no. of products can be produced within a very limited time period.

The advantages of using procedural knowledge are as follows:

1. Domain specific knowledge can be easily represented.
2. Extended logical inferences, such as default reasoning facilitated.
3. Side effects of actions may be modeled.

Some disadvantages of procedural knowledge are

1. **Completeness:** In procedural knowledge not all cases may be represented.
2. **Consistency:** Not all deductions may be correct.
3. **Modularity:** Changes in knowledge base might have far-reaching effects.

Heuristic Knowledge: Heuristic knowledge refers to rules of thumb or general guidelines that help in problem-solving or decision-making. These rules are based on experience, intuition, or expert knowledge and provide strategies or approaches to tackle complex problems. Heuristic knowledge is often used in AI systems to guide search algorithms, optimization techniques, or decision-making processes.

Meta-Knowledge: Meta-knowledge refers to knowledge about knowledge itself. It involves knowledge about the structure, organization, and usage of knowledge. Meta-knowledge is used to manage and manipulate other types of knowledge, such as knowledge about the reliability of information, knowledge about the sources of knowledge, or knowledge about the context in which knowledge is applied.

Structural knowledge refers to the understanding of the organization, relationships, and interconnections among different elements or components within a system or domain. It focuses on the underlying structure or framework that governs the behavior and properties of the system.

In the context of artificial intelligence, structural knowledge is particularly relevant in areas such as knowledge representation, reasoning, and problem-solving. It involves capturing and representing the hierarchical, spatial, temporal, or causal relationships between entities or concepts in a domain.

Knowledge Representation Techniques

There are several knowledge representation techniques used in artificial intelligence to capture and represent knowledge in a structured and meaningful way. Here are some commonly used techniques:

Logic-Based Representation

Predicate Logic: Represents knowledge using logical predicates, variables, quantifiers, and logical operators. It allows for precise and formal representation of relationships and constraints. First-Order Logic (FOL): Extends predicate logic by incorporating quantifiers to express statements about objects and their properties. Description Logic: Provides a formal framework for representing knowledge using concepts, roles, and individuals, allowing for reasoning and inference.

A logic is a formal language, with precisely defined syntax and semantics, which supports sound inference. Different logics exist, which allow you to represent different kinds of things, and which allow more or less efficient inference. The logic may be different types like propositional logic, predicate logic, temporal logic, description logic etc. But representing something in logic may not be very natural and inferences may not be efficient.

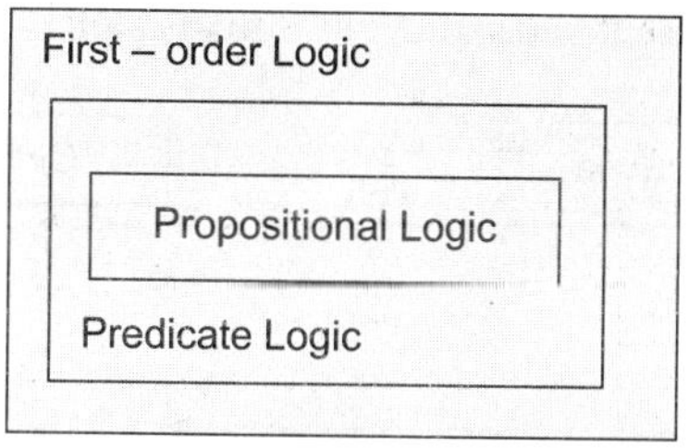

Fig. 1.7.

Semantic Networks

Directed Graphs: Represent knowledge as nodes and edges, where nodes represent concepts or entities, and edges represent relationships between them. Conceptual Dependency Graphs: Capture the conceptual relationships and dependencies between actions, events, and objects in a domain. Frame-Based Systems: Represent knowledge using frames or schema, which define the structure and attributes of objects or concepts.

A semantic network is a graphical knowledge representation technique. This knowledge representation system is primarily on network structure. The semantic networks were basically developed to model human memory. A semantic net consists of nodes connected by arcs. The arcs are defined in a variety of ways, depending upon the kind of knowledge being represented.

The main idea behind semantic net is that the meaning of a concept comes, from the ways in which it is connected to other concepts. The semantic network consists of different nodes and arcs. Each node should contain the information about objects and each arc should contain the relationship between objects. Semantic nets are used to find relationships among objects by spreading activation about from each of two nodes and seeing where the activation met this process is called intersection search.

For example: Ram is a boy.

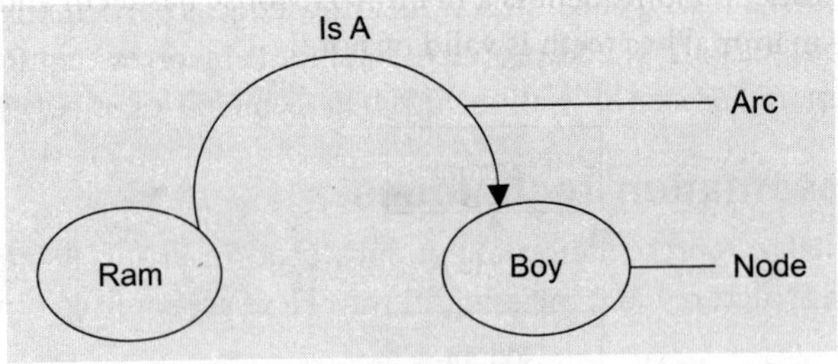

Fig. 1.8.

Semantic Network by using Instances

The semantic network based knowledge representation mechanism is useful where an object or concept is associated with many attributes and where relationships between objects are important. Semantic nets have also been used in natural language research to represent complex sentences expressed in English. The semantic representation is useful because it provides a standard way of analyzing the meaning of sentence. It is a natural way to represent relationships that would appear as ground instances of binary predicates in predicate logic. In this case we can create one instance of each object. In instance based semantic net representations some keywords are used like: IS A, INSTANCE, AGENT, HAS-PARTS etc.

Consider the following examples:

1. Suppose we have to represent the sentence "Sima is a girl".

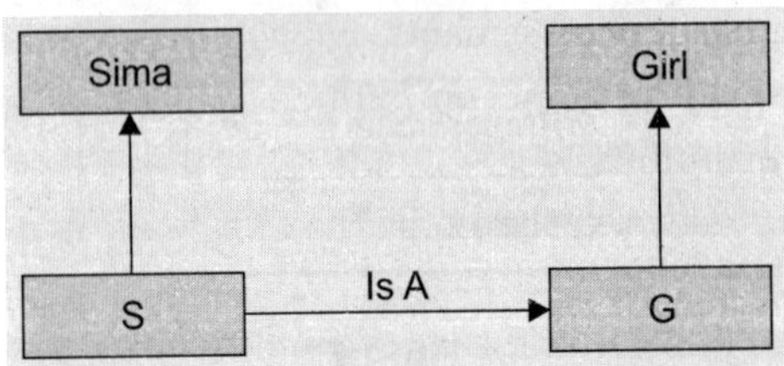

2. Ram is taller than Hari

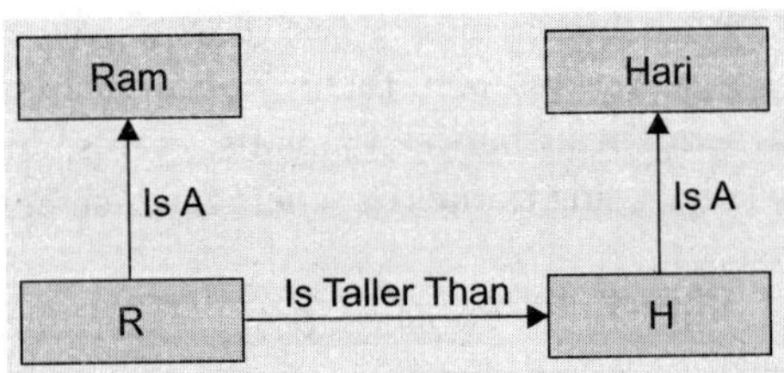

It can also be represented as

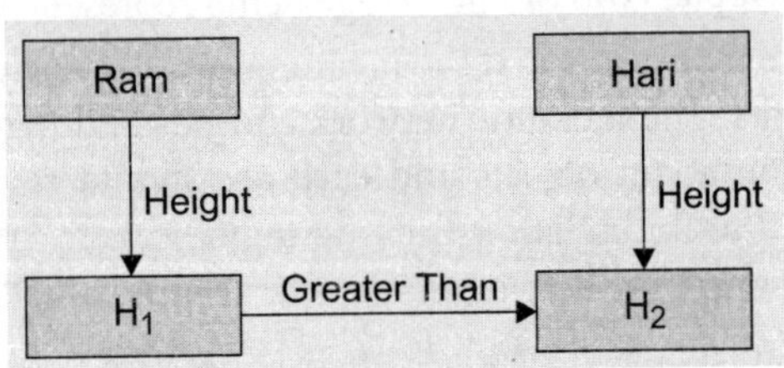

"Mouse is a Rodent and Rodent is a mammal. Mouse has teeth and etas grass". Check whether the sentence mammal has teeth is valid or not.]

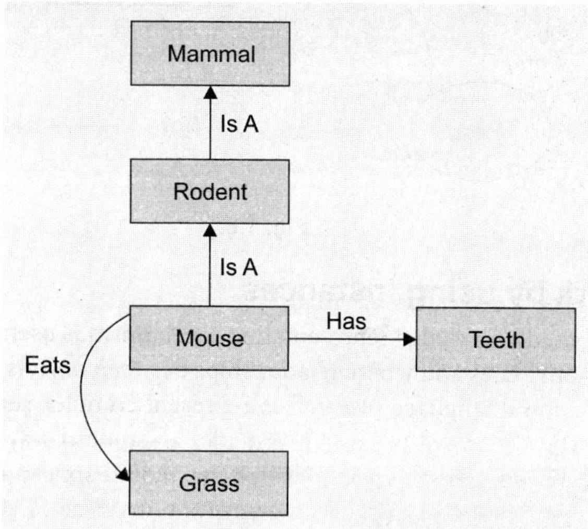

Partitioned Semantic Network

Some complex sentences are there which cannot be represented by simple semantic nets and for this we have to follow the technique partitioned semantic networks. Partitioned semantic net allow for

1. Propositions to be made without commitment to truth.
2. Expressions to be quantified.

In partitioned semantic network, the network is broken into spaces which consist of groups of nodes and arcs and regard each space as a node.

Let us consider few examples. Draw the partitioned semantic network structure for the followings:

Sima is eating an apple.

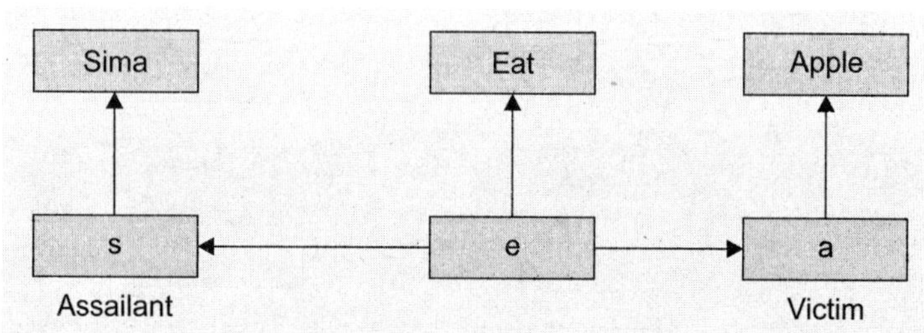

All Sima are eating an apple.

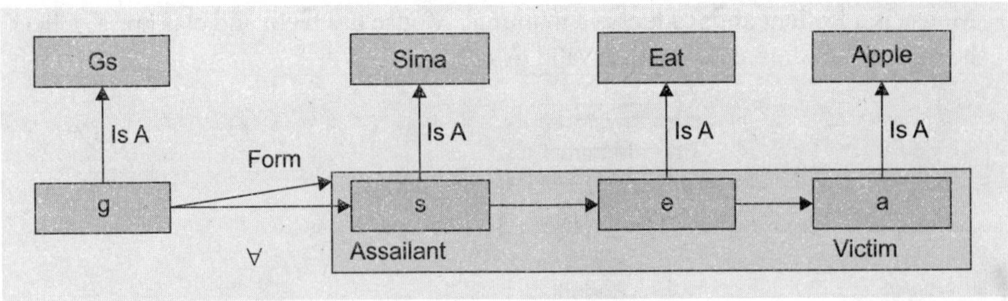

All Sima are eating some apple.

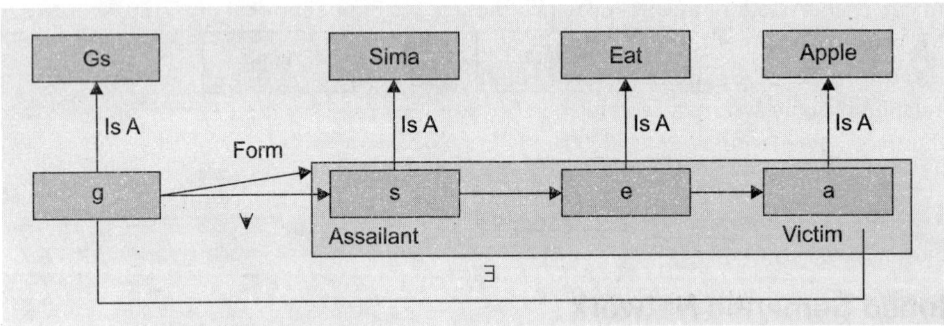

All men are mortal

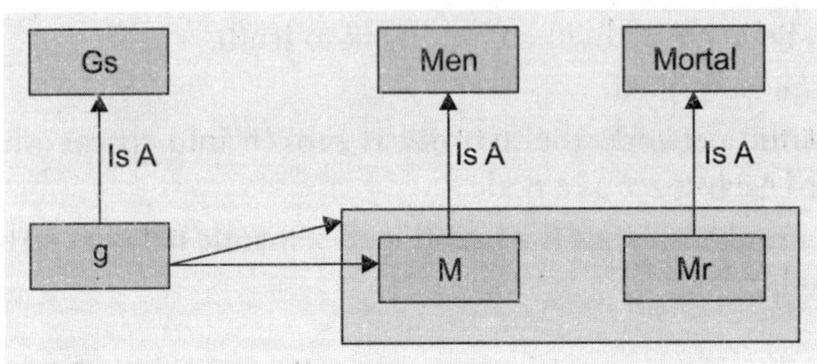

Every dog has bitten a shopkeeper

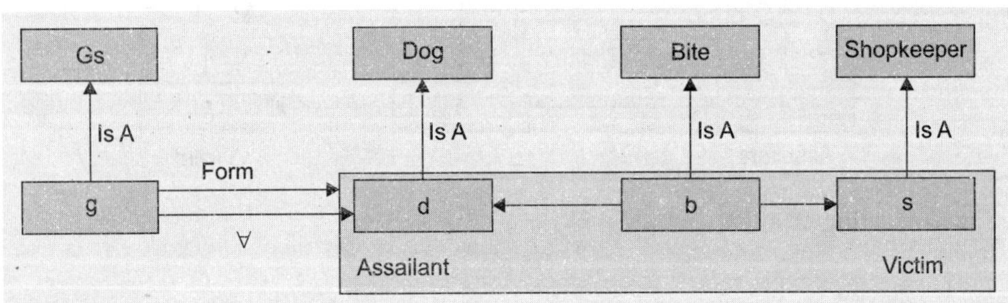

Every dog in town has bitten a shopkeeper.

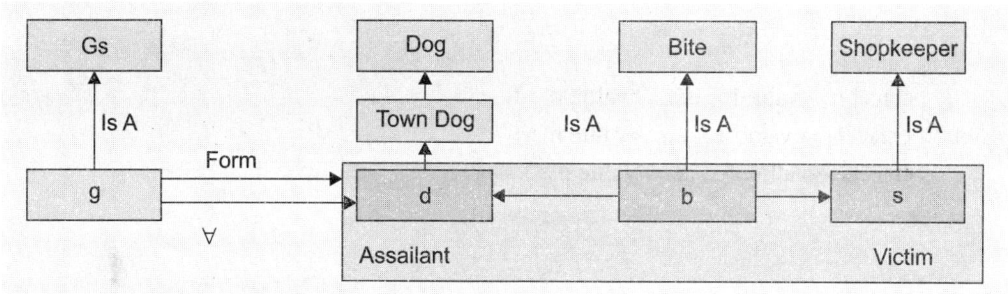

Note: On the above semantic network structures, the instance "IS A" is used. Also two terms like assailant and victim are used. Assailant means "by which the work is done" and that of victim refers to "on which the work is applied". Another term namely GS, which refers to General Statement. For GS, make a node g which is an instance of Gs. Every element will have at least two attributes. Firstly, a form that states which a relation is being asserted. Secondly, one or more for all (∀) or there exists (∃) connections which represent universally quantifiable variables.

FRAME

A frame is a data structure used in knowledge representation that represents an entity or object in the world. It consists of a collection of attributes and associated values, which describe various properties and characteristics of the entity.

Frames are similar to record-like structures, where each attribute is represented by a slot. A slot can have a name and a value, and it may also have subfields called facets, which provide additional information or constraints on the attribute value. The values in facets can be of any type and can have multiple occurrences.

A frame can have multiple slots, each representing a different attribute or property of the entity. The slots can contain information such as attribute-value pairs, default values, conditions for filling the slot, pointers to other related frames, or procedures that are activated when needed.

Frames can represent entities in an absolute sense, providing a comprehensive description of the entity, or they can represent the entity from a specific perspective or point of view.

In a frame system, multiple frames are connected to each other through relationships, where the value of one attribute in a frame may refer to another frame. This allows for the organization and interconnection of knowledge about various entities and their relationships.

It's important to note that a single frame taken alone is rarely useful. It is the collection of interconnected frames that forms a meaningful knowledge representation system. Each frame is typically represented with an opening parenthesis and closed with a closing parenthesis to denote its boundaries.

Syntax of a Frame

(<frame name>

(<slot1> (<facet1><value 1> .... <value n_1>)

(<facet2><value1> .... <value n_2>)

.

.

.

.

(<facet n><value1> .... <value n_n>))

(<slot 2> (<facet1><value 1> .... <value n_1>)

(<facet2><value2> .... <value n_2>)

.

.

))

Let us consider the below examples.

1. Create a frame of the person Ram who is a doctor. He is of 40. His wife name is Sita. They have two children Babu and Gita. They live in 100 kps street in the city of Delhi in India. The zip code is 756005.

   (Ram
   (PROFESSION (VALUE Doctor))
   (AGE (VALUE 40))
   (WIFE (VALUE Sita))
   (CHILDREN (VALUE Bubu, Gita))
   (ADDRESS
      (STREET (VALUE 100 kps))
      (CITY(VALUE Delhi))
      (COUNTRY(VALUE India))
      (ZIP (VALUE 756005))))

2. Create a frame of the person Anand who is a chemistry professor in RD Women's College. His wife name is Sangita having two children Rupa and Shipa.

   (Anand
      (PROFESSION (VALUE Chemistry Professor))
      (ADDRESS (VALUE RD Women's College))
      (WIFE (VALUE Sangita))
      (CHILDREN(VALUE RupaShipa)))

3. Create a frame of the person Akash who has a white maruti car of LX-400 Model. It has 5 doors. Its weight is 225kg, capacity is 8, and mileage is 15 km /lit.

   (Akash
      (CAR (VALUE Maruti))
      (COLOUR (VALUE White))
      (MODEL (VALUE LX-400))
      (DOOR (VALUE 5))
      (WEIGHT (VALUE 225kg))
      (CAPACITY (VALUE 8))
      (MILAGE (VALUE 15km/lit)))

Frames can indeed be connected to other frames, forming a network or hierarchy of interconnected frames. One type of frame that facilitates procedural attachment and supports the reasoning process is an action frame. Action frames are used to represent actions or procedures that can be performed within a knowledge representation system. They provide a structure for organizing the steps or processes involved in performing an action.

When reasoning using frames, the process of instantiation is employed. Instantiation occurs when a given situation is matched with existing frames in the network. The reasoning process then attempts to match the current problem state with the slots of the frames and assigns appropriate values to those slots. The values assigned to the slots within the frames represent specific situations or conditions. By assigning values to the slots, the reasoning process progresses towards achieving a goal or desired outcome. The reasoning process, in this context, can be seen as the process of filling slot values in frames to represent and manipulate knowledge. Overall, frames and their interconnections, along with the reasoning process of instantiation and slot value assignment, provide a mechanism for representing and reasoning about knowledge in a structured and goal-directed manner.

Conceptual Graphs

Conceptual graphs are another knowledge representation technique that extends the idea of semantic networks. They provide a graphical representation of knowledge using concepts, relationships, and propositions.

In conceptual graphs, concepts are represented as nodes, and relationships between concepts are represented as labeled arcs. These arcs capture the semantic connections between concepts, indicating how they are related to each other.

Conceptual graphs also include propositions, which are statements or assertions about the relationships between concepts. Propositions are represented as labeled arcs connecting the concepts involved in the statement. For example, a proposition "John is the father of Mary" would be represented as arcs connecting the concepts "John," "father," and "Mary."

One of the key features of conceptual graphs is their ability to express complex relationships and logical reasoning. They provide a formalism for representing logical operations such as conjunction, disjunction, negation, and implication. This allows for the representation of complex knowledge and the ability to perform inferencing and reasoning tasks.

Conceptual graphs are used in various domains, including artificial intelligence, natural language processing, and knowledge representation. They provide a flexible and expressive way to represent knowledge and facilitate the development of intelligent systems that can reason and understand natural language statements.

In conceptual graphs, the representation of individual and generic concepts follows a specific format in both graphical and linear representations.

For individual concepts, they are represented within a rectangle in graphical representation. This rectangle contains the concept name, which represents the type of the concept, followed by the reference field, which represents a specific instance of that concept. In linear representation, individual concepts are enclosed within square brackets.

On the other hand, generic concepts are represented within an oval in graphical representation. These concepts represent categories or classes of objects or concepts. In linear representation, generic concepts are enclosed within parentheses.

Conceptual graphs serve as the basic building blocks for associative networks. They provide a foundation for representing and organizing knowledge by using standard concepts like AGENT, OBJECT, INSTRUMENT, and PART. These basic concepts can be combined to define new concepts and relations.

A linear conceptual graph is a simplified form of the graphical representation, where a single conceptual graph corresponds to a natural language sentence. In this linear form, concepts are depicted as words, and the relationships between them are represented by their arrangement in the sentence. Overall, conceptual graphs offer a structured and graphical representation of concepts, relationships, and propositions, enabling the representation and manipulation of knowledge in a concise and meaningful way.

Consider an example

"Ram is eating an apple "

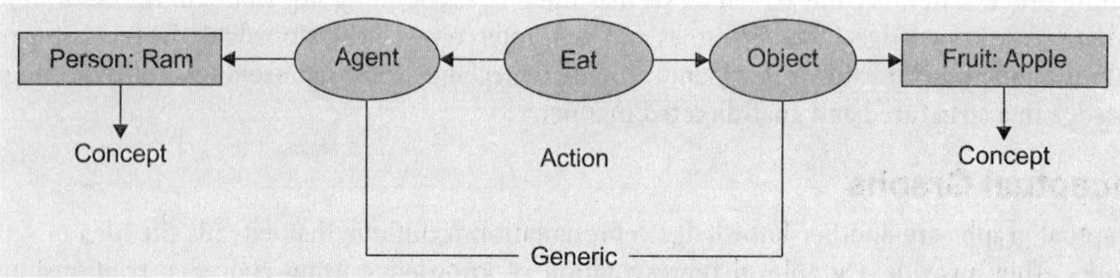

Fig. 1.9. Graphical Representation

[Person: Ram] ⟵ (Agent) ⟵ [Eat] ⟶ (Object) ⟶ [Fruit: Apple]

Conceptual Dependency

We may represent any type of knowledge using this additional technique for knowledge representation. It is based on the representation of any natural language assertion using a small set of simple concepts and formation principles. The foundation of conceptual dependence theory is the knowledge representation approach, which was initially created to comprehend and express the structures of natural language. Roger C. Shank created the conceptual dependence structures for the first time in 1977.

The knowledge representation needs to be strong enough to represent these ideas if a computer program is to be created that can comprehend a wide range of phenomena expressed in natural languages. The canonical form of sentence meaning is provided by the conceptual dependency representation, which captures the most concepts. Generally speaking, the conceptual dependence structure can be expressed using four primitives. Those are

(*a*) **ACTS:** Actions

(*b*) **PPs:** Objects (Picture Producers)

(*c*) **AAs:** Modifiers of Actions (Action Aiders)

(*d*) **PAs:** Modifiers of PPs (Picture Aiders)

(*e*) **TS:** Time of action

Conceptual dependency provides both a structure and a specific set of primitives at a particular level of granularity, out of which representation of particular pieces of information can be constructed.

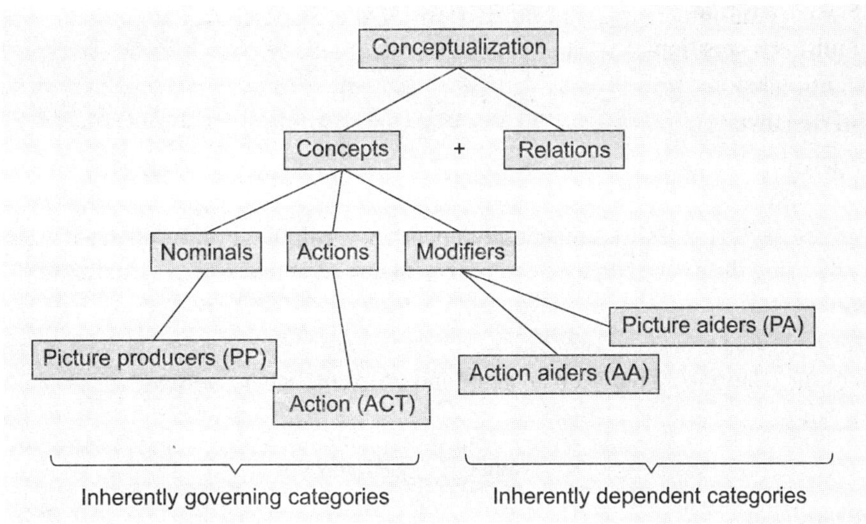

The main idea behind Conceptual Dependency is to break down sentences into a set of elementary concepts and their relationships. These elementary concepts represent the basic meaning of the sentence, independent of the specific words used. For example, the sentence "John gives the book to Mary" can be broken down into elementary concepts like "John", "give", "book", and "Mary", along with the relationships between them (e.g., John is the giver, book is the object, and Mary is the receiver).

In CD, representation of actions are built from a set of primitive acts.

1. **ATRANS:** Transfer of an abstract relationship (give, accept, take)
2. **PTRANS:** Transfer the physical location of an object (Go, Come, Run, Walk)
3. **MTRANS:** Transfer the mental information (Tell)
4. **PROPEL:** Application of physical force to an object (push, pull, throw)
5. **MOVE:** Movement of a body part by its owner (kick).
6. **GRASP:** Grasping of an object by an action (clutch)
7. **INGEST:** Ingestion of an object by an animal (eat)
8. **EXPEL:** Expel from an animal body (cry)
9. **MBUILD:** Building new information out of old (decide)
10. **SPEAK:** Production of sounds (say)
11. **ATTEND:** Focusing of a sense organ towards a stimulus (Listen)

The main goal of CD representation is to capture the implicit concept of a sentence and make it explicit. In normal representation of the concepts, besides actor and object, other concepts of time, location, source and destination are also mentioned. Following conceptual tenses are used in CD representation.

1. **O:** Object case relationship
2. **R:** Recipient case relationship
3. **P:** Past
4. **F:** Future
5. **Nil:** Present
6. **T:** Transition

7. **Ts:** Start Transition
8. **Tf:** Finisher Transition
9. **K:** Continuing
10. **?:** Interrogative
11. **/:** Negative
12. **C:** Conditional

Also there are several rules in conceptual dependency combination of all sense organs like eye, ear, nose etc.) By using the above rules we can represent any sentence. Let us visualize few examples on conceptual dependency.

Rule 1: PP ⟺ ACT

It describes the relationship between an actor and en event, he/she causes.

E.g., Ram ran

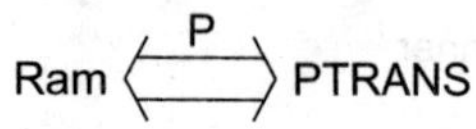

Where P: Past Tense

Rule 2: PP ⟺ PA

It describes the relationship between a PP and PA where the PA indicates one characteristics of PP. E.g., Ram is tall.

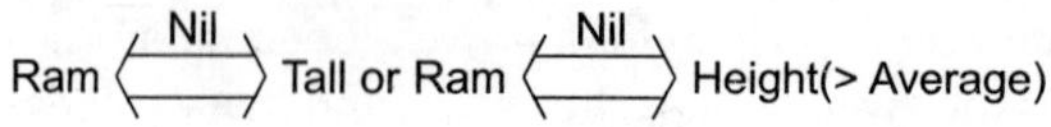

Rule 3: PP ⟺ PP

It describes the relationship between two PPs where one PP is defined by other.

E.g., Ram is a doctor

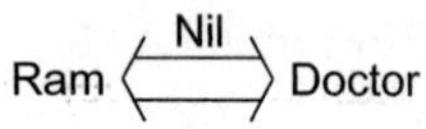

Rule 4:

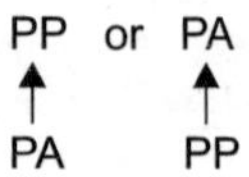

It describes the relationship between the PP and PA, where PA indicates one attributes of PP.

E.g., A nice boy is a doctor.

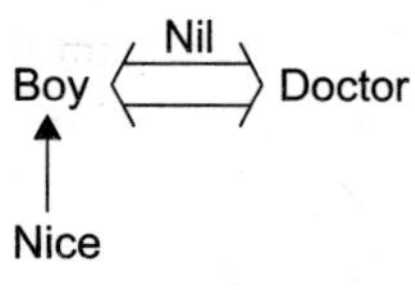

Rule 5:

It describes the relationship between 3 PP's where one PP is the owner of another PP.

E.g., Ram's Cat

Rule 6: Act $\xleftarrow{O}$ PP Where O: Object

It describes the relationship between the PP and ACT. Where PP indicates the object of that action. E.g., Ram is eating an apple.

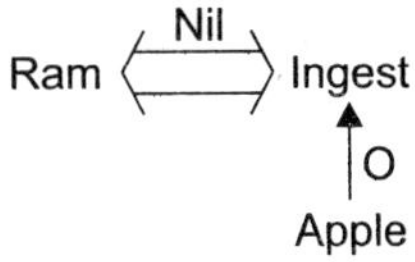

Rule 7:

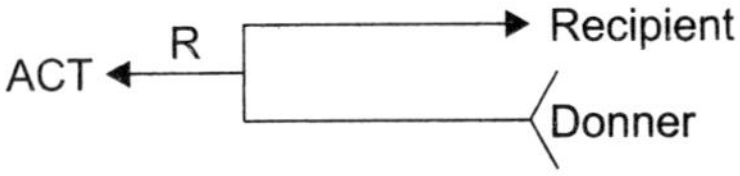

(R: Recipient)

Here one PP describes the recipients and another PP describes the donner

E.g., Rahul gave a book to Sourav.

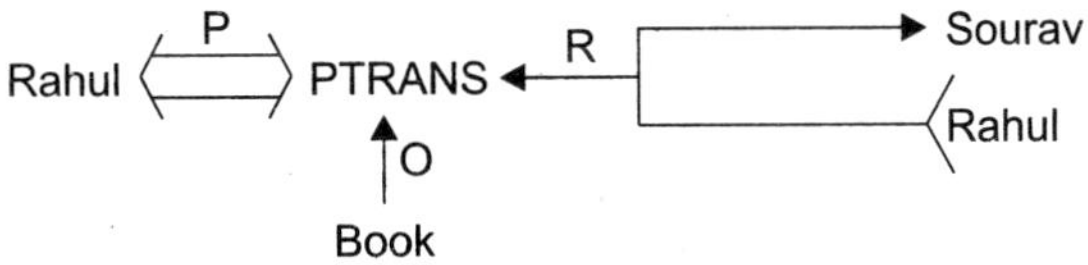

Rule 8:

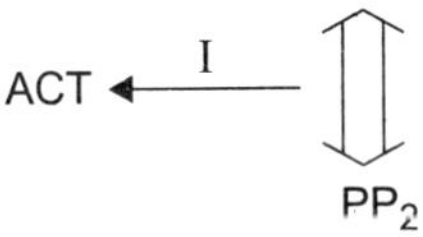

(I: Instrument used in the action)

Here PP_1 indicates the agent and PP_2 indicates the object that is used in the action.

E.g., Tapash ate the ice cream with the spoon.

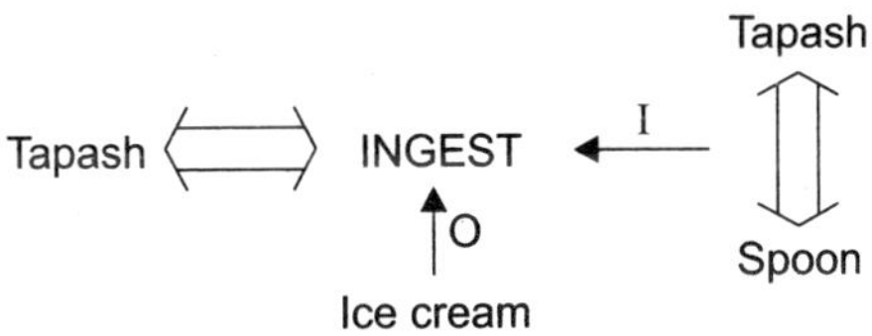

Rule 9:

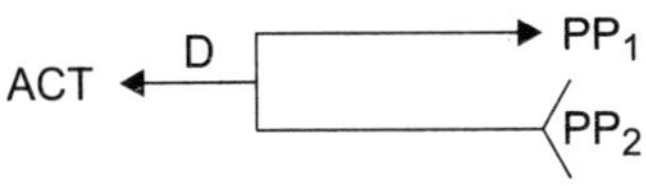

Here D indicates destination, PP_1 indicates destination and PP_2 indicates the source.

E.g., the bucket is filled with milk.

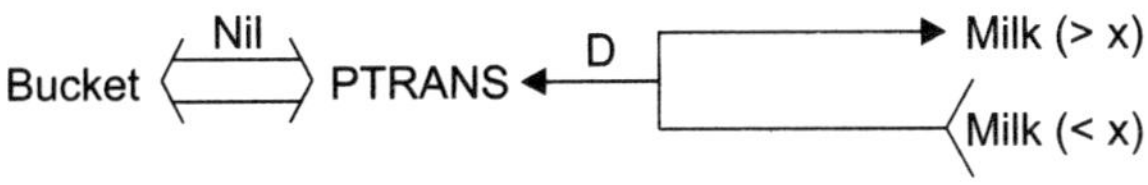

Xindicates the average milk and the source, i.e., bucket is dry which is hidden.

Rule 10:

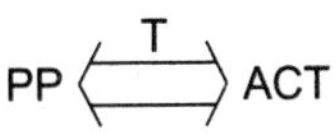

(T: Time)

It describes the relationship between a conceptualization and the time at which the event is described occurs.

E.g., Sita ate the apple yesterday.

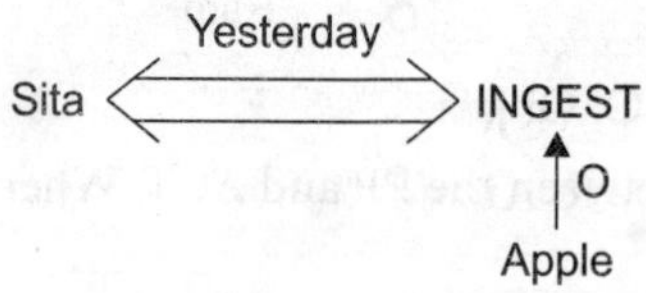

Rule 11: 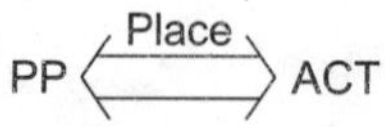

It describes the relationship between a conceptualization and the place at which it is occurred.

E.g., Shanu ate the apple at VRS hotel yesterday

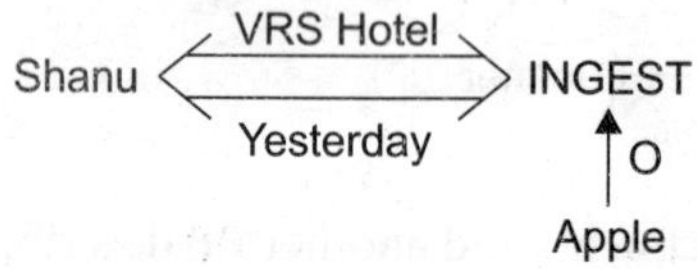

Rule 12: 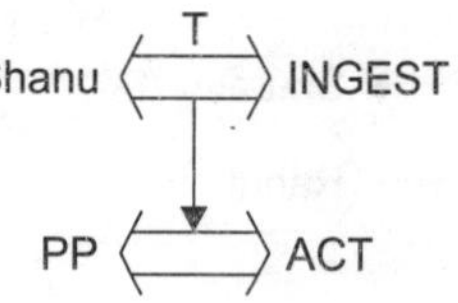

It describes the relationship between one conceptualization with another.

E.g., while I was going to college, I saw a snake.

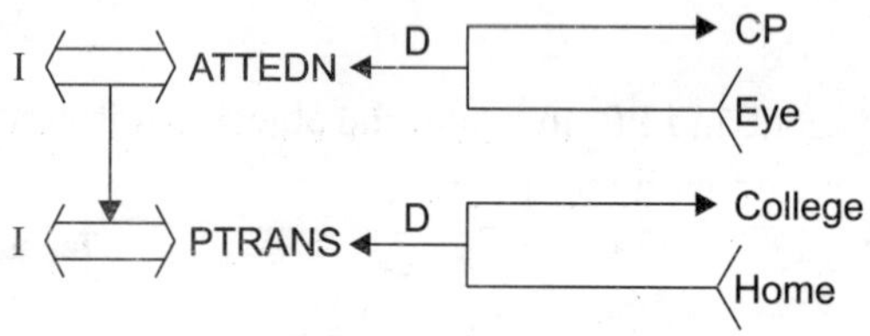

(Where CP: Conscious Processor, i.e., the combination of all sense organs like eye, ear, nose etc.)

By using the above rules we can represent any sentence. Let us visualize few examples on conceptual dependency.

(1) Sima gave a book to Niki

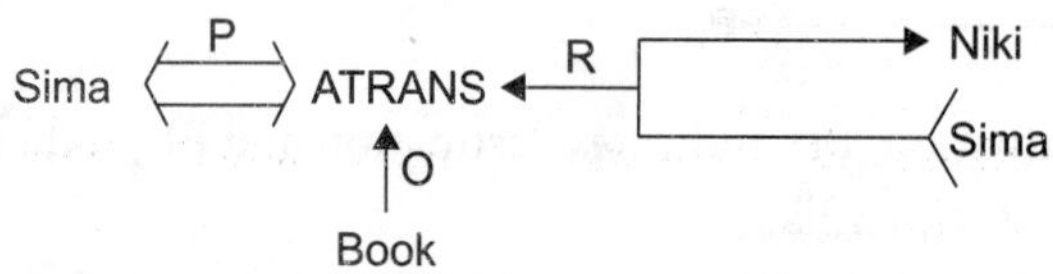

Where O: Object, P: Past Tense, R: Recipient, Sima: PP, Book: PP, Niki: PP, ATRANS: give

(2) Bhabani cuts an apple with a knife

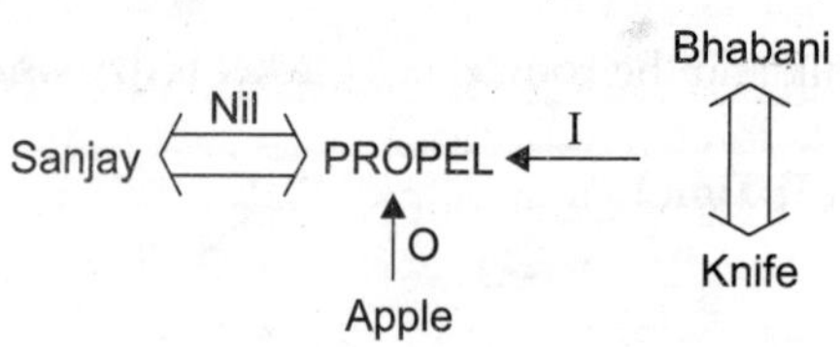

(3) Sanjay drove the car fast

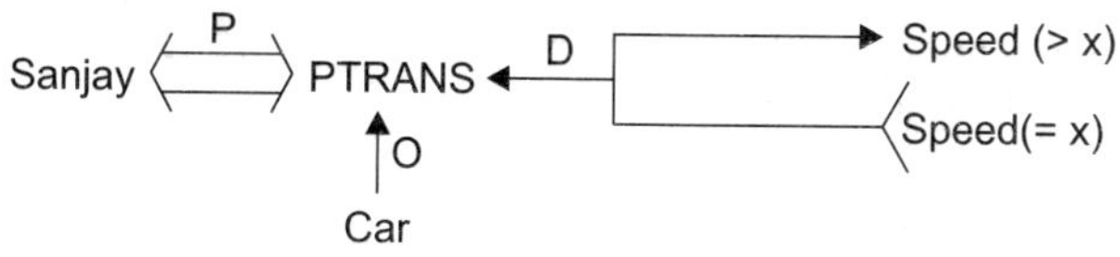

(4) The rose was given by Rupa to Anand

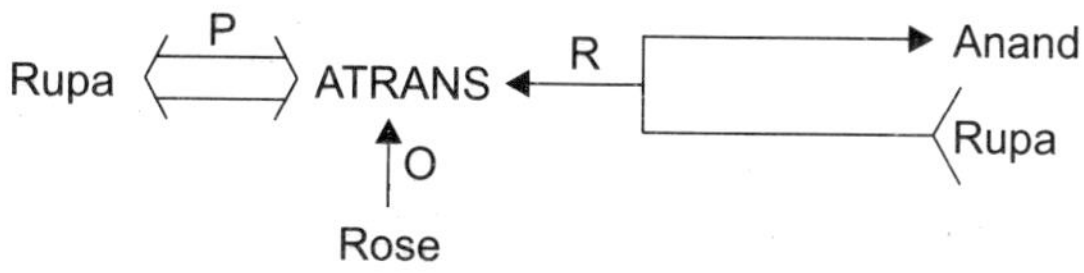

(5) Shruti pushed the door.

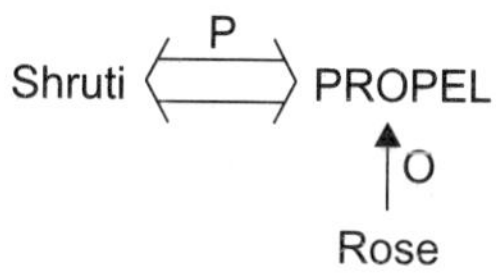

(6) The man took a book

Here man is the doctor and book is the object of the action took.

(7) My grandfather told me a story

(8) Ira gave the man a dictionary

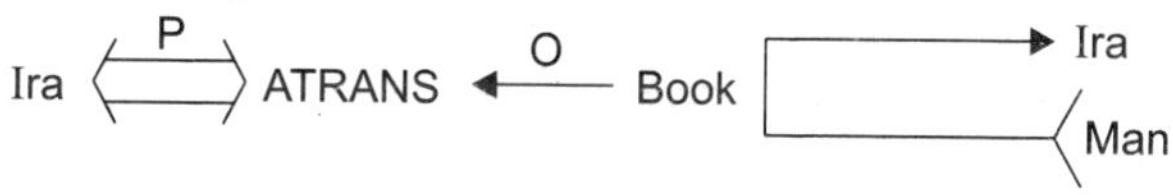

SCRIPT

It is another method of knowledge representation. Scripts are frame-like structures that are used to portray everyday situations like going to a restaurant or seeing the doctor. A script is a formal description of a predetermined course of action in a certain situation. A script is made up of a number of slots. Each slot might have some information about the kinds of values it might hold as well as a default value that would be used in the absence of any further information. In the actual world, there are no consistent patterns to how events occur, therefore scripts are helpful. These patterns develop as a result of causal connections between occurrences. An enormous casual chain is formed by the occurrences in a script. The entrance conditions that allow the script's first events to happen make up the beginning of the chain. The set of outcomes at the chain's conclusion may allow for the occurrence of subsequent events. All of a script's headers may be used to signal that the script has to be run.

There are several ways a script can be helpful in analyzing a certain circumstance once it has been activated. A script has the power to foretell future events that have not yet been explicitly observed. Using scripts to create a single cohesive interpretation out of a set of observations is an essential application.

Scripts are less universal than frames, hence they cannot be used to represent all types of knowledge. Scripts are excellent tools for illustrating the particular types of knowledge for which they were intended.

A script has various components like:

1. **Entry condition:** It must be true before the events described in the script can occur. E.g. in a restaurant script the entry condition must be the customer should be hungry and the customer has money.
2. **Tracks:** It specifies particular position of the script e.g. In a supermarket script the tracks may be cloth gallery, cosmetics gallery etc.
3. **Result:** It must be satisfied or true after the events described in the script have occurred. e.g. In a restaurant script the result must be true if the customer is pleased. The customer has less money.
4. **Probs:** It describes the inactive or dead participants in the script e.g. In a supermarket script, the probes may be clothes, sticks, doors, tables, bills etc.
5. **Roles:** It specifies the various stages of the script. E.g. In a restaurant script the scenes may be entering, ordering etc. Now let us look on a movie script description according to the above component.
   (*a*) **Script name:** Movie
   (*b*) **Track:** CINEMA HALL
   (*c*) **Roles:** Customer(c), Ticket seller(TS), Ticket Checker(TC), Snacks Sellers (SS)
   (*d*) **Probes:** Ticket, snacks, chair, money, Ticket, chart
   (*e*) **Entry condition:** The customer has money The customer has interest to watch movie.
6. **Scenes:**
   (a) SCENE-1 (Entering into the cinema hall)
   C PTRANS C into the cinema hall
   C ATTEND eyes towards the ticket counter
   C PTRANS C towards the ticket counters
   C ATTEND eyes to the ticket chart
   C MBUILD to take which class ticket
   C MTRANS TS for ticket
   C ATRANS money to TS
   TS ATRANS ticket to C
   (b) SCENE-2 (Entering into the main ticket check gate)
   C PTRANS C into the queue of the gate
   C ATRANS ticket to TC
   TC ATTEND eyes onto the ticket
   TC MBUILD to give permission to C for entering into the hall
   TC ATRANS ticket to C C PTRANS C into the picture hall.
   (c) SCENE-3 (Entering into the picture hall)
   C ATTEND eyes into the chair
   TC SPEAK where to sit

C PTRANS C towards the sitting position
C ATTEND eyes onto the screen

(d) SCENE-4 (Ordering snacks)
C MTRANS SS for snacks SS ATRANS snacks to C
C ATRANS money to SS C INGEST snacks

(e) SCENE-5 (Exit) C ATTEND eyes onto the screen till the end of picture
C MBUILD when to go out of the hall
C PTRANS C out of the hall 7)

Result: The customer is happy
The customer has less money

Syntax and Semantics of First-order Logic

First-order logic (FOL), also known as first-order predicate calculus, is a formal language used to represent statements and relationships in logic and mathematics. It is a type of formal logic that extends propositional logic by introducing quantifiers and variables.

Symbols and Interpretations

The basic syntactic elements of first-order logic are the symbols that stand for objects, relations, and functions. The symbols, therefore, come in three kinds: constant symbols, which stand for objects; predicate symbols, which stand for relations; and function symbols, which stand for functions.

As in propositional logic, every model must provide the information required to determine if any given sentence is true or false. Thus, in addition to its objects, relations, and functions, each model includes an interpretation that specifies exactly which objects, relations and functions are referred to by the constant, predicate, and function symbols.

$$
\begin{aligned}
\text{Sentence} &\rightarrow \text{AtomicSentence} \mid \text{ComplexSentence} \\
\text{AtomicSentence} &\rightarrow \text{Predicate} \mid \text{Predicate(Term, ...)} \mid \text{Term} = \text{Term} \\
\text{ComplexSentence} &\rightarrow \text{(Sentence)} \mid \text{[Sentence]} \\
&\mid \neg\, \text{Sentence} \\
&\mid \text{Sentence} \wedge \text{Sentence} \\
&\mid \text{Sentence} \vee \text{Sentence} \\
&\mid \text{Sentence} \Rightarrow \text{Sentence} \\
&\mid \text{Sentence} \Leftrightarrow \text{Sentence} \\
&\mid \text{Quantifier Variable, ... Sentence} \\
\text{Term} &\rightarrow \text{Function(Term, ...)} \\
&\mid \text{Constant} \\
&\mid \text{Variable} \\
\text{Quantifier} &\rightarrow \forall \mid \exists \\
\text{Constant} &\rightarrow A \mid X_1 \mid \text{John} \mid \ldots \\
\text{Variable} &\rightarrow a \mid x \mid s \mid \ldots \\
\text{Predicate} &\rightarrow \text{True} \mid \text{False} \mid \text{After} \mid \text{Loves} \mid \text{Raining} \mid \ldots \\
\text{Function} &\rightarrow \text{Mother} \mid \text{LeftLeg} \mid \ldots
\end{aligned}
$$

Operator Precedence : $\neg, =, \wedge, \vee, \Rightarrow, \Leftrightarrow$

Fig. 1. The syntax of first-order logic with equality, specified in Backus–Naur form (see page 1060 if you are not familiar with this notation). Operator precedences are specified, from highest to lowest. The precedence of quantifiers is such that a quantifier holds over everything to the right of it.

In summary, a model in first-order logic consists of a set of objects and an interpretation that maps constant symbols to objects, predicate symbols to relations on those objects, and function symbols to functions on those objects. Just as with propositional logic, entailment, validity, and so on are defined in terms of all possible models.

Terms

In first-order logic, a term is a logical expression that refers to an object or a value. Constant symbols are examples of terms because they directly represent specific objects or values, like "John," "Mary," or "42."

However, in some cases, it may not be practical or convenient to have a distinct constant symbol for every object or value in a domain. For instance, if we want to refer to "King John's left leg," it might be cumbersome to create a constant symbol for this specific object. Instead, we can use function symbols to represent such complex expressions.

Function symbols are used to define functions that take arguments and produce a value or an object as a result. They allow us to represent expressions like "King John's left leg" as a single term. In this case, we can define a function symbol "LeftLeg" that takes "John" as an argument and returns the object representing his left leg. So, instead of using a constant symbol, we write "LeftLeg(John)" as a term to refer to "King John's left leg."

Function symbols extend the expressiveness of first-order logic by allowing us to build more complex terms that represent relationships and properties of objects in a domain. They are a powerful tool for creating compact and expressive expressions in formal logic languages, such as first-order logic.

Atomic Sentences

Now that we have both terms for referring to objects and predicate symbols for referring to relations, we can put them together to make atomic sentences that state facts. An atomic sentence (or atom for short) is formed from a predicate symbol optionally followed by a ATOM parenthesized list of terms, such as Brother (Richard, John).

This states, under the intended interpretation given earlier, that Richard the Lionheart is the brother of King John.6 Atomic sentences can have complex terms as arguments. Thus, Married(Father (Richard), Mother (John)) states that Richard the Lionheart's father is married to King John's mother (again, under a suitable interpretation).

An atomic sentence is true in a given model if the relation referred to by the predicate symbol holds among the objects referred to by the arguments.

Complex Sentences

We can use logical connectives to construct more complex sentences, with the same syntax and semantics as in propositional calculus. Here are four sentences that are true in the model of Figure 8.2 under our intended interpretation:

Brother (LeftLeg(Richard), John)

Brother (Richard, John) $\wedge$ Brother (John, Richard)

King(Richard) ∨ King(John)
¬King(Richard) ⇒ King(John) .

Quantifiers

Quantifiers are an essential part of first-order logic that allows us to express statements about entire sets of objects or properties rather than individual objects. There are two main quantifiers in first-order logic:

Universal Quantifier (∀): The universal quantifier (∀) is used to express that a statement holds for all objects or elements in a specific domain. For example, ∀x P(x) asserts that the predicate P(x) is true for every individual x in the domain.

- **∀x (Even(x) → Integer(x)):** This statement asserts that for all elements x in the domain, if x is even, then x is an integer.
- **∀n (Prime(n) → Odd(n)):** This statement asserts that for all numbers n, if n is prime, then n is odd.

Existential Quantifier (∃): The existential quantifier (∃) is used to express that there exists at least one object in the domain for which a statement is true. For example, ∃x Q(x) asserts that there is at least one individual x in the domain for which the predicate Q(x) is true.

- **∃x (Positive(x) ∧ Negative(x)):** This statement asserts that there exists at least one element x in the domain that is both positive and negative (which is not possible in real numbers, but demonstrates the usage of quantifiers).
- **∃n (Even(n) ∧ Prime(n)):** This statement asserts that there exists at least one number n that is both even and prime.

"All kings are persons," is written in first-order logic as ∀ x King(x) ⇒ Person(x) . ∀ is usually pronounced "For all ...". (Remember that the upside-down A stands for "all.") Thus, the sentence says, "For all x, if x is a king, then x is a person." The symbol x is called a variable.

Quantifiers are often used in conjunction with variables to create quantified statements. For example:

∀x (P(x) → Q(x)): This statement asserts that for all elements x in the domain, if P(x) is true, then Q(x) must also be true.

∃y (R(y) ∧ S(y)): This statement asserts that there exists at least one element y in the domain for which both R(y) and S(y) are true.

Quantifiers play a crucial role in formalizing mathematical statements, defining the scope of variables, and expressing general properties and relationships within a logical system. They allow us to make precise statements about sets of objects, making first-order logic a powerful tool for reasoning and deduction.

Nested Quantifiers

Nested quantifiers are a powerful feature in first-order logic that allows us to express more complex statements involving multiple quantified variables. With nested quantifiers, we can quantify over multiple variables, making it possible to reason about relationships between elements in a domain more precisely.

Let's consider an example involving nested quantifiers:

Domain: A set of students in a school.

Predicates:

- "Likes(x, y)": Student x likes student y.
- "Studying(x, course)": Student x is studying course y.

Statement: $\exists x \exists y (Likes(x, y) \land \forall z\, Studying(z, Math) \rightarrow Likes(x, z))$

This statement can be read as: "There exist two students x and y, where student x likes student y, and for all students z who are studying Math, student x also likes student z."

For example, to say that siblinghood is a symmetric relationship, we can write
$\forall x, y\ Sibling(x, y) \Leftrightarrow Sibling(y, x)$.

In other cases we will have mixtures. "Everybody loves somebody" means that for every person, there is someone that person loves:
$\forall x \exists y\ Loves(x, y)$. On the other hand, to say "There is someone who is loved by everyone," we write
$\exists y \forall x\ Loves(x, y)$.

The order of quantification is therefore very important. It becomes clearer if we insert parentheses. $\forall x\ (\exists y\ Loves(x, y))$ says that everyone has a particular property, namely, the property that they love someone. On the other hand, $\exists y\ (\forall x\ Loves(x, y))$ says that someone in the world has a particular property, namely the property of being loved by everybody.

In other words, the statement asserts that there are two students in the domain (x and y) such that student x likes student y. Furthermore, for all students z who are studying the course Math, student x also likes student z.

Nested quantifiers allow us to express complex relationships involving different variables in a succinct and precise manner, making first-order logic a powerful tool for formalizing statements and reasoning about various domains and their relationships.

Connections between ∀ and ∃

(1) **Negation:** The negation of a universal quantification ($\forall x\, P(x)$) is an existential quantification ($\exists x\, \neg P(x)$), and vice versa. For example, $\neg(\forall x\, P(x))$ is equivalent to $\exists x\, \neg P(x)$, and $\neg(\exists x\, P(x))$ is equivalent to $\forall x\, \neg P(x)$. This is known as De Morgan's Law for quantifiers.

(2) **Relation in terms of Domain Size:** $\forall x\, P(x)$ means that P(x) is true for every individual x in the entire domain. On the other hand, $\exists x\, P(x)$ means that there exists at least one individual x in the domain for which P(x) is true. These quantifiers express different properties related to the size of the domain.

(3) **Combined Statements:** Universal and existential quantifiers can be combined in complex statements. For example, the statement $\forall x \exists y\, R(x, y)$ means "For every individual x, there exists at least one individual y such that R(x, y) is true." This type of statement makes a claim about every individual and also asserts the existence of specific elements satisfying the condition R(x, y) for each x.

In summary, "∀" and "∃" are fundamental quantifiers in first-order logic that express different types of statements about variables in a domain. Universal quantification asserts that a statement is true for all elements in the domain, while existential quantification asserts that there exists at least one element for which the statement is true. Both quantifiers can be used independently or in combination to express various logical statements.

Let's consider a domain of natural numbers (N) and define two predicates:

P(x): "x is an even number."

Q(x): "x is a prime number."

Example 1: $\forall x\, P(x)$ means "For all natural numbers x, x is an even number." This statement asserts that every natural number is even. Since this is not true (e.g., 1 is not even), the statement is false.

Example 2: $\exists x\, Q(x)$ means "There exists a natural number x such that x is a prime number." This statement asserts that there is at least one prime number in the domain. Since this is true (e.g., 2 is a prime number), the statement is true.

Example 3: $\forall x\ Q(x)$ means "For all natural numbers x, x is a prime number." This statement asserts that every natural number is a prime number. Since this is not true (e.g., 1 is not prime), the statement is false.

Example 4: $\exists x\ P(x)$ means "There exists a natural number x such that x is an even number." This statement asserts that there is at least one even number in the domain. Since this is true (e.g., 2 is even), the statement is true.

Example 5: $\forall x\ (P(x) \rightarrow Q(x))$ means "For all natural numbers x, if x is even, then x is prime." This statement makes a claim about the relationship between even and prime numbers. Since this statement is not universally true (e.g., 4 is even but not prime), the statement is false.

Example 6: $\exists x\ (P(x) \wedge Q(x))$ means "There exists a natural number x such that x is both even and prime." This statement asserts the existence of a number that is both even and prime. Since there is no such number in the domain, the statement is false.

These examples demonstrate how the universal and existential quantifiers can be used to make statements about the properties of elements in a domain and their relationships. The truth or falsity of these statements depends on the specific properties of the domain and the predicates involved.

Equality

In first-order logic, the equality symbol (=) is used to express the concept of equality between two terms. It is a binary relation that indicates that two terms refer to the same object or have the same value.

For example, if we have the constant symbols a and b, the expression $a = b$ asserts that a and b refer to the same object or have the same value.

Properties of Equality

Reflexivity: For any term t, $t = t$. This means every term is equal to itself.

Symmetry: If $t1 = t2$, then $t2 = t1$. This means the order of terms in an equality does not matter.

Transitivity: If $t1 = t2$ and $t2 = t3$, then $t1 = t3$. This means if two terms are equal and the second term is equal to a third term, then the first term is also equal to the third term.

In first-order logic, the equality symbol can be used in formulas to state that certain terms are equal, and these formulas can be part of quantified statements or logical implications.

Example 1: Let's consider a domain of natural numbers (N) and define the constant symbols $a = 5$ and $b = 2$. The formula $a = b$ asserts that 5 is equal to 2, which is false.

Example 2: In a more complex example, let's consider the formula $\forall x\ (x + 1 = x + 1)$. This formula uses the universal quantifier to state that for all natural numbers x, the term $(x + 1)$ is equal to itself. This is true because of the reflexivity property of equality.

Example 3: Consider the formula $\exists x\ (x^\wedge 2 = 9)$. This formula uses the existential quantifier to state that there exists a number x such that x^2 is equal to 9. This is true because $x = 3$ satisfies the equation.

These examples illustrate how the equality symbol is used to make statements about the equality of terms and how it interacts with quantified formulas. It plays a fundamental role in expressing relationships and properties in first-order logic.

Using First-Order Logic

We provide more systematic representations DOMAIN of some simple domains. In knowledge representation, a domain is just some part of the world about which we wish to express some knowledge.

Assertions and queries in first-order logic

In first-order logic, assertions and queries are two types of statements used to represent knowledge and make logical inquiries about the domain of interest. These statements are formulated using logical formulas and symbols, including quantifiers, predicates, and connectives.

Assertions:

Assertions in first-order logic are statements that assert or represent some knowledge about the domain. They are used to express facts or properties that are believed to be true in the given domain. Assertions are typically represented as logical sentences or formulas.

Examples of Assertions:

(*a*) **P(x):** "x is a prime number." (P is a unary predicate)

(*b*) **Q(x, y):** "x is the parent of y." (Q is a binary predicate)

(c) **∀x P(x):** "All numbers are prime." (Universal quantification)

(*d*) **∃x Q(x, John):** "There exists a parent of John." (Existential quantification)

Queries

Queries in first-order logic are statements used to ask questions or inquire about the truth of certain properties in the domain. They are used to seek answers to specific questions based on the given knowledge and logical rules.

Examples of Queries:

(*a*) **Q(2, y):** "Who is the parent of 2?" (Variable y is used to represent the answer)

(*b*) **∃x P(x):** "Is there a prime number in the domain?"

(*c*) **¬∀x P(x):** "Is it not true that all numbers are prime?" (Negation of the assertion in example c)

In both assertions and queries, quantifiers (universal and existential) play a crucial role in determining the scope of the statement. Universal quantifiers (∀) express that the statement holds for all elements in the domain, while existential quantifiers (∃) indicate the existence of at least one element that satisfies the statement.

Logical formulas can be constructed using predicates, constants, variables, and logical connectives (negation, conjunction, disjunction, implication, and biconditional) to express complex relationships and properties within the domain.

To evaluate the truth value of assertions and answer queries, first-order logic relies on inference rules and reasoning mechanisms. Model theory and deduction techniques are used to derive conclusions and answers based on the given knowledge and logical rules.

Overall, assertions and queries in first-order logic form the basis for representing knowledge and making inquiries in a formal and logical manner, facilitating the development of powerful reasoning systems and artificial intelligence applications.

The Kinship Domain

The kinship domain is a classical example used in the study of first-order logic and artificial intelligence. It involves representing family relationships and using logical statements to describe the kinship relations between different individuals in a family.

In this domain, individuals are represented as constant symbols, and kinship relations are expressed using predicates. For example, we can have predicates like "parent(x, y)" to represent that "x" is the parent of "y," "sibling(x, y)" to denote that "x" is a sibling of "y," and so on.

With these predicates, we can define various relationships and make assertions or queries about family members. For instance, we can write assertions like "parent(john, mary)" to state that John is the parent of Mary, or "sibling(mary, david)" to assert that Mary is a sibling of David.

Additionally, we can pose queries like "∃ x parent(x, john)" to ask if there exists any person who is the parent of John. This query would be true if there is at least one individual who is the parent of John, and it would be false otherwise.

The kinship domain is a fundamental example used in the study of first-order logic and provides insights into how logical expressions can be used to represent complex relationships and answer questions about a given domain. It serves as a foundation for more sophisticated applications in knowledge representation and reasoning.

Let's dive deeper into the kinship domain and explore some additional examples and concepts related to first-order logic.

In the kinship domain, we can represent individuals with constant symbols. For instance, let's consider the following constants:

- **john:** representing an individual named John
- **mary:** representing an individual named Mary
- **david:** representing an individual named David
- **alice:** representing an individual named Alice
- ... and so on for other family members

We can then use predicates to represent different kinship relations:

- **parent(x, y):** This predicate represents that "x" is the parent of "y."
- **sibling(x, y):** This predicate denotes that "x" is a sibling of "y."
- **grandparent(x, y):** This predicate expresses that "x" is the grandparent of "y."
- **cousin(x, y):** This predicate indicates that "x" is a cousin of "y."
- ...

With these predicates, we can make assertions about the relationships between family members. For example:

(1) **parent(john, mary):** This statement asserts that John is the parent of Mary.

(2) **sibling(mary, david):** This statement asserts that Mary is a sibling of David.

(3) **grandparent(john, alice):** This statement asserts that John is the grandparent of Alice.

(4) **cousin(mary, david):** This statement asserts that Mary is a cousin of David.

In first-order logic, we can also use quantifiers to make more complex statements and queries. For instance:

- ∃ **x parent(x, john):** This query asks if there exists an individual "x" who is the parent of John. If there is at least one such person, the query is true.
- ∀ **x sibling(x, mary):** This statement asserts that every individual "x" is a sibling of Mary. If all family members are siblings of Mary, the statement is true.
- ∃ **x grandparent(x, alice) ∧ parent(john, x):** This query asks if there exists an individual "x"

who is both a grandparent of Alice and a child of John. If there is at least one such person, the query is true.

The kinship domain provides a rich example to understand how first-order logic can be used to represent relationships and make logical assertions and queries about family members. It is a foundational concept in knowledge representation and reasoning and finds applications in various AI systems and databases.

Numbers, Sets, and Lists

Numbers are perhaps the most vivid example of how a large theory can be built up from a tiny kernel of axioms. We describe here the theory of natural numbers or non-negative integers. We need a predicate NatNum that will be true of natural numbers; we need one PEANO AXIOMS constant symbol, 0; and we need one function symbol, S (successor). The Peano axioms define natural numbers and addition.9 Natural numbers are defined recursively:

NatNum(0).

$\forall$ n NatNum(n) $\Rightarrow$ NatNum(S(n)).

That is, 0 is a natural number, and for every object n, if n is a natural number, then S(n) is a natural number. So the natural numbers are 0, S(0), S(S(0)), and so on. We also need axioms to constrain the successor function:

$$\forall n\ 0 \neq S)n).$$

$$\forall m, n\ m \neq n \Rightarrow S(m) \neq S(n).$$

Now we can define addition in terms of the successor function:

$$\forall m\ NatNum(m) \Rightarrow +(0, m) = m.$$

$$\forall m, n\ NatNum(m) \wedge NatNum(n) \Rightarrow +(S(m), n) = S(+(m, n)).$$

The first of these axioms says that adding 0 to any natural number m gives m itself. Notice the use of the binary function symbol "+" in the term +(m, 0); in ordinary mathematics, the term would be written m + 0 using infix notation. (The notation we have used for first-order logic is called **prefix**.) To make our sentences about numbers easier to read, we allow the use of infix notation. We can also write S(n) as n + 1, so the second axiom becomes

$$\forall m, n\ NatNum(m) \wedge NatNum(n) \Rightarrow (m + 1) + n = (m + n) + 1$$

The axiom reduces addition to repeated application of the successor function.

The use of infix notation is an example of **syntactic sugar**, that is, an extension to or abbreviation of the standard syntax that does not change the semantics. Any sentence that uses sugar can be "desugared" to produce an equivalent sentence in ordinary first-order logic.

Once we have addition, it is straightforward to define multiplication as repeated addition, exponentiation as repeated multiplication, integer division and remainders, prime numbers, and so on. Thus, the whole of number theory (including cryptography) can be built up from one constant, one function, one predicate and four axioms.

The domain of **sets** is also fundamental to mathematics as well as to commonsense reasoning. (In fact, it is possible to define number theory in terms of set theory.) We want to be able to represent individual sets, including the empty set. We need a way to build up sets by adding an element to a set or taking the union or intersection of two sets. We will want to distinguish sets from objects that are not sets.

We will use the normal vocabulary of set theory as syntactic sugar. The empty set is a constant written as { }. There is one unary predicate, Set, which is true of sets. The binary predicates are $x \in s$(x is a member of set s) and $s_1 \subseteq s_2$ (set s_1 is a subset, not necessarily proper, of set s_2). The binary functions are $s_1 \cap s_2$ (the intersection of two sets), $s_1 \cup s_2$ (the union of two sets), and $\{x|s\}$ (the set resulting from adjoining element x to set s). One possible set of axioms is as follows:

1. The only sets are the empty set and those made by adjoining something to a set:
$$\forall s\ Set(s) \Leftrightarrow (s = \{\ \}) \vee (\exists x, s_2\ Set(s_2) \wedge s = \{x|s_2\}).$$
2. The empty set has no elements adjoined into it. In other words, there is no way to decompose { } into a smaller set and an element:
$$\neg\exists x, s\ \{x|s\} = \{\ \}.$$
3. Adjoining an element already in the set has no effect:
$$\forall x, s\ x \in s \Leftrightarrow s = \{x|s\}.$$
4. The only members of a set are the elements that were adjoined into it. We express this recursively, saying that x is a member of s if and only if s is equal to some set s_2 adjoined with some element y, where either y is the same as x or x is a member of s_2:
$$\forall x, s\ x \in s \Leftrightarrow \exists y, s_2\ (s = \{y|s_2\} \wedge (x = y \vee x \in s_2)).$$
5. A set is a subset of another set if and only if all of the first set's members are members of the second set:
$$\forall s_1, s_2\ s_1 \subseteq s_2 \Leftrightarrow (\forall x\ x \in s_1 \Rightarrow x \in s_2).$$
6. Two sets are equal if an only if each is a subset of the other:
$$\forall s_1, s_2\ (s_1 = s_2) \Leftrightarrow (s_1 \subseteq s_2 \wedge s_2 \subseteq s_1).$$
7. An object is in the intersection of two sets if and only if it is a member of both sets:
$$\forall x, s_1, s_2\ x \in (s_1 \cap s_2) \Leftrightarrow (x \in s_1 \wedge x \in s_2).$$
8. An object is in the union of two sets if and only if it is a member of either set:
$$\forall x, s_1, s_2\ x \in (s_1 \cup s_2) \Leftrightarrow (x \in s_1 \vee x \in s_2).$$

Lists are similar to sets. The differences are that lists are ordered and the same element can appear more than once in a list. We can use the vocabulary of Lisp for lists: Nil is the constant list with no elements; Cons, Append, First, and Rest are functions; and Find is the predicate that does for lists what Member does for sets, List? is a predicated that is true only of lists. As with sets, it is common to used syntactic sugar in logical sentences involving lists. The empty list is []. The term Cons(x, y), where y is a non-empty list, is written [x|y]. The term Cons(x, Nil)(i.e., the list containing the element x) is written as [x]. A list of several elements, such as [A, B, C], corresponds to the nested term Cons(A, Cons(B, Cons(C, Nil))).

The Wumpus World

The Wumpus World is a classic artificial intelligence (AI) problem used as a testbed for various intelligent agents and reasoning systems. It was introduced by Stuart Russell and Peter Norvig in their book "Artificial Intelligence: A Modern Approach."

In the Wumpus World, the agent (usually represented as a robot or explorer) is placed in a square grid, typically of size 4×4 or 5×5, where it needs to navigate through the environment to accomplish certain goals. The grid contains various elements, including:

(1) **Wumpus:** A dangerous creature that can kill the agent if it moves to the same cell as the Wumpus.

(2) **Pits:** Deadly holes in the ground that can cause the agent to fall and fail the mission if it moves into a pit.

(3) **Gold:** A treasure that the agent needs to collect to achieve its objective.

(4) **Stench:** A percept or clue that indicates the presence of the Wumpus in adjacent cells.

(5) **Breeze:** A percept or clue that indicates the presence of a pit in adjacent cells.

The agent can perceive the current state of the environment through sensors. These sensors provide perceptual information such as stench, breeze, and glimmer (indicating the presence of gold nearby).

The agent's task is to navigate through the Wumpus World to find the gold while avoiding the Wumpus and pits. It needs to reason about its actions and make decisions based on the available information and knowledge about the environment.

(1) **The Agent:** The agent is the intelligent entity that explores the Wumpus World. It has limited perception and can sense its surroundings using perceptual information such as stench, breeze, and glimmer. The agent's goal is to find the gold and safely return to the starting point without getting killed by the Wumpus or falling into pits.

(2) **Grid Environment:** The Wumpus World is represented as a grid of cells, usually a 4x4 or 5x5 grid. Each cell can be either clear, containing no hazards, or occupied by the Wumpus, a pit, or the gold.

(3) **Wumpus:** The Wumpus is a dangerous creature that resides in one of the cells. If the agent enters the same cell as the Wumpus, it gets killed, and the mission fails.

(4) **Pits:** The Wumpus World contains pits, which are holes in the ground that the agent must avoid. If the agent enters a cell with a pit, it falls into the pit, and the mission fails.

(5) **Gold:** The agent's objective is to find the gold and pick it up. Once the agent collects the gold, it must return to the starting point to complete the mission successfully.

(6) **Percepts:** The agent's sensors provide perceptual information about the surrounding cells. The agent can perceive stench if the Wumpus is present in adjacent cells, breeze if there is a pit nearby, and glimmer if there is gold in an adjacent cell.

(7) **Actions:** The agent can take various actions to move through the environment, including moving forward, turning left or right, and grabbing the gold.

Solving the Wumpus World problem involves creating an intelligent agent capable of reasoning about its actions based on the perceptual information received. The agent must make decisions on which actions to take to reach its goal while avoiding hazards and maximizing the chances of success.

To approach this problem, AI researchers and practitioners use search algorithms to explore the possible paths in the environment, planning techniques to strategize the agent's moves, and reasoning methods to infer the presence of hazards based on perceptual information.

The Wumpus World is a classic example of an uncertain and partially observable environment, which poses challenges for AI agents. It serves as an excellent testbed for evaluating the performance of different AI algorithms and reasoning systems in real-world-like scenarios.

To solve the Wumpus World problem, AI agents typically use various search algorithms, such as depth-first search, breadth-first search, A* search, or other informed search techniques. They may also employ knowledge representation and reasoning methods, such as propositional logic or first-order logic, to infer the presence of hazards based on perceptual information.

The Wumpus World is an interesting and challenging problem in AI, as it requires agents to deal with uncertainty, partial information, and potential dangers while making decisions to achieve a specific goal. It serves as a popular benchmark to evaluate the performance of intelligent agents and reasoning systems in dynamic and uncertain environments.

A variety of "worlds" are being used as examples for Knowledge Representation, Reasoning, and Planning. Among them the Vacuum World, the Block World, and the Wumpus World. We will examine the Wumpus World and in this context introduce the Situation Calculus, the Frame Problem, and a variety of axioms.

The Wumpus World was introduced by Genesereth, and is discussed in Russell-Norvig. The Wumpus World is a simple world (as is the Block World) for which to represent knowledge and to reason.

It is a cave with a number of rooms, represented as a 4×4 square.

4	Stench		Breeze	Breeze
3	Wumpus	Stench breeze gold	Pit	Breeze
2	Stench		Breeze	
1	Start ⇒	Breeze	Pit	Breeze
	1	2	3	4

Rules of the Wumpus World

The neighborhood of a node consists of the four squares north, south, east, west of the given square.

In a square the agent gets a vector of percepts, with components

Stench,Breeze,Glitter,Bump,Scream

For example [Stench,None,Glitter,None,None]

- Stench is perceived at a square iff the wumpus is at this square or in its neighborhood.
- Breeze is perceived at a square iff a pit is in the neighborhood of this square.
- Glitter is perceived at a square iff gold is in this square
- Bump is perceived at a square iff the agent goes Forward into a wall
- Scream is perceived at a square iff the wumpus is killed anywhere in the cave

An agent can do the following actions (one at a time):

Turn(Right), Turn(Left), Forward, Shoot, Grab, Release, Climb

- The agent can go Forward in the direction it is currently facing, or Turn Right, or Turn Left. Going Forward into a wall will generate a Bump percept.
- The agent has a single arrow that it can Shoot. It will go straight in the direction faced by the agent until it hits (and kills) the wumpus, or hits (and is absorbed by) a wall.
- The agent can Grab a portable object at the current square or it can Release an object that it is holding.
- The agent can Climb out of the cave if at the Start square.

The Start square is (1,1) and initially the agent is facing east. The agent dies if it is in the same square as the wumpus. The objective of the game is to kill the wumpus, to pick up the gold, and to climb out with it.

The Situation Calculus

The Situation Calculus is used in cases as the one that we are now considering. With the name Situation we mean a state of the world. The Situation Calculus is used to reason about actions and their effect on the possible states of the world.

We will limit our discussion of the Situation Calculus to the case of the Wumpus World.

The Frame Problem

We are reasoning about possible states of the world, where the states are identified by the actions by which we got to that state from the initial state. The Frame Problem is concerned with the question of what happens to the truth-value of the statements that describe the world as we go from one world to the world resulting by application of an action.

We deal with the frame problem by introducing a certain number of axioms, that go by names such as Effect Axioms, Frame Axioms, and Successor-State Axioms.

Representing our Knowledge about the Wumpus World

Percept(x,y)

where x must be a percept vector and y must be a situation. It means that at situation y the agent perceives x.

For convenience we introduce the following definitions:

- Percept([Stench,y,z,w,v],t) = > Stench(t)
- Percept([x,Breeze,z,w,v],t) = > Breeze(t)
- Percept([x,y,Glitter,w,v],t) = > AtGold(t)

Holding(x,y)

where x is an object and y is a situation. It means that the agent is holding the object x in situation y.

Action(x,y)

where x must be an action (i.e. Turn(Right), Turn(Left), Forward, ..) and y must be a situation. It means that at situation y the agent takes action x.

At(x,y,z)

where x is an object, y is a Location, i.e. a pair [u,v] with u and v in {1,2,3,4}, and z is a situation. It means that the agent x in situation z is at location y.

Present(x,s)

means that object x is in the current room in the situation s.

Result(x,y)

It means that the result of applying action x to the situation y is the situation Result(x,y). Note that Result(x,y) is a term, not a statement.

For example we can say

- Result(Forward, S0) = S1
- Result(Turn(Right),S1) = S2

These definitions could be made more general. Since in the Wumpus World there is a single agent, there is no reason for us to make predicates and functions relative to a specific agent. In other "worlds" we should change things appropriately.

Another generalization is possible, to write all assertions about the world as terms, and then add the predicates

T(situation assertion-term)

to mean that in the specified situation the specified assertion is true.

Belief(agent situation assertion-term)

to mean that the specified agent in the specified situation believes the specified assertion to be true.

Here are a series of statements about the Wumpus World.

Effect Axioms

Effect axioms characterize what is changed because of an action. For example:

- Present(x, s) & Portable(x) ⇒ Holding(x, Result(Grab,s))
- Not Holding(x, Result(Release,s))

Frame Axioms

Frame axioms characterize what has remained the same because of an action. For example:

- Holding(x, s) & (a/=Release) ⇒ Holding(x, Result(a,s))
- NOT Holding(x, s) & ((a/=Grab)) | NOT(Present(x,s) & Portable(x)) ⇒ NOT Holding(x, Result (a, s))

Successor-State Axioms

For each predicate that can change over time they characterize the actions under which it changes and the actions under which it remains the same. For example:

- Holding(x,Result(a,s)) IFF [(a=Grab & Present(x,s) & Portable(x)) OR (Holding(x,s) & (a/=Release))

Model-Based and Diagnostic Reasoning

Causal Rules specify how aspects of the state of the world determine our percepts. Model-Based **Reasoning** is what we do when we use causal rules. Here are some causal rules:

- At(Wumpus, l_1, s) & Adjacent(l_1, l_2) ⇒ Smelly(l_2)
- At(Pit, l_1, s) & Adjacent(l_1, l_2) ⇒ Breezy(l2)

Diagnostic Rules specify how to go from percepts to assertions about the state of the world. **Diagnostic Reasoning** is what we do when we use diagnostic rules. Here are some diagnostic rules:

- At(Agent,l,s) & Breeze(s) ⇒ Breezy(l)
- At(Agent,l,s) & Stench(s) ⇒ Smelly(l)
- Smelly(l1) = > (EXISTS l_2 At(Wumpus, l_2, s) & ($l_2 = l_1$ OR Adjacent(l_1, l_2)))
- At(Wumpus, x, t) & NOT Pit(x) IFF OK(x)

Linear Algebra

Linear algebra is a branch of mathematics that deals with the study of vectors, vector spaces, and linear transformations. It forms the foundation for various mathematical and computational techniques used in science, engineering, and data analysis. Key concepts in linear algebra include:

Vector Spaces

Vector spaces are the basic setting in which linear algebra happens. A vector space V is a set (the elements of which are called vectors) on which two operations are defined: vectors can be added together, and vectors can be multiplied by real number s_1 called scalars. V must satisfy

(*i*) There exists an additive identity (written 0) in V such that $x + 0 = x$ for all $x \in V$

(*ii*) For each $x \in V$, there exists an additive inverse (written $-x$) such that $x + (-x) = 0$

(*iii*) There exists a multiplicative identity (written 1) in R such that $1x = x$ for all $x \in V$

(*iv*) **Commutativity:** $x + y = y + x$ for all $x, y \in V$

(v) **Associativity:** $(x + y) + z = x + (y + z)$ and $\alpha(\beta x) = (\alpha\beta)x$ for all $x, y, z \in V$ and $\alpha, \beta \in R$

(vi) **Distributivity:** $\alpha(x + y) = \alpha x + \alpha y$ and $(\alpha + \beta)x = \alpha x + \beta x$ for all $x, y \in V$ and $\alpha, \beta \in R$

A set of vectors $v_1, \ldots, v_n \in V$ is said to be linearly independent if

$$\alpha_1 v_1 + \cdots + \alpha_n v_n = 0 \text{ implies } \alpha_1 = \cdots = \alpha_n = 0.$$

The span of $v_1, \ldots, v_n \in V$ is the set of all vectors that can be expressed of a linear combination of them:

$$\text{span}\{v_1, \ldots, v_n\} = \{v \in V : \exists \alpha_1, \ldots, \alpha_n \text{ such that } \alpha_1 v_1 + \cdots + \alpha_n v_n = v\}$$

If a set of vectors is linearly independent and its span is the whole of V , those vectors are said to be a basis for V . In fact, every linearly independent set of vectors forms a basis for its span.

If a vector space is spanned by a finite number of vectors, it is said to be finite-dimensional. Otherwise it is infinite-dimensional. The number of vectors in a basis for a finite-dimensional vector space V is called the dimension of V and denoted dim V .

Euclidean Space

The quintessential vector space is Euclidean space, which we denote R^n. The vectors in this space consist of n-tuples of real numbers:

$$x = (x_1, x_2, \ldots, x_n)$$

For our purposes, it will be useful to think of them as $n \times 1$ matrices, or column vectors:

$$x = \begin{bmatrix} x_1 \\ x_2 \\ \vdots \\ x_n \end{bmatrix}$$

Addition and scalar multiplication are defined component-wise on vectors in R^n:

$$x + y = \begin{bmatrix} x_1 + y_1 \\ \vdots \\ x_n + y_n \end{bmatrix}, \quad \alpha x = \begin{bmatrix} \alpha x_1 \\ \vdots \\ \alpha x_n \end{bmatrix}$$

Euclidean space is used to mathematically represent physical space, with notions such as distance, length, and angles. Although it becomes hard to visualize for $n > 3$, these concepts generalize mathematically in obvious ways. Even when you're working in more general settings than R^n, it is often useful to visualize vector addition and scalar multiplication in terms of 2D vectors in the plane or 3D vectors in space.

Subspaces

Vector spaces can contain other vector spaces. If V is a vector space, then $S \subseteq V$ is said to be a subspace of V if

(i) $0 \in S$

(ii) S is closed under addition: $x, y \in S$ implies $x + y \in S$

(iii) S is closed under scalar multiplication: $x \in S, \alpha \in R$ implies $\alpha x \in S$

Note that V is always a subspace of V , as is the trivial vector space which contains only 0. As a concrete example, a line passing through the origin is a subspace of Euclidean space. If U and W are subspaces of V , then their sum is defined as

$$U + W = \{u + w \mid u \in U, w \in W\}$$

It is straightforward to verify that this set is also a subspace of V . If $U \cap W = \{0\}$, the sum is said to be a direct sum and written $U \oplus W$. Every vector in $U \oplus W$ can be written uniquely as u + w for some u ∈ U and w ∈ W. (This is both a necessary and sufficient condition for a direct sum.)

The dimensions of sums of subspaces obey a friendly relationship :

$$\dim(U + W) = \dim U + \dim W - \dim(U \cap W)$$

It follows that $\dim(U \oplus W) = \dim U + \dim W$

Since $\dim(U \cap W) = \dim(\{0\}) = 0$ if the sum is direct.

Linear Maps

A linear map is a function $T : V \rightarrow W$, where V and W are vector spaces, that satisfies

(*i*) $T(x + y) = Tx + Ty$ for all $x, y \in V$

(*ii*) $T(\alpha x) = \alpha Tx$ for all $x \in V, \alpha \in R$

The standard notational convention for linear maps (which we follow here) is to drop unnecessary parentheses, writing Tx rather than T(x) if there is no risk of ambiguity, and denote composition of linear maps by ST rather than the usual S (T.

A linear map from V to itself is called a linear operator.

Observe that the definition of a linear map is suited to reflect the structure of vector spaces, since it preserves vector spaces' two main operations, addition and scalar multiplication. In algebraic terms, a linear map is called a homomorphism of vector spaces. An invertible homomorphism (where the inverse is also a homomorphism) is called an isomorphism. If there exists an isomorphism from V to W, then V and W are said to be isomorphic, and we write V ~= W. Isomorphic vector spaces are essentially "the same" in terms of their algebraic structure. It is an interesting fact that finite dimensional vector spaces? of the same dimension are always isomorphic; if V, W are real vector spaces with dim V = dim W = n, then we have the natural isomorphism

$$\phi : V \rightarrow W$$

$$\alpha_1 v_1 + \dots + \alpha_n v_n \rightarrow \alpha_1 w_1 + \dots + \alpha_n w_n$$

where $v_1, \dots, v_n$ and $w_1, \dots, w_n$ are any bases for V and W. This map is well-defined because every vector in V can be expressed uniquely as a linear combination of $v_1, \dots, v_n$. It is straightforward to verify that ϕ is an isomorphism, so in fact V ~= W. In particular, every real n-dimensional vector space is isomorphic to R^n.

The Matrix of a Linear Map

Vector spaces are fairly abstract. To represent and manipulate vectors and linear maps on a computer, we use rectangular arrays of numbers known as matrices.

Suppose V and W are finite-dimensional vector spaces with bases $v_1, \dots, v_n$ and $w_1, \dots, w_m$, respectively, and $T : V \rightarrow W$ is a linear map. Then the matrix of T, with entries A_{ij} where i = 1, ..., m, j = 1, ... , n, is defined by

$$Tv_j = A_{1j}W_1 + \dots + A_{mj}W_m$$

That is, the jth column of A consists of the coordinates of T_{vj} in the chosen basis for W. Conversely, every matrix $A \in R^{m \times n}$ induces a linear map $T : R^n \rightarrow R^m$ given by

$$Tx = Ax$$

and the matrix of this map with respect to the standard bases of R^n and R^m is of course simply A. If $A \in R^{m\times n}$, its transpose $A > \in R^{n\times m}$ is given by $(A^T)ij = Aji$ for each (i, j). In other words, the columns of A become the rows of A^T, and the rows of A become the columns of A^T.

The transpose has several nice algebraic properties that can be easily verified from the definition:

(*i*) $(A^T)^T = A$

(*ii*) $(A + B)^T = A^T + B^T$

(*iii*) $(aA)^T = aA^T$

(*iv*) $(AB)^T = B^TA^T$

Nullspace, Range

Some of the most important subspaces are those induced by linear maps. If $T : V \rightarrow W$ is a linear map, we define the nullspace[3] of T as

$$\text{null}(T) = \{v \in V | Tv = 0\}$$

and the range of T as

$$\text{range}(T) = \{w \in W \mid v \in V \text{ such that } Tv = w\}$$

It is a good exercise to verify that the nullspace and range of a linear map are always subspaces of its domain and codomain, respectively

The columnspace of a matrix $A \in R^{m\times n}$ is the span of its columns (considered as vectors in R^m), and similarly the rowspace of A is the span of its rows (considered as vectors in R^n). It is not hard to see that the columnspace of A is exactly the range of the linear map from R^n to R^m which is induced by A, so we denote it by range(A) in a slight abuse of notation. Similarly, the rowspace is denoted range(A^T).

It is a remarkable fact that the dimension of the columnspace of A is the same as the dimension of the rowspace of A. This quantity is called the rank of A, and defined as

rank(A) = dim range(A)

Metric Spaces

Metrics generalize the notion of distance from Euclidean space (although metric spaces need not be vector spaces).

A metric on a set S is a function $d : S \times S \rightarrow R$ that satisfies

(*i*) $d(x, y) \geq 0$, with equality if and only if $x = y$

(*ii*) $d(x, y) = d(y, x)$

(*iii*) $d(x, z) \leq d(x, y) + d(y, z)$ (the so-called triangle inequality)

For all $x, y, z \in S$

A key motivation for metrics is that they allow limits to be defined for mathematical objects other than real numbers. We say that a sequence $\{x_n\} \subseteq S$ converges to the limit x if for any $\in > 0$, there exists $N \in N$ such that $d(x_n, x) < \in$ for all $n \geq N$. Note that the definition for limits of sequences of real numbers, which you have likely seen in a calculus class, is a special case of this definition when using the metric $d(x, y) = |x - y|$.

Normed Spaces

Norms generalize the notion of length from Euclidean space.

A norm on a real vector space V is a function $\|\cdot\|\ V \rightarrow \mathbb{R}$ that satisfies

(i) $||x|| \geq 0$, with equality if and only if $x = 0$
(ii) $||\alpha x|| = |\alpha|||x||$
(iii) $||x + y|| \leq ||x|| + ||y||$ (the triangle inequality again)

for all x, y ∈ V and all α ∈ R. A vector space endowed with a norm is called a normed vector space, or simply a normed space.

Note that any norm on V induces a distance metric on V:

$$d(x, y) = ||x - y||$$

One can verify that the axioms for metrics are satisfied under this definition and follow directly from the axioms for norms. Therefore any normed space is also a metric space.4

We will typically only be concerned with a few specific norms on R^n:

$$||x||_1 = \sum_{i=1}^{n} |x_i|$$

$$||x||_2 = \sqrt{\sum_{i=1}^{n} x_i^2}$$

$$||x|_p = \left(\sum_{i=1}^{n} |x_i|^p\right)^{1/p} \quad (p \geq 1)$$

$$||x||_\infty = \max_{1''i''n} |x_i|$$

Note that the 1- and 2-norms are special cases of the p-norm, and the ∞-norm is the limit of the p-norm as p tends to infinity. We require $p \geq 1$ for the general definition of the p-norm because the triangle inequality fails to hold if $p < 1$.

Here's a fun fact: For any given finite-dimensional vector space V, all norms on V are equivalent in the sense that for two norms $|| \cdot ||_A$, $|| \cdot ||_B$, there exist constants α, β > 0 such that

$$\alpha||x||_A \leq ||x||_B \leq \beta||x||_A$$

for all x ∈ V. Therefore convergence in one norm implies convergence in any other norm. This rule may not apply in infinite-dimensional vector such as function spaces, though.

Inner Product Spaces

An inner product on a real vector space V is a function $\langle \cdot, \cdot \rangle : V \times V \rightarrow \mathbb{R}$ satisfying

(i) $\langle x, x \rangle \geq 0$, with equality if and only if $x = 0$
(ii) **Linearity in the first slot:** $\langle x + y, z \rangle = \langle x, z \rangle + \langle y, z \rangle$ and $\langle \alpha x, y \rangle = \alpha \langle x, y \rangle$
(iii) $\langle x, y \rangle = \langle y, x \rangle$

for all x, y, z ∈ V and all α ∈ R. A vector space endowed with an inner product is called an inner product space.

Note that any inner product on V induces a norm on V:

$$||x|| = \sqrt{\langle x, x \rangle}$$

One can verify that the axioms for norms are satisfied under this definition and follow (almost) directly from the axioms for inner products. Therefore any inner product space is also a normed space (and hence also a metric space).5

Two vectors x and y are said to be orthogonal if hx, yi = 0; we write $x \perp y$ for shorthand. Orthogonality generalizes the notion of perpendicularity from Euclidean space. If two orthogonal vectors x and y additionally have unit length (i.e., $||x|| = ||y|| = 1$), then they are described as orthonormal.

The standard inner product on R^n is given by

$$\langle x, y\rangle = \sum_{i=1}^{n} x_i y_i = x^T y$$

The matrix notation on the right-hand side arises because this inner product is a special case of matrix multiplication where we regard the resulting 1×1 matrix as a scalar. The inner product on R n is also often written $x \cdot y$ (hence the alternate name dot product). The reader can verify that the two-norm $|| \cdot ||_2$ on $\mathbb{R}^n$ is induced by this inner product.

Eigenthings

For a square matrix $A \in R^{n\times n}$, there may be vectors which, when A is applied to them, are simply scaled by some constant. We say that a nonzero vector $x \in R^n$ is an eigenvector of A corresponding to eigenvalue λ if

$$Ax = \lambda x$$

The zero vector is excluded from this definition because $A_0 = 0 = \lambda_0$ for every λ.

We now give some useful results about how eigenvalues change after various manipulations.

Proposition 3. Let x be an eigenvector of A with corresponding eigenvalue λ. Then

(*i*) For any $\gamma \in \mathbb{R}$, x is an eigenvector of $A + \gamma I$ with eigenvalue $\lambda + \gamma$.

(*ii*) If A is invertible, then x is an eigenvector of A^{-1} with eigenvalue λ^{-1}.

(*iii*) $A^k x = \lambda^k x$ for any $k \in \mathbb{Z}$ (where $A^0 = I$ by definition).

Proof.

(*i*) **Follows readily:**

$$(A + \lambda I)x = Ax + \lambda Ix = \lambda x + \gamma x = (\lambda + \gamma)x$$

(*ii*) Suppose A is invertible. Then

$$x = A^{-1}Ax = A^{-1}(\lambda x) = \lambda A^{-1}x$$

Dividing by λ, which is valid because the invertibility of A implies $\lambda \neq 0$, gives $\lambda^{-1}x = A^{-1}x$.

(*iii*) The case $k \geq 0$ follows immediately by induction on k. Then the general case $k \in Z$ follows by combining the $k \geq 0$ case with (*ii*).

Trace

The trace of a square matrix is the sum of its diagonal entries:

$$tr(A) = \sum_{i=1}^{n} A_{ii}$$

The trace has several nice algebraic properties:

(*i*) trA + B) = tr(A) + tr(B)

(*ii*) $tr(\alpha A) = \alpha tr(A)$

(*iii*) $tr(A^T) = tr(A)$

(*iv*) tr(ABCD) = tr(BCDA) = tr(CDAB) = tr(DABC)

The first three properties follow readily from the definition. The last is known as invariance under cyclic permutations. Note that the matrices cannot be reordered arbitrarily, for example tr(ABCD) 6= tr(BACD) in general. Also, there is nothing special about the product of four matrices – analogous rules hold for more or fewer matrices.

Interestingly, the trace of a matrix is equal to the sum of its eigenvalues (repeated according to multiplicity):

$$\text{tr}(A) = \sum_i \lambda_i(A)$$

Determinant

The determinant of a square matrix can be defined in several different confusing ways, none of which are particularly important for our purposes; go look at an introductory linear algebra text (or Wikipedia) if you need a definition. But it's good to know the properties:

(i) $\det(I) = 1$

(*ii*) $\det(A^T) = \det(A)$

(*iii*) $\det(AB) = \det(A)\det(B)$

(*iv*) $\det(A^{-1}) = \det(A)^{-1}$

(*v*) $\det(\alpha A) = \alpha^n \det(A)$

Interestingly, the determinant of a matrix is equal to the product of its eigenvalues (repeated according to multiplicity)

$$\det(A) = \prod_i \lambda_i(A)$$

Orthogonal Matric

A matrix $Q \in \mathbb{R}^{n\times n}$ is said to be **orthogonal** if its columns are pairwise orthonormal. This definition implies that

$$Q^TQ = QQ^T = I$$

or equivalently, $Q^T = Q^{-1}$. A nice thing about orthogonal matrices is that they preserve inner products:

$$(Qx)^T(Qy) = x^TQ^TQy = x^TIy = x^Ty$$

A direct result of this fact is that they also preserve 2-norms:

$$||Qx||_2 = \sqrt{(Qx)^T(Qx)} = \sqrt{x^Tx} = ||x||_2$$

Therefore multiplication by an orthogonal matrix can be considered as a transformation that preserves length, but may rotate or reflect the vector about the origin.

Symmetric Matrices

A matrix $A \in \mathbb{R}^{n\times n}$ is said to be **symmetric** if it is equal to its own transpose ($A = A^T$), meaning that $A_{ij} = A_{ji}$ for all (i, j). This definition seems harmless enough but turns out to have some strong implications. We summarize the most important of these as

Theorem 2. (Spectral Theorem) If $A \in \mathbb{R}^{n\times n}$ is symmetric, then these exists an orthonormal basis $\mathbb{R}^n$ consisting of eigenvectors of A.

The practical application of this theorem is a particular factorization of symmetric matrices, referred to as the eigencomposition or spectral decomposition. Denote the orthonormal basis of eigenvectors q_1, ..., q_n and their eigenvalues $\lambda_1, ..., \lambda_n$. Let Q be an orthogonal matrix with $q_1, ..., q_n$ as its columns, and $\Lambda = \text{diag}(\lambda_1, ..., \lambda_n)$. Since by definition $Aq_i = \lambda_i q_i$ for every i, the following relationship holds:

$$AQ = Q\Lambda$$

Right-multiplying by Q^T, we arrive at the decomposition

$$A = Q\Lambda Q^T$$

Rayleigh Quotients

Let $A \in \mathbb{R}^{n\times n}$ be a symmetric matrix. The expression x^TAx is called a **quadratic form.**

There turns out to be an interesting connection between the quadratic form of a symmetric matrix and its eigenvalues. This connection is provided by the **Rayleigh quotient.**

$$R_A(x) = \frac{x^TAx}{x^Tx}$$

The Rayleigh quotient has a couple of important properties which the reader can (and should!) easily verify from the definition:

(*i*) **Scale invariance:** For any vector $x \neq 0$ and any scalar $\alpha \neq 0$, $R_A(x) = R_A(\alpha x)$.

(*ii*) If x is an eigenvector of A with eigenvalue λ, then $R_A(x) = \lambda$.

We can further show that the Rayleigh quotient is bounded by the largest and smallest eigenvalues of A. But first we will show a useful special case of the final result.

Proposition 4. For any x such that $||x||_2 = 1$,

$$\lambda_{min}(A) \leq x^TAx \leq \lambda_{max}(A)$$

with equality if and only if x is a corresponding eigenvector.

Proof. We show only the max case because the argument for the min case is entirely analogous.

Since A is symmetric, we can decompose it as $A = Q\Lambda Q^T$. Then use the change of variable $y = Q^Tx$, noting that the relationship between x and y is one-to-one and that $||y||_2 = 1$ since Q is orthogonal.

Hence, $$\max_{||x||_2=1} x^TAx = \max_{||y||_2=1} y^T\Lambda y = \max_{y_1^2+...+y_n^2=1} \sum_{i=1}^{n}\lambda_i y_i^2$$

Written this way, it is clear that y maximizes this expression exactly if and only if it satisfies $\sum_{i\in I} y_i^2 = 1$ where $I = \{i : \lambda_i = \max_{j=1,...,n}\lambda_j = \lambda_{max}(A)\}$ and $y_j = 0$ for $j \notin I$. That is, I contains the index or indices of the largest eigenvalue. In this case, the maximal value of the expression is

$$\sum_{i=1}^{n}\lambda_i y_i^2 = \sum_{i\in I}\lambda_i y_i^2 = \lambda_{max}(A)\sum_{i\in I} y_i^2 = \lambda_{max}(A)$$

Then writing $q_1, ..., q_n$ for the columns of Q, we have

$$x = QQ^Tx = Qy = \sum_{i=1}^{n} y_i q_i = \sum_{i\in I} y_i q_i$$

where we have used the matrix-vector product identity.

Recall that $q_1, ..., q_n$ are eigenvectors of A and form an orthonormal basis for $\mathbb{R}^n$. Therefore by construction, the set $\{q_i : i \in I\}$ forms an orthonormal basis for the eigenspace of $\lambda_{max}(A)$. Hence x, which is a linear combination of these, lies in that eigenspace and thus is an eigenvector of A corresponding to $\lambda_{max}(A)$.

We have shown that $\max_{||x||_2=1} x^TAx = \lambda_{max}(A)$, from which we have the general inequality $x^TAx \leq$

$\lambda_{max(}(A)$ for all unit-length x.

By the scale invariance of the Rayleigh quotient, we immediately have as a corollary (since $x^TAx = R_A(x)$ for unit x)

Theorem 3. (Min-max theorem) For all $x \neq 0$,

$$\lambda_{min}(A) \leq R_A(x) \leq \lambda_{max}(A)$$

with equality if and only if x is a corresponding eigenvector.

This is sometimes referred to as a **variational characterization of eigenvalues** because it expresses the smallest/largest eigenvalue of A in terms of a minimization/maximization problem:

$$\lambda_{min/max}(A) = \min_{x \uparrow 0} / \max_{x \uparrow 0} R_A(x)$$

Positive (Semi-)Definite Matrices

A symmetric matrix A is **positive semi-definite** if for all $x \in \mathbb{R}^n$, $x^TAx \leq 0$. Sometimes people write $A \succeq 0$ to indicate that A is positive semi-definite.

A symmetric matrix A is positive definite if for all non-zero $x \in \mathbb{R}^n$, $x^TAx > 0$. Sometimes people write $A \succ 0$ to indicate that A is positive definite. Note that positive definiteness is a strictly stronger property than positive semi-definiteness, in the sense that every positive definite matrix is positive semi-definite but not vice-versa.

These properties are related to eigenvalues in the following way.

Proposition 5. A symmetric matrix is positive semi-definite if and only if all of its eigenvalues are non-negative, and positive definite if and only if all of its eigenvalues are positive.

Proof. Suppose A is positive semi-definite, and let x be an eigenvector of A with eigenvalue λ. Then

$$0 \leq x^TAx = x^T(\lambda x) = \lambda x^Tx = 1||x||_2^2$$

Since $x \neq 0$ (by the assumption that it is an eigenvector), we have $||x||_2^2 > 0$, so we can divide both sides by $||x||_2^2$ to arrive at $\lambda \geq 0$. If A is positive definite, the inequality above holds strictly, so $\lambda > 0$. This proves one direction.

To simplify the proof of the other direction, we will use the machinery of Rayleigh quotients. Suppose that A is symmetric and all its eigenvalues are non-negative. Then for all $x \neq 0$.

$$0 \leq \lambda_{min}(A) \leq R_A(x)$$

Since x^TAx matches $R_A(x)$ in sign, we conclude that A is positive semi-definite. If the eigenvalues of A are all strictly positive, then $0 < \lambda_{min}(A)$, whence it follows that A is positive definite.

As an example of how these matrices arise, consider

Proposition 6. Suppose $A \in \mathbb{R}^{m\times n}$. Then A^TA is positive semi-definite. If nul(A) = {0}, then A^TA is positive definite.

Proof. For any $x \in \mathbb{R}^n$,

$$x^T(A^TA)x = (Ax)^T(Ax) = ||Ax||_2^2 \geq 0$$

So A^TA is positive semi-definite. If null(A) = {0}, then $Ax \neq 0$ whenever $x \neq 0$, so $||Ax||_2^2 > 0$, and thus A^TA is positive definite.

Positive definite matrices are invertible (since their eigenvalues are non-zero), whereas positive semi-definite matrices might not be. However, if you already have a positive semi-definite matrix, it is possible to perturb its diagonal slightly to produce a positive definite matrix.

Proposition 7. If A is positive semi-definite and $\in > 0$, then $A + \in I$ is positive definite.

Proof. Assuming A is positive semi-definite and $\in > 0$, we have for $x \neq 0$ that

$$x^T(A + \in I)x = x^TAx + \in x^TIx = \underbrace{x^TAx}_{\geq 0} + \underbrace{\in \|x\|_2^2}_{>0} > 0$$

as claimed.

An obvious but frequently useful consequence of the two propositions we have just shown is that $A^TA + \in I$ is positive definite (and is particular, invertible) for any matrix A and any $\in > 0$.

Some Useful Matrix Identities

Matrix-vector product as linear combination of matrix columns

Proposition 10. Let $x \in \mathbb{R}^n$ be a vector and $A \in \mathbb{R}^{m\times n}$ a matrix with columns $a_1, ..., a_n$. Then

$$Ax = \sum_{i=1}^{n} x_i a_i$$

This identity is extremely useful in understanding linear operators in terms of their matrices' columns. The proof is very simple (consider each element of Ax individually and expand by definitions) but it is a good exercise to convince yourself.

Sum of outer products as matrix-matrix product

An **outer product** is an expression of the form ab^T, where $a \in \mathbb{R}^m$ and $b \in \mathbb{R}^n$. By inspection it is not hard to see that such an expression yields an $m \times n$ matrix such that

$$[ab^T]_{ij} = a_i b_j$$

It is not immediately obvious, but the sum of outer products is actually equivalent to an appropriate matrix-matrix product! We formalize this statement as

Preposition 11. Let $a_1, ..., a_k \in \mathbb{R}^m$ and $b_1, ..., b_k \in \mathbb{R}^n$. Then

$$\sum_{l=1}^{k} a_l b_l^T = AB^T$$

where $\quad A = [a_1 \dots a_k], \quad b = [b_1 \dots b_k]$

Proof. For each (i, j), we have

$$\left[\sum_{l=1}^{k} a_l b_l^T\right] = \sum_{l=1}^{k} [a_l b_l^T]_{ij} = \sum_{l=1}^{k} [a_l]_i [b_l]_j = \sum_{l=1}^{k} A_{il} B_{jl}$$

This last expression should be recognized as an inner product between the ith row of A and the jth row of B, or equivalently the jth column of B^T. Hence by the definition of matrix multiplication, it is equal to $[AB^T]_{ij}$.

Quadratic Forms

Let $A \in \mathbb{R}^{n\times n}$ be a symmetric matrix, and recall that the expression x^TAx is called a quadratic form of A. It is in some cases helpful to rewrite the quadratic form in terms of the individual elements that make up A and x:

$$x^TAx = \sum_{i=1}^{n} \sum_{j=1}^{n} A_{ij} x_i x_j$$

This identity is valid for any square matrix (need not be symmetric), although quadratic forms are usually only discussed in the context of symmetric matrices.

What Is Statistics?

Statistics is a branch of mathematics and a scientific discipline that deals with the collection, analysis, interpretation, presentation, and organization of data. It involves the study of data patterns, trends, and relationships to draw meaningful conclusions and make informed decisions. Statistics is widely used in various fields, including social sciences, business, economics, medicine, engineering, and natural sciences, to gain insights and make predictions based on empirical evidence.

The main objectives of statistics are:

1. **Describing Data:** Statistics helps in summarizing and describing data using various measures such as mean, median, mode, standard deviation, and percentiles. It allows researchers to understand the distribution and variability of data. Descriptive statistics involves the use of various techniques to summarize and describe data. It includes measures of central tendency, such as the mean, median, and mode, which provide information about the typical or central value of a dataset. Measures of variability, such as the range, variance, and standard deviation, quantify the spread or dispersion of the data points. Visualization tools like histograms, bar charts, and scatter plots help to present the data in a graphical format for better understanding.
2. **Drawing Inferences:** Statistics enables researchers to make inferences about a population based on sample data. By using statistical methods, they can estimate population parameters and draw conclusions about the entire group. Inferential statistics aims to make predictions or draw conclusions about a population based on a sample of data. It involves hypothesis testing, where researchers test a hypothesis about a population parameter using sample data. The process of drawing inferences involves estimating parameters, calculating confidence intervals, and conducting hypothesis tests to assess the significance of results.
3. **Hypothesis Testing:** Statistics is used to test hypotheses and make decisions about the validity of certain assumptions or claims based on sample data. Hypothesis testing is a fundamental concept in statistics used to make inferences about population parameters based on sample data. It is a formal procedure that allows us to test whether there is enough evidence to support or reject a specific claim or hypothesis about a population.
4. **Prediction and Forecasting:** Through statistical modeling and analysis, researchers can make predictions and forecasts about future events or outcomes. Prediction and forecasting are important aspects of statistics that involve making predictions or estimates about future events or outcomes based on past data and patterns. While they are related, they have different contexts and applications:
   - **Prediction:** Prediction focuses on making inferences about specific future events or values based on historical data. It is commonly used in machine learning and statistical modeling to build predictive models that can make accurate predictions about new and unseen data. In prediction, the goal is to estimate a specific outcome, and the accuracy of the prediction is evaluated based on how well the model performs on new data. Examples of prediction include predicting stock prices, customer churn, weather conditions, or the likelihood of a disease occurrence based on risk factors.
   - **Forecasting:** Forecasting, on the other hand, is the process of making predictions about future trends, patterns, or values based on historical data. It is widely used in time series

analysis and business planning to anticipate future behavior and make strategic decisions. In forecasting, the focus is on predicting the overall trend or direction of a series rather than specific individual values. The accuracy of a forecast is evaluated based on how well it captures the underlying patterns and trends in the data. Examples of forecasting include predicting sales, demand for products, or economic indicators like GDP growth.

Both prediction and forecasting rely on various statistical and machine learning techniques, such as regression analysis, time series analysis, and machine learning algorithms like decision trees, neural networks, and support vector machines. The choice of the method depends on the nature of the data and the specific problem at hand.

5. **Experimental Design:** Statistics plays a crucial role in designing experiments and studies to ensure reliable and valid results. Experimental design is a fundamental concept in statistics that involves planning, conducting, and analyzing experiments to draw valid conclusions about cause-and-effect relationships between variables. It is an essential tool for researchers and scientists to make meaningful inferences and test hypotheses in controlled settings.

Key concepts in statistics include data types (quantitative and qualitative), measures of central tendency and variability, probability theory, sampling techniques, hypothesis testing, regression analysis, and statistical inference. The field of statistics has also evolved with the development of modern computational tools and software, making it more accessible and applicable in various domains.

Overall, statistics is a powerful tool for researchers, analysts, and decision-makers to analyze and understand complex data, make evidence-based decisions, and gain valuable insights into various phenomena in the real world.

Population and Sample

In statistics, a population refers to the entire group or set of individuals, objects, or events that we are interested in studying. It represents the complete collection of units that possess the characteristics of interest. For example, if we are studying the heights of all adults in a country, the entire adult population of that country would be the target group.

On the other hand, a sample is a subset of the population, selected from the entire population, to represent and draw inferences about the characteristics of the entire population. It is impractical, time-consuming, and sometimes impossible to collect data from the entire population. Therefore, a sample is taken to estimate or infer the population parameters, such as the mean, proportion, or standard deviation.

The process of selecting a sample from the population is known as sampling. Various sampling methods, such as random sampling, stratified sampling, cluster sampling, and convenience sampling, can be used to ensure that the sample is representative of the population.

For example, if we are interested in studying the average income of all working professionals in a city, it would be difficult to survey every working professional. Instead, we can randomly select a sample of working professionals and collect their income data. By analyzing the sample data, we can estimate the average income of the entire population of working professionals in the city.

The accuracy and reliability of the conclusions drawn from a sample depend on the sampling method used and the size of the sample. Properly designed and representative samples help in making valid inferences about the population parameters, even though we do not have data for the entire population.

Measures of Central Tendency

Measures of central tendency are statistical values that represent the central or typical value of a dataset. They provide a single value that summarizes the entire dataset, making it easier to understand and interpret the distribution of the data. The three main measures of central tendency are:

Mean: The mean is the most common measure of central tendency and is also known as the average. It is calculated by summing all the values in the dataset and then dividing by the total number of values. If there are n number of observations and x_i is the ith observation, then mean is:

$$\bar{x} = \frac{\sum_{i=1}^{n} x_i}{n}$$

For example, if we have the dataset {2, 5, 8, 10, 12}, the mean would be (2 + 5 + 8 + 10 + 12)/5 = 7.4.

Median: The median is the middle value of a dataset when the data is arranged in ascending or descending order. If the dataset has an odd number of values, the median is the middle value. If the dataset has an even number of values, the median is the average of the two middle values. The median is less sensitive to extreme values, making it a robust measure of central tendency.

If the total number of data points (n) is odd, the median is the value at position (n+1)/2.

When the total number of observations (n) is even, the median is the average value of observations at n/2 and (n+2)/2 positions.

For example, in the dataset {2, 5, 8, 10, 12}, the median is 8. If we add another value 15 to the dataset {2, 5, 8, 10, 12, 15}, the median would still be 8.

Mode: The mode is the value that occurs most frequently in the dataset. A dataset may have multiple modes (bimodal, trimodal, etc.), or it may have no mode if all values occur with the same frequency.

The mode is the observation (value) that occurs most frequently in the data set. There can be over one mode in a dataset.

For example, in the dataset {2, 5, 8, 8, 10, 12}, the mode is 8 as it occurs twice, which is more frequent than any other value.

Variance and Standard Deviation

Variance and standard deviation are two important measures of dispersion or spread in a dataset. They quantify how much the individual data points deviate from the central tendency (mean) of the data.

Variance: Variance is a statistical measure that indicates the average squared difference between each data point and the mean of the dataset. It measures the spread of data points around the mean. A higher variance indicates greater variability in the data, while a lower variance indicates less variability. The formula to calculate variance is:

Variance is used to measure the variability in the data from the mean.

$$\sigma^2 = \frac{\sum_{i=1}^{n} (x_i - \mu)^2}{n}$$

Standard Deviation: Standard deviation is another measure of the spread of data points around the mean. It is simply the square root of the variance and is expressed in the same units as the original data. Variance and standard deviation represent the measures of fit, meaning how well the mean represents the data. The formula to calculate standard deviation is:

$$\sigma = \sqrt{\frac{\sum_{i=1}^{n}(x_i - \mu)^2}{n}}$$

It provides a more interpretable value compared to variance, as it is in the same units as the data.

Example: Let's consider a simple example to calculate the variance and standard deviation for a dataset:

Suppose we have the following dataset representing the ages of a group of people (in years):

{25, 30, 28, 35, 32}

Step 1: Calculate the mean (μ):

$$\mu = (25 + 30 + 28 + 35 + 32) / 5 = 30$$

Step 2: Calculate the variance:

$$\text{Variance} = ((25 - 30)^2 + (30 - 30)^2 + (28 - 30)^2 + (35 - 30)^2 + (32 - 30)^2) / 5$$

$$\text{Variance} = (25 + 0 + 4 + 25 + 4)/5$$

$$\text{Variance} = 58/5$$

$$\text{Variance} = 11.6$$

Step 3: Calculate the standard deviation:

Standard Deviation = $\sqrt{11.6} \approx 3.41$

So, for this dataset, the variance is 11.6, and the standard deviation is approximately 3.41. These measures tell us that the ages of the people in the group are spread out from the mean age of 30, with an average squared difference of 11.6 and a typical deviation of approximately 3.41 years from the mean.

Range and Interquartile Range

Range and Interquartile Range (IQR) are measures used to describe the spread or variability of a dataset.

Range: The range is the simplest measure of variability and represents the difference between the maximum and minimum values in the dataset. It provides a rough idea of how spread out the data is.

Example: Consider the following dataset representing the scores of students in a test:

{80, 85, 90, 75, 95}

$$\text{Range} = \text{Maximum value} - \text{Minimum value}$$

$$\text{Range} = 95 - 75 = 20$$

Interquartile Range (IQR)

The interquartile range is a more robust measure of variability than the range. It is calculated as the difference between the third quartile (Q_3) and the first quartile (Q_1) of the dataset. Quartiles divide the data into four equal parts.

Steps to calculate the IQR:

(*a*) Sort the dataset in ascending order.

(*b*) Find the median (Q_2) of the data.

(*c*) Calculate the first quartile (Q_1), which is the median of the lower half of the data (excluding the median itself).

(*d*) Calculate the third quartile (Q_3), which is the median of the upper half of the data (excluding the median itself).

(*e*) $IQR = Q_3 - Q_1$

Example: Consider the following dataset representing the ages of a group of people:

{20, 22, 24, 25, 27, 29, 31, 35}

Sorted dataset: {20, 22, 24, 25, 27, 29, 31, 35}

$$\text{Median } (Q_2) = (25 + 27) / 2 = 26$$
$$Q_1 = (22 + 24) / 2 = 23$$
$$Q_3 = (29 + 31) / 2 = 30$$
$$IQR = Q_3 - Q_1 = 30 - 23 = 7$$

In this example, the interquartile range is 7, indicating that the middle 50% of the ages lie within a range of 7 years.

Skewness and Kurtosis

Skewness and kurtosis are two important measures used to describe the shape of a probability distribution or the distribution of a dataset.

Skewness

Skewness measures the asymmetry of the probability distribution or dataset. It indicates whether the data is concentrated more to the left or right of the mean. A positive skewness value indicates that the tail of the distribution extends to the right, meaning the dataset has a longer right tail. Conversely, a negative skewness value indicates that the tail of the distribution extends to the left, indicating a longer left tail.

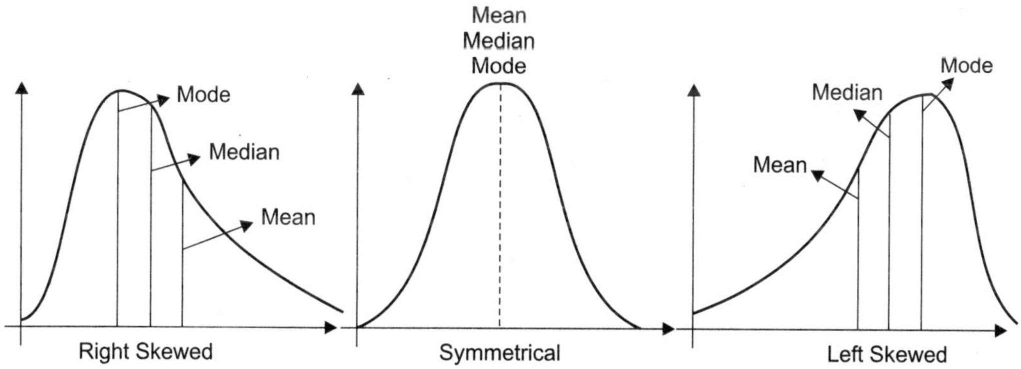

Example: Consider the following dataset representing exam scores:

{60, 70, 75, 80, 85, 90, 95}

$$\text{Skewness} = 0.2 \text{ (approximately)}$$

The positive skewness value suggests that the data is slightly skewed to the right.

Kurtosis

Kurtosis measures the peakedness or flatness of the probability distribution or dataset compared to the normal distribution (bell-shaped curve). It describes the tails' thickness and height relative to the central peak. A positive kurtosis value indicates a more peaked distribution with heavier tails, while a negative kurtosis value indicates a flatter distribution with lighter tails.

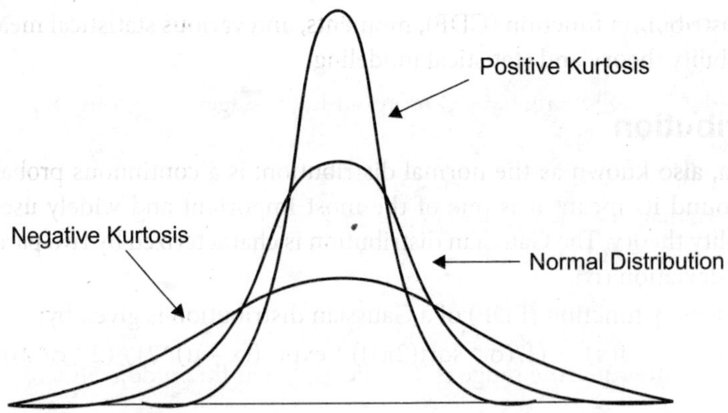

Example: Consider the following dataset representing exam scores:

{60, 70, 75, 80, 85, 90, 95}

Kurtosis ≈ −1.238

The negative kurtosis value suggests that the dataset is flatter than a normal distribution.

In summary, skewness and kurtosis are useful tools for understanding the shape of data distributions. Skewness helps identify the direction of asymmetry, while kurtosis provides insights into the peakedness or flatness of the distribution. These measures are important in various statistical analyses and can help identify deviations from normality.

Probability Density Function (PDF)

The Probability Density Function (PDF) is a fundamental concept in probability theory and statistics. It describes the probability distribution of a continuous random variable and provides a way to analyze the likelihood of the variable taking specific values within a given range.

Mathematically, the PDF of a continuous random variable X is denoted as f(x) and satisfies the following properties:

1. **Non-negativity:** $f(x) \geq 0$ for all x in the range of X.
2. **Total Area Under the Curve:** The area under the PDF curve over the entire range of X is equal to 1.
3. **Probability Interpretation:** The probability that X lies within a specific interval [a, b] is given by the area under the PDF curve between a and b.

The probability that X takes on a specific value x (i.e., $P(X = x)$) is technically zero for continuous random variables since the area under a single point is zero. Instead, we consider the probability that X falls within a small interval around x, which is represented by the infinitesimal width of the PDF curve at that point.

Graphically, the PDF of a continuous random variable is represented as a smooth curve. The height of the curve at any point x indicates the probability density of X taking that particular value. The area under the curve between two points represents the probability of X falling within that interval.

The PDF is an essential tool for statistical analysis and inference. It helps to calculate probabilities, determine the likelihood of certain outcomes, and make informed decisions based on the characteristics of a continuous random variable. Additionally, the PDF is closely related to other statistical concepts, such as cumulative distribution function (CDF), moments, and various statistical measures, making it a cornerstone of probability theory and statistical modeling.

Gaussian Distribution

Gaussian distribution, also known as the normal distribution, is a continuous probability distribution that is symmetric around its mean. It is one of the most important and widely used distributions in statistics and probability theory. The Gaussian distribution is characterized by two parameters: the mean (μ) and the standard deviation (σ).

The probability density function (PDF) of a Gaussian distribution is given by:

$$f(x) = (1/(\sigma * \text{sqrt}(2\pi))) * \exp(-((x - \mu)^\wedge 2) / (2 * \sigma^\wedge 2))$$

Where:

- f(x) is the probability density function at the point x.
- μ is the mean of the distribution, representing the central value.
- σ is the standard deviation, determining the spread or dispersion of the data.
- π is the mathematical constant Pi (approximately 3.14159).
- exp() is the exponential function.

The normal distribution is symmetric around its mean, with the highest probability density at the mean. As we move away from the mean, the probability density decreases, forming the characteristic bell-shaped curve.

Properties of the Gaussian Distribution

1. The mean, median, and mode are all equal and located at the center of the distribution.
2. The total area under the curve is equal to 1, representing the probability of the entire distribution.
3. Approximately 68% of the data falls within one standard deviation of the mean ($\mu \pm \sigma$).
4. Approximately 95% of the data falls within two standard deviations of the mean ($\mu \pm 2\sigma$).
5. Almost all of the data (about 99.7%) falls within three standard deviations of the mean ($\mu \pm 3\sigma$).

The Gaussian distribution is widely used in various fields such as statistics, physics, finance, engineering, and machine learning. It serves as an essential model for many real-world phenomena due to its prevalence and mathematical simplicity.

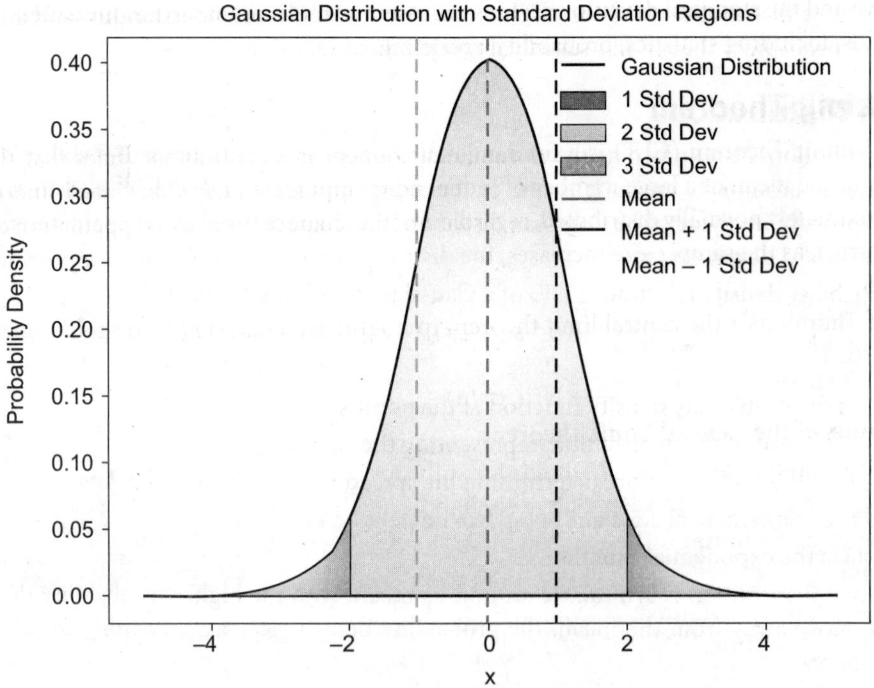

The plot shows a Gaussian distribution, which is a bell-shaped curve, also known as the normal distribution. The curve represents the probability density function (PDF) of a random variable that follows the Gaussian distribution.

Here's an explanation of the plot:

1. **Bell-shaped curve:** The smooth curve represents the Gaussian distribution. The highest point of the curve corresponds to the mean of the distribution.
2. **Mean (μ):** The red vertical line indicates the mean of the distribution. The mean represents the central tendency or the average value of the data.
3. **Standard Deviation (σ):** The blue vertical lines on either side of the mean represent one standard deviation away from the mean. In this plot, the region between the two blue lines covers approximately 68% of the data, as about 68% of the data points fall within one standard deviation of the mean.
4. **Shaded regions:** The plot is shaded in three regions. The light blue region covers data points within one standard deviation from the mean. The light green region covers data points within two standard deviations from the mean. The light coral region covers data points within three standard deviations from the mean.
5. **Probability Density:** The y-axis represents the probability density, which shows the relative likelihood of a random variable taking a particular value. The higher the curve at a specific point, the higher the probability of the variable taking that value.

In summary, the plot visually illustrates the characteristics of the Gaussian distribution, with the mean and standard deviation regions highlighted. It provides valuable insights into how data is distributed and the probability of data points falling within different ranges from the mean. The bell-shaped curve and the standard deviation regions are essential tools for understanding and analyzing data in many fields, including statistics, probability, and machine learning.

Central Limit Theorem

The Central Limit Theorem (CLT) is a fundamental concept in statistics that states that the sampling distribution of the mean of a large number of independent and identically distributed random variables will be approximately normally distributed, regardless of the shape of the original population distribution. In simpler terms, as the sample size increases, the distribution of the sample mean approaches a normal distribution.

Rule of Thumb: For the central limit theorem to hold true, the sample size should be greater than or equal to 30.

$$x_i \longrightarrow N(\mu, \sigma^2/n)$$

Key points of the Central Limit Theorem:

1. **Large Sample Size:** The CLT holds for sufficiently large sample sizes. Generally, a sample size greater than 30 is considered large enough for the CLT to apply.
2. **Random Sampling:** The samples must be drawn randomly and independently from the population.
3. **Identically Distributed:** The random variables in the sample should have the same distribution as the population.
4. **Sample Mean:** The CLT refers specifically to the distribution of the sample mean. As the sample size increases, the sample mean becomes a more reliable estimator of the population mean.

Why is the Central Limit Theorem important?

The CLT has profound implications in statistics and real-world applications:

1. **Normal Approximation:** It allows us to approximate the sampling distribution of the mean, even when the population distribution is not normal.
2. **Inference:** The CLT is the foundation of many statistical inference techniques, such as hypothesis testing and confidence intervals, which rely on the assumption of a normal distribution.
3. **Decision Making:** It simplifies decision-making processes by enabling analysts to use the normal distribution as a powerful and well-understood tool.
4. **Sampling Efficiency:** It explains why the sample mean is an efficient estimator of the population mean, and why smaller sample sizes are often sufficient to make reliable inferences.

In summary, the Central Limit Theorem is a critical concept in statistics that provides a powerful tool for analyzing and understanding sample means and their distributions. It is widely used in various statistical methods and is essential for making sound statistical inferences and predictions in practice.

Review Questions

Solved Questions

Q.1. Fill in the blanks

(*a*) Artificial Intelligence (AI) is the **simulation of human intelligence** in computer systems to perform tasks that typically require human intelligence.

(*b*) Weak AI, also known as **Narrow AI**, is designed for a specific task, while Strong AI aims to possess general intelligence comparable to human intelligence.

(*c*) The concept of Artificial Intelligence dates back to **ancient mythology**, where myths and stories depicted mechanical beings with human-like characteristics.

Q.2. Is AI a science, or is it engineering? Or neither or both? Explain.

Ans. Science: AI involves scientific inquiry into understanding intelligence, cognition, and learning processes. Researchers in AI study huan cognition, behaviour, and neural mechanisms to develop models and theories of intelligence.

Engineering: AI is also an engineering discipline focused on designing, developing, and deploying practical AI systems to solve real-world problems.

Overall, AI encompasses both scientific exploration and engineering implementation, with researchers and practitioners working together to advance the field and develop intelligent systems that benefit society.

Q.3. Define in your own words: (a) intelligence, (b) artificial intelligence, (c) agent, (d) rationality, (e) logical reasoning.

Ans.

(*a*) Dictionary definitions of intelligence talk about "the capacity to acquire and apply knowledge" or "the faculty of thought and reason" or "the ability to comprehend and profit from experience." These are all reasonable answers, but if we want something quantifiable we would use something like "the ability to apply knowledge in order to perform better in an environment."

(*b*) We define artificial intelligence as the study and construction of agent programs that perform well in a given environment, for a given agent architecture.

(*c*) We define an agent as an entity that takes action in response to percepts from an environment.

(*d*) We define rationality as the property of a system which does the "right thing" given what it knows. See Section 2.2 for a more complete discussion. Both describe perfect rationality.

(*e*) We define logical reasoning as the process of deriving new sentences from old, such that the new sentences are necessarily true if the old ones are true.

Q.4. How does the concept of problem spaces apply to puzzle-solving?

Ans. In puzzle-solving, the problem space consists of all the possible states of the puzzle and the legal moves or actions that can be taken to manipulate the puzzle. The initial state represents the starting configuration of the puzzle, and the goal state represents the desired solution. By exploring different states and actions within the problem space, the solver attempts to reach the goal state and solve the puzzle.

Q.5. Provide an example of a production system in real-world applications.

Ans. An example of a production system is an expert system used in medical diagnosis. The production memory contains rules based on medical knowledge, such as symptoms and corresponding diseases. The working memory stores information about the patient's symptoms. The inference engine matches the symptoms in working memory with the rules in production memory to identify possible diseases and recommend appropriate actions or treatments.

Q.6. When developing a search engine for a large online database of scientific research papers. How would you apply searching algorithms to retrieve relevant documents based on user queries and preferences?

Ans. In the search engine, we can represent the research papers and user queries as nodes in a graph, where the edges represent the relevance or similarity between papers based on factors like keywords, topics, and citations. We can apply searching algorithms like A* or iterative deepening search to traverse the graph and identify papers that are most relevant to the user's query, considering factors such as citation networks, author reputation, and publication dates.

Q.7. Solve the tower of hanoi problem for 3 disks, showing each step.

Ans. Here's the step-by-step solution for moving 3 disks from peg A (source) to peg C (destination), using peg B (auxiliary) as the intermediate peg:

1. Move disk 1 from A to C.
2. Move disk 2 from A to B.
3. Move disk 1 from C to B.
4. Move disk 3 from A to C.
5. Move disk 1 from B to A.
6. Move disk 2 from B to C.
7. Move disk 1 from A to C.

Q.8. Prove each of the following statements, or give a counterexample:

(*a*) Breadth-first search is a special case of uniform-cost search.

(*b*) Depth-first search is a special case of best-first tree search.

Ans.

(*a*) When all step costs are equal, (n)g(n) is directly proportional to the depth of node nn in the search tree. In such scenarios, the cost of reaching a node is solely determined by its depth in the tree, as every step has an equal cost.

Here's how uniform-cost search (UCS) reproduces breadth-first search (BFS) when all step costs are equal:

UCS Behaviour: UCS expands nodes based solely on their path cost from the initial node. Since all step costs are equal, UCS prioritizes nodes solely based on their depth in the search tree. Nodes at shallower depths have lower cumulative path costs compared to nodes at deeper depths.

BFS Behaviour: BFS explores nodes level by level, starting from the initial node. It expands all neighboring nodes at a given level before moving to deeper levels.The priority in BFS is also given to nodes based on their depth in the search tree, with shallower nodes being expanded first.

Given that UCS and BFS both prioritize nodes based on their depth in the search tree, and all step costs are equal in this scenario, UCS effectively reproduces the behavior of BFS. In essence, UCS behaves like BFS when all step costs are equal, making it a special case of BFS in such situations.

(*b*) breadth-first search (BFS), depth-first search (DFS), and uniform-cost search can all be seen as special cases of best-first search with different evaluation functions:

Breadth-First Search (BFS): In BFS, the evaluation function (n)f(n) is equal to the depth of the node nn. This means that BFS expands nodes level by level, exploring all nodes at the current level before moving to the next level.

Therefore, BFS can be considered as best-first search with (n) = depth(n).

Depth-First Search (DFS): In DFS, the evaluation function n(n)f(n) is equal to the negative depth of the node nn. DFS explores as far as possible along each branch before backtracking, prioritizing deeper nodes over shallower ones.

Thus, DFS can be viewed as best-first search with (n) = –depth(n).

Uniform-Cost Search: In uniform-cost search, the evaluation function (n)f(n) is equal to the actual cost n(n)g(n) of reaching node nn. This means that uniform-cost search expands nodes based on their path cost from the initial state.

Therefore, uniform-cost search can be seen as best-first search with (n) = n(n).

Q.9. Consider a vocabulary with only four propositions, A, B, C, and D. How many models are there for the following sentences?

(*a*) $\neg A \vee \neg B \vee \neg C \vee \neg D$. (*b*) $(A \Rightarrow B) \wedge A \wedge \neg B \wedge C \wedge D$

Ans. These can be computed by counting the rows in a truth table that come out true, but each has some simple property that allows a short-cut:

(*a*) Each proposition A, B, C, and D can either be true or false, resulting in 24=16 possible combinations of truth values for all propositions.

The sentence is false only if all propositions A, B, C, and D are false. The number of models where all propositions are false is 24–1=15. since we exclude the case where all propositions are false.

Therefore, there are 15 models for this sentence.

(*b*) The sentence consists of five conjuncts: $(A \Rightarrow B)$, A, $\neg B$, C, and D.

Each proposition A, B, C, and D can be either true or false.

To satisfy the conjunction, all five conjuncts must be true simultaneously. Let's analyze each conjunct:

($A \Rightarrow B$): This conjunct is true if A is false or if both A and B are true. Therefore, if A is true and B is false, this conjunct is false.

- **A:** This conjunct requires A to be true.
- **¬B:** This conjunct requires B to be false.
- **C:** This conjunct requires C to be true.
- **D:** This conjunct requires D to be true.

Now, let's consider the possibilities:

If A is true, B is false, and C and D are true, the first conjunct ($A \Rightarrow B$) is false, making the entire sentence false.

Since the last four conjuncts specify a model in which the first conjunct ($A \Rightarrow B$) is false, there are 0 models for the sentence.

Q.10. Is the sentence $\exists$ x, y x = y valid? Explain.

Ans. The sentence $\exists$ x, y x = y is valid. A sentence is valid if it is true in every model. An existentially quantified sentence is true in a model if it holds under any extended interpretation in which its variables are assigned to domain elements. According to the standard semantics of FOL as given in the chapter, every model contains at least one domain element, hence, for any model, there is an extended interpretation in which x and y are assigned to the first domain element. In such an interpretation, x = y is true.

Q.11. Write down a logical sentence such that every world in which it is true contains exactly one object.

Ans. $\forall$ x, y x = y stipulates that there is exactly one object. If there are two objects, then there is an extended interpretation in which x and y are assigned to different objects, so the sentence would be false. Some students may also notice that any unsatisfiable sentence also meets the criterion, since there are no worlds in which the sentence is true.

Q.12. Write event calculus axioms to describe the actions in the wumpus world.

Ans. Event calculus is a logical formalism used to represent and reason about actions and events. In the context of the Wumpus World, we can define Event Calculus axioms to describe the actions taken by the agent in the environment. Here are some axioms that can be used:

Fluent Predicates:

- **At (x,y):** The agent is at position (x,y) in the grid.
- **Facing(d):** The agent is facing direction d (north, south, east, west).
- **HasArrow:** Indicates whether the agent has an arrow.
- **WumpusAlive:** Indicates whether the Wumpus is alive.

Initial State Axioms:

- **At (1,1):** The agent starts at position (1,1).
- **Facing(east):** The agent initially faces east.
- **HasArrow:** The agent starts with an arrow.
- **WumpusAlive:** Initially, the Wumpus is alive.

Action Axioms:

- **Forward:** Moving forward from position (x,y) to position (x′, y′) is an action if the agent is at (x, y) and there are no obstacles in the direction it is facing.
- **Turn (d1, d2):** Turning from direction d1 to direction d2 is an action.
- **Shoot:** Shooting the arrow is an action if the agent has an arrow and is facing the Wumpus.
- **Grab:** Grabbing the gold is an action if the agent is at the same position as the gold.
- **Climb:** Climbing out of the cave is an action if the agent is at position (1,1) and has the gold.

Effect Axioms:

- At(x′, y′) holds after Forward if there are no obstacles in the way.
- Facing (d2) holds after Turn (d1, d2).
- ¬WumpusAlive holds after Shoot if the agent is facing the Wumpus.
- ¬HasArrow holds after Shoot.

- Glitter holds after Grab if the gold is at the same position as the agent.
- ¬Gold holds after Grab (the gold is removed from the cave).
- HaveGold holds after Climb if the agent has grabbed the gold.

Inertia Axioms:

- At (x, y) at time t+1 if At(x, y) at time t and no actions affect the agent's position.

These axioms provide a logical framework for describing the agent's actions, their effects, and the resulting state changes in the Wumpus World. They can be used for reasoning about the consequences of actions and for planning the agent's behavior.

Multiple Choice Questions

Q.1. What is the primary goal of Artificial Intelligence (AI)?

(*a*) To develop robots with human-like emotions
(*b*) To develop systems that can perform tasks requiring human intelligence
(*c*) To create computers that can think and feel like humans
(*d*) To replace human workers with machines

Q.2. Which of the following is an example of Narrow (Weak) AI?

(*a*) Self-driving cars
(*b*) Siri or Alexa virtual assistants
(*c*) IBM's Watson
(*d*) Human-like robots capable of performing various tasks

Q.3. The Turing Test is used to assess:

(*a*) The computational power of a computer
(*b*) The ability of a computer to understand and process natural language
(*c*) Whether a computer can exhibit intelligent behavior indistinguishable from that of a human
(*d*) The accuracy of a machine learning algorithm

Q.4. Which of the following is NOT a subfield of AI?

(*a*) Machine Learning
(*b*) Natural Language Processing (NLP)
(*c*) Robotics
(*d*) Cryptography

Q.5. What does the term "Deep Learning" refer to?

(*a*) A type of neural network with multiple hidden layers
(*b*) Learning through trial and error
(*c*) Learning from labeled data
(*d*) Learning from reinforcement

Q.6. Which programming language is commonly used for AI development?

(*a*) C++ (*b*) Java (*c*) Python (*d*) Ruby

Q.7. What is the main purpose of an Expert System in AI?

(*a*) To mimic human decision-making in specific domains
(*b*) To create virtual reality environments
(*c*) To automate physical tasks in industrial settings
(*d*) To simulate natural language conversations

Q.8. Which of the following is NOT a component of an Intelligent Agent?

(*a*) Perception (*b*) Knowledge Base
(*c*) Decision Making (*d*) Database Management

Q.9. What is the primary challenge in developing Artificial General Intelligence (AGI)?

(*a*) Designing algorithms for specific tasks (*b*) Ensuring ethical behavior of AI systems
(*c*) Replicating human-level intelligence across a wide range of tasks
(*d*) Improving computational efficiency

Q.10. Which AI technique involves training a computer to learn from experience without being explicitly programmed?

(*a*) Rule-based Systems (*b*) Expert Systems
(*c*) Machine Learning (*d*) Genetic Algorithms

Q.11. What is a problem in the context of problem-solving in Artificial Intelligence (AI)?

(*a*) Any situation that requires a solution
(*b*) A discrepancy between the current state and the desired state
(*c*) A set of rules and constraints
(*d*) A specific algorithm for finding solutions

Q.12. In problem-solving, what does the problem space represent?

(*a*) The physical environment in which the problem occurs
(*b*) The set of possible states and actions that can lead from the initial state to the goal state
(*c*) The set of all possible solutions to the problem
(*d*) The time it takes to solve the problem

Q.13. Which of the following is NOT an example of a problem space?

(*a*) The set of all possible moves in a game of chess
(*b*) The set of all possible routes in a traveling salesperson problem
(*c*) The set of all possible solutions to a mathematical equation
(*d*) The set of all possible configurations of a Rubik's Cube

Q.14. What is search in the context of problem-solving?

(*a*) The process of identifying and defining a problem
(*b*) The process of finding a solution to a problem by exploring the problem space
(*c*) The process of generating new problems from existing ones
(*d*) The process of evaluating the effectiveness of a solution

Q.15. Which of the following is an example of an uninformed search algorithm?

(*a*) A* search (*b*) Depth-first search
(*c*) Best-first search (*d*) Hill climbing

Q.16. What is the main difference between depth-first search and breadth-first search?

(*a*) Depth-first search explores nodes in the order they are encountered, while breadth-first search explores nodes level by level.
(*b*) Depth-first search always finds the shortest path to the goal, while breadth-first search may not.

(*c*) Depth-first search is a blind search algorithm, while breadth-first search is an informed search algorithm.
(*d*) Depth-first search uses a heuristic function to guide the search, while breadth-first search does not.

Q.17. In heuristic search algorithms, what is a heuristic function used for?
(*a*) To determine the optimal path from the initial state to the goal state
(*b*) To evaluate the cost of reaching the goal state from each state in the search space
(*c*) To estimate the distance from each state to the goal state
(*d*) To prioritize the expansion of nodes in the search space

Q.18. Which of the following search algorithms guarantees finding the optimal solution?
(*a*) Depth-first search (*b*) Breadth-first search
(*c*) A* search (*d*) Hill climbing

Q.19. What is the purpose of pruning in search algorithms?
(*a*) To remove unnecessary nodes from the search space to improve efficiency
(*b*) To add new nodes to the search space to explore alternative paths
(*c*) To expand the search space by generating new nodes
(*d*) To backtrack and explore previously visited nodes

Q.20. Which search algorithm is commonly used for solving problems with large search spaces?
(*a*) Depth-first search (*b*) Breadth-first search
(*c*) A* search (*d*) Greedy best-first search

Q.21. What is the median of the following set of numbers: 12, 15, 18, 20, 25, 30?
(*a*) 18 (*b*) 20 (*c*) 22.5 (*d*) 25

Q.22. What does the standard deviation measure in a data set?
(*a*) The average value (*b*) The spread of data around the mean
(*c*) The total range of data (*d*) The central tendency of data

Q.23. In a normal distribution, approximately what percentage of data falls within one standard deviation of the mean?
(*a*) 34% (*b*) 50% (*c*) 68% (*d*) 95%

Q.24. Which measure of central tendency is most affected by outliers?
(*a*) Mean (*b*) Median (*c*) Mode (*d*) Range

Q.25. If the correlation coefficient between two variables is -0.75, it indicates:
(*a*) Strong positive correlation (*b*) Weak negative correlation
(*c*) Strong negative correlation (*d*) No correlation

Q.26. What does a p-value in statistical hypothesis testing represent?
(*a*) The probability of rejecting the null hypothesis when it is true
(*b*) The probability of accepting the null hypothesis when it is true
(*c*) The probability of observing the data given that the null hypothesis is true
(*d*) The probability of observing the data given that the alternative hypothesis is true

Q.27. Which statistical test is used to determine if there is a significant difference between the means of two independent groups?

(*a*) Paired t-test (*b*) Chi-square test
(*c*) Analysis of variance (ANOVA) (*d*) Pearson correlation test

Q.28. What is the formula to calculate the probability of an event in a uniform distribution?

(*a*) P(x) = (x – μ)/σ (*b*) P(x) = 1 / (b – a)
(*c*) P(x) = e^(–λ) * (λ^x)/x! (*d*) P(x) = (x – a)/(b – a)

Q.29. What is the mode of the following set of numbers: 5, 7, 7, 9, 10, 10, 12?

(*a*) 7 (*b*) 9 (*c*) 10 (*d*) There is no mode

Q.30. What is the formula to calculate the coefficient of variation?

(*a*) CV = (Standard deviation / Mean) * 100% (*b*) CV = (Mean / Standard deviation) * 100%
(*c*) CV = Mean - Standard deviation (*d*) CV = Standard deviation / Mean

Answers

1. (*b*)	2. (*b*)	3. (*c*)	4. (*d*)	5. (*a*)	6. (*c*)	7. (*a*)	8. (*d*)	9. (*c*)
10. (*c*)	11. (*b*)	12. (*b*)	13. (*c*)	14. (*b*)	15. (*b*)	16. (*a*)	17. (*c*)	18. (*c*)
19. (*a*)	20. (*c*)	21. (*b*)	22. (*b*)	23. (*c*)	24. (*a*)	25. (*c*)	26. (*c*)	27. (*c*)
28. (*b*)	29. (*c*)	30. (*a*)						

Unsolved Questions

1. Define Artificial Intelligence (AI) and explain its significance in modern computing.
2. What are the primary goals of Artificial Intelligence?
3. Give an example of a task that falls under the domain of Artificial Intelligence.
4. Distinguish between Narrow (Weak) AI and General (Strong) AI. Provide examples for each.
5. Explain the concept of "thinking humanly" and "thinking rationally" in the context of AI.
6. Outline the key milestones in the history of Artificial Intelligence.
7. Name some of the early pioneers and contributors to the field of AI.
8. Discuss the AI winter periods and their impact on the development of AI.
9. What is Computational Intelligence, and how does it differ from traditional AI approaches?
10. Provide examples of applications where Computational Intelligence techniques are commonly used.
11. Explain the importance of AI in various industries. Provide examples of AI applications in real-world scenarios.
12. Define the terms "Problem" and "Problem Space" in the context of problem-solving.
13. Explain how defining a problem as a state space search helps in finding solutions.
14. What is a Production System, and how does it contribute to problem-solving?
15. Discuss the importance of searching in problem-solving.
16. What are the key components of a search algorithm?
17. Differentiate between Uninformed and Informed Search Algorithms. Provide examples for each type.
18. Explain the concept of heuristics in the context of Informed Search Algorithms.

19. Prove that if a heuristic is consistent, it must be admissible. Construct an admissible heuristic that is not consistent.
20. Define knowledge and provide an example of tacit knowledge.
21. Explain the role of knowledge-based systems in artificial intelligence.
22. Discuss the importance of knowledge acquisition in developing knowledge-based systems.
23. Compare and contrast semantic networks and frames as knowledge representation techniques.
24. What is the significance of logic-based representation in AI systems?
25. Explain the difference between syntax and semantics in the context of first-order logic.
26. How is linear algebra used in the context of vector spaces and matrices in AI?
27. Discuss the role of linear maps in AI applications.
28. Why is statistics important in the field of artificial intelligence?
29. Compare and contrast population and sample in statistical analysis.
30. Measures of Central Tendency and Dispersion.
31. Calculate the mean, median, and mode for a given dataset.
32. Explain the importance of variance and standard deviation in understanding data variability.
33. Define probability density function (PDF) and its role in probability theory.
34. Discuss the application of the Central Limit Theorem in AI.
35. Choose a specific scenario and propose a suitable knowledge representation technique (e.g., frame, semantic network) for that scenario.
36. Discuss the challenges and considerations in building a knowledge base for an AI application.
37. This corresponds to the following open formula:

    $\text{Man}(x) \wedge \exists s_1, s_2, s_3\ \text{Son}(s_1 x) \wedge \text{Son}(s_2, x) \wedge \text{Son}(s_3, x)$

    $\wedge s_1 \neq s_2 \wedge s_1 \neq s_3 \wedge s_2 \neq s_3$

    $\wedge \neg\exists\ d_1, d_2, d_3\ \text{Daughter}\ (d_1, x) \wedge \text{Daughter}(d_2, x) \wedge \text{Daughter}(d_3, x)$

    $\wedge\ d_1 \neq d_2 \wedge d_1 \neq d_3 \wedge d_2 \neq d_3$

    $\wedge \forall s\ \text{Son}(s, x) \Rightarrow \text{Unemployed}(s) \wedge \text{Married}(s) \wedge \text{Doctor}(\text{Spouse}(s))$

    $\wedge \forall d\ \text{Daughter}(d, x) \Rightarrow \text{Professor}(d) \wedge$

    $(\text{Department}(d) = \text{Physics} \vee \text{Department}(d) = \text{Math}).$
38. Consider a vocabulary with the following symbols:

    Occupation(p, o): Predicate. Person p has occupation o.

    Customer (p1, p2): Predicate. Person p1 is a customer of person p2.

    Boss(p1, p2): Predicate. Person p1 is a boss of person p2.

    Doctor, Surgeon, Lawyer , Actor: Constants denoting occupations.

    Emily, Joe: Constants denoting people.

    Use these symbols to write the following assertions in first-order logic:

    (*a*) Emily is either a surgeon or a lawyer. (i.e., O(E,S) ∨ O(E,L).)

    (*b*) Joe is an actor, but he also holds another job.

    (*c*) All surgeons are doctors.

    (*d*) Joe does not have a lawyer (i.e., is not a customer of any lawyer).

    (*e*) Emily has a boss who is a lawyer.

39. Which of the following are valid (necessarily true) sentences?
    (*a*) $(\exists x\ x = x) \Rightarrow (\forall y\ \exists z\ y = z)$.
    (*b*) $\forall x\ P(x) \vee \neg P(x)$.
    (*c*) $\forall x\ Smart(x) \vee (x = x)$.

Fill in the Blanks

1. During an AI winter, there is a slowdown in AI research and funding due to _________ and unmet expectations.
2. Machine Learning, Natural Language Processing (NLP), and Computer Vision are examples of _________ techniques used in AI.
3. Reactive Machines operate based on pre-defined rules and lack the ability to learn from _________.
4. Symbolic AI relies on the manipulation of _________ and logic to solve problems.
5. Computational Intelligence includes approaches like _________, fuzzy logic, and evolutionary algorithms.
6. In problem-solving, a _________ is a situation that needs to be addressed or resolved.
7. A _________ represents all possible states that can be reached from the initial state in the process of solving a problem.
8. A _________ is a set of rules or operations that can be applied to transform the current state into a new state.
9. Searching is a fundamental component of problem-solving, where algorithms explore the _________ for a solution.
10. Uninformed Search Algorithms make decisions solely based on _________ information.
11. In Informed Search Algorithms, _________ are used to guide the search toward the goal state.
12. The Missionaries and Cannibals Problem involves transporting missionaries and cannibals across a river while respecting certain _________ constraints.
13. The 8-Queen Problem requires placing eight queens on a chessboard in such a way that no two queens _________ each other.
14. The Tower of Hanoi Problem involves moving a stack of disks from one rod to another, following the rules of _________.
15. Knowledge refers to _________ acquired through experience or education.
16. Knowledge-based systems are computer programs that utilize _________ to perform tasks typically requiring human intelligence.
17. Types of knowledge include declarative knowledge (), procedural knowledge (), and contextual knowledge (_________).
18. Knowledge acquisition is the process of gathering and collecting information to build a _________.
19. Knowledge representation involves organizing and structuring knowledge in a form suitable for _________ by a computer.
20. Properties for knowledge representation include _________, efficiency, expressiveness, and ease of maintenance.
21. Requirements for knowledge representation systems include the ability to represent incomplete or uncertain knowledge, support for efficient _________, and adaptability to changing domains.

22. Different types of knowledge include explicit knowledge (__________ and codified) and tacit knowledge (personal, subjective, and hard to __________).
23. Semantic networks represent knowledge using nodes and links, capturing __________ between concepts.
24. Frames are a knowledge representation technique that organizes information into hierarchical structures with __________ and values.
25. Conceptual graphs provide a formalism for knowledge representation using graphs with nodes and labeled __________.
26. Conceptual dependency is a knowledge representation technique that focuses on __________ and their effects on the world.
27. Scripts represent stereotypical sequences of __________, providing a structured way to represent common activities or scenarios.
28. Logic-based representation involves expressing knowledge using __________ and rules.
29. The syntax and semantics of first-order logic provide rules for constructing and __________ logical statements.
30. In first-order logic, symbols represent __________, and interpretations define the meaning of these symbols.
31. Linear Algebra involves the study of __________ in vector spaces and matrices.
32. Vector spaces are mathematical structures that consist of vectors and satisfy certain __________.
33. Euclidean space is a specific type of vector space representing geometric space with the __________ metric.
34. Subspaces are subsets of a vector space that also form a vector space under the same __________.
35. Linear maps, or linear transformations, are functions between vector spaces that preserve __________ operations.
36. The matrix of a linear map is a matrix that represents the __________ in a particular basis.
37. Statistics is the study of collecting, analyzing, interpreting, presenting, and __________ data.
38. In statistics, a population is the entire set of individuals or instances, and a sample is a subset used to make inferences __________ the population.
39. Measures of central tendency, such as mean, median, and mode, summarize the center or __________ of a set of values.
40. Variance and standard deviation measure the __________ or dispersion of a set of values.
41. Range and interquartile range provide information about the __________ of values in a dataset.
42. A probability density function describes the likelihood of different outcomes in a __________ random variable.
43. The Central Limit Theorem states that the distribution of the sum (or __________) of a large number of independent, identically distributed random variables approaches a normal distribution.

2

(Idea of Machine Learning)

INTRODUCTION

Machines have made tremendous progress since the Industrial Revolution, evolving from simple tools to sophisticated systems capable of performing cognitive tasks that were once exclusive to humans. In addition to their presence in factories and manufacturing plants, machines now excel in activities like judging competitions, driving cars, and defeating professional chess players, showcasing their ability to replicate complex human tasks.

However, this advancement in machine capabilities has raised concerns and fears among some individuals. These concerns often stem from deep-rooted insecurities about the potential consequences. People wonder what could happen if intelligent machines were to pose a threat to human survival or if they were to develop capabilities beyond what humans intended. Questions also arise about the possibility of machines surpassing human intelligence, a concept known as the singularity.

Despite these apprehensions, it is essential to approach the development of intelligent machines with responsible and ethical practices to ensure that they benefit humanity without posing risks. By focusing on beneficial applications and incorporating appropriate safety measures, we can harness the potential of intelligent machines for the betterment of society.

One significant fear surrounding the advancement of AI and machine learning is the potential threat to job security. Certain professions, such as truck drivers, accountants, bar workers, waiters, chartered accountants, receptionists, and taxi drivers, face a high risk of becoming automated by 2035, according to BBC's analysis.

However, predictions about job automation should be taken with caution. While AI technology is progressing rapidly, widespread adoption is still uncertain and comes with both known and unforeseen challenges. Implementing AI solutions is not as simple as flipping a switch; it requires careful development and expertise.

Machine learning, in particular, relies on statistical algorithms managed and overseen by skilled professionals known as data scientists and machine learning engineers. Currently, there is a shortage of qualified professionals in this field, which is a significant obstacle to the progress of AI. The demand for experts in machine learning is high, but the supply of qualified professionals is struggling to meet it.

While job automation is a reality that cannot be ignored, the complexity of AI technology and the need for skilled professionals ensure that there will be a gradual transition rather than an immediate replacement of human jobs. Moreover, the growth of AI also presents new job opportunities in the field of data science and machine learning, offering potential avenues for individuals to adapt and contribute to this evolving industry.

According to Charles Green, the Director of Thought Leadership at Belatrix Software: "It's a huge challenge to find data scientists, people with machine learning experience, or people with the skills to analyze and use the data, as well as those who can create the algorithms required for machine learning. Secondly, while the technology is still emerging, there are many ongoing developments. It's clear that AI is a long way from how we might imagine it."

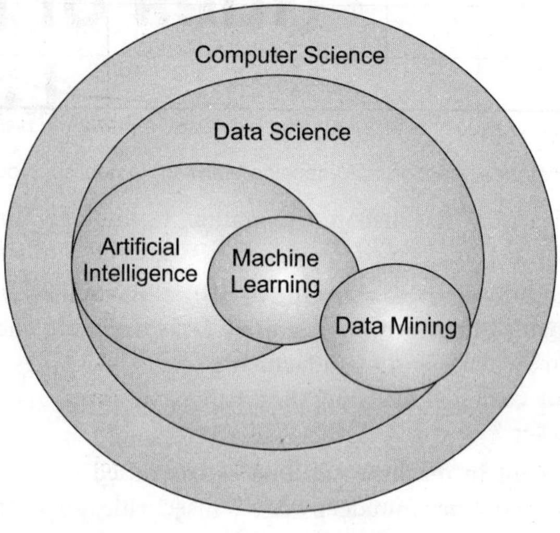

Fig. 2.1. Visual representation of the relationship between data-related fields

WHAT IS MACHINE LEARNING?

In 1959, IBM published a paper in the IBM Journal of Research and Development with an, at the time, obscure and curious title. Authored by IBM's Arthur Samuel, the paper invested the use of machine learning in the game of checkers "to verify the fact that a computer can be programmed so that it will learn to play a better game of checkers than can be played by the person who wrote the program."

Arthur Samuel is often credited as one of the pioneers of machine learning, as he is widely recognized for coining and defining the term "machine learning" in the form we know today. While he was not the first to use the term, his landmark journal submission titled "Some Studies in Machine Learning Using the Game of Checkers" marked a significant milestone in the field of artificial intelligence and the application of learning principles to machines. In this work, Samuel explored the concept of training computers to play checkers and demonstrated their ability to improve their performance through experience, laying the foundation for modern machine learning techniques.

This early work by Samuel reflects the human desire to impart our own learning capabilities to artificial systems, showcasing our determination to develop machines that can learn from data and improve their performance over time. Samuel's contributions have had a lasting impact on the field of artificial intelligence, inspiring subsequent researchers and practitioners to further explore and develop machine learning algorithms and applications.

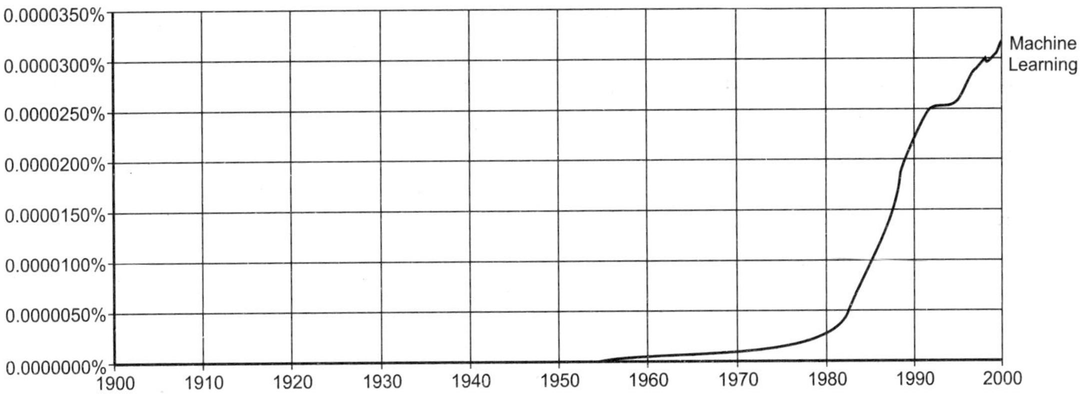

Fig. 2.2. Historical mentions of "machine learning" in published books.

As of today, machine learning has become a mature technology that finds applications in almost every aspect of life. It has transformed various industries and domains, making personalized recommendations, predicting future trends, optimizing processes, and aiding in critical decision-making. Machine learning algorithms can recommend toys to toddlers, suggest technology books to tech enthusiasts, and recommend literature titles to writers. They can predict market trends to help amateur traders compete with seasoned professionals, assist oncologists in diagnosing diseases, and optimize energy consumption for a greener environment.

Google is at the forefront of machine learning and artificial intelligence research, with ambitious projects like the Google self-driving car and Google Brain. These initiatives demonstrate the rapid advancement and innovation in the field of machine learning, which has become an integral part of our daily lives.

Machine learning's journey started with pioneers like Arthur Samuel, who laid the groundwork for training machines to learn and improve their performance through experience. Over the years, the field has grown exponentially, incorporating various algorithms, techniques, and approaches, making it a fundamental aspect of modern technology and science.

As we move forward, machine learning will continue to evolve and shape our lives in ways we cannot yet fully imagine, driving innovation and progress in various industries and solving complex problems that were once unimaginable. It is an exciting time for machine learning and artificial intelligence, with endless possibilities waiting to be explored and harnessed for the benefit of humanity.

Machine learning is defined by Tom M. Mitchell, a Professor of Machine Learning at Carnegie Mellon University's School of Computer Science, as follows:

"A computer program is said to learn from experience E with respect to some task T and performance measure P if its performance on T, as measured by P, improves with experience E."

In this definition, "experience E" refers to the data that the machine learning algorithm learns from, "task T" represents the specific problem or task the algorithm aims to solve, and "performance measure P" evaluates how well the algorithm performs on the task. The essence of machine learning lies in its ability to improve its performance on the given task by learning from the provided data or experience.

Exactly, defining the problem correctly is a crucial step in any project, including machine learning projects. It sets the foundation for the entire project and determines the goals and objectives that need to be achieved. A well-defined problem statement ensures that the project remains focused and aligned with the desired outcomes.

The three fundamental steps of the machine learning process:

1. **Data Input:** In this step, historical data or information is gathered and used as the input to the machine learning model. The data could be structured (tabular data) or unstructured (text, images, etc.). It is essential to ensure that the data is of high quality, relevant to the problem, and free from biases.
2. **Abstraction:** Once the data is collected, machine learning algorithms are applied to process and analyze it. During this step, the model extracts patterns, relationships, and insights from the data. The abstraction process involves transforming the raw data into a more meaningful representation, such as feature engineering, to capture the essential characteristics of the data.

   Knowledge is fed into the machine learning process and how abstraction helps in deriving a summarized representation of the data, known as a model. The model serves as a knowledge representation of the raw data and can take various forms, depending on the type of machine learning algorithm used and the nature of the data. Some common forms of models include:

   - **Computational Blocks like If/Else Rules:** In certain cases, machine learning models can be expressed as simple conditional statements, such as if/else rules. These rules define specific conditions and actions to be taken based on those conditions. This form of model is often used in decision trees and rule-based systems.
   - **Mathematical Equations:** Many machine learning algorithms, particularly those in regression and optimization tasks, utilize mathematical equations to model relationships between input variables and output predictions. These equations represent the learned patterns and can be used to make predictions on new data.
   - **Specific Data Structures like Trees or Graphs:** Some machine learning algorithms, like decision trees and neural networks, use specific data structures like trees or graphs to represent the learned knowledge. These structures capture hierarchical relationships and complex interactions between features.
   - **Logical Groupings of Similar Observations:** In clustering algorithms, the model represents knowledge by grouping similar data points together based on their attributes. Clusters of similar observations are formed, allowing the model to identify patterns and similarities in the data.

   Overall, the choice of the model depends on the problem domain, the type of data available, and the specific goals of the machine learning task. The model serves as a condensed form of knowledge that can be used for making predictions, classifications, or decisions on new, unseen data.

   A great example to illustrate the process of fitting a model and training in machine learning.

   Let's take the simple linear regression model 'y = c + c x' as an example. In this equation, 'y' represents the output variable, 'x' represents the input variable, and 'c' represents the coefficients or constants that we need to find to make predictions.

   To fit the model, we need to determine the values of 'c' and 'c' based on the input data we have. This process is known as training the model. During training, the model is adjusted and optimized to learn the underlying patterns and relationships present in the training data.

   The training data consists of pairs of input 'x' and output 'y' values, which are used to estimate the values of 'c' and 'c' that best fit the data. The goal of training is to minimize the error or the difference between the predicted output 'y' (based on the model) and the actual output 'y' from the training data.

Once the model is trained and the values of 'c' and 'c' are determined, the model can be used to make predictions on new, unseen data. It can take new input values 'x' and use the learned coefficients to predict the corresponding output 'y'.

In summary, fitting the model involves finding the optimal values of the model's parameters (coefficients) based on the training data. This process of learning from the data and adjusting the model is called training, and the data used for training is known as training data. Once the model is trained, it can be used to make predictions on new data.

3. **Generalization:** After abstraction, the model is trained on the processed data to learn patterns and relationships between inputs and outputs. The trained model is then generalized to make predictions or decisions on new, unseen data. Generalization ensures that the model can perform well on new data and not just the training data.

   After the model is trained and abstracted from the input data, it's essential to generalize its knowledge to handle new, unseen data or test data. Generalization allows the model to make predictions and decisions beyond the specific data it was trained on.

   However, generalization comes with its challenges. When the trained model is too closely aligned with the training data, it may not accurately represent the underlying trends in the real-world data. This phenomenon is called overfitting, where the model fits the noise or random variations in the training data rather than the true patterns.

   On the other hand, when the test data has certain characteristics that were not present in the training data, the model may struggle to make accurate predictions. This is called underfitting, where the model lacks the capacity to capture the complexity of the underlying patterns in the data.

   To achieve successful generalization, it is essential to strike a balance between overfitting and underfitting. Machine learning algorithms aim to find this balance by adjusting their parameters during the training process.

   An important aspect of generalization is to assess the model's performance on a separate set of data called the validation or test set. This allows us to evaluate how well the model performs on unseen data and make any necessary adjustments to improve its performance.

   In summary, generalization is the process of making the trained model capable of handling new, unseen data and making decisions beyond the training data. It involves striking a balance between overfitting and underfitting to ensure that the model can make accurate predictions in real-world scenarios

TOP OF FORM

These steps are at the core of most machine learning algorithms and form the foundation for creating models that can learn from data and make accurate predictions or decisions. The process of data input, abstraction, and generalization is iterative, where models are continuously refined and improved based on feedback and new data.

Well-posed Learning Problem

A well-posed learning problem is a precisely defined problem in the context of machine learning. The framework presented here is a simple and effective way to approach problem-solving using machine learning. Let's explore each question in more detail:

1. **What is the problem?**
Clearly define the problem you want to solve using machine learning. This involves understanding the nature of the problem, its scope, and the specific task that needs to be accomplished. For example, if the problem is to predict customer churn in a subscription-based service, the task is a binary classification problem where the goal is to determine whether a customer will churn or not.
2. **Why does the problem need to be solved?**
Identify the motivation or rationale behind solving the problem using machine learning. This step involves understanding the impact of the problem on the business or domain you are working in. For example, reducing customer churn can lead to increased revenue and customer satisfaction for a subscription-based service.
3. **How to solve the problem?**
Determine the appropriate machine learning approach and methodology to tackle the problem. This step involves selecting the right algorithms, preparing the data, and evaluating the performance of the model. It's essential to consider the availability of data, the complexity of the problem, and the resources required to implement the solution.

By answering these three questions, you can gain a clear understanding of the problem and its significance. It will also help you assess whether machine learning is a suitable approach for solving the problem. Additionally, it will guide you in choosing the appropriate techniques and methodologies to develop an effective machine learning solution.

Following this framework ensures that you approach the problem in a systematic and well-informed manner, increasing the likelihood of success in solving real-world challenges with machine learning.

Types of Machine Learning

Machine learning encompasses a diverse set of algorithms and methodologies, making the selection of the right algorithm a crucial aspect of any machine learning project. Understanding the three fundamental categories of machine learning is essential to determine the appropriate approach for a given problem:

1. **Supervised Learning:** In supervised learning, the algorithm is trained on labeled data, where the input data and corresponding output (labels) are provided. The goal is to learn a mapping between input features and their corresponding target values. The algorithm makes predictions on unseen data based on the learned relationships from the training data. Common tasks in supervised learning include classification, where the output is a category or class, and regression, where the output is a continuous value. Examples of supervised learning algorithms include Support Vector Machines (SVM), Decision Trees, and Neural Networks.
2. **Unsupervised Learning:** Unsupervised learning operates on unlabeled data, where the algorithm does not have access to any predefined target output. The objective is to discover patterns, structures, or clusters within the data. Unsupervised learning algorithms group similar data points together based on their intrinsic properties without explicit guidance. Clustering and dimensionality reduction are typical tasks in unsupervised learning. Popular unsupervised learning algorithms include K-Means, Hierarchical Clustering, and Principal Component Analysis (PCA).
3. **Reinforcement Learning:** In reinforcement learning, an agent learns to interact with an environment to achieve a specific goal. The agent receives feedback in the form of rewards or penalties based on its actions, guiding it towards optimal decision-making. The objective is to

maximize the cumulative reward over time through a series of interactions. Reinforcement learning is often used in applications like robotics, game playing, and autonomous systems. Q-Learning and Deep Q-Networks (DQNs) are examples of reinforcement learning algorithms.

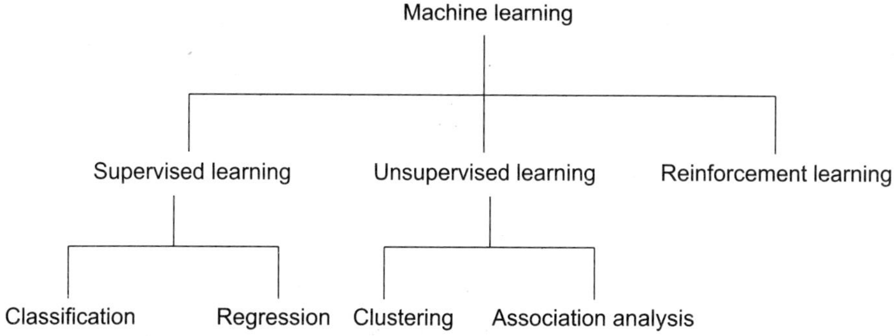

Fig. 2.3. Types of machine learning

Supervised Learning

In supervised learning, the machine needs access to past information or experiences to learn and make predictions. This past information comes in the form of labeled data, where the input data is accompanied by corresponding output labels that represent the desired or correct answers.

Imagine that a machine is given input of photographs of various items, and its purpose is to sort the images according to the object's shape or colour. Depending on shape, the pictures that are of Images of triangular-shaped things, for example, must be segregated from those of objects with a circular shape. photos of blue things must be separated from photos of green objects if segregation is required based on colour. But how can a machine tell the difference between a triangle and a circle? In a similar vein, how can a machine tell whether an image of an object is blue or green? A machine is very similar to a young child who must first be taught the fundamentals of shape and colour by his parents or other people in order for him to begin doing the work. A machine has to be given the fundamental data. Training data serves as this fundamental input or experience in the machine learning paradigm. Training data is historical information about a certain task. The training data will include historical information on various facets or features on a variety of images, as well as a tag indicating whether the image is round or triangular or blue or green in hue. In the case of supervised learning, the tag is referred to as "label," and we say that the training data is labelled.

A straightforward illustration of the supervised learning procedure. The input consists of labelled training data that includes historical data. The computer creates a prediction model based on the training data, which it then applies to the test data to classify each record.

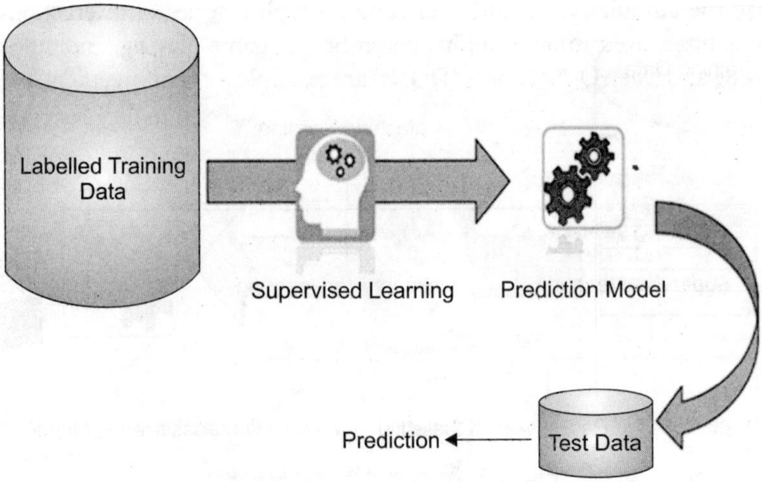

Fig. 2.4. Supervised learning

Some examples of supervised learning are

1. **Image Classification:** Given a dataset of images with corresponding labels indicating different objects or scenes, the task is to build a model that can classify new images into appropriate categories. For example, distinguishing between images of cats and dogs.
2. **Sentiment Analysis:** In this task, the model analyzes text data (e.g., customer reviews, social media posts) and predicts the sentiment expressed, such as positive, negative, or neutral.
3. **Spam Detection:** Supervised learning can be used to classify emails as either spam or not spam based on labeled data containing examples of spam and non-spam emails.
4. **Handwriting Recognition:** The model is trained on a dataset of handwritten digits or characters along with their corresponding labels. It can then recognize handwritten digits or characters in new input data.
5. **Credit Risk Assessment:** In this application, historical data on credit applicants along with their creditworthiness (good or bad credit) is used to build a model for predicting the credit risk of new applicants.
6. **Medical Diagnosis:** Supervised learning can be applied to predict medical conditions based on patient data and diagnostic tests, using historical data with known diagnoses.
7. **Stock Price Prediction:** By using historical stock market data, a model can be developed to predict the future price movements of stocks.
8. **Speech Recognition:** The model is trained on labeled audio data containing speech samples and their corresponding transcripts to recognize and transcribe spoken words.

A classification problem is one in which we are attempting to predict a nominal or category variable. When attempting to predict a real-valued variable, however, the issue is classified as a regression problem.

Classification is a supervised learning technique in machine learning, where the primary goal is to categorize or label data instances into predefined classes or categories based on their input features. It involves training a model on a labeled dataset, where each data point is associated with a specific class label. The model learns patterns and relationships from this training data and uses them to classify new, unseen data instances into the appropriate classes.

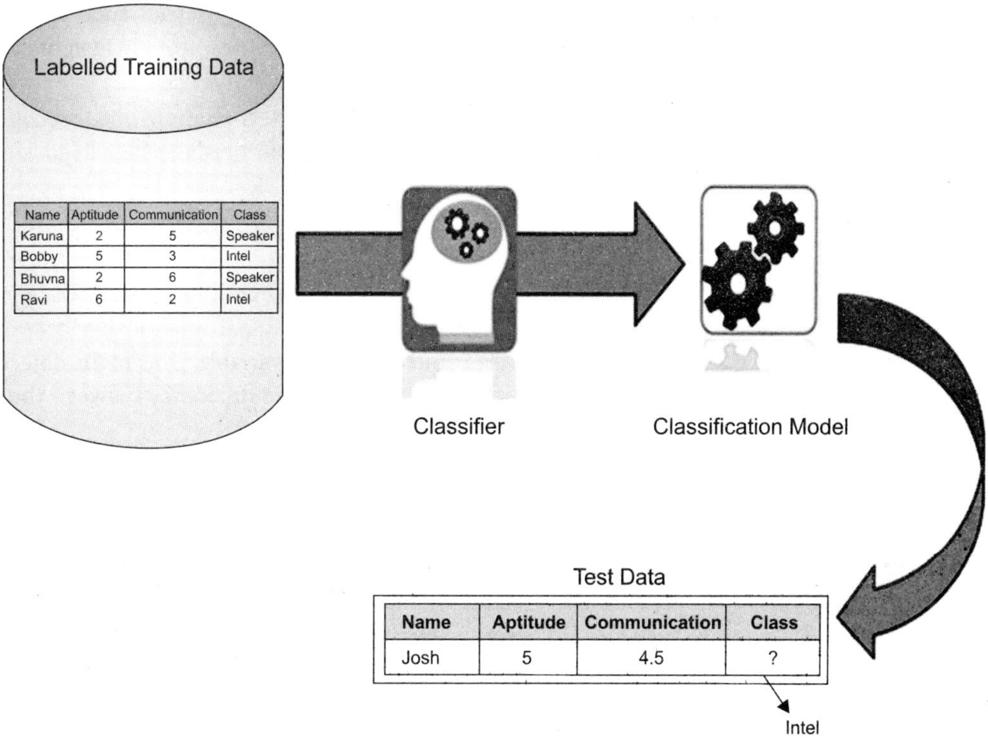

Fig. 2.5. Classification

In classification, the input features are also known as independent variables or predictors, while the class labels represent the target variable or dependent variable. The model's objective is to find a decision boundary that separates the data points into distinct classes, allowing it to make accurate predictions on unseen data.

The classification process can be summarized as follows:

1. **Input Data:** The model receives input data, which consists of features or attributes describing each data instance.
2. **Training:** The model is trained on a labeled dataset, where the class labels are known for each data instance. During training, the model adjusts its parameters to find the best decision boundary that minimizes the classification error.
3. **Decision Rule:** Once the model is trained, it establishes a decision rule based on the learned patterns. This rule allows the model to assign new data instances to specific classes.
4. **Prediction:** The trained model is then used to predict the class labels of unseen data instances. The model takes the input features as input and outputs the predicted class label.

Classification problems can have two main types of outputs:

- **Binary Classification:** The target variable has only two classes, typically represented as positive and negative, 1 and 0, or true and false.
- **Multi-class Classification:** The target variable has more than two classes, and the model needs to classify the data instances into multiple distinct categories.

The performance of a classification model is typically evaluated using metrics such as accuracy, precision, recall, F1 score, and confusion matrix, among others. These metrics provide insights into the model's effectiveness in correctly classifying data instances into their respective classes.

Classification is widely used in various applications, including text categorization, image recognition, medical diagnosis, sentiment analysis, and many other fields where data needs to be categorized into specific classes.

Regression

Linear regression is a supervised learning technique used for predicting continuous numerical values, also known as the target or dependent variable. It aims to establish a linear relationship between the predictor variables, also called independent variables, and the target variable. The main objective of linear regression is to find the best-fitted straight line that minimizes the difference between the actual and predicted values of the target variable using the least squares method.

In simple linear regression, there is only one predictor variable, while in multiple linear regression, there are multiple predictor variables that contribute to predicting the target variable. Linear regression is commonly used in various applications, including predicting house prices, stock market trends, weather forecasting, and many other situations where the relationship between variables can be approximated by a straight line. It provides a simple and interpretable way to understand the relationship between the predictor variables and the target variable. However, it may not be suitable for complex datasets with non-linear relationships, where other advanced regression techniques or machine learning models may be more appropriate.

Let's consider a simple example of linear regression to predict the salary of employees based on their years of experience. In this scenario, the years of experience will be the predictor variable (x), and the salary will be the target variable (y).

Suppose we have the following data:

Years of Experience (x)	Salary (y)
1	30,000
2	35,000
3	40,000
4	45,000
5	50,000

We want to find a linear relationship between years of experience and salary, so we can predict the salary for employees with different levels of experience.

Data Collection: We have collected data on employees' years of experience and their corresponding salaries.

Visualization: We plot the data points on a scatter plot to visualize the relationship between years of experience and salary.

Model Fitting: We fit a straight line to the data using linear regression. The equation of the line will be in the form of $y = mx + b$, where 'm' is the slope and 'b' is the intercept. The goal is to find the values of 'm' and 'b' that best fit the data.

Model Evaluation: We use the least squares method to find the values of 'm' and 'b' that minimize the sum of squared differences between the actual salaries and the predicted salaries based on the linear regression model.

Prediction: Once the model is trained, we can use it to predict the salary for employees with different years of experience. For example, if an employee has 6 years of experience, we can use the linear regression equation to predict their salary.

After fitting the model, we may find that the linear regression line is y = 10000x + 20000. This means that for each additional year of experience, the salary is expected to increase by $10,000, and employees with zero years of experience (new hires) can expect a starting salary of $20,000.

Now, we can use this linear regression model to predict the salary of an employee with, let's say, 8 years of experience. We plug in the value of x (years of experience) into the equation:

$$y = 10000 * 8 + 20000 = 100,000$$

So, an employee with 8 years of experience is predicted to have a salary of $100,000 based on the linear regression model.

In the context of the Iris dataset, suppose we want to perform a simple linear regression to predict the sepal length (target variable) based on the petal length (predictor variable). We can use the petal length as our independent variable (x) and the sepal length as our dependent variable (y).

Here's a step-by-step explanation of how to perform simple linear regression using the Iris dataset:

1. Load the Iris dataset and extract the petal length and sepal length columns as our predictor and target variables, respectively.
2. Split the dataset into training and testing sets. The training set will be used to train the linear regression model, and the testing set will be used to evaluate its performance.
3. Fit the linear regression model using the training data.
4. Make predictions on the test data using the trained model.
5. Evaluate the performance of the model by comparing the predicted sepal lengths with the actual sepal lengths from the test data.

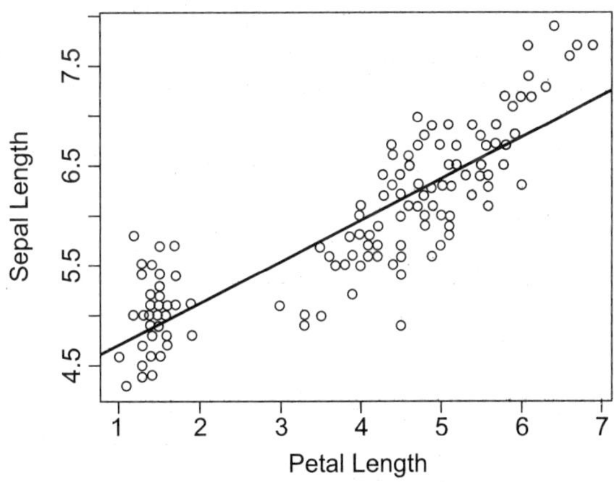

Fig. 2.6. Regression

Typical applications of regression can be seen in various fields and industries. Here are some common examples:

1. **Predicting Sales:** Regression can be used to predict future sales based on historical sales data, marketing efforts, and other relevant factors.

2. **Financial Forecasting:** Regression models can help forecast stock prices, exchange rates, or interest rates based on historical market data.
3. **Housing Prices:** Regression can be used to predict house prices based on features such as location, size, number of rooms, and amenities.
4. **Healthcare:** Regression models can be employed to predict patient outcomes, disease progression, or the effectiveness of medical treatments.
5. **Risk Assessment:** In insurance and finance, regression can be used to assess risk and predict potential losses.
6. **Marketing:** Regression analysis can be applied to analyze customer behavior, predict customer preferences, and optimize marketing campaigns.
7. **Climate Science:** Regression models can help study climate patterns, temperature changes, and their impact on the environment.
8. **Quality Control:** Regression can be used to predict product quality based on various manufacturing parameters.
9. **Sports Analytics:** Regression analysis is commonly used in sports to predict player performance, team outcomes, and game results.
10. **Education:** Regression can help predict student performance, graduation rates, and academic achievements based on various factors.

These are just a few examples of the wide range of applications for regression analysis. It is a versatile and powerful tool used in many domains to make data-driven predictions and decisions.

Unsupervised Learning

In unsupervised learning, the primary goal is to explore and discover patterns or structures within the data without the use of labeled training examples. Unlike supervised learning, where the algorithm is trained on known outcomes and then used to predict new data, unsupervised learning works with raw data and tries to identify inherent relationships or groupings.

The process of unsupervised learning is often referred to as pattern discovery or knowledge discovery because it uncovers valuable insights and patterns hidden within the data. It allows us to understand the underlying structure of the data and gain valuable knowledge about the dataset.

One critical application of unsupervised learning is customer segmentation. In this context, unsupervised learning algorithms can analyze customer data, such as purchase behavior, demographics, and online activity, to identify distinct groups or segments of customers with similar characteristics. These segments can then be used for targeted marketing, personalized recommendations, and better understanding customer preferences.

Other applications of unsupervised learning include anomaly detection, where the algorithm identifies unusual patterns or outliers in the data, dimensionality reduction, where the algorithm simplifies high-dimensional data for visualization and analysis, and clustering, where the algorithm groups similar data points together based on their features.

Overall, unsupervised learning plays a crucial role in data exploration and analysis, enabling businesses and researchers to gain valuable insights and make data-driven decisions without the need for labeled training data or explicit predictions.

Clustering is indeed a significant type of unsupervised learning that aims to group similar objects together based on their characteristics or features. The primary objective of clustering is to discover inherent patterns and groupings within unlabelled data, allowing data points with similar properties to be grouped together in clusters while keeping dissimilar data points in separate clusters.

Distance is a commonly used similarity measure for clustering. Data points that are closer to each other in terms of distance are more likely to belong to the same cluster, while those with a higher distance are less likely to be part of the same cluster. This approach is known as distance-based clustering, where the clustering algorithm calculates the distances between data points and assigns them to clusters accordingly.

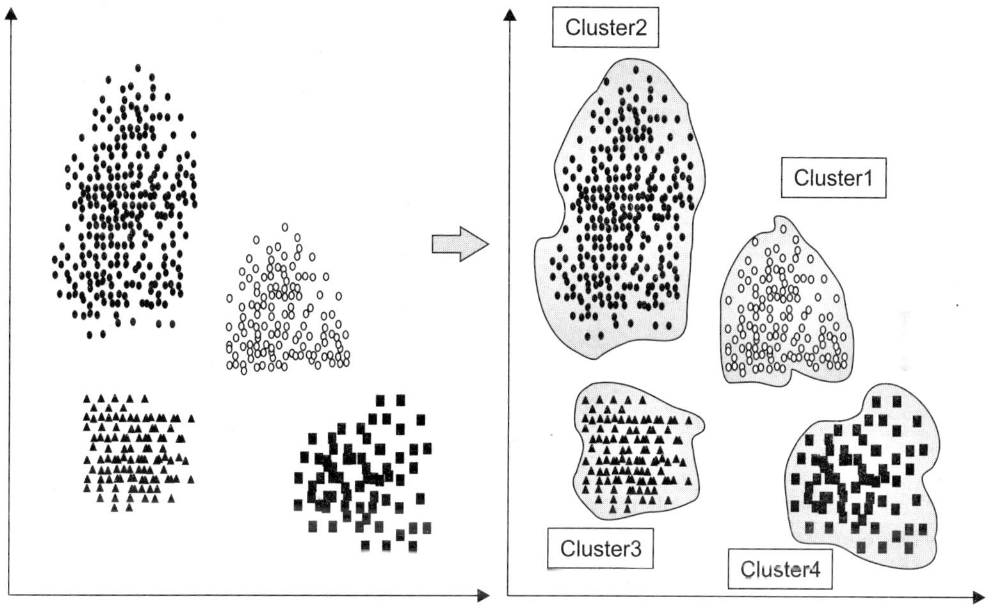

Fig. 2.7. Distance-based clustering

The clustering process can be depicted at a high level, as shown in Figure 1.8. Initially, the algorithm starts with all data points as individual clusters. It then iteratively merges or splits clusters based on the similarity or distance between data points until the desired clusters are formed. The clustering process may involve various algorithms, such as k-means, hierarchical clustering, and density-based clustering, each with its own approach and characteristics.

Clustering has numerous applications in various fields, such as customer segmentation, image and pattern recognition, data analysis, and anomaly detection. It helps in organizing large datasets, identifying natural groupings, and gaining valuable insights from unstructured data.

Overall, clustering is a fundamental technique in unsupervised learning that plays a crucial role in data exploration, organization, and analysis by revealing underlying patterns and relationships within the data.

Association analysis is another essential variant of unsupervised learning. It involves discovering interesting relationships and associations between different items or variables in a large dataset. The primary goal of association analysis is to identify frequent itemsets, which are sets of items that often co-occur together.

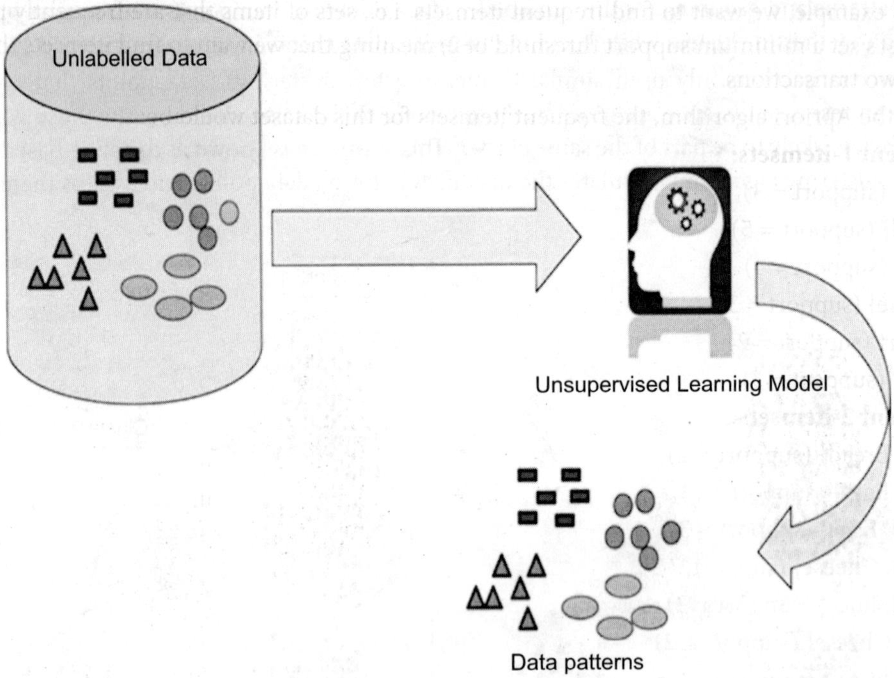

Fig. 2.8. Unsupervised learning

One of the most well-known algorithms used in association analysis is the Apriori algorithm. It searches for frequent itemsets by generating candidate itemsets and then pruning them based on their support, which is the frequency of occurrence of the itemset in the dataset.

Association analysis is commonly used in market basket analysis, where it helps identify products that are often purchased together. Retailers can use this information to optimize product placements and offer personalized recommendations to customers.

For example, by analyzing customer purchase data, association analysis may reveal that customers who buy diapers are also likely to buy baby wipes. This information can be leveraged by a store to place these items close to each other, leading to increased sales and customer satisfaction.

In summary, association analysis is a valuable technique in unsupervised learning that helps discover hidden patterns and relationships in large datasets, providing valuable insights for businesses and decision-making processes.

Let's consider a hypothetical example of association analysis in a retail setting. Suppose we have a transaction dataset from a grocery store, where each transaction represents a customer's purchase. The dataset may look like this:

Transaction 1: {Milk, Bread, Eggs, Cheese}
Transaction 2: {Bread, Butter, Juice}
Transaction 3: {Milk, Bread, Butter, Eggs}
Transaction 4: {Bread, Cheese, Juice}
Transaction 5: {Milk, Eggs, Juice}
Transaction 6: {Bread, Eggs, Cheese}

In this example, we want to find frequent itemsets, i.e., sets of items that are frequently purchased together. Let's set a minimum support threshold of 2, meaning that we want to find itemsets that appear in at least two transactions.

Using the Apriori algorithm, the frequent itemsets for this dataset would be:

Frequent 1-itemsets:

{Milk} (support = 3)

{Bread} (support = 5)

{Eggs} (support = 4)

{Cheese} (support = 3)

{Butter} (support = 2)

{Juice} (support = 3)

Frequent 2-itemsets:

{Milk, Bread} (support = 2)

{Milk, Eggs} (support = 2)

{Bread, Eggs} (support = 3)

{Bread, Cheese} (support = 2)

{Bread, Juice} (support = 2)

{Eggs, Cheese} (support = 2)

{Eggs, Juice} (support = 2)

From the frequent itemsets, we can identify interesting associations between items. For example, we can see that Bread and Eggs appear together in three transactions (Bread, Eggs), indicating a strong association between these items. The store can use this information to optimize product placement, create targeted promotions, or suggest product recommendations to customers based on their purchases.

Association analysis provides valuable insights into customer behavior and product relationships, enabling businesses to make data-driven decisions that can lead to increased sales and customer satisfaction.

Reinforcement Learning

This natural process of learning to walk is analogous to how machines learn through reinforcement learning. In reinforcement learning, an agent learns to interact with an environment to achieve a specific goal. The agent takes actions in the environment and receives feedback in the form of rewards or penalties based on its actions.

In the example of the baby learning to walk, the environment is the physical surroundings, and the goal is to walk smoothly without falling. The baby takes actions by moving its legs and feet, and the feedback it receives is the result of its actions - either successfully walking or falling down.

Similarly, in reinforcement learning, the agent takes actions in the environment, and the environment provides rewards or penalties based on the agent's actions. The agent's objective is to learn the best sequence of actions that will maximize the cumulative reward over time.

Through this trial-and-error process, the baby (and the reinforcement learning agent) learns from its mistakes and gradually improves its walking skills. In the case of reinforcement learning, the agent uses algorithms to explore different actions, learn from the rewards or penalties it receives, and update its strategies to make better decisions in the future.

Reinforcement learning has shown great success in various fields, including robotics, gaming, and autonomous systems. It enables machines to learn complex tasks by interacting with the environment and receiving feedback, similar to how babies learn to walk by exploring and adapting to their surroundings.

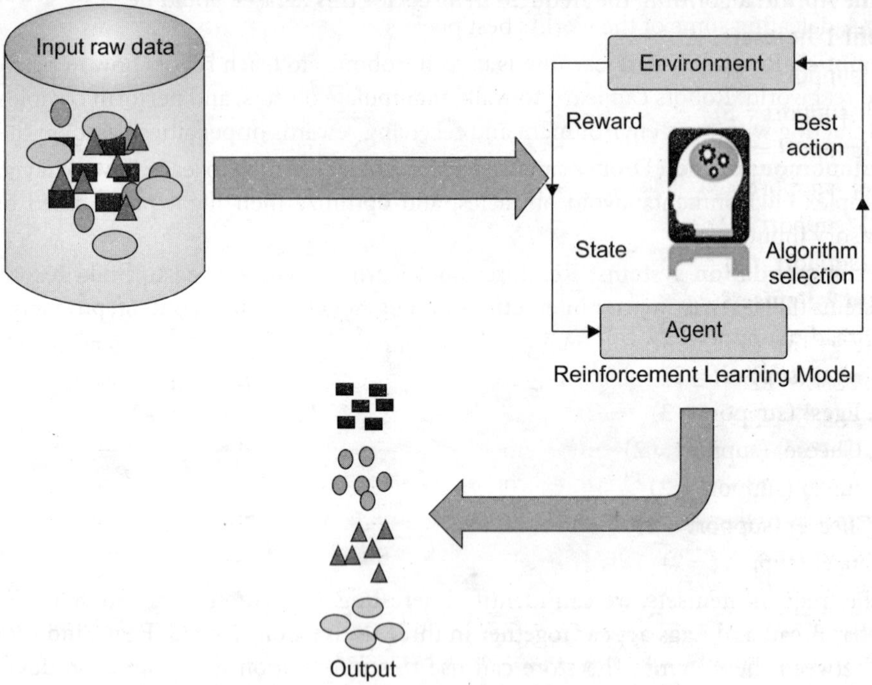

Fig. 2.9. Reinforcement learning

Examples: Self-driving cars are a prime example of reinforcement learning in action. These autonomous vehicles learn to navigate and make driving decisions based on real-time data from their sensors and the environment. The critical information they need to consider includes road speed limits, traffic conditions, road conditions, weather, and more.

The self-driving car's objective is to reach its destination safely and efficiently, and it achieves this by taking various actions such as starting and stopping, accelerating and decelerating, and making turns to the left or right.

Reinforcement learning algorithms enable self-driving cars to learn from their interactions with the environment and adjust their behavior accordingly. For example, if a self-driving car successfully navigates through a busy intersection, it may receive a positive reward. On the other hand, if it experiences difficulties or unsafe situations, it may receive a negative reward.

Over time, the self-driving car learns the best strategies to handle different road scenarios by maximizing the cumulative rewards it receives. This learning process allows the vehicle to adapt to various road conditions, handle unexpected situations, and improve its driving performance.

Reinforcement learning is a powerful approach for developing intelligent and adaptive systems like self-driving cars, as it enables them to continuously learn and make decisions in complex and dynamic environments.

Here are a few more examples of reinforcement learning in different domains:

1. **Game playing:** Reinforcement learning has been successfully applied to various games, including board games like Chess and Go, as well as video games. For instance, the DeepMind's AlphaGo program uses reinforcement learning to play the ancient game of Go at a superhuman level, defeating some of the world's best players.
2. **Robotics:** Reinforcement learning is used in robotics to teach robots how to perform tasks in the real world. Robots can learn to walk, manipulate objects, and perform complex actions by interacting with their environment and receiving rewards or penalties based on their actions.
3. **Autonomous drones:** Drones can use reinforcement learning to learn how to navigate through complex environments, avoid obstacles, and optimize their flight paths based on real-time sensory input.
4. **Recommendation systems:** Reinforcement learning can be used to build recommendation systems that learn from user interactions to suggest personalized content, products, or services.
5. **Energy management:** In energy management systems, reinforcement learning can be employed to optimize energy usage and reduce consumption based on real-time data and user preferences.
6. **Industrial automation:** Reinforcement learning can be used in industrial settings to optimize manufacturing processes, control robotic arms, and improve overall efficiency.
7. **Natural language processing:** In conversational AI applications, reinforcement learning can be used to train chatbots or virtual assistants to interact with users and learn from user feedback to improve their responses.
8. **Finance and trading:** Reinforcement learning can be applied to trading strategies to optimize investments and manage risks in financial markets.

These examples demonstrate the versatility and effectiveness of reinforcement learning in a wide range of applications, showcasing its potential to create intelligent, adaptive systems in various domains.

Comparison – Supervised, Unsupervised, and Reinforcement Learning

Supervised, unsupervised, and reinforcement learning are three major categories of machine learning, each with its distinct characteristics and applications. Here's a comparison of these three types:

Data Requirement:

- **Supervised Learning:** Requires labeled training data, where input data is paired with corresponding target labels.
- **Unsupervised Learning:** Works with unlabeled data and focuses on finding patterns and groupings within the data.
- **Reinforcement Learning:** Does not require explicit labeled data but instead uses a reward system to learn from interactions with an environment.

Objective:

- **Supervised Learning:** Predicts the target label for new, unseen data points based on patterns learned from labeled training data.
- **Unsupervised Learning:** Discovers hidden structures, patterns, and relationships within the data, such as clustering similar data points together.
- **Reinforcement Learning:** Learns to take actions in an environment to maximize a cumulative reward, optimizing a policy to achieve long-term goals.

Training Process:

- **Supervised Learning:** The model is trained on labeled data, adjusting its parameters to minimize prediction errors.
- **Unsupervised Learning:** The model learns to find structure within the data without explicit guidance, such as clustering or dimensionality reduction techniques.
- **Reinforcement Learning:** The agent learns through trial and error, exploring different actions and receiving feedback in the form of rewards or penalties.

Application Areas:

- **Supervised Learning:** Used for tasks like classification and regression problems, where the goal is to make accurate predictions based on historical data.
- **Unsupervised Learning:** Commonly used for tasks like clustering, anomaly detection, and dimensionality reduction to gain insights from unlabeled data.
- **Reinforcement Learning:** Applied to dynamic decision-making problems, such as robotics, game playing, and autonomous systems, where the agent learns to optimize its behavior over time.

Label Requirement:

- **Supervised Learning:** Labels are essential for training and evaluating the model's performance.
- **Unsupervised Learning:** Does not require labels but can benefit from labeled data for evaluation purposes.
- **Reinforcement Learning:** Labels are not necessary; the agent learns through rewards and feedback.

Algorithm:

Supervised Learning Algorithms:

- **Linear Regression:** Predicts continuous values based on linear relationships between features and the target variable.
- **Logistic Regression:** Used for binary classification problems, predicting probabilities of an instance belonging to a particular class.
- **Decision Trees:** Builds tree-like models to make decisions based on features' values.
- **Random Forest:** An ensemble method combining multiple decision trees to improve predictive accuracy.
- **Support Vector Machines (SVM):** Classifies data points by finding the optimal hyperplane that maximizes the margin between classes.
- **Naive Bayes:** Uses Bayes' theorem to calculate the probability of an instance belonging to a certain class based on feature probabilities.

Unsupervised Learning Algorithms:

- **K-means:** A popular clustering algorithm that groups data points into k clusters based on their similarities.
- **Hierarchical Clustering:** Builds a tree-like structure of nested clusters by iteratively merging or splitting clusters.
- **Principal Component Analysis (PCA):** A dimensionality reduction technique that transforms data into a lower-dimensional space while retaining important information.

- **Gaussian Mixture Model (GMM):** A probabilistic model that estimates multiple Gaussian distributions to cluster data.
- **DBSCAN (Density-Based Spatial Clustering of Applications with Noise):** Identifies clusters based on density-connected data points.
- **Autoencoders:** A type of neural network used for unsupervised learning and feature extraction.

Reinforcement Learning Algorithms:

- **Q-Learning:** An off-policy algorithm used for solving Markov Decision Processes (MDPs).
- **Deep Q Network (DQN):** A variant of Q-learning that uses deep neural networks to approximate the Q-values.
- **Policy Gradient Methods:** Algorithms that optimize the policy directly to maximize the expected reward.
- **Actor-Critic:** Combines value-based (Critic) and policy-based (Actor) methods for more stable learning.
- **Proximal Policy Optimization (PPO):** A policy gradient algorithm that prevents large policy updates.
- **Deep Deterministic Policy Gradient (DDPG):** Used for continuous action spaces and utilizes deep neural networks to approximate the policy.

These are just a few examples of machine learning algorithms for each category. There are many other algorithms and variations used for different types of tasks and data structures. The choice of algorithm depends on the specific problem, the nature of the data, and the desired outcomes.

In summary, supervised learning deals with labeled data to make predictions, unsupervised learning focuses on discovering patterns in unlabeled data, and reinforcement learning learns to interact with an environment to optimize actions based on rewards. Each type of learning has its strengths and weaknesses, and the choice of the learning approach depends on the specific problem and available data.

APPLICATIONS OF MACHINE LEARNING

Wherever there is a substantial amount of past data, machine learning can be used to generate actionable insight from the data. Though machine learning is adopted in multiple forms in every business domain, we have covered below three major domains just to give some idea about what type of actions can be done using machine learning.

Machine learning is a powerful and versatile tool that is used in various fields and industries. Here are some situations where machine learning is commonly applied:

1. **Pattern Recognition:** Machine learning algorithms excel at recognizing patterns in large datasets. This is particularly useful in fields such as finance, weather forecasting, and marketing, where historical data is analyzed to identify patterns and make predictions. For example, in finance, machine learning algorithms can analyze stock market data to predict future trends and make investment decisions.
2. **Data Analysis and Insights:** Machine learning enables us to extract valuable insights from large and complex datasets. By analyzing patterns, correlations, and relationships within the data, machine learning algorithms can uncover hidden trends and provide meaningful information. This is beneficial in fields like marketing, customer relationship management, and business intelligence, where understanding customer behavior and market trends is crucial for decision-making.

3. **Automation and Efficiency:** Machine learning can automate repetitive tasks and streamline processes, leading to increased efficiency and productivity. By learning from historical data, machine learning models can make predictions and decisions without explicit programming. This is useful in various industries, such as manufacturing, supply chain management, and customer service, where repetitive tasks can be automated to save time and resources.
4. **Personalization and Recommendation Systems:** Machine learning is extensively used in recommendation systems to provide personalized suggestions to users. By analyzing user preferences, behavior, and historical data, machine learning algorithms can recommend products, services, or content tailored to individual interests. This is seen in platforms like streaming services (Netflix), e-commerce (Amazon), and music platforms (Spotify), where personalized recommendations enhance user experiences and drive engagement.
5. **Natural Language Processing:** Machine learning techniques are applied in natural language processing (NLP) to understand and interpret human language. This enables applications such as voice assistants, chatbots, sentiment analysis, language translation, and text summarization. NLP powered by machine learning helps computers understand and interact with human language, enabling more intuitive and effective communication.
6. **Image and Speech Recognition:** Machine learning algorithms are crucial in image and speech recognition tasks. By learning from vast amounts of labeled data, these algorithms can accurately identify objects, faces, and speech patterns. This technology has applications in autonomous vehicles, security systems, medical imaging, speech-to-text conversion, voice authentication, and more.
7. **Fraud Detection and Cybersecurity:** Machine learning plays a vital role in detecting patterns and anomalies that may indicate fraudulent activities or cybersecurity threats. By analyzing large volumes of data and identifying unusual patterns, machine learning algorithms can detect fraudulent transactions, intrusions, and anomalies in real-time. This is essential for industries such as banking, e-commerce, and network security, where timely detection and prevention of fraud are critical.
8. **Healthcare and Medical Diagnosis:** Machine learning is increasingly utilized in healthcare for various applications. It can aid in medical diagnosis by analyzing patient data, medical images, and genetic information to assist healthcare professionals in making accurate diagnoses. Machine learning can also be used for personalized treatment recommendations, drug discovery, patient monitoring, and predicting disease outcomes.
9. **Predictive Maintenance:** Machine learning algorithms can analyze sensor data from machines and equipment to predict maintenance needs and prevent costly breakdowns. By monitoring patterns, anomalies, and performance metrics, machine learning can identify potential issues before they occur. This helps optimize maintenance schedules, reduce downtime, and improve operational efficiency in industries such as manufacturing, transportation, and energy.
10. **Financial Forecasting:** Machine learning is widely applied in finance for tasks such as stock market prediction, credit scoring, fraud detection, and algorithmic trading. By analyzing historical financial data, market trends, and economic indicators, machine learning models can make informed predictions and decisions. These applications assist financial institutions and investors in making better investment choices, managing risks, and detecting fraudulent activities.

Overall, machine learning is needed when we have large amounts of data, complex patterns or relationships to uncover, repetitive tasks to automate, and the need for accurate predictions or personalized recommendations. It offers significant advantages in numerous domains, empowering businesses and industries to leverage data-driven insights for better decision-making, efficiency, and innovation. These are just a few examples of the many areas where machine learning is applied. The versatility and predictive power of machine learning make it valuable in numerous industries, helping businesses gain insights, automate processes, and make data-driven decisions.

STATE-OF-THE-ART LANGUAGES/TOOLS IN MACHINE LEARNING

Several programming languages and tools are widely used in the field of machine learning. The popularity of these languages and tools may vary over time, but here are some state-of-the-art languages and tools commonly used in machine learning:

Python: Python is the most popular and versatile language for machine learning. It offers numerous libraries and frameworks, making it easy to implement machine learning algorithms and work with large datasets. Some popular Python libraries for machine learning include:

- **Scikit-learn:** A comprehensive machine learning library with various algorithms and tools for data preprocessing, model selection, and evaluation.
- **TensorFlow:** An open-source deep learning framework developed by Google for building and training neural networks.
- **PyTorch:** Another deep learning framework popular for its dynamic computation capabilities and ease of use.

R: R is a programming language specifically designed for statistical computing and data analysis. It has an extensive collection of packages for machine learning and statistical modeling. Some popular R packages for machine learning include:

- **caret:** A comprehensive package for building and evaluating predictive models.
- **randomForest:** Implements the random forest algorithm for classification and regression tasks.
- **xgboost:** Implements the gradient boosting algorithm for improved performance.

Julia: Julia is a high-level, high-performance language designed for numerical and scientific computing. It is gaining popularity in the machine learning community due to its speed and ease of use for data analysis and model training. Julia is a high-level, high-performance programming language designed for technical computing, data science, and machine learning. It was created to address the need for a language that combines the ease of use of dynamic languages like Python with the performance of compiled languages like C or Fortran.

Julia's performance and easy-to-use syntax make it an excellent choice for machine learning tasks, especially when dealing with large datasets and computationally intensive algorithms. Its growing ecosystem of machine learning packages and libraries provides ample resources for developing sophisticated machine learning models and applications. As Julia continues to evolve, it is expected to gain more popularity in the data science and machine learning communities.

Java: Java is a popular programming language in enterprise applications and is also used for machine learning. Libraries like Deeplearning4j and Weka are commonly used for Java-based machine learning tasks.

MATLAB: MATLAB is widely used in academic and research settings for numerical computation and data analysis. It has a strong set of built-in functions for machine learning and statistics. MATLAB is indeed a powerful commercial software widely used for numerical computing, data analysis, and machine learning. Its extensive capabilities and user-friendly interface have made it a popular choice among researchers, engineers, and data scientists in both industry and academia.

MATLAB's combination of powerful numerical computing capabilities, extensive machine learning support, and scalability for large datasets makes it a valuable tool for researchers and practitioners working on machine learning projects across various domains.

C++: While not as common as Python or R for machine learning, C++ is used for its performance and efficiency in building machine learning models, especially in applications requiring real-time processing.

Microsoft Azure Machine Learning: A cloud-based service that provides tools and services for building, training, and deploying machine learning models. Microsoft Azure Machine Learning (Azure ML) is a cloud-based platform provided by Microsoft that enables data scientists and developers to build, deploy, and manage machine learning models at scale. It is part of the broader Microsoft Azure ecosystem and offers a wide range of tools and services to streamline the end-to-end machine learning workflow.

Microsoft Azure Machine Learning provides a powerful, flexible, and user-friendly platform for developing and deploying machine learning models in the cloud. It empowers data scientists and developers with a wide range of tools and services to accelerate their machine learning projects and deliver insights and predictions to applications and services at scale.

Google Cloud AI Platform: A cloud-based service from Google that allows developers to build and deploy machine learning models on Google Cloud. Google Cloud AI Platform is a cloud-based machine learning platform provided by Google Cloud that enables data scientists and developers to build, train, deploy, and manage machine learning models at scale. It is part of the Google Cloud Platform (GCP) and offers a comprehensive suite of tools and services to support the end-to-end machine learning workflow.

Google Cloud AI Platform provides a robust and flexible environment for developing and deploying machine learning models in the cloud. With its managed services, integration with popular libraries, and scalable infrastructure, it empowers data scientists and developers to build and deploy sophisticated machine learning solutions that can be seamlessly integrated with other Google Cloud services.

Amazon SageMaker: A fully managed service from Amazon Web Services (AWS) for building, training, and deploying machine learning models. Amazon SageMaker is a fully managed service offered by Amazon Web Services (AWS) that allows developers and data scientists to build, train, and deploy machine learning models at scale. It provides a complete end-to-end platform to streamline the machine learning workflow, from data preprocessing and model training to deployment and monitoring.

Amazon SageMaker provides a comprehensive and user-friendly environment for building, training, and deploying machine learning models. With its managed infrastructure, AutoML capabilities, and integration with AWS services, it empowers developers and data scientists to focus on building sophisticated machine learning solutions without worrying about the underlying infrastructure and operations.

The choice of language and tools often depends on the specific project requirements, the team's expertise, and the ecosystem in which the project is deployed. Python, with its vast libraries and active community, is currently the most popular choice for most machine learning tasks. However, other languages and tools mentioned above are also widely used in specific domains or scenarios.

Python is one of the most widely used tools for machine learning and data science. There are several reasons why Python is highly popular in these domains:

1. **Versatility:** Python is a versatile programming language that can be used for a wide range of tasks, including web development, scripting, automation, and data analysis. Its flexibility makes it a natural choice for data science and machine learning projects.
2. **Rich Ecosystem:** Python has a vast ecosystem of libraries and frameworks specifically designed for data science and machine learning. Popular libraries like NumPy, Pandas, Matplotlib, SciPy, and scikit-learn provide robust tools for data manipulation, visualization, and machine learning algorithms.
3. **Easy to Learn:** Python is known for its clear and readable syntax, making it easy for beginners to learn and understand. This accessibility attracts a large number of data scientists, researchers, and developers to choose Python as their preferred language.
4. **Community Support:** Python has a strong and active community of data scientists, machine learning practitioners, and developers. This vibrant community contributes to the development of new libraries, tools, and resources that benefit the entire data science ecosystem.
5. **Integration with other Tools:** Python seamlessly integrates with other popular tools and languages, such as TensorFlow, Keras, PyTorch, and Apache Spark, further expanding its capabilities for machine learning and data analysis.
6. **Scalability:** Python's versatility extends to its scalability, allowing it to handle both small and large-scale machine learning projects. With libraries like Dask and joblib, Python can efficiently utilize multiple cores and distributed systems.
7. **Popularity in Industry:** Python's widespread adoption in the industry has led to its integration into many data science and machine learning projects. Its presence in various domains, from tech to finance and healthcare, further reinforces its popularity.
8. **Learning Resources:** Due to its widespread use, there are numerous learning resources available for Python, such as online tutorials, courses, and books, which facilitate the learning process for aspiring data scientists and machine learning practitioners.

While Python is a dominant language in the data science and machine learning space, it's worth noting that other tools like R, Julia, and commercial platforms like MATLAB and TensorFlow have also gained traction in specific areas and use cases. The choice of the most suitable tool often depends on the specific project requirements, existing infrastructure, and individual preferences of data scientists and developers.

PREPARING TO MODEL

Introduction

Despite the fact that machine learning technology has undergone substantial progress and is now widely used, in order to become a practitioner, we must first acquire some basic comprehension. To address a problem, we need to know how to use the variety of machine learning techniques and technologies that are available. In actuality, that will be highly particular to the kind of problem we are attempting to solve. The types of actions that will be involved will be entirely different depending on whether the challenge is one of prediction or one in which we are attempting to uncover a pattern in data without prior knowledge of the data. Therefore, whether a machine learning project is in the supervised, unsupervised, or reinforcement learning areas will determine how it appears or what the key activities are that make up its core. Regardless of the variation, some fundamental information must be developed before we begin with the fundamental ideas and critical algorithms of machine learning. We'll take a quick look at a few common machine learning tasks in this section and concentrate on some of the fundamental ideas that all practitioners should understand before beginning their work in the field of machine learning.

MACHINE LEARNING ACTIVITIES

Machine learning activities begin with data as their first step. The labelled training data set is followed by unlabeled test data in supervised learning. The aim in unsupervised learning is to identify patterns in the input data; there is no need for tagged data in this situation. To comprehend the type of data, the quality of the data, and the connections between the various data parts, a thorough review and exploration of the data are required. Accordingly, a number of pre-processing operations on the input data may be required before we can move on to the main machine learning operations. After the input data enters the machine learning system, the following typical preparation tasks are carried out:

Step by Step Learning of Machine learning-

Step 1: Understand the Basics

1.1 **Introduction to Machine Learning**

- Definition and applications of machine learning
- Types of machine learning: supervised, unsupervised, reinforcement learning
- Machine learning workflow and common terminology

1.2 **Mathematics and Statistics for Machine Learning**

- Linear algebra: vectors, matrices, operations, linear equations
- Calculus: derivatives, gradients
- Probability theory and statistics: probability distributions, hypothesis testing

1.3 **Programming Fundamentals**

- Introduction to Python or R programming language
- Syntax, variables, data types, control structures, and functions
- Working with libraries for data manipulation and analysis: NumPy, Pandas, scikit-learn (for Python) or tidy verse (for R)

Step 2: Data Pre-processing and Exploration

2.1 **Data Collection and Understanding**

- Data sources and formats
- Exploratory Data Analysis (EDA): data summary, visualization, identifying patterns, outliers, and missing values

2.2 **Data Cleaning and Pre-processing**

- Handling missing data: imputation, deletion, or advanced techniques
- Handling outliers: detection, removal, or transformation
- Feature scaling: normalization, standardization
- Feature encoding: categorical variables, one-hot encoding
- Feature engineering: creating new features, dimensionality reduction

2.3 **Data Splitting and Cross-Validation**

- Train-test split for model evaluation
- Cross-validation techniques: k-fold cross-validation, stratified cross-validation

Step 3: Supervised Learning Algorithms

3.1 **Linear Regression**
- Simple linear regression
- Multiple linear regression
- Evaluation metrics: mean squared error, R-squared

3.2 **Logistic Regression**
- Binary logistic regression
- Multiclass logistic regression
- Evaluation metrics: accuracy, precision, recall, F1-score

3.3 **Decision Trees and Random Forests**
- Building decision trees
- Ensemble learning with random forests
- Feature importance and interpretation

3.4 Support Vector Machines (SVM)
- Linear SVM
- Nonlinear SVM with kernel methods
- Margin, support vectors, and hyperplane

3.5 **k-Nearest Neighbors (k-NN)**
- k-NN algorithm and distance metrics
- Choosing the optimal k value
- Curse of dimensionality

Step 4: Unsupervised Learning Algorithms

4.1 **Clustering Algorithms**
- K-means clustering
- Hierarchical clustering
- Evaluation metrics: inertia, silhouette score

4.2 **Dimensionality Reduction Techniques**
- Principal Component Analysis (PCA)
- t-SNE (t-Distributed Stochastic Neighbor Embedding)
- Application of dimensionality reduction in visualization

4.3 **Association Rule Learning**
- Apriori algorithm
- Support, confidence, and lift

Step 5: Advanced Topics in Machine Learning

5.1 **Ensemble Methods**
- Bagging and boosting techniques
- AdaBoost, Gradient Boosting, XGBoost
- Stacking and voting classifiers

5.2 **Neural Networks and Deep Learning**
- Introduction to artificial neural networks (ANN)

- Feedforward neural networks and backpropagation
- Deep learning architectures: convolutional neural networks (CNN), recurrent neural networks (RNN), and more

5.3 **Natural Language Processing (NLP)**
- Text pre-processing: tokenization, stemming, lemmatization
- Text representation: Bag-of-Words, TF-IDF
- Text classification and sentiment analysis

5.4 **Reinforcement Learning**
- Markov Decision Processes (MDP)
- Q-learning and policy iteration algorithms
- Applications in game playing and robotics

Step 6: Model Evaluation and Optimization

6.1 **Model Evaluation Metrics**
- Accuracy, precision, recall, F1-score
- Receiver Operating Characteristic (ROC) curve, Area Under the Curve (AUC)

6.2 **Overfitting, Underfitting, and Regularization**
- Bias-variance trade-off
- Regularization techniques: L1 and L2 regularization

6.3 **Hyperparameter Tuning and Model Selection**
- Grid search, random search
- Cross-validation for hyperparameter tuning
- Model selection based on performance metrics

Step 7: Real-World Projects and Practical Applications

7.1 **Implement end-to-end Machine Learning Projects**
- Data pre-processing, model training, evaluation, and deployment
- Working with real-world datasets and challenges

7.2 **Participate in Kaggle competitions or similar projects**
- Collaborate with other data scientists and learn from their approaches
- Gain hands-on experience and sharpen your skills

7.3 **Stay updated with the latest research and industry trends**
- Read research papers, articles, and blogs
- Attend conferences, webinars, or online courses

By following these steps, you can gradually progress from the basics to a professional level in machine learning. Remember to practice what you learn through coding exercises, projects, and continuous learning. The key is to apply your knowledge to real-world problems and gain practical experience.

BASIC TYPES OF DATA IN MACHINE LEARNING

A data set is a collection of related information or records. Each record represents a specific entity or subject area and contains information about that entity. The data set consists of rows, and each row is called a record. Each data set also has multiple attributes, which provide information about specific characteristics of the entity.

Here's a breakdown of the key elements of a data set:

1. **Data Set:** A collection of related information or records. A data set is a structured collection of data, where each record represents a single entity or observation, and each attribute contains specific information about that entity. It can be represented in various formats, such as tables, spreadsheets, or databases, depending on the application and requirements. Data sets are widely used in various fields, including business, healthcare, finance, science, and research.
2. **Record:** Each row in the data set represents a specific entity or subject and contains information about that entity. A record is a single row in the data set, containing all the information or data related to a specific entity or observation. For example, in a data set about students, each record may represent a single student and include attributes such as Roll Number, Name, Gender, and Age.
3. **Attribute (Feature, Variable, Dimension, or Field):** Each data set has multiple attributes, which represent specific characteristics of the entity. For example, in the data set on students, attributes could include Roll Number, Name, Gender, and Age. An attribute is a column in the data set that represents a specific characteristic or property of the entity being observed. Attributes are also known by other names, such as features, variables, dimensions, or fields.
4. **Data Space:** The number of attributes in the data set determines the data space. In the example, since there are four attributes (Roll Number, Name, Gender, and Age), the data space is referred to as four-dimensional. Data space refers to the number of attributes or dimensions in the data set. Each record can be seen as a point in this multi-dimensional space, with the attributes defining the coordinates of that point.
5. **Value:** Each attribute has a specific value for each record. The value of an attribute may vary from one record to another, representing different characteristics for different entities. Each attribute has a specific value for each record in the data set. The value of an attribute represents the specific information or characteristic of the corresponding entity in that record. For example, the Roll Number attribute may have values like "101," "102," "103," and so on for each student record.

Overall, a data set allows us to organize and represent information in a structured format, enabling further analysis and machine learning tasks. The records and attributes together form the foundation for understanding and extracting insights from the data set. Data sets play a fundamental role in machine learning as they serve as the foundation for building and training models. Data scientists and analysts use data sets to gain insights, identify patterns, and make predictions based on the information contained within them. Proper data preprocessing and analysis are crucial to ensure the data set's quality and relevance for successful machine learning tasks. Additionally, data sets need to be adequately prepared before feeding them into machine learning algorithms to achieve accurate and meaningful results.

Here's an example of a simple data set representing information about students in a school:

Roll Number	Name	Gender	Age	Grade
101	John Smith	Male	15	A
102	Emma Jones	Female	16	B
103	Mike Brown	Male	14	C
104	Lisa Green	Female	15	A
105	Jack White	Male	16	B

In this data set, each row represents a single student, and each column represents a specific attribute or characteristic of the students. The attributes include:

1. **Roll Number:** The unique identification number assigned to each student.
2. **Name:** The name of the student.
3. **Gender:** The gender of the student (Male or Female).
4. **Age:** The age of the student.
5. **Grade:** The grade or academic performance of the student (e.g., A, B, C).

This data set is a four-dimensional data space because it has four attributes (Roll Number, Name, Gender, Age). Each record (row) represents a point in this four-dimensional space, with specific values for each attribute. For example, the first record represents a male student named John Smith with Roll Number 101, age 15, and Grade A.

Data sets like this can be used for various purposes, such as analyzing student performance, predicting academic achievements, or understanding gender distribution in the school population. Machine learning algorithms can be applied to such data sets to discover patterns, make predictions, and gain insights from the data.

Let's try to comprehend the various forms of data that we typically encounter in machine learning challenges now that the context of the data sets has been provided. Data can be broadly categorised into the two basic categories:

1. Quality information
2. numerical information

1. **Qualitative Data:** Qualitative data, also known as categorical data, represents characteristics or attributes that are not numerical in nature. Qualitative data offers information that cannot be assessed regarding the quality of an object or information. The quality of student performance, for instance, as measured by the phrases "Good," "Average," and "Poor," falls under the heading of qualitative data. Additionally, student names and roll numbers are data that cannot be measured using a scale. Therefore, they would be considered qualitative data. Categorical data is another name for qualitative data. This type of data is descriptive and can be divided into different categories or groups. Qualitative data can be further classified into two subtypes:
   (*a*) **Nominal Data:** Nominal data consists of categories with no specific order or ranking. Nominal data are those that only have a named value rather than a number value. It is employed to provide attributes named values. Nominal values are impossible to quantify. Examples of nominal data include gender (Male/Female), color (Red/Blue/Green), or city names (New York/London/Paris).
   (*b*) **Ordinal Data:** Ordinal data also consists of categories, but they have a specific order or ranking. Ordinal data can be naturally organised in addition to having the same qualities as nominal data. By extension, this means that ordinal data similarly gives named values to characteristics, but unlike nominal data, they can be organised in a sequence of increasing or decreasing value so that we can express whether one value is superior to or greater than another. However, the intervals between the categories may not be uniform. Examples of ordinal data include education levels (High School/Diploma/Graduate), customer satisfaction ratings (Poor/Good/Excellent), or age groups (Young/Middle-aged/Senior).

2. **Quantitative Data:** Quantitative data, also known as numerical data, represents quantities or measurements that can be expressed with numbers. Quantitative data can be measured because it pertains to information about an object's amount. Consider the attribute "marks," for instance. It can be quantified using a scale of measurement. Numeric data is another name for quantitative data. This type of data is usually associated with numeric values and can be further divided into two subtypes:

   There are two types of quantitative data:

   1. **Interval data:** Numeric data that is known for both the order and the precise difference between values is referred to as interval data. Temperature in Celsius is a perfect illustration of interval data. The temperature difference between each value stays constant in Celsius. For instance, the difference between 12 and 18 degrees Celsius is measured and is 6 degrees Celsius, just like the difference between 15.5 and 21.5 degrees Celsius. Date, time, and so on are further examples.

      Mathematical operations like addition and subtraction are possible for interval data. Because of this, the central tendency for interval data can be calculated using the mean, median, or mode. Additionally, standard deviation can be determined.

      Interval data, however, lack what is referred to be a "true zero" value. For instance, neither "0 temperature" nor "no temperature" exist. Thus, for interval data, only addition and subtraction apply. You cannot use the ratio. As a result, we may state that a temperature of 40 °C is equivalent to a temperature of 20 °C plus 20 °C.

      We cannot, however, claim that a temperature of 40°C suggests anything is twice as hot as one of 20°C.

   2. **Ratio data:** Numeric data that can be precisely measured is represented as ratio data. For ratio data, there is absolute zero.

      Additionally, these variables may be multiplied, divided, added, or subtracted. By using the mean, median, or mode as well as dispersion methods like standard deviation, the central tendency can be calculated. Height, weight, age, pay, and other ratio data examples are provided.

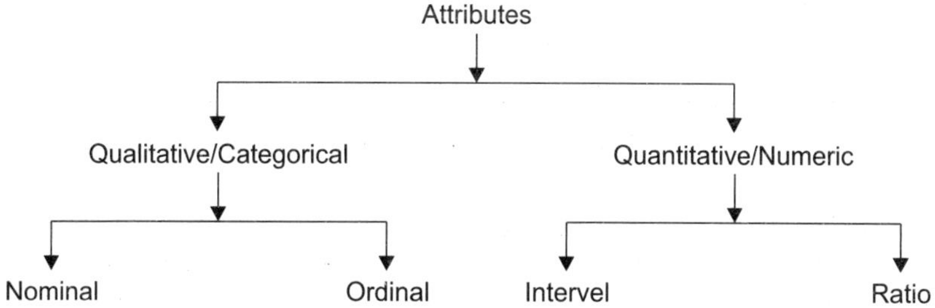

Fig. 2.10. Types of data

EXPLORING STRUCTURE OF DATA

We now know that categorical and numeric data are the two most common categories of data encountered in machine learning. We can go deeper into analysing a data set with this context in mind. It's important to know which attributes in a data set are category and which are numerical. This is so because examining numerical data requires a different strategy than examining categorical data does. If the data set is typical, we might have the data dictionary on hand for reference. A data dictionary is a repository for metadata, which is all the details about how each data piece in the data set is organised. Each attribute's description, data type, and other pertinent information are provided in detail in the data dictionary.

If the data dictionary is not available, we must obtain the information using the machine learning tool's standard library function. Let's proceed with a common data set from the UCI machine learning repository for the time being.

The Auto MPG data set provided in the UCI repository is the one we use as a reference. The first few rows of the data set are shown in Figure 2.5.

mpg	cylinder	displace-ment	horse-power	weight	accel-eration	model year	origin	car name
18	8	307	130	3504	12	70	1	Chevrolet chevelle malibu
15	8	350	165	3693	11.5	70	1	Buick skylark 320
18	8	318	150	3436	11	70	1	Plymouth satellite
16	8	304	150	3433	12	70	1	Amc rebel sst
17	8	302	140	3449	10.5	70	1	Ford torino
15	8	429	198	4341	10	70	1	Ford galaxie 500
14	8	454	220	4354	9	70	1	Chevrolet impala
14	8	440	215	4312	8.5	70	1	Plymouth fury iii
14	8	455	225	4425	10	70	1	Pontiac catalina
15	8	390	190	3850	8.5	70	1	Amc acbassador dpl
15	8	383	170	3563	10	70	1	Dodge challenger se
14	8	340	160	3609	8	70	1	Plymouth' cuda 340
15	8	400	150	3761	9.5	70	1	Chevrolet monte carlo
14	8	455	225	3086	10	70	1	Buick estate wagon (sw)
24	4	113	95	2372	15	70	3	Toyota corona mark ii
22	6	198	95	2933	15.5	70	1	Plymouth duster
18	6	199	97	2774	15.5	70	1	Amc hornet

Fig. 1. Auto MPG data set

As is quite evident from the data, the attributes such as 'mpg', 'cylinders', 'displacement', 'horsepower', 'weight', 'acceleration', 'model year', and 'origin' are all numeric. Out of these attributes, 'cylinders', 'model year', and 'origin' are discrete in nature as the only finite number of values can be assumed by these attributes. The remaining of the numeric attributes, i.e., 'mpg', 'displacement', 'horsepower', 'weight', and 'acceleration' can assume any real value.

Hence, these attributes are continuous in nature. The only remaining attribute 'car name' is of type categorical, or more specifically nominal. This data set is regarding prediction of fuel consumption in miles per gallon, i.e., the numeric attribute 'mpg' is the target attribute. With this understanding of the data set attributes, we can start exploring the numeric and categorical attributes separately.

Exploring Numerical Data

Box plots and histograms are powerful graphical tools used to explore and visualize numerical data in machine learning and data analysis. Let's delve into each of them:

1. **Box Plot (Box-and-Whisker Plot):** A box plot provides a visual summary of the distribution of numerical data through five key statistics: the minimum, first quartile (Q1), median (Q2), third quartile (Q3), and maximum. The box represents the interquartile range (IQR) and covers the central 50% of the data. The median is shown as a horizontal line within the box. Whiskers extend from the edges of the box to the minimum and maximum data points within a certain range (often defined as 1.5 times the IQR). Data points outside this range are considered outliers and are displayed as individual points beyond the whiskers.
2. **Histogram:** A histogram is a graphical representation of the frequency distribution of numerical data. It divides the data into intervals or bins and shows the number of occurrences (frequency) of data points falling within each bin. The x-axis represents the data range divided into bins, and the y-axis shows the frequency count. Histograms provide valuable insights into the distribution of data, helping to identify patterns, skewness, and central tendencies.

Both box plots and histograms are invaluable tools for understanding the distribution of data, identifying outliers, and detecting patterns. They assist data analysts and machine learning practitioners in making informed decisions during the exploratory data analysis phase, enabling them to gain a deeper understanding of the underlying data characteristics before proceeding with model building and analysis.

Understanding Data Spread

After examining the central tendency of the various numerical attributes, we can now identify those that have a significant departure from the mean or median.

Let's examine those qualities in more detail. In order to drill down further, we must examine the whole range of values for each attribute, but not at the level of individual data components because that level may be too large to manually evaluate. So we will take a granular view of the data spread in the form of

1. Dispersion of data
2. Position of the different data values

Measuring Data Dispersion

Consider the data values of two attributes

1. **Attribute 1 values:** 44, 46, 48, 45, and 47
2. **Attribute 2 values:** 34, 46, 59, 39, and 52

Both the set of values have a mean and median of 46. However, the first set of values that is of attribute 1 is more concentrated or clustered around the mean/median value whereas the second set of values of attribute 2 is quite spread out or dispersed. To measure the extent of dispersion of a data, or to find out how much the different values of a data are spread out, the variance of the data is measured. The variance of a data is measured using the formula given below:

$$\text{Variance}(x) = \frac{\sum_{i=1}^{n} x_i^2}{n} - \left(\frac{\sum_{i=1}^{n} x_i}{n}\right)^2$$

where x is the variable or attribute whose variance is to be measured and n is the number of observations or values of variable x.

Standard deviation of a data is measured as follows:

$$\text{Standard deviation (x)} = \sqrt{\text{Variance (x)}}$$

Standard deviation (x) =

Larger value of variance or standard deviation indicates more dispersion in the data and vice versa. In the above example, let's calculate the variance of attribute 1 and that of attribute 2. For attribute 1,

$$\text{Variance} = \frac{\sum_{i=1}^{n} x_i^2}{n} - \left(\frac{\sum_{i=1}^{n} x_i}{n}\right)^2 = \frac{44^2 + 46^2 + 48^2 + 45^2 + 47^2}{5} - \left(\frac{44 + 46 + 48 + 45 + 47}{5}\right)^2$$

$$= \frac{1936 + 2116 + 2304 + 2025 + 2209}{5} - \left(\frac{230}{5}\right)^2 = \frac{10590}{5} - (46)^2 = 2$$

For attribute 2,

$$\text{Variance} = \frac{\sum_{i=1}^{n} x_i^2}{n} - \left(\frac{\sum_{i=1}^{n} x_i}{n}\right)^2 = \frac{34^2 + 46^2 + 59^2 + 39^2 + 52^2}{5} - \left(\frac{34 + 46 + 59 + 39 + 52}{5}\right)^2$$

$$= \frac{1156 + 2116 + 3481 + 1521 + 2704}{5} - \left(\frac{230}{5}\right)^2 = \frac{10978}{5} - (46)^2 = 79.6$$

So it is quite clear from the measure that attribute 1 values are quite concentrated around the mean while attribute 2 values are extremely spread out. Since this data was small, a visual inspection and understanding were possible and that matches with the measured value.

Measuring Data Value Position

When the data values of an attribute are arranged in an increasing order, we have seen earlier that median gives the central data value, which divides the entire data set into two halves. Similarly, if the first half of the data is divided into two halves so that each half consists of one-quarter of the data set, then that median of the first half is known as first quartile or Q . In the same way, if the second half of the data is divided into two halves, then that median of the second half is known as third quartile or Q . The overall median is also known as second quartile or Q . So, any data set has five values - minimum, first quartile (Q1), median (Q2), third quartile (Q3), and maximum.

Let's review these values for the attributes 'cylinders', 'displacement', and 'origin'. Figure 2.8 captures a summary of the range of statistics for the attributes. If we take the example of the attribute 'displacement', we can see that the difference between minimum value and Q1 is 36.2 and the difference between Q1 and median is 44.3. On the contrary, the difference between median and Q3 is 113.5 and Q3 and the maximum value is 193. In other words, the larger values are more spread out than the smaller ones. This helps in understanding why the value of mean is much higher than that of the median for the attribute 'displacement'. Similarly, in case of attribute 'cylinders', we can observe that the difference between minimum value and median is 1 whereas the difference between median and the maximum value is 4. For the attribute 'origin', the difference between minimum value and median is 0 whereas the difference between median and the maximum value is 2.

	Cylinders	Displacement	Origin
Minimum	3	68	1
Q1	4	104.2	1
Median	4	148.5	1
Q3	8	262	2
Maximum	8	455	3

Fig. 2.11. Attribute value drill-down for Auto MPG

However, we still cannot ascertain whether there is any outlier present in the data. For that, we can better adopt some means to visualize the data. Box plot is an excellent visualization medium for numeric data.

Plotting and Exploring Numerical Data

Box plots, also known as box-and-whisker plots, are graphical representations used to visualize the distribution of numerical data. They display the spread and central tendency of the data through five summary statistics: minimum, maximum, first quartile (Q1), median (Q2), and third quartile (Q3). Here's how to interpret a box plot:

1. **Box**: The box represents the interquartile range (IQR) and contains the middle 50% of the data. It is defined by the first quartile (Q1) at the bottom and the third quartile (Q3) at the top. The length of the box shows the spread of the central data.
2. **Median (Q2):** The median is represented by a line within the box, dividing the data into two equal halves. It is the value at which 50% of the data falls below and 50% above.
3. **Whiskers:** The whiskers extend from the edges of the box to the minimum and maximum values within a certain range. The range is typically 1.5 times the IQR. Data points beyond the whiskers are considered outliers and are represented as individual points.
4. **Outliers:** Outliers are data points that fall outside the whiskers. They are often represented as individual dots or asterisks.

Box plots are particularly useful for comparing the distribution of data among different groups or categories. They help identify potential skewness, the presence of outliers, and the spread of data within each group. Box plots provide a concise summary of the data's central tendencies and spread, making them valuable tools in exploratory data analysis and statistical inference.

- The central rectangle or the box spans from first to third quartile (i.e., Q1 to Q3), thus giving the inter-quartile range (IQR).
- Median is given by the line or band within the box.
- The lower whisker extends up to 1.5 times of the inter-quartile range (or IQR) from the bottom of the box, i.e., the first quartile or Q1. However, the actual length of the lower whisker depends on the lowest data value that falls within (Q1 – 1.5 times of IQR). Let's try to understand this with an example. Say for a specific set of data, Q1 = 73, median = 76 and Q3 = 79. Hence, IQR will be 6 (i.e. Q3 – Q1).So, lower whisker can extend maximum till (Q1 – 1.5 × IQR) = 73 – 1.5 × 6 = 64. However, say there are lower range data values such as 70, 63, and 60. So, the lower whisker will come at 70 as this is the lowest data value larger than 64.

- The upper whisker extends up to 1.5 as times of the inter-quartile range (or IQR) from the top of the box, i.e. the third quartile or Q3. Similar to lower whisker, the actual length of the upper whisker will also depend on the highest data value that falls within (Q3 + 1.5 times of IQR). Let's try to understand this with an example. For the same set of data mentioned in the above point, upper whisker can extend maximum till (Q3 + 1.5 × IQR) = 79 + 1.5 × 6 = 88. If there is higher range of data values like 82, 84, and 89. So, the upper whisker will come at 84 as this is the highest data value lower than 88.
- The data values coming beyond the lower or upper whiskers are the ones which are of unusually low or high values respectively. These are the outliers, which may deserve special consideration.

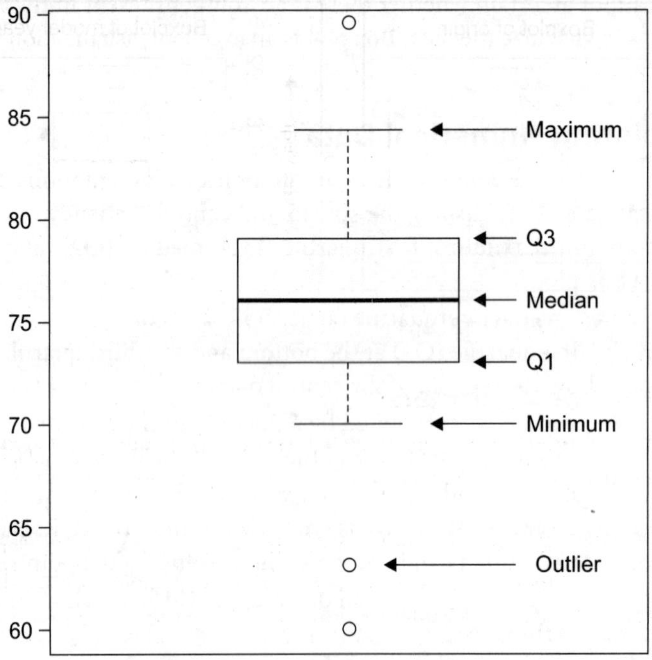

Fig. 2.12. Box plot

Let's visualize the box plot for the three attributes - 'cylinders', 'displacement', and 'origin'. We will also review the box plot of another attribute in which the deviation between mean and median is very little and see what the basic difference in the respective box plots is. Figure 2.10 presents the respective box plots.

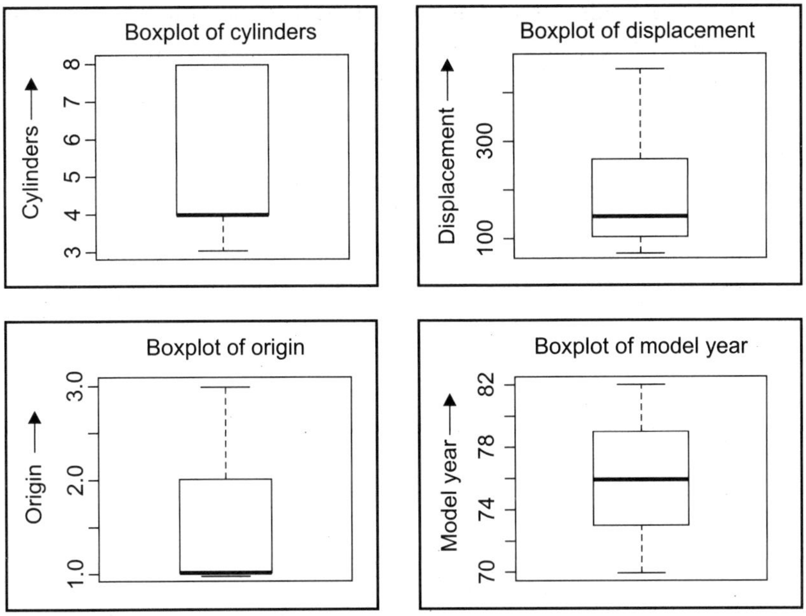

Fig. 2.13. Box plot of auto MPG attributes

Analysing Box Plot for 'Cylinders'

The box plot for attribute 'cylinders' looks pretty weird in shape. The upper whisker is missing, the band for median falls at the bottom of the box, even the lower whisker is pretty small compared to the length of the box! Is everything right?

The answer is a big YES, and you can figure it out if you delve a little deeper into the actual data values of the attribute. The attribute 'cylinders' is discrete in nature having values from 3 to 8. Table 2.2 captures the frequency and cumulative frequency of it.

Table 2. Frequency of "Cylinders" Attribute

Cylinders	Frequency	Cumulative Frequency
3	4	4
4	204	208 (= 4 + 204)
5	3	211 (= 208 + 3)
6	84	295 (= 211 + 84)
7	0	295 (= 295 + 0)
8	103	398 (= 295 + 103)

As can be observed in the table, the frequency is extremely high for data value 4. Two other data values where the frequency is quite high are 6 and 8. So now if we try to find the quartiles, since the total frequency is 398, the first quartile (Q1), median (Q2), and third quartile (Q3) will be at a cumulative frequency 99.5 (i.e., average of 99th and 100th observation), 199 and 298.5 (i.e. average of 298th and 299th observation), respectively. This way Q1 = 4, median = 4 and Q3 = 8. Since there is no data value beyond 8, there is no upper whisker. Also, since both Q1 and median are 4, the band for median falls on the bottom of the box. Same way, though the lower whisker could have extended till -2 (Q1 – 1.5 × IQR = 4 – 1.5 × 4 = –2), in reality, there is no data value lower than 3. Hence, the lower whisker is also short. In any case, a value of cylinders less than 1 is not possible.

Analysing Box Plot for 'Origin'

Like the box plot for attribute 'cylinders', the box plot for attribute 'cylinders' also looks pretty weird in shape. Here the lower whisker is missing and the band for median falls at the bottom of the box! Let's verify if everything right?

Just like the attribute 'cylinders', attribute 'origin' is discrete in nature having values from 1 to 3. Table 2.3 captures the frequency and cumulative frequency (i.e., a summation of frequencies of all previous intervals) of it.

Origin	Frequency	Cumulative Frequency
1	249	249
2	70	319 (= 249 + 70)
3	79	398 (= 319 + 79)

As can be observed in the table, the frequency is extremely high for data value 1. Since the total frequency is 398, the first quartile (Q1), median (Q2), and third quartile (Q3) will be at a cumulative frequency 99.5 (i.e., average of 99th and 100th observation), 199 and 298.5 (i.e., average of 298th and 299th observation), respectively. This way Q1 = 1, median = 1, and Q3 = 2. Since Q1 and median are same in value, the band for median falls on the bottom of the box. There is no data value lower than Q1. Hence, the lower whisker is missing.

Analysing Box Plot for 'Displacement'

The box plot for the attribute 'displacement' looks better than the previous box plots. However, still, there are few small abnormalities, the cause of which needs to be reviewed. Firstly, the lower whisker is much smaller than an upper whisker. Also, the band for median is closer to the bottom of the box.

Let's take a closer look at the summary data of the attribute 'displacement'. The value of first quartile, Q1 = 104.2, median = 148.5, and third quartile, Q3 = 262. Since (median – Q1) = 44.3 is greater than (Q3 – median) = 113.5, the band for the median is closer to the bottom of the box (which represents Q1). The value of IQR, in this case, is 157.8. So the lower whisker can be 1.5 times 157.8 less than Q1. But minimum data value for the attribute 'displacement' is 68. So, the lower whisker at 15% [(Q1 – minimum)/1.5 × IQR = (104.2 – 68) / (1.5 × 157.8) = 15%] of the permissible length. On the other hand, the maximum data value is 455. So the upper whisker is 81% [(maximum – Q3)/1.5 × IQR = (455 – 262)/ (1.5 × 157.8) = 81%] of the permissible length. This is why the upper whisker is much longer than the lower whisker.

Analysing Box Plot for 'Model Year'

The box plot for the attribute 'model. year' looks perfect. Let's validate is it really what expected to be. For the attribute 'model.year': First quartile, Q1 = 73 Median, Q2 = 76 Third quartile, Q3 = 79

So, the difference between median and Q1 is exactly equal to Q3 and median (both are 3). That is why the band for the median is exactly equidistant from the bottom and top of the box.

IQR = Q3 9 Q1 = 7 9 – 7 3 = 6

Difference between Q1 and minimum data value (i.e., 70) is also same as maximum data value (i.e. 82) and Q3 (both are 3). So both lower and upper whiskers are expected to be of the same size which is 33% [3/(1.5 × 6)] of the permissible length.

Histogram

Another plot that aids in the efficient visualisation of numerical properties is the histogram. It aids in comprehending how numerical data is distributed into intervals, sometimes known as "bins." The key distinction between a histogram and a box plot is

- The goal of a histogram is to plot ranges of data values, or "bins," where the amount of data pieces in each range depends on the distribution of the data. The size of each bar corresponding to the various ranges will change as a result.
- The main goal of a box plot is to divide a data set into four equal pieces, with the same number of data components in each portion.

Depending on the characteristics of the data, such as skewness, histograms can take on many shapes. The many histogram shapes that are typically constructed are shown in Figure 2.11. These patterns help us quickly comprehend the data and serve as an excellent tool for data research.

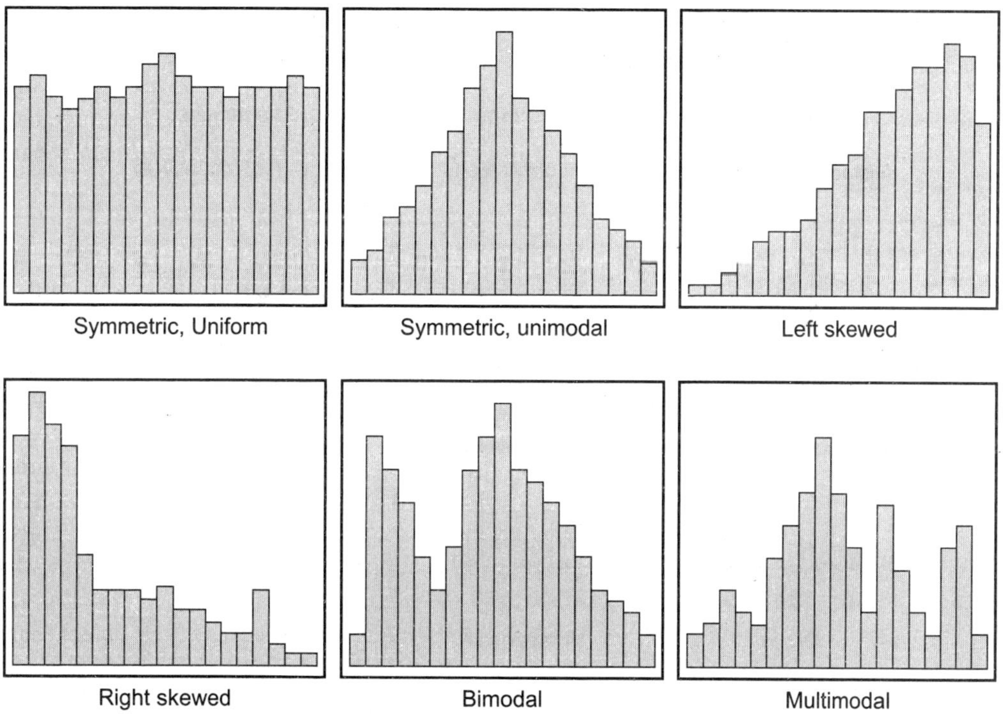

Fig. 2.14. General histogram shapes

Let's now examine the histograms for the different attributes of Auto MPG data set presented in Figure 2.12. The histograms for 'mpg' and 'weight' are right-skewed. The histogram for 'acceleration' is symmetric and unimodal, whereas the one for 'model.year' is symmetric and uniform. For the remaining attributes, histograms are multimodal in nature.

Now let's dig deep into one of the histograms, say the one for the attribute 'acceleration'. The histogram is composed of a number of bars, one bar appearing for each of the 'bins'. The height of the bar reflects the total count of data elements whose value falls within the specific bin value, or the frequency. Talking in context of the histogram for acceleration, each 'bin' represents an acceleration value interval of 2 units. So the second bin, e.g., reflects acceleration value of 10 to 12 units. The corresponding bar chart height reflects the count of all data elements whose value lies between 10 and 12 units. Also, it is evident from the histogram that it spans over the acceleration value of 8 to 26 units. The frequency of data elements corresponding to the bins first keep on increasing, till it reaches the bin of range 14 to 16 units. At this range, the bar is tallest in size. So we can conclude that a maximum number of data elements fall within this range. After this range, the bar size starts decreasing till the end of the whole range at the acceleration value of 26 units.

Please note that when the histogram is uniform, as in the case of attribute 'model. year', it gives a hint that all values are equally likely to occur.

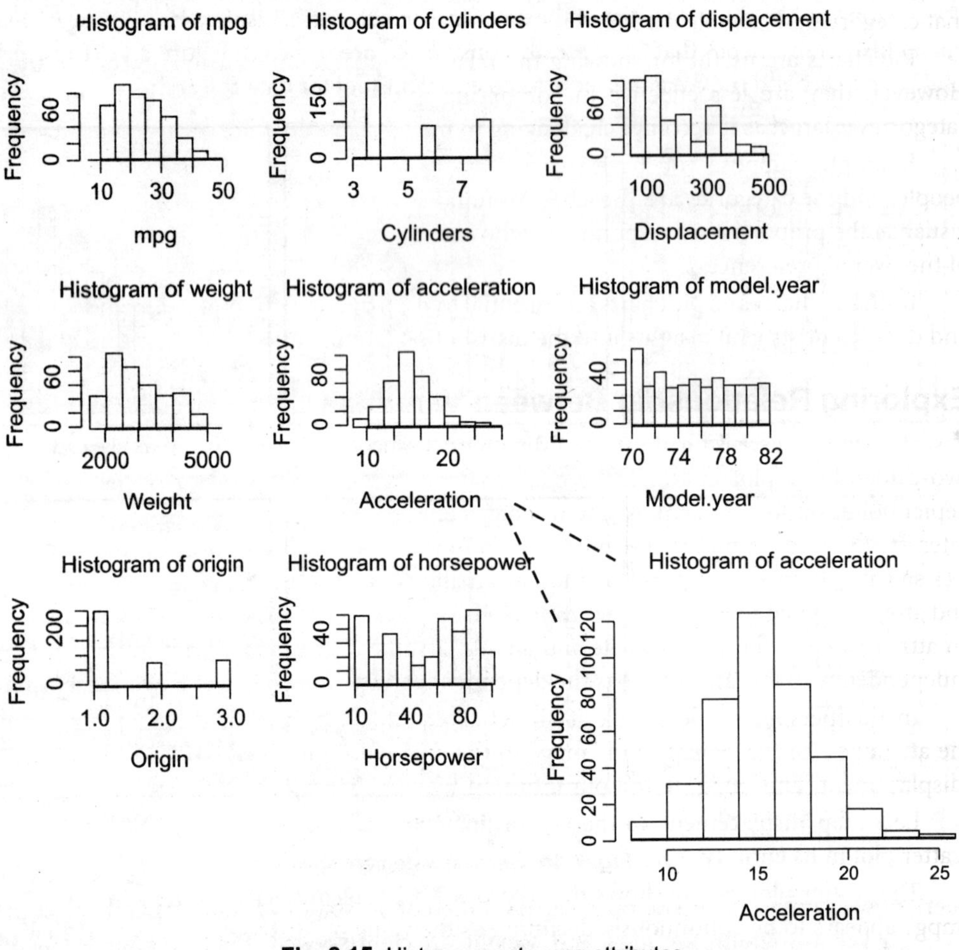

Fig. 2.15. Histogram auto mpg attributes

Exploring Categorical Data

When exploring categorical data, one of the most common graphical representations used is the bar chart (also known as bar graph). A bar chart displays the frequency or count of each category in a dataset as rectangular bars. Each category is represented on the x-axis, and the height of the bar corresponds to the frequency or count of that category.

Bar charts are effective in visualizing the distribution of categorical data and comparing the frequency of different categories. They help identify the most common categories and any significant variations between the categories.

Example: Suppose you have survey data of favorite colors among a group of people, and the categories are "Red," "Blue," "Green," and "Yellow." You can use a bar chart to visualize the frequency of each color and compare the popularity of different colors among the respondents.

Another graphical representation for exploring categorical data is the pie chart. In a pie chart, each category is represented as a slice of the pie, and the size of each slice corresponds to the proportion of that category in the whole dataset.

Pie charts are useful for showing the relative contribution of each category to the entire dataset. However, they are less effective in comparing multiple categories, especially when the number of categories is large, as it becomes challenging to interpret the different slice sizes accurately.

Example: Suppose you have survey data of preferred vacation destinations among a group of people, and the categories are "Beach," "Mountain," "City," and "Wilderness." You can use a pie chart to visualize the proportion of respondents who prefer each destination type, giving you a quick overview of the overall preferences.

Both bar charts and pie charts are essential tools in data exploration and analysis, helping researchers and data scientists gain insights into the distribution and patterns within categorical datasets.

Exploring Relationship Between Variables

A scatter plot is useful for illustrating bivariate relationships, or those involving two variables. It is a two-dimensional plot in which the coordinates provided by the values of the attributes are used to depict points or dots. As an illustration, a data collection has the characteristics attr_1 and attr_2. We are interested in understanding the link between two attributes, specifically how the value of one attribute, let's say attr_1, affects the value of another attribute, let's say attr_2. With attr_1 assigned to the x-axis and attr_2 mapped to the y-axis, we can create a scatter plot. As a result, each point on the plot will have an attr_1 value in the x-coordinate and an attr_2 value in the y-coordinate. Attr_1 is referred to as the independent variable and attr_2 as the dependent variable, much like in a two-dimensional plot.

In this perspective, let's look at an actual example. There should be some relationship between the attributes "displacement" and "mpg" in the data collection Auto MPG. Let's use the scatter plot of "displacement" and "mpg" to test our intuition.

Let's map 'displacement' to the x-coordinate and'mpg' to the y-coordinate. Figure 2.13 shows the scatter plot in its entirety.

The scatter plot clearly shows that there is a relationship between the two variables. The value of "mpg" appears to be continuously declining as the value of "displacement" rises. What is the nature of the partnership, we might wonder? The correlation between the variables can be calculated to review it. If you want to learn more about correlation and how to calculate it, please go to chapter 5.

There are some data values that stand out from the others, which is another intriguing point to note. One data element, for instance, has an mpg of 37 for a displacement of 250.

This record is entirely distinct from other data points with comparable displacement values but mpg values between 15 and 25. This indicates the possibility of having outlier data values.

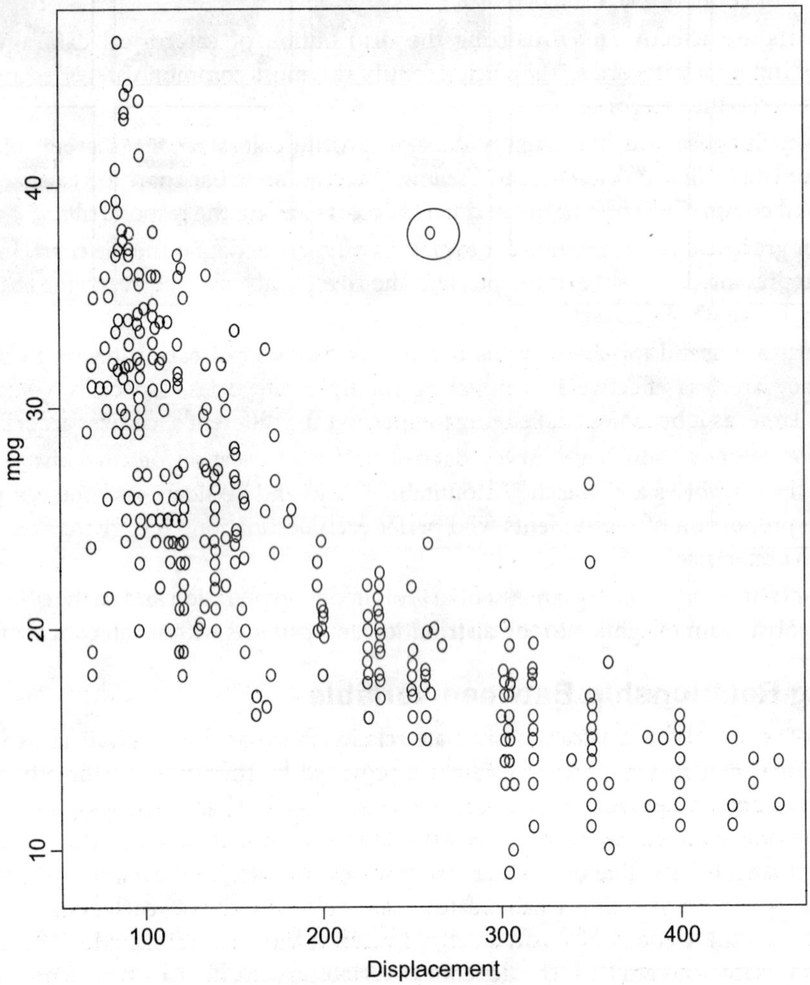

Fig. 2.16. Scatter plot of 'displacement' and 'mpg'

In Figure 2.14, the pair wise relationship among the features – 'mpg', 'displacement', 'horsepower', 'weight', and 'acceleration' have been captured. As you can see, in most of the cases, there is a significant relationship between the attribute pairs. However, in some cases, e.g., between attributes 'weight' and 'acceleration', the relationship doesn't seem to be very strong.

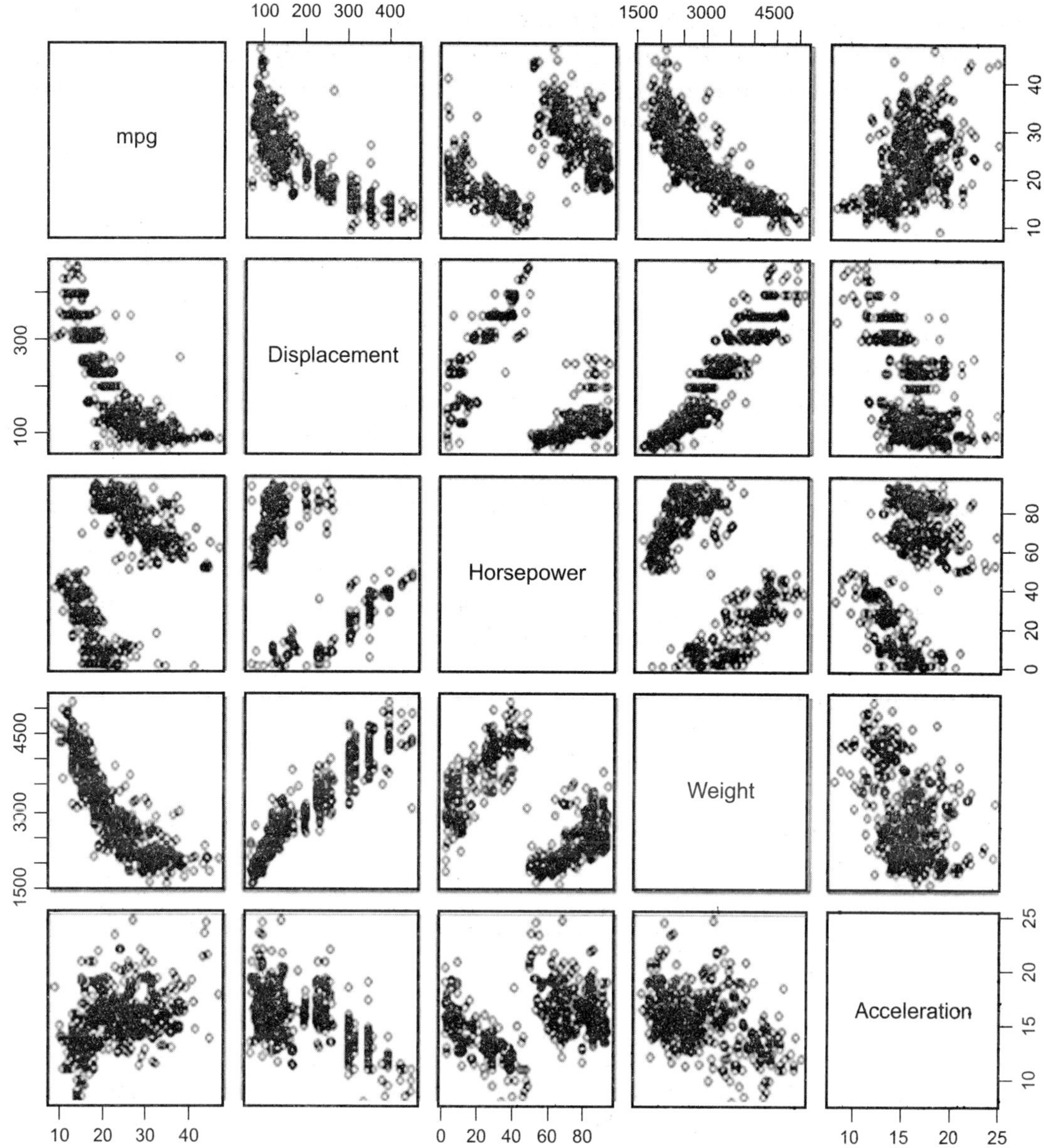

Fig. 2.17. Pair wise scatter plot between different attributes of Auto MPG

Two-Way Cross-Tabulations

Two-way cross-tabulations, also known as contingency tables, are a statistical method used to summarize and analyze the relationship between two categorical variables. They provide a compact representation of the joint distribution of the two variables, allowing us to observe the frequency of combinations of categories for each variable.

To create a two-way cross-tabulation, follow these steps:

1. **Identify the two categorical variables of interest:** Choose two categorical variables from your dataset that you want to analyze together. For example, you might want to study the relationship between "Gender" and "Educational Level."
2. **Create a table:** Set up a table with rows representing the categories of one variable and columns representing the categories of the other variable. The cells of the table will contain the frequency or count of observations that fall into each category combination.
3. **Fill in the table:** Count the number of occurrences for each combination of categories and place the counts in the appropriate cells of the table.
4. **Calculate proportions:** If desired, you can convert the counts to proportions to observe the relative distribution of the categories.
5. **Analyze the results:** Examine the cross-tabulation to understand the relationship between the two variables. Look for patterns, associations, or differences between categories to gain insights into their connections.

Let's assume the attributes 'cylinders', 'model.year', and 'origin' as categorical and try to examine the variation of one with respect to the other. As we understand, attribute 'cylinders' reflects the number of cylinders in a car and assumes values 3, 4, 5, 6, and 8. Attribute 'model.year' captures the model year of each of the car and 'origin' gives the region of the car, the values for origin 1, 2, and 3 corresponding to North America, Europe, and Asia. Below are the cross-tabs

'Model Year' vs. 'Origin'

Table 3. Cross-tab for 'Model year' vs. 'Origin'

Origin/Model Year	70	71	72	73	74	75	76	77	78	79	80	82	82
1	22	20	18	29	15	20	22	19	22	23	7	13	20
2	5	4	5	7	6	6	8	4	6	4	9	4	2
3	2	4	5	4	6	4	4	6	8	2	13	12	9

Data Quality

The success of machine learning models heavily relies on the quality of the data used for training and testing. As you mentioned, data may have various imperfections like missing values and outliers, which can significantly impact the performance of the models. Dealing with these issues is an essential part of data preprocessing and cleaning.

1. **Missing Values:** Missing data can occur for various reasons, such as data entry errors, system failures, or non-response from survey participants. When dealing with missing values, one common approach is to impute them, which means filling in the missing values with estimated values based on other data points or statistical methods. The imputation technique used should be carefully selected to avoid biasing the data.
2. **Outliers:** Outliers are data points that deviate significantly from the majority of the data. They can occur due to measurement errors, data entry mistakes, or rare events. Outliers can distort the model and lead to inaccurate predictions. One approach to handle outliers is to remove

them from the data set. However, the decision to remove outliers should be made cautiously, as sometimes they might be genuine and meaningful data points.

Data quality improvement techniques, such as data validation, normalization, and feature engineering, also play a crucial role in enhancing the quality of the data. It is essential to understand the nature of the data and the domain to make informed decisions regarding data preprocessing.

Overall, addressing data quality issues is a critical step in the machine learning process to ensure that the models are trained on reliable and accurate data, leading to more robust and accurate predictions.

Data quality refers to the reliability, accuracy, consistency, completeness, and relevance of data for a specific purpose. It is crucial in any data-driven analysis or machine learning project as the quality of the data directly impacts the validity and reliability of the results and insights obtained from the analysis. Poor data quality can lead to incorrect conclusions and unreliable predictions, while high-quality data ensures more accurate and trustworthy outcomes.

There are multiple factors which lead to these data quality issues. Following are some of them:

Incorrect Sample Set Selection

Data that do not accurately reflect normal or regular quality may have been chosen for the sample set incorrectly. For instance, if we were to choose a representative sample of sales transactions from a holiday season and attempt to utilize such information to forecast future sales. Because the sample set was chosen at the wrong time, the forecast in this situation will be very different from the actual scenario. Similar to this, any attempt to forecast poll results using training data that does not include the proper mixture of voters from various categories, such as age, sex, ethnic diversity, etc., is doomed to failure. A bad sample size could also be at blame. For instance, a small sample size may not be able to collect all characteristics or information required for the model to be learned properly.

Errors in Data Collection

A person or group of people are frequently in charge of gathering the information that will be used in a learning activity. In this manual process, there is a chance that data will be entered incorrectly, either in terms of value (for example, 20.67 might be entered incorrectly as 206.7 or 2.067) or in terms of a unit of measurement (for example, cm could be entered incorrectly as m or mm). This could lead to data elements that are excessively high or low in comparison to other elements. We refer to these records as outliers.

Additionally, it is possible that no data is ever recorded. It is even more likely in the case of a survey used to gather data because survey participants may decide not to answer a particular question. Therefore, there is no data value for that data element in the responder's record.

Several factors contribute to data quality, including:

1. **Accuracy:** Data should be free from errors and reflect the true values of the measured or recorded attributes.
2. **Completeness:** Data should contain all the required information for the analysis or task at hand, without missing values or gaps.
3. **Consistency:** Data should be uniform and coherent, with consistent formats, units, and definitions across different sources and records.
4. **Timeliness:** Data should be up-to-date and relevant to the current context, ensuring that decisions are based on the most recent information.

5. **Validity:** Data should be relevant to the problem being addressed and should accurately represent the concepts it intends to measure.
6. **Relevance:** Data should be meaningful and relevant to the specific analysis or decision-making process.

To ensure data quality, various data validation and cleaning techniques are employed, such as outlier detection, handling missing values, data normalization, deduplication, and data profiling. Data quality assessment is an ongoing process, and data practitioners often work closely with domain experts to validate and verify the data for accuracy and relevance.

Data Remediation

Data remediation refers to the process of identifying and resolving data quality issues in a dataset to improve its accuracy, consistency, completeness, and reliability. It involves various techniques and methodologies to clean, correct, and enhance the data, ensuring it is suitable for analysis, reporting, and machine learning tasks. Data remediation is a crucial step in data management, as poor data quality can lead to erroneous insights and inaccurate decision-making.

The data remediation process typically includes the following steps:

1. **Data Profiling:** Analyzing the dataset to understand its structure, data types, and potential issues. Data profiling helps in identifying missing values, duplicates, outliers, and other anomalies.
2. **Data Cleaning:** Removing or correcting data errors, such as missing values, duplicates, and inconsistencies. Data cleaning techniques involve imputing missing values, removing duplicates, and resolving inconsistencies within the dataset.
3. **Data Standardization:** Ensuring that data follows a consistent format and adheres to predefined standards. Standardizing data helps in comparing and integrating data from different sources.
4. **Data Enrichment:** Enhancing the dataset by adding additional relevant information or attributes. Data enrichment can involve merging data from external sources or using domain-specific knowledge to supplement the existing dataset.
5. **Data Validation:** Verifying the accuracy and correctness of the data through validation rules and checks. Data validation helps in ensuring that the data meets specific quality criteria and is suitable for analysis.
6. **Data Transformation:** Converting data into a suitable format for analysis or modeling. Data transformation may involve normalization, scaling, or encoding categorical variables.
7. **Data Integration:** Combining data from multiple sources and resolving conflicts to create a unified and comprehensive dataset.
8. **Data Monitoring:** Establishing processes to continuously monitor data quality over time and identifying any new issues that may arise.

Data remediation is an iterative process that requires collaboration between data experts, domain experts, and stakeholders to ensure that the data is of high quality and fit for its intended use. By addressing data quality issues through remediation, organizations can make better-informed decisions and derive more accurate insights from their data.

Handling outliers is an essential step in data remediation to improve the quality and reliability of the dataset. Outliers are data points that deviate significantly from the rest of the data, and they can negatively impact statistical analysis, machine learning algorithms, and other data-driven processes. Dealing with outliers involves various techniques, and here are some common approaches:

1. **Identify Outliers:** The first step is to detect outliers in the dataset. This can be done using statistical methods like the Z-score, modified Z-score, or interquartile range (IQR) method. Data points with values beyond a certain threshold are considered outliers.
2. **Remove Outliers:** In some cases, outliers can be removed from the dataset if they are the result of data entry errors or measurement inaccuracies. However, caution should be exercised when removing outliers, as they might contain valuable information or indicate important insights.
3. **Transform Data:** Another approach is to transform the data using mathematical functions to reduce the impact of outliers. Common transformations include logarithmic, square root, or inverse transformations, which can help make the distribution more normal and stabilize variance.
4. **Winsorization:** Winsorization involves capping the extreme values of the dataset. Instead of removing outliers, the values beyond a specified threshold are replaced with the nearest non-outlier value.
5. **Binning or Discretization:** Binning involves dividing the continuous data into intervals or bins and assigning all outliers to the nearest bin. This can help reduce the influence of outliers and make the data more manageable.
6. **Imputation:** Outliers in missing value data can be imputed using various techniques, such as mean, median, or regression-based imputation, to replace the extreme values with more representative ones.
7. **Model-Based Approaches:** In some cases, advanced statistical methods or machine learning models can be used to identify and handle outliers more effectively.
8. **Separate Analysis:** In certain scenarios, outliers can be analyzed separately to understand their impact on the overall dataset and make informed decisions about handling them.

It's crucial to remember that the choice of handling outliers depends on the context, the nature of the data, and the specific problem at hand. Domain knowledge, understanding of the data, and the intended use of the dataset play a significant role in determining the appropriate approach to handle outliers effectively.

Handling missing values is a critical step in data remediation as incomplete data can lead to biased analysis and inaccurate predictions in machine learning models. There are several approaches to dealing with missing values:

1. **Deletion:** In cases where the missing values are minimal, and their impact on the analysis is negligible, rows or columns with missing values can be deleted. However, this method should be used with caution as it can lead to a reduction in the size of the dataset and the loss of valuable information.
2. **Imputation:** Imputation involves filling in the missing values with estimated or substituted values. Common imputation techniques include:

   Mean or Median Imputation: Replacing missing values with the mean or median of the available data for that attribute.

   Regression Imputation: Using regression models to predict missing values based on other attributes.

   Hot Deck Imputation: Replacing missing values with values from similar records in the dataset.

   K-Nearest Neighbors (KNN) Imputation: Predicting missing values by averaging the values of the k-nearest neighbors.

3. **Flagging or Indicator Variable:** In some cases, it is beneficial to create an additional binary variable that indicates whether the original value was missing or not. This approach can help preserve the information about missingness and may be useful in certain analyses.
4. **Meaningful Default Value:** For categorical variables, a meaningful default value can be used to fill in the missing values. This approach is suitable when a particular category is absent and can be assigned a unique label.
5. **Multiple Imputations:** In more complex cases, where the pattern of missingness is not entirely random, multiple imputations can be performed to generate several datasets with different imputed values. The final analysis is then conducted on each of these datasets, and the results are combined.
6. **Domain Knowledge:** In some situations, domain knowledge can provide insights into handling missing values. Experts in the field may have an understanding of how missing values should be treated based on the nature of the data and the specific context.

Choosing the appropriate method for handling missing values depends on the dataset's characteristics, the amount of missing data, and the specific analytical goals. It is essential to consider the potential biases and uncertainties introduced by the chosen method and to document the approach taken to ensure the transparency and reproducibility of the analysis.

In the case of Auto MPG data set, only in 6 out of 398 records, the value of attribute 'horsepower' is missing. If we get rid of those 6 records, we will still have 392 records, which is definitely a substantial number. So, we can very well eliminate the records and keep working with the remaining data set

Dimensionality Reduction

Dimensionality reduction is a technique used in machine learning and data analysis to reduce the number of features or variables in a dataset while preserving essential information. It is particularly useful when dealing with high-dimensional data, as reducing the number of dimensions can lead to more efficient computation, visualization, and better model performance.

The main goals of dimensionality reduction are:

- **Simplification:** By reducing the number of features, the complexity of the data is reduced, making it easier to interpret and understand.
- **Computational Efficiency:** High-dimensional data can be computationally expensive to process and analyze. Dimensionality reduction helps in reducing computational overhead.
- **Visualization:** Reducing data to a lower-dimensional space allows for easier visualization and exploration of data patterns.
- **Noise Reduction:** By eliminating irrelevant or noisy features, dimensionality reduction can lead to improved model performance by focusing on the most informative variables.

There are two main categories of dimensionality reduction techniques:

1. **Feature Selection:** In feature selection, a subset of the original features is selected based on their relevance to the target variable or their contribution to the model's performance. Common feature selection methods include backward elimination, forward selection, and recursive feature elimination.
2. **Feature Extraction:** Feature extraction techniques transform the original high-dimensional data into a lower-dimensional space by creating new features that represent combinations or projections of the original features. Principal Component Analysis (PCA) and Singular Value Decomposition (SVD) are popular feature extraction methods.

Principal Component Analysis (PCA) is one of the most widely used dimensionality reduction techniques. It identifies the principal components, which are orthogonal vectors that capture the most significant variance in the data. These components can then be used as new features, and the number of components can be chosen based on the desired level of data compression or explained variance.

Dimensionality reduction should be applied with care, as reducing dimensions can lead to the loss of some information. It is essential to balance the benefits of simplification and computational efficiency with the potential loss of information and model performance. Dimensionality reduction should be combined with thorough data analysis and domain knowledge to ensure that the reduced dataset remains meaningful and appropriate for the specific analysis or model-building task.

Feature Subset Selection

Feature subset selection is a specific type of dimensionality reduction technique that focuses on selecting a subset of relevant features from the original set of features in a dataset. The goal of feature subset selection is to retain the most informative and discriminative features while discarding irrelevant or redundant ones, thus improving the performance of machine learning models and reducing computation time.

There are various approaches to feature subset selection, and they can be broadly categorized into three types:

1. **Filter Methods:** Filter methods use statistical metrics to rank the individual features based on their relevance to the target variable, such as correlation coefficients, mutual information, or statistical tests. Features are selected based on their scores, and a predefined threshold is often used to determine the subset of features to retain.
2. **Wrapper Methods:** Wrapper methods assess the performance of a machine learning model using different subsets of features. It involves training and evaluating the model on different feature subsets, and the selection of the best subset is based on model performance metrics like accuracy, precision, recall, etc. Wrapper methods are computationally expensive since they require training and evaluating the model for each subset.
3. **Embedded Methods:** Embedded methods integrate feature selection into the model training process. They work by adding or removing features while training the model, and feature selection is inherently part of the learning algorithm. Techniques like L1 regularization (Lasso) and tree-based methods (e.g., Random Forests) are examples of embedded feature selection.

The choice of the feature subset selection method depends on the characteristics of the dataset and the specific machine learning task at hand. Some datasets may have many irrelevant or redundant features, making filter methods more efficient. On the other hand, wrapper methods can be more effective when the dataset is small and model performance is crucial.

Feature subset selection plays a vital role in machine learning model development by improving model accuracy, reducing overfitting, and speeding up computation time. However, it is essential to balance the trade-off between reducing dimensionality and preserving critical information, as aggressive feature selection may lead to information loss and suboptimal model performance. It is often recommended to combine feature subset selection with other dimensionality reduction techniques like PCA or feature extraction methods to achieve better results.

Review Questions

Multiple Choice Questions

Q.1. What is machine learning?

(*a*) A type of computer programming language
(*b*) A branch of Artificial Intelligence focused on algorithms that learn from data
(*c*) The process of automating manual tasks using robots
(*d*) A technique for optimizing computer hardware performance

Q.2. Which of the following tasks is NOT typically associated with machine learning?

(*a*) Image recognition
(*b*) Language translation
(*c*) Sorting algorithms
(*d*) Stock market prediction

Q.3. What is the primary goal of supervised learning?

(*a*) To uncover hidden patterns and structures in data
(*b*) To learn from input-output pairs to predict outputs for new inputs
(*c*) To classify data into discrete categories
(*d*) To optimize decision-making based on trial and error

Q.4. Which of the following algorithms is commonly used for regression tasks in Machine Learning?

(*a*) K-nearest neighbors (KNN)
(*b*) Support Vector Machines (SVM)
(*c*) Decision Trees
(*d*) Linear Regression

Q.5. What is the main objective of unsupervised learning?

(*a*) To predict outputs for new inputs based on historical data
(*b*) To classify data into predefined categories
(*c*) To discover hidden patterns or structures in data without explicit labels
(*d*) To optimize decision-making based on feedback

Q.6. Which of the following is an example of a clustering algorithm in Machine Learning?

(*a*) Linear Regression
(*b*) K-means
(*c*) Random Forest
(*d*) Gradient Descent

Q.7. What is the purpose of feature engineering in Machine Learning?

(*a*) To design and build hardware components for Machine Learning systems
(*b*) To extract and select relevant features from raw data to improve model performance
(*c*) To interpret and visualize the results of Machine Learning algorithms
(*d*) To generate synthetic data for training Machine Learning models

Q.8. Which of the following evaluation metrics is commonly used for classification tasks?

(*a*) Mean Squared Error (MSE)
(*b*) Root Mean Squared Error (RMSE)
(*c*) Accuracy
(*d*) R-squared (R^2)

Q.9. What is overfitting in the context of Machine Learning?

(*a*) When a model performs well on new, unseen data
(*b*) When a model performs poorly on the training data but generalizes well to new data
(*c*) When a model captures noise or random fluctuations in the training data
(*d*) When a model is too simple to capture the underlying patterns in the data

Q.10. Which of the following techniques can help prevent overfitting in Machine Learning models?

(*a*) Adding more layers to the neural network
(*b*) Increasing the complexity of the model
(*c*) Regularization
(*d*) Decreasing the size of the training dataset

Q.11. What is the purpose of data preprocessing in Machine Learning?

(*a*) To visualize the data
(*b*) To clean and transform raw data into a usable format for modeling
(*c*) To evaluate the performance of the model
(*d*) To train the model using the processed data

Q.12. Which of the following techniques is commonly used for handling missing values in a dataset?

(*a*) Deleting the rows with missing values
(*b*) Replacing missing values with the mean or median of the column
(*c*) Ignoring the missing values during model training
(*d*) All of the above

Q.13. What is feature scaling in Machine Learning?

(*a*) Transforming categorical features into numerical ones
(*b*) Scaling the target variable to a specific range
(*c*) Standardizing or normalizing numerical features to a similar scale
(*d*) Selecting the most relevant features for model training

Q.14. Which of the following is NOT a dimensionality reduction technique?

(*a*) Principal Component Analysis (PCA)
(*b*) t-Distributed Stochastic Neighbor Embedding (t-SNE)
(*c*) Random Forest
(*d*) Linear Discriminant Analysis (LDA)

Q.15. What is the purpose of feature encoding in Machine Learning?

(*a*) To remove redundant features from the dataset
(*b*) To transform categorical variables into a numerical format that can be used for modeling
(*c*) To scale numerical features to a similar range
(*d*) To visualize the relationship between features and the target variable

Q.16. Which of the following is a supervised learning technique for feature selection?

(*a*) Principal Component Analysis (PCA)
(*b*) Recursive Feature Elimination (RFE)
(*c*) t-Distributed Stochastic Neighbor Embedding (t-SNE)
(*d*) K-means clustering

Q.17. What is the purpose of train-test splitting in Machine Learning?

(*a*) To preprocess the data before model training
(*b*) To evaluate the performance of the model on unseen data
(*c*) To visualize the relationship between features and the target variable
(*d*) To select the most relevant features for model training

Q.18. Which evaluation metric is commonly used for regression tasks in Machine Learning?

(*a*) Accuracy (*b*) Precision
(*c*) Mean Squared Error (MSE) (*d*) F1-score

Q.19. In cross-validation, how many subsets is the training data typically divided into?

(*a*) Two (*b*) Three (*c*) Five (*d*) Ten

Q.20. What is the purpose of hyperparameter tuning in Machine Learning?

(*a*) To preprocess the data before model training
(*b*) To evaluate the performance of the model on unseen data
(*c*) To select the most relevant features for model training
(*d*) To optimize the parameters that control the learning process of the model

Answers

1. (*b*)	2. (*c*)	3. (*b*)	4. (*d*)	5. (*c*)	6. (*b*)	7. (*b*)	8. (*c*)	9. (*c*)
10. (*c*)	11. (*b*)	12. (*d*)	13. (*c*)	14. (*c*)	15. (*b*)	16. (*b*)	17. (*b*)	18. (*c*)
19. (*c*)	20. (*d*)							

Unsolved Questions

1. Define machine learning and provide an example of a real-world application where machine learning is used.
2. Explain the concept of a well-posed learning problem and why it is important in machine learning.
3. Differentiate between supervised, unsupervised, and reinforcement learning with examples for each.
4. Discuss a scenario where reinforcement learning would be more suitable than supervised learning.
5. Identify and describe three diverse applications of machine learning in different industries.
6. Explore the challenges and opportunities associated with implementing machine learning in real-world scenarios.
7. Compare and contrast supervised and unsupervised learning in terms of data requirements and use cases.
8. Discuss the unique characteristics of reinforcement learning and its potential applications.
9. Choose a specific machine learning tool (e.g., TensorFlow, PyTorch) and explain its key features and advantages.
10. Discuss the importance of selecting the right programming language for machine learning tasks.

Fill in the Blanks

1. Machine learning is a field of artificial intelligence that focuses on the development of algorithms and models that enable computers to __________ from data.

2. A well-posed learning problem consists of a __________, a set of input data, and a performance metric that defines the success criteria.
3. The three main types of machine learning are supervised learning, unsupervised learning, and __________ learning.
4. In supervised learning, the algorithm learns from a labeled dataset, where the input data is paired with corresponding __________.
5. Unsupervised learning involves training a model on __________ data without labeled outputs.
6. Reinforcement learning is a type of machine learning where an agent learns to make decisions by interacting with an __________ and receiving feedback in the form of rewards.
7. Supervised learning is characterized by labeled data and a clear mapping between inputs and outputs, while unsupervised learning deals with __________ patterns in unlabeled data. Reinforcement learning focuses on learning optimal actions in a dynamic environment.
8. Machine learning finds applications in various domains, including __________, healthcare, finance, and natural language processing.
9. Some state-of-the-art languages and tools in machine learning include __________, TensorFlow, PyTorch, and scikit-learn.

Fill in the Blanks with Answers

1. Machine learning is a subset of __________ intelligence that focuses on systems learning from __________.
2. In supervised learning, the algorithm is trained on a dataset that includes both __________ and their corresponding __________.
3. The goal of unsupervised learning is to find __________ and patterns in data without labelled .
4. The performance of a machine learning model is often assessed using __________ and __________ metrics.
5. Feature engineering involves selecting and transforming __________ to improve a model's __________.
6. The process of dividing a dataset into training and testing sets is crucial to evaluate a model's __________ on new, unseen data.
7. __________ learning is a type of machine learning where the algorithm learns by interacting with its __________.
8. The function that a machine learning algorithm is trying to optimize or minimize is called the __________ function.
9. Decision trees and random forests are examples of __________ learning algorithms used for both classification and __________ tasks.
10. Overfitting occurs when a model performs well on the __________ data but fails to generalize to __________ data.
11. In a confusion matrix, the true positive and true negative values represent the number of __________ predictions.
12. The process of adjusting the parameters of a machine learning model to improve its performance is known as __________.

13. Cross-validation is a technique used to assess a model's __________ and reduce the risk of overfitting.
14. The acronym __________ stands for Artificial Neural Network, a model inspired by the human __________.
15. In reinforcement learning, the __________ provides feedback to the agent based on its actions in the __________.
16. Machine learning algorithms can be categorized into three main types: supervised learning, unsupervised learning, and __________ learning.
17. In supervised learning, the input data is often denoted as __________ and the corresponding output as labels or __________.
18. The process of transforming categorical variables into numerical representations is called __________.
19. In machine learning, a model that is too simple to capture the underlying patterns in the data is said to suffer from __________.
20. The __________ is a parameter that controls the trade-off between model complexity and training data fitting in algorithms like Support Vector Machines.
21. The process of preparing the input data for machine learning algorithms, including cleaning and scaling, is known as __________.
22. In unsupervised learning, a common clustering algorithm is __________, which aims to partition data points into groups with similar characteristics.
23. A neural network layer that reduces the dimensionality of the input data is called a __________ layer.
24. The process of adjusting the learning rate during training to reach the minimum of the loss function is known as __________.
25. The area under the Receiver Operating Characteristic (ROc) curve is a metric used to evaluate the performance of __________ models.

Answer

1. artificial intelligence, data.
2. inputs, outputs.
3. structures, outputs.
4. accuracy, precision
5. features, performance.
6. generalization
7. Reinforcement, environment.
8. objective
9. supervised, regression
10. training, testing
11. correct
12. tuning
13. performance
14. ANN, brain.
15. environment, world
16. Reinforcement
17. Features, targets
18. Encoding
19. Underfitting
20. cost
21. Preprocessing
22. K-Means
23. Dense
24. Learning rate annealing
25. Binary classification

Exercise

Data Preprocessing:

Load and Explore Data:

Load a dataset using a library like Pandas.

Explore basic statistics, such as mean, median, and standard deviation.

Handling Missing Data:

Identify and handle missing values in the dataset using techniques like imputation or removal.

Data Scaling:

Apply Min-Max scaling or Standardization to the numerical features in the dataset.

Encoding Categorical Variables:

Encode categorical variables using techniques like one-hot encoding or label encoding.

❑❑❑

3

Linear Regression

INTRODUCTION

Regression is a statistical method used to analyze the relationship between a dependent variable and one or more independent variables. The regression method aims to estimate the values of the dependent variable based on the values of the independent variables. For example, we could ask for the relationship between people's weights 13 and heights, or study time and test scores, the relationship between rainfall and soil erosion.

What are the Purposes of Regression Analysis?

Regression Analysis has two main purposes:

Explanatory: A regression analysis explains the relationship between the response and predictor variables. For example, it can answer questions such as, does kidney function increase the severity of symptoms in some particular disease process?

Predictive: A regression model can give a point estimate of the response variable based on the value of the predictors.

There are several regression methods available, and the choice of which method to use depends on the nature of the data and the research question at hand. Here are some commonly used regression methods:

1. **Linear Regression:** Linear regression is the most basic and widely used regression method. It assumes a linear relationship between the dependent variable and the independent variables. The goal is to find the best-fit line that minimizes the difference between the predicted and actual values. Linear regression is suitable when the relationship between variables can be approximated by a straight line.

   Example: Suppose we have a dataset of houses with their respective sizes and prices. We want to build a linear regression model to predict the price of a house based on its size.

   Mathematical Representation: In linear regression, the model represents a linear relationship between the independent variable x (house size) and the dependent variable y (house price) as:

   $$y = \theta 0 + \theta 1 * x$$

   Here, θ0 represents the y-intercept (the price when the size is zero), and θ1 represents the slope (the rate of change of price with respect to size). The goal is to estimate the optimal values of θ0 and θ1 that minimize the difference between the predicted and actual prices.

2. **Polynomial Regression:** Polynomial regression is an extension of linear regression where higher-order polynomial terms (such as quadratic or cubic terms) are included in the model. It allows for curved relationships between variables. Polynomial regression can capture more complex patterns in the data but may be prone to overfitting if not properly regularized.

   Example: Suppose we have a dataset of students' study hours and their corresponding exam scores. We want to predict the scores based on the study hours using polynomial regression.

   Mathematical Representation: In polynomial regression, the model represents a polynomial relationship between the independent variable x (study hours) and the dependent variable y (exam scores) as:

   $$y = \theta 0 + \theta 1 * x + \theta 2 * x^\wedge 2 + \theta 3 * x^\wedge 3 + \ldots$$

   Here, θ0, θ1, θ2, θ3, etc., are the coefficients representing the effect of each polynomial term on the prediction. By including higher-order polynomial terms, we can capture non-linear relationships between variables.

3. **Ridge Regression:** Ridge regression is a variant of linear regression that includes a regularization term to prevent overfitting. It adds a penalty term to the cost function, encouraging smaller and more balanced coefficient values. Ridge regression is useful when dealing with multicollinearity (high correlation between independent variables).

   Example: Let's consider a dataset with various features such as age, income, and education level, and we want to predict a person's credit score. However, the features are highly correlated, leading to multicollinearity.

   Mathematical Representation: In ridge regression, the model representation is similar to linear regression, but with an additional regularization term to prevent overfitting:

   $$y = \theta 0 + \theta 1 * x1 + \theta 2 * x2 + \ldots + \theta n * xn + \lambda * (\theta 1^\wedge 2 + \theta 2^\wedge 2 + \ldots + \theta n^\wedge 2)$$

   Here, λ (lambda) is the regularization parameter that controls the amount of shrinkage applied to the coefficients. Ridge regression shrinks the coefficient values towards zero, encouraging more balanced and stable models.

4. **Lasso Regression:** Lasso regression, similar to ridge regression, adds a regularization term to the cost function. However, lasso regression uses the L1 norm penalty, which has the effect of shrinking some coefficient values to exactly zero. This feature makes lasso regression useful for feature selection and producing sparse models.

   Example: Let's consider a dataset with multiple features, and we want to predict a person's house price. However, we suspect that only a few important features are truly influential in determining the price.

   Mathematical Representation: In lasso regression, the model representation is similar to linear regression, but with an additional L1 regularization term:

   $$y = \theta 0 + \theta 1 * x1 + \theta 2 * x2 + \ldots + \theta n * xn + \lambda * (|\theta 1| + |\theta 2| + \ldots + |\theta n|)$$

   The L1 norm penalty encourages sparsity by shrinking some coefficient values to exactly zero. This property makes lasso regression useful for feature selection.

5. **Elastic Net Regression:** Elastic Net regression combines the L1 and L2 norm penalties of lasso and ridge regression, respectively. It offers a balance between the two methods, allowing for both coefficient shrinkage and feature selection. Elastic Net regression is helpful when dealing with high-dimensional datasets with many correlated variables.

   Example: Suppose we have a dataset of housing prices with many features, and we want to predict the price based on these features. However, some features are highly correlated, and we also want to perform feature selection.

Mathematical Representation: In elastic net regression, the model representation combines the L1 and L2 regularization terms from lasso and ridge regression:

$$y = \theta 0 + \theta 1 * x1 + \theta 2 * x2 + ... + \theta n * xn$$
$$+ \lambda 1 * (|\theta 1| + |\theta 2| + ... + |\theta n|) + \lambda 2 * (\theta 1^\wedge 2 + \theta 2^\wedge 2 + ... + \theta n^\wedge 2)$$

Here, λ1 and λ2 are the regularization parameters controlling the amount of L1 and L2 regularization, respectively. Elastic net regression offers a balance between lasso and ridge regression, allowing for both coefficient shrinkage and feature selection.

6. **Logistic Regression:** Logistic regression is a regression method used for binary classification problems, where the dependent variable is binary (e.g., yes/no, true/false). It models the probability of belonging to a particular class using a logistic function. Logistic regression estimates the coefficients that maximize the likelihood of the observed data.

   Example: Suppose we have a dataset of patients with information about their age and whether they have a certain medical condition. We want to predict the probability of a person having the condition based on their age.

   Mathematical Representation: In logistic regression, the model represents the probability of a binary outcome (e.g., having the medical condition) based on the independent variable x (age) using a logistic function:

$$p = 1/(1 + \exp(-(\theta 0 + \theta 1 * x)))$$

   Here, p represents the probability of the event occurring, θ0 is the intercept, θ1 is the coefficient associated with the independent variable x (age), and exp() is the exponential function. The logistic function ensures that the predicted probabilities range from 0 to 1.

   These are just a few examples of regression methods, and there are many other specialized regression techniques available, such as Poisson regression, time series regression, and quantile regression. The choice of method depends on the specific problem, the nature of the data, and the assumptions that can be made.

Linear regression is a supervised learning algorithm used to model the relationship between a dependent variable and one or more independent variables. It assumes a linear relationship between the variables, where the dependent variable can be predicted as a linear combination of the independent variables. Mathematically, linear regression represents the relationship between a dependent variable y and one or more independent variables x. The goal is to find the best-fit line that minimizes the difference between the predicted values and the actual values.

Let's consider the case of simple linear regression with one independent variable x:

Given a dataset with n data points {(x1, y1), (x2, y2), ..., (xn, yn)}, the mathematical representation of linear regression can be expressed as:

$$y = \theta 0 + 7\theta 1 * x + \varepsilon \qquad ...(1)$$

Here,

- y represents the dependent variable (the variable we want to predict).
- x represents the independent variable (the variable used to predict y).
- θ0 is the y-intercept, which represents the value of y when x is zero.
- θ1 is the slope, which represents the rate of change of y with respect to x.
- ε represents the error term or residual, which captures the deviation between the predicted and actual values.

The goal is to estimate the optimal values of θ0 and θ1 that minimize the sum of squared residuals (also known as the least squares method). The estimated coefficients (θ0 and θ1) can be obtained through various methods, such as ordinary least squares (OLS), gradient descent, or matrix operations.

Once the coefficients are estimated, the linear regression model can be used to make predictions on new data points by plugging in the values of x into the equation:

$$y\_predicted = \theta 0 + \theta 1 * x\_new \quad ...(2)$$

By calculating the predicted values, we can assess the relationship between the variables and make predictions on unseen data.

It's important to note that the example above represents simple linear regression with one independent variable. In multiple linear regression, the equation extends to include more independent variables:

$$y = \theta 0 + \theta 1 * x1 + \theta 2 * x2 + ... + \theta n * xn + \varepsilon \quad ...(3)$$

In this case, each θ coefficient represents the effect of a specific independent variable on the dependent variable, while other variables are held constant. The estimation process remains similar, but with the inclusion of multiple coefficients to determine their respective contributions to the prediction.

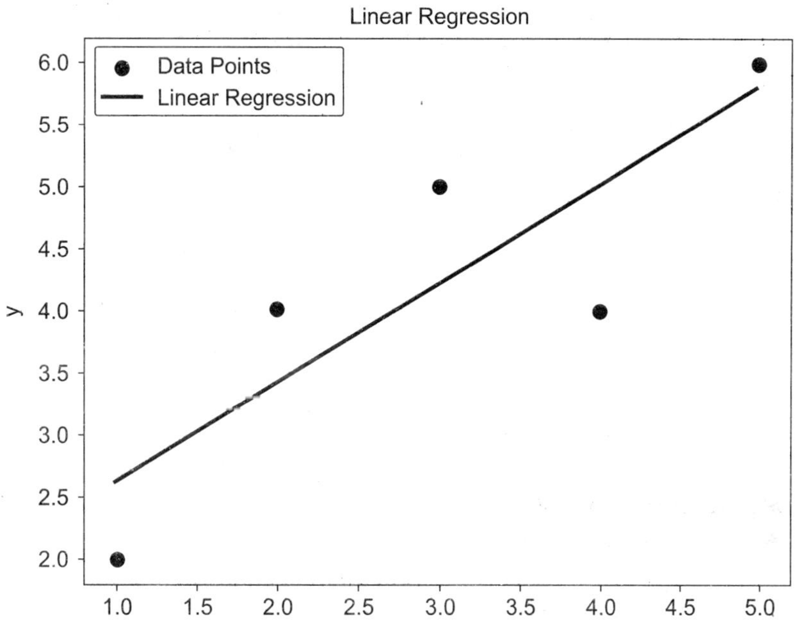

From the plot, we can derive several insights about the linear regression model and it's fit to the data:

1. **Relationship:** The scatter plot shows the relationship between the independent variable (X) and the dependent variable (y). In this example, we see a generally positive relationship, whereas X increases, y tends to increase as well.
2. **Linearity:** The regression line visually represents the linear relationship between X and y. It provides an approximation of the underlying trend in the data. In this case, the red line demonstrates a straight-line relationship, indicating that a linear regression model is appropriate for this dataset.
3. **Fit:** The regression line aims to minimize the distance between the line and the data points. The better the line fits the data, the more accurately it can predict y values for new X values. By visually inspecting the plot, we can get an idea of how well the line fits the data. If the line closely aligns with the majority of the data points, it suggests a good fit.

4. **Outliers:** By examining the scatter plot, we can identify any outliers, which are data points that deviate significantly from the general trend. Outliers can impact the fit of the regression line and should be investigated further to determine if they are genuine observations or anomalies.
5. **Variability:** The spread of the data points around the regression line indicates the variability in the relationship. If the points are tightly clustered around the line, it suggests a low level of variability, indicating a stronger relationship. Conversely, if the points are scattered widely, it suggests higher variability and potentially a weaker relationship.

These insights derived from the plot can provide a visual assessment of how well the linear regression model captures the relationship between the variables and help in interpreting the results. Additionally, they can guide further analysis, such as examining residuals or evaluating the model's performance metrics.

Example: An example of linear regress is to predict the housing prices based on the area, given a training set shown in the following table.

Size in feet2 (x) (predictors or features)	Prices in $1000 (y) (target or label)
2104	430
1810	312
950	200
1500	280
...	...

To predict target y given a value of variable x, first we need to estimate the coefficients θ0, θ1 based on m observations $(x^{(1)}, y^{(1)}), (x^{(2)}, y^{(2)})\ldots (x^{(m)}, y^{(m)})$. Then y is predicted by the hypothesis $\hat{y} = h_\theta(x) = \theta 0 + \theta 1 x$

To find the optimal coefficients, a cost function is defined as mean square error.

Solution: To estimate the coefficients θ0 and θ1, we can use the following steps:

1. **Calculate the mean values of x and y:**

x_mean = mean of x values

y_mean = mean of y values

x_mean = (2104 + 1810 + 950 + 1500)/4 = 1341

y_mean = (430 + 312 + 200 + 280)/4 = 305

2. **Calculate the differences between each x value and the mean of x (x_mean), and the differences between each y value and the mean of y (y_mean):**

diff_x = x – x_mean

diff_y = y – y_mean

diff_x = [2104 – 1341, 1810 – 1341, 950 – 1341, 1500 – 1341]

= [763, 469, −391, 159]

diff_y = [430 – 305, 312 – 305, 200 – 305, 280 – 305] = [125, 7, −105, −25]

3. **Calculate the numerator and denominator for θ1:**

numerator = sum (diff_x * diff_y)

denominator = sum (diff_x * diff_x)

numerator = (763 * 125) + (469 * 7) + (-391 * -105) + (159 * -25) = 193732

denominator = (763 * 763) + (469 * 469) + (-391 * -391) + (159 * 159) = 963968

4. **Calculate the optimal coefficient θ1:**

$$\theta 1 = \text{numerator/denominator} = 193732/963968 \approx 0.201$$

5. **Calculate the optimal coefficient θ0:**

$$\theta 0 = \text{y\_mean} - \theta 1 * \text{x\_mean} = 305 - (0.201 * 1341) \approx 58.155$$

Therefore, the regression equation for predicting house prices based on area is:

$$\hat{y} = 58.155 + 0.201x$$

Using this equation, you can make predictions for new values of x.

By minimizing the mean squared error (MSE) cost function, we find the coefficients that best fit the training data and provide the most accurate predictions for the given linear regression problem.

Now, let's calculate the mean squared error (MSE) using the predicted values and the actual values from the training set:

Step 1: Calculate the predicted values ($\hat{y}$) using the regression equation $\hat{y} = 58.155 + 0.201x$ for each data point in the training set.

Size in feet 2 (x)	Prices in $1000 (y)	Predicted Prices ($\hat{y}$)
2104	430	$\hat{y}$ = 58.155 + 0.201 * 2104
1810	312	$\hat{y}$ = 58.155 + 0.201 * 1810
950	200	$\hat{y}$ = 58.155 + 0.201 * 950
1500	280	$\hat{y}$ = 58.155 + 0.201 * 1500

Step 2: Calculate the squared differences between the predicted values and the actual values:

Squared Differences (squared_diff) = $(\hat{y} - \text{y\_actual})^2$ for each data point.

Step 3: Calculate the mean of the squared differences to obtain the mean squared error (MSE):

$$\text{MSE} = \text{sum(squared\_diff)}/n, \text{ where n is the number of data points.}$$

By calculating the MSE, we can quantify the average squared difference between the predicted house prices and the actual house prices in the training set. This provides a measure of how well the linear regression model fits the training data.

Linear Regression- Methods to Get Best

Gradient descent is an optimization algorithm commonly used in machine learning, including in the training process of linear regression models. It iteratively updates the parameters of a model to minimize a cost function, such as the mean squared error (MSE). Here's an explanation of gradient descent:

Given the training set:

$$x = [x_1, x_2, ..., x_n] \text{ (predictor variable)}$$
$$y = [y_1, y_2, ..., y_n] \text{ (target variable)}$$

1. Initialization: Initialize the parameters of the model, such as the coefficients θ_0 and θ_1 in linear regression, with random or predefined values.

$$\theta_0 = 0 \text{ (initial value for intercept)}$$
$$\theta_1 = 0 \text{ (initial value for slope)}$$

2. **Define the cost function:** Choose a suitable cost function, such as MSE, that measures the error between the predicted values and the actual values.
   Define the cost function (MSE):
   $$J(\theta0, \theta1) = (1/2n) * \Sigma_i(y_i - (\theta0 + \theta1x_i))^2$$
3. **Calculate the gradient:** Compute the gradient of the cost function with respect to the model parameters. In linear regression, the gradient is calculated by taking the partial derivatives of the cost function with respect to θ0 and θ1.
   Perform gradient descent:
   Repeat until convergence {
   Compute the predicted values:
   $$\hat{y}_i = \theta0 + \theta1x_i\}$$
4. **Update the parameters:** Adjust the parameters in the direction that minimizes the cost function. This is done by taking steps proportional to the negative gradient. The learning rate (alpha) determines the step size.
   In each iteration, we update the parameters θ0 and θ1 by subtracting the learning rate α multiplied by the partial derivatives of the cost function with respect to θ0 and θ1. The learning rate α determines the step size of the parameter updates.
   The partial derivatives are given by:
   $$\partial J/\partial\theta0 = (1/n) * \Sigma_i(\hat{y}_i - y_i)$$
   $$\partial J/\partial\theta1 = (1/n) * \Sigma_i((\hat{y}_i - y_i) * x_i)$$
   Where n is the number of data points.
5. **Iterate until convergence:** Repeat steps 3 and 4 until the cost function converges or reaches a predefined threshold, indicating that the model has reached the optimal values of the parameters.

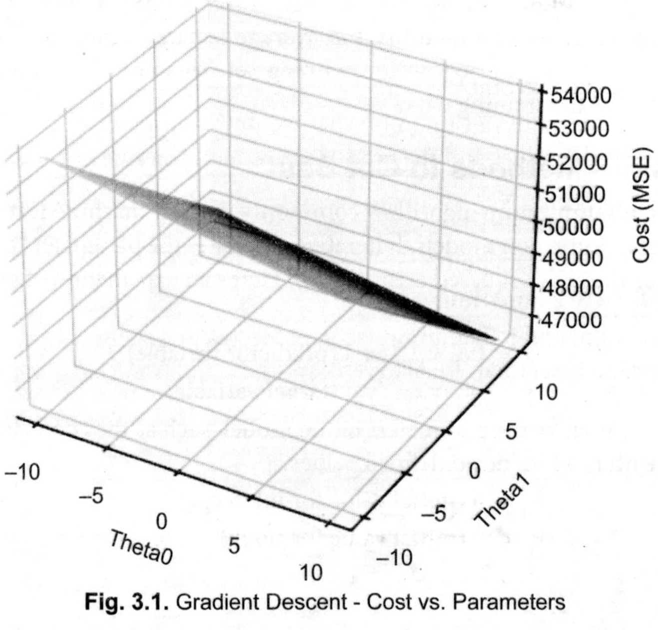

Fig. 3.1. Gradient Descent - Cost vs. Parameters

Gradient descent allows the model to iteratively update the parameters by following the negative gradient direction, gradually approaching the minimum of the cost function. The learning rate controls the size of each step taken during the parameter updates. It is essential to choose an appropriate learning rate to ensure convergence and avoid overshooting or slow convergence.

The process continues until the cost function is minimized or until a maximum number of iterations is reached. At the end of the iterations, the final parameters represent the optimal values that minimize the cost function, and the model is ready to make predictions.

Gradient descent is a powerful optimization algorithm and is widely used in training various machine learning models, including linear regression, logistic regression, and neural networks. It enables the models to learn from data and find the best parameters that fit the given training set.

Least Square Method

The Least Squares Method is a common technique used in linear regression to find the best-fitting line that minimizes the sum of the squared differences between the observed data points and the corresponding values predicted by the linear model. It aims to find the coefficients of the linear equation that provide the best fit to the data. The method is also known as the Ordinary Least Squares (OLS) method.

Here's how the Least Squares Method works in linear regression

Formulate the Linear Equation

Start with the general linear equation for a simple linear regression:

1. **Formulate the Linear Equation:**

   Start with the general linear equation for a simple linear regression:

   $$y = mx + b$$

   where:

   - y is the dependent variable (target),
   - x is the independent variable (feature),
   - m is the slope of the line,
   - b is the y-intercept

2. **Define the Objective Function:**

   The goal is to find the values of m and b that minimize the sum of the squared differences between the observed y values and the predicted y values from the linear equation:

   $$\text{Objective Function} = \sum_{i=1}^{n}(y_i - (mx_i + b))^2$$

   where n is the number of data points.

3. **Minimize the Objective Function:**

   To find the values of m and b that minimize the objective function, take the partial derivatives with respect to m and b, set them equal to zero, and solve for m and b. This leads to the following equations:

   $$m = \frac{n\sum_{i=1}^{n} x_i y_i - \sum_{i=1}^{n} x_i \sum_{i=1}^{n} y_i}{n\sum_{i=1}^{n} x_i^2 - \left(\sum_{i=1}^{n} x_i\right)^2}$$

$$b = \frac{\sum_{i=1}^{n} y_i - m\sum_{i=1}^{n} x_i}{n}$$

4. **Calculate the Coefficients:**
   Use the derived values of m and b to obtain the coefficients that define the best-fitting line for the linear regression equation.
5. **Evaluate the Model:**
   Once you have the coefficients, you can use them to make predictions for new data points and evaluate the model's performance using metrics like Mean Squared Error (MSE) or R-squared.

The Least Squares Method seeks to minimize the residual sum of squares, which represents the difference between the observed y values and the predicted y values from the linear equation. By finding the values of m and b that minimize this sum, the method finds the line that best represents the linear relationship between the variables.

Example: Suppose you have a dataset of pairs of x and y values representing a relationship between two variables. Your goal is to find the best-fitting line that minimizes the sum of squared differences between the observed y values and the predicted y values from the line.

Here's a step-by-step example using simple data:

1. **Sample Data:**
   Let's consider the following data points:

x	y
1	2
2	3
3	3.5
4	4.5
5	5

2. **Calculate Mean x and y:**
   Calculate the mean of x and y values:

$$\bar{x} = \frac{\bullet\ x}{n} \quad \text{and} \quad \bar{y} = \frac{\bullet\ y}{n}$$

   For our data, $\bar{x} = 3$ and $\bar{y} = 3.4$

3. **Calculate Slope (m):**
   Calculate the slope of the best-fitting line using the formula:

$$m = \frac{\sum((x-\bar{x})(y-\bar{y}))}{\sum((x-\bar{x})^2)}$$

   For our data:

$$m = \frac{(1-3)(2-3.4)+2-3)(3-3.4)+(3-3)(3.5-3.4)+(4-3(4.5-3.4)}{(1-3)^2+(2-3)^2+(3-3)^2+(4-3)^2+(5-3)^2}$$

$$m \approx 0.9$$

4. **Calculate Y-intercept (b):**
   Calculate the y-intercept of the best-fitting line using the formula:
   $$b = \bar{y} - m \cdot \bar{x}$$
   Using the mean values we calculated earlier:
   $$b = 3.4 - 0.9 \cdot 3$$
   $$b = 0.7$$
5. **Best-Fitting Line:**
   The equation of the best-fitting line is:
   $$y = mx + b$$
   Substituting the values of m and b:
   $$y = 0.9x + 0.7$$

Multiple Linear Regression

Linear regression for multiple features, also known as multiple linear regression, is an extension of simple linear regression that involves more than one predictor variable. It allows us to predict a target variable based on multiple input features.

Consider a dataset with m observations, where each observation has n predictor variables (x_1, x_2, ..., x_n) and a target variable (y). The goal is to find a linear relationship between the predictors and the target variable.

Mathematically, the hypothesis for multiple linear regression can be expressed as:

$$h\theta(x) = \theta0 + \theta1 * x1 + \theta2 * x2 + ... + \theta n * xn + \varepsilon$$

Here,

- hθ(x) represents the predicted value of the target variable y for a given set of predictor variables x.
- θ0, θ1, θ2, ..., θn are the coefficients or parameters that we need to estimate.

To estimate the optimal values of the coefficients, we use a cost function that measures the difference between the predicted values and the actual values. The mean squared error (MSE) is a commonly used cost function for multiple linear regression. It is defined as:

$$J(\theta0, \theta1, \theta2, ..., \theta n) = (1/(2 * m)) * \Sigma(h\theta(x_i) - y_i)^2$$

Here,

- m is the number of training examples (observations).
- $h\theta(x_i)$ is the predicted value for the i-th training example.
- y_i is the actual value for the i-th training example.

The goal is to minimize the cost function by finding the optimal values of the coefficients θ0, θ1, θ2, ..., θn.

To estimate the optimal coefficients, we can use the normal equation, which provides a closed-form solution. The normal equation is given by:

$$\theta = (X^TX)^{-1}X^Ty$$

Here,

- X is the feature matrix that contains the predictor variables x_1, x_2, ..., x_n. It has dimensions mx (n + 1), where the first column is filled with 1s to account for the intercept term.

- X^T is the transpose of X.
- y is the vector of the target variable values.
- $(X^TX)^{-1}$ is the inverse of the matrix product of X^T and X.

By calculating the values of θ using the normal equation, we obtain the optimal coefficients that minimize the mean squared error.

Let's take an example to demonstrate multiple linear regression:

Suppose we want to predict the price of a house based on three features: the area of the house in square feet, the number of bedrooms, and the age of the house in years. We have a training dataset that includes the following observations:

Area (x1)	Bedrooms (x2)	Age (x3)	Price (y)
2104	3	20	400
1600	3	15	330
2400	4	18	550
1416	2	25	260
...	...	...	...

Maximum likelihood estimation (MLE) provides a probabilistic interpretation of linear regression. It is a method used to estimate the parameters of a statistical model by maximizing the likelihood of the observed data.

In the case of linear regression, we assume that the target variable (y) follows a Gaussian (normal) distribution with a mean predicted by the linear regression model. The goal of MLE is to find the parameters (θ) that maximize the likelihood of observing the given data.

Let's denote the likelihood function as L(θ), which represents the probability of observing the given data points (X, Y) given the parameter values θ. In linear regression, assuming a Gaussian distribution, the likelihood function can be written as:

$$L(\theta) = P(Y|X; \theta) = \pi[1/\sqrt{(2\pi\sigma^2)}] * \exp[-(y - \theta^\wedge Tx)^2/(2\sigma^2)]$$

where:

Y represents the label vector

X represents the feature matrix

θ represents the parameter vector

σ^2 represents the variance of the Gaussian distribution

Model Assumption

- We assume that the target variable (y) follows a Gaussian (normal) distribution with a mean μ and constant variance σ^2. This assumption implies that the distribution of the target variable is symmetric around the mean.
- The relationship between the features (x) and the target variable is assumed to be linear. In other words, we assume that the target variable can be expressed as a linear combination of the features, with some error term ε. Mathematically, it is represented as: $y = \theta^\wedge Tx + \varepsilon$.
- Here, θ is the parameter vector, representing the coefficients that weigh each feature in the linear equation.

Likelihood Function

- The likelihood function represents the probability of observing the given data points (X, y) given the parameter values θ.
- Assuming independent and identically distributed (i.i.d.) samples, the likelihood function is the product of the individual likelihoods.
- In the case of linear regression, assuming a Gaussian distribution, the likelihood function for each data point can be represented using the probability density function (PDF) of the Gaussian distribution.
- The PDF of a Gaussian distribution is given by $P(y_i|\theta) = (1/\sqrt{(2\pi\sigma^2)}) * \exp[-(y_i - \theta^T x_i)^2/(2\sigma^2)]$, where y_i is the observed target value for the ith data point, x_i is the corresponding feature vector, $\theta^T x_i$ is the predicted value based on the linear regression model, and σ^2 is the variance.

Log-Likelihood Function

- To simplify calculations and avoid numerical issues associated with multiplying many small probabilities, it is common to work with the log-likelihood function.
- Taking the logarithm of the likelihood function, we get the log-likelihood function: $\log L(\theta) = \log P(y_1|\theta) + \log P(y_2|\theta) + ... + \log P(y_n|\theta)$.
- For the Gaussian distribution, the logarithm of the PDF simplifies the expression as $\log P(y_i|\theta) = \log(1/\sqrt{(2\pi\sigma^2)}) - (y_i - \theta^T x_i)^2/(2\sigma^2)$.
- Summing up the log-likelihood terms, we get $\log L(\theta) = \Sigma[\log(1/\sqrt{(2\pi\sigma^2)}) - (y_i - \theta^T x_i)^2/(2\sigma^2)]$.

Cost Function

- In MLE, we aim to maximize the likelihood function, which is equivalent to minimizing the negative log-likelihood.
- Thus, the cost function in MLE is the negative log-likelihood function, denoted as $J(\theta) = -\log L(\theta)$.
- The negative log-likelihood can be written as $J(\theta) = 0.5 * n * \log(2\pi\sigma^2) + 0.5 * \Sigma[(y_i - \theta^T x_i)^2/(\sigma^2)]$, where n is the number of data points.

Parameter Estimation

- The goal of MLE is to find the parameter values θ that maximize the likelihood (or minimize the cost).
- This is typically achieved using optimization algorithms such as gradient descent, where the cost function is iteratively minimized by adjusting the parameter values.
- Alternatively, closed-form solutions like the normal equation can be used to directly calculate the optimal parameter values.
- For linear regression, the normal equation is $\theta* = (X^TX)^{-1}X^Ty$, where X is the design matrix containing the feature values of the data points, X^T is the transpose of X, and y is the target vector.
- By solving the normal equation, we obtain the optimal parameter values that maximize the likelihood of the observed data.

In summary, MLE in linear regression involves assuming a Gaussian distribution for the target variable, expressing the likelihood function based on the assumed distribution, deriving the log-likelihood function, defining the cost function as the negative log-likelihood, and estimating the optimal parameter values that minimize the cost function using optimization algorithms or closed-form solutions.

The loss function is a critical piece for turning the model-fitting problem into an optimization problem. In the case of least-squares regression, we used a squared loss

$$l(\hat{y}, y) = (\hat{y} - y)^2 \qquad ...(1)$$

An alternative view on fitting a model is to think about a probabilistic procedure that might've given rise to the data. This probabilistic procedure would have parameters and then we can take the approach of trying to identify which parameters would assign the highest probability to the data that was observed. When we talk about probabilistic procedures that generate data given some parameters or covariates, we are really talking about conditional probability distributions.

Let's step away from regression for a minute and just talk about how we might think about a probabilistic procedure that generates data from a Gaussian distribution with a known variance but an unknown mean. Consider a set of data $\{yn\}_{n=1}^{N}$ where $yn \in R$ and we assume that they are all independently and identically distributed according to a Gaussian distribution with unknown mean μ and variance σ^2. We would write this as a conditional probability as

$$yn \mid \mu, \sigma^2 \sim N(yn \mid \mu, \sigma^2) \qquad ...(2)$$

The probability density function associate with this conditional distribution isthe familiar univariate Gaussian.

$$\Pr(y_n|\mu, \sigma^2) = \frac{1}{\sigma\sqrt{2\pi}} \exp\left\{-\frac{1}{2\sigma^2}(y_n - \mu)^2\right\} \qquad ...(3)$$

We have N i.i.d. data, however, and so we write the conditional distribution for all of them as a product

$$\Pr(\{y_n\}_{n=1}^{N}|\mu, \sigma^2) = \prod_{n=1}^{N} \frac{1}{\sigma\sqrt{2\pi}} \exp\left\{-\frac{1}{2\sigma^2}(y_n - \mu)^2\right\} \qquad ...(4)$$

This function, which we are here thinking of as being parameterized by μ is what we call the likelihood. When we maximize this with respect to μ, we are asking "what μ would assign the highest probability to the data we've seen?" This inductive criterion of selecting model parameters based on their ability to probabilistically explain the data is what we refer to as maximum likelihood estimation (MLE). Maximum likelihood estimation is a cornerstone of statistics and it has many wonderful properties that are out of scope for this course. At the end of the day, however, we can think of this as being a different (negative) loss function:

$$\mu^* = \mu^{MLE} = \arg\max_{\mu} \Pr(\{y_n\}_{n=1}^{N} | \mu, \sigma^2) = \prod_{n=1}^{N} \frac{1}{\sigma\sqrt{2\pi}} \exp\left\{-\frac{1}{2\sigma^2}(y_n - \mu)^2\right\} \qquad ...(5)$$

In practice, this isn't exactly the problem that we like to solve. Rather, we actually prefer to maximize the log likelihood because it turns all of our products into sums, which are easier to manipulate and differentiate, while preserving the location of the maximum. Also, when we take the product of many things that may be less than 1, the floating point numbers on our computer may become very close to zero and the maximization may not be numerically stable; taking the log makes those small positive numbers into better behaved negative numbers. As such, our (negative) loss function becomes

$$L(\mu) = \log \Pr(\{x_n\}_{n=1}^N \mid \mu, \sigma^2) = \sum_{n=1}^{N} \log\left(\frac{1}{\sigma\sqrt{2\pi}} \exp\left\{-\frac{1}{2\sigma^2}(y_n - \mu)^2\right\}\right) \quad ...(6)$$

$$= -N \log \sigma - \frac{N}{2}\log 2\pi - \frac{1}{2\sigma^2}\sum_{n=1}^{N}(y_n - \mu)^2 \quad ...(7)$$

Figure 1 shows the likelihood function $L(\mu)$ that arises from a small set of data. Note in particular how the vertical scale of the likelihood is very small; this is one reason we transform it with the natural logarithm. We can go on and find the maximum likelihood estimate of μ by following the same kind of procedure that we used for least squares regression: differentiate, set to zero, and solve for μ.

$$\frac{d}{d\propto} L(\propto) = \frac{1}{\sigma^2}\sum_{n=1}^{N}(y_n - \mu) \quad ...(8)$$

$$\frac{1}{\sigma^2}\sum_{n=1}^{N} y_n - \frac{N}{\sigma^2}\mu = 0 \quad ...(9)$$

$$\mu = \frac{1}{N}\sum_{n=1}^{N} y_n \quad ...(10)$$

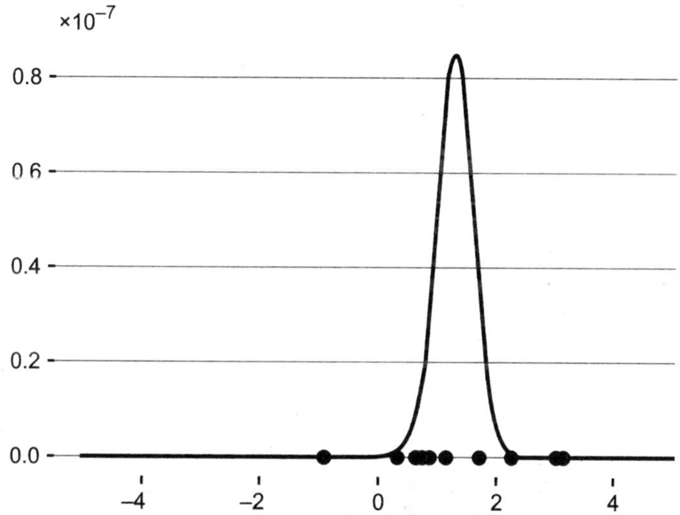

Figure 1: The black dots are ten (N = 10) data from a Gaussian distribution with σ2 = 1 and μ = 1.4. The red line is the likelihood as a function of μ. The maximum likelihood estimate is the peak of the red line. The red line is proportional to a Gaussian distribution but it is not generally true that likelihoods will have the same shape as the data distribution; this is a property that happens to arise when the location parameter is the quantity being estimated. Note also that the scale of the likelihood is tiny.

Unsurprisingly, the maximum likelihood estimate in this model (regardless of σ2) is the sample average of the data.

MLE Regression with Gaussian Noise

We now revisit the linear regression problem with a maximum likelihood approach. As in the previous lecture, we assume our data are tuples of the form $\{x_n, y_n\}_{n=1}^N$, where $x_n \in$ RD and $y_n \in$ R. Rather than having a least-squares loss function, however, we now have to construct an explicit model for the noise that lets us reason about the conditional probability of the label. That is, we're now going to say that our data arise from a process like

$$y = x^T w + \varepsilon \qquad ...(11)$$

where $\varepsilon \in R$ is a random variable capturing the noise. Just like we can construct different loss functions, we can think about different noise models for ε. Generalizing the previous section, a very natural idea is to say that this noise is from a zero-mean Gaussian distribution with variance σ2,

$$\varepsilon|\sigma^2 \sim N(\varepsilon|0, \sigma^2). \qquad ...(12)$$

Adding a constant to a Gaussian just has the effect of shifting its mean, so the resulting conditional probability distribution for our generative probabilistic process is

$$\Pr(y_n|x_n, w, \sigma^2) = \frac{1}{\sigma\sqrt{2\pi}} \exp\left\{-\frac{1}{2\sigma^2}(y_n - x_n^T w)^2\right\} \qquad ...(13)$$

This is very similar to Eq. 3, except now rather than conditioning on μ, we're conditioning on x_n and w. Those two quantities combine to form the mean of the Gaussian distribution on y_n. We denote the noise associated with the nth observation as ε_n and we will take these to be independent and identically distributed. This allows us to write the overall likelihood function as a product over these N terms

$$\Pr(\{y_n\}_{n=1}^N | \{x_n\}_{n=1}^N, w, \sigma^2) = \prod_{n=1}^N \frac{1}{\sigma\sqrt{2\pi}} \exp\left\{-\frac{1}{2\sigma^2}(y_n - x_n^T w)^2\right\} \qquad ...(14)$$

Again, this is a function of w, as that is the parameter we are seeking to fit to the data. In the previous lecture, we employed some more compact notation and aggregated the labels into a vector y and the features into a design matrix X. We do the same trick here, but with a new twist: we're going to turn this univariate Gaussian distribution into a multivariate Gaussian distribution with a diagonal covariance matrix. Recall that the PDF for a D-dimensional Gaussian distribution is

$$\Pr(z|\mu, \Sigma) = |\Sigma|^{-1/2} (2\pi)^{-D/2} \exp\left\{-\frac{1}{2}(z-\mu)^T \Sigma^{-1}(z-\mu)\right\} \qquad ...(15)$$

The covariance matrix Σ must be square, symmetric, and positive definite. When Σ is diagonal, the D dimensions are independent of each other. Putting our regression likelihood into this form we write:

$$\Pr(y|X, w, \sigma^2) = N(y|Xw, \sigma^2 I) = (2\sigma^2\pi)^{-N/2} \exp\left\{-\frac{1}{2\sigma^2}(Xw-y)^T(Xw-y)\right\} \qquad ...(16)$$

We can now think about how we'd maximize this with respect to w in order to find the maximum likelihood estimate. As in the simple Gaussian case, it is helpful to take the natural log first

$$\log \Pr(y|X, w, \sigma^2) = -\frac{N}{2}\log(2\sigma^2\pi) - \frac{1}{2\sigma^2}(Xw-y)^T(Xw-y) \qquad ...(17)$$

The additive term doesn't have a w. We are then left with the following optimization problem:

$$w^{MLE} = \arg\max_w \left\{-\frac{1}{2\sigma^2}(Xw-y)^T(Xw-y)\right\} \qquad ...(18)$$

The $1/2\sigma^2$ does not change the solution to this problem and of course could change the sign and make this maximization into a minimization

$$w^{MLE} = \arg\min_w (Xw-y)^T(Xw-y) \qquad ...(19)$$

This is exactly the same optimization problem that we solved for the least-squares linear regression! While itseems like the loss function view and the maximum likely hood view are different, this reveals that they are often the same under the hood: least squares can be interpreted as assuming Gaussian noise, and particular choices of likelihood can be interpreted directly as (usually exponentiated) loss functions

Fitting σ^2

One thing that is different about maximum likelihood, however, is that it gives us an additional parameter to play with that helps us reason about the predictive distribution. The predictive distribution is the distribution over the label, given parameters we have just fit. Rather than simply producing a single estimate, when we have a probabilistic model we can account for noise when we look at test data. That is, after finding w^{MLE} if we have a query input x_{pred} for which we don't know the y, we could compute a guess via $y_{pred} = x^T{}_{pred}\, w^{MLE}$, or we could actually construct a whole distribution

$$Pr(y_{pred}, w^{MLE}, \sigma^2) = N(y_{pred}|x^T_{pred}w^{MLE}, \sigma^2) \quad ...(20)$$

This sounds great, but σ^2 went away when we constructed the optimization problem for w. Why would it be any good? Well, it won't be any good — unless you fit it also. Fortunately, maximum likelihood estimation tells us how to do that one also, and we can start out by assuming that we've already computed w^{MLE}. We set up the problem the same way except we keep the additive term in Eq. 17

$$\sigma^{MLE} = \arg\max_{\sigma}\left\{-\frac{N}{2}\log(2\sigma^2\pi)-\frac{1}{2\sigma^2}(Xw^{MLE}-y)^T(Xw^{MLE}-y)\right\} \quad ...(21)$$

Solving this maximization problem is again just a question of differentiating and setting to zero:

$$\frac{\partial}{\partial\sigma^2}\left[-\frac{N}{2}\log\sigma^2-\frac{1}{2\sigma^2}(Xw^{MLE}-y)^T(Xw^{MLE}-y)\right] = 0 \quad ...(22)$$

$$-\frac{N}{2\sigma^2}+\frac{1}{2\sigma^4}(Xw^{MLE}-y)^T(Xw^{MLE}-y) = 0 \quad ...(23)$$

$$-N+\frac{1}{\sigma^2}(Xw^{MLE}-y)^T(Xw^{MLE}-y) = 0 \quad ...(24)$$

$$\sigma^2 = \frac{1}{N(Xw^{MLE}-y)^T(Xw^{MLE}-y)} \quad ...(25)$$

This is a satisfying result because it is just finding the sample average of the squared deviations between what w^{MLE} predicts and what the training data actually are. It feels exactly like what happens when you compute the maximum likelihood estimate of the variance of a univariate Gaussian distribution.

Linear Basis Function Models

In the linear regression model, we have a linear combination of the input features and parameters, as shown in equation (25):

$$\hat{y} = h_\theta(x) = \theta^T x \quad ...(1)$$

To model nonlinear relationships between the input features and the target output, we can generalize the linear model by introducing basis functions, as shown in equation (3.26):

$$\hat{y} = h_\theta(x) = \theta^T\phi(x) = \Sigma\theta_j\phi_j(x) \quad ...(2)$$

Here, $\phi_j(x)$ represents the jth basis function, and $\phi(x)$ is a vector of basis functions. The linear combination of the basis functions allows us to model nonlinear relationships between the inputs and the target output.

For example, equation (3)shows a set of quadratic basis functions:

$$\phi(x) = [1, x_1, x_2, x_1x_2, x_1^2, x_2^2] \quad ...(3)$$

Using these basis functions, we can model quadratic surfaces. Each basis function represents a different aspect or interaction between the input features.

Similarly, polynomial regression can be represented using basis functions, where $\phi_j(x) = \hat{x}_j$ for $j = 0, 1, ..., m$. Here, m is the order of the polynomial model.

In practice, implementing the model in equation (3.26) often involves pre-processing or feature extraction on the original data variables x. This allows us to express the extracted features in terms of the chosen basis functions. The choice of basis functions depends on the problem and the types of nonlinear relationships we want to capture.

By using appropriate basis functions, we can extend the linear regression model to handle nonlinear relationships between the input features and the target variable, providing more flexibility and accuracy in modeling real-world data.

Practice for Linear Regression

Before applying data to a machine learning algorithm, there are two practical issues that need to be addressed: feature scaling and learning rate selection.

Feature scaling is the process of ensuring that all features in the dataset have comparable numerical values. This is important because features with different scales can have a disproportionate impact on the learning algorithm. For example, if one feature ranges from 0 to 1 and another feature ranges from 0 to 1000, the latter feature may dominate the learning process. To avoid this, it is common practice to scale the features to a similar range, such as between 0 and 1 or using standardization (mean of 0 and standard deviation of 1). This ensures that all features contribute equally to the learning algorithm and helps improve convergence and performance.

The second issue is selecting an appropriate learning rate (α) for the learning algorithm. The learning rate determines the step size at each iteration of the learning algorithm and plays a crucial role in achieving convergence. If the learning rate is too small, the algorithm may take a long time to converge or get stuck in a local minimum. On the other hand, if the learning rate is too large, the algorithm may fail to converge or overshoot the optimal solution. Selecting an appropriate learning rate involves a trade-off between convergence speed and accuracy. It often requires experimentation and fine-tuning to find the optimal learning rate for a specific problem.

Addressing these practical issues, feature scaling and learning rate selection, can significantly impact the performance and convergence of machine learning algorithms. By scaling the features appropriately and choosing an optimal learning rate, we can improve the effectiveness and efficiency of the learning process.

Feature scaling is a process of transforming the numerical values of different features in a dataset to a common scale. The reason we do this is that features often have different scales and units, which can create issues when training machine learning models.

In unbalanced feature scaling, the input features have significantly different numerical ranges or scales. For example, one feature may have values in the range of 0-1, while another feature may have values in the range of 1000-10000. This unbalanced scaling can cause issues because features with larger scales can dominate the learning process and have a disproportionate impact on the algorithm's performance. The contour plot for unbalanced feature scaling shows elongated and distorted contours due to the difference in scales.

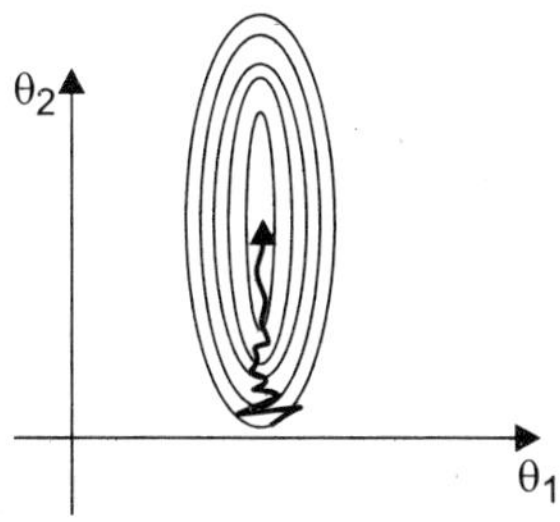

Fig. 3.2. Contour plots and converge path(red arrow lines) unbalanced feature scaling

On the other hand, balanced feature scaling aims to normalize the input features so that they have similar numerical ranges or scales. This is typically done using techniques like standardization or normalization. Standardization scales the features to have zero mean and unit variance, while normalization scales the features to a specific range, such as 0-1. By balancing the feature scales, the learning algorithm can effectively consider the contributions from each feature without any bias towards features with larger scales. The contour plot for balanced feature scaling shows more symmetric and well-proportioned contours.

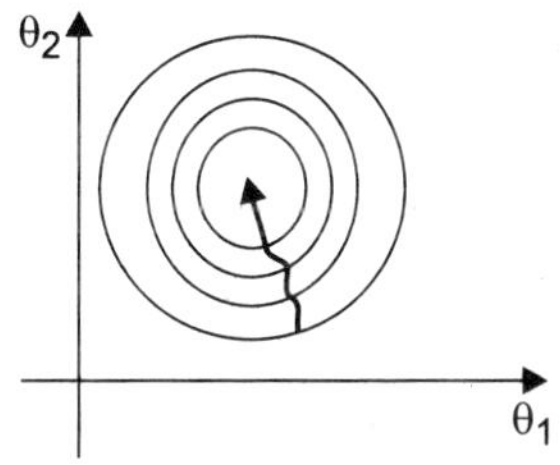

Fig. 3.3. Balanced Feature Scaling

For example, consider a dataset with two features: "age" and "income." The "age" feature ranges from 0 to 100, while the "income" feature ranges from 0 to 100,000. If we don't scale these features, the difference in their scales can lead to problems. Machine learning algorithms often rely on distance calculations or optimization techniques, and having features with different scales can cause one feature to dominate the others.

To address this issue, we apply feature scaling techniques. There are two common methods: normalization and standardization.

Normalization (min-max scaling): This method scales the values of a feature to a range between 0 and 1. It preserves the relative relationships between the data points. The formula for normalization is:

x_scaled = (x – min(x))/(max(x) – min(x))

Here, x is the original feature value, x_scaled is the scaled feature value, min(x) is the minimum value of the feature, and max(x) is the maximum value of the feature.

This formula ensures that the minimum value of the feature is transformed to 0, the maximum value is transformed to 1, and the rest of the values are scaled proportionally within the range. Normalization preserves the relative relationships between the data points and is suitable when the distribution of the data is not necessarily Gaussian.

One benefit of normalization is that it maintains the original range of the data, which can be useful if the range carries important information. It is also less affected by outliers compared to standardization. However, normalization does not handle outliers well, as they can disproportionately impact the scaling.

Standardization: This method transforms the values of a feature to have a mean of 0 and a standard deviation of 1. It assumes that the data follows a Gaussian distribution. The formula for standardization is:

x_scaled = (x - mean(x))/std(x)

Here, x is the original feature value, x_scaled is the scaled feature value, mean(x) is the mean of the feature, and std(x) is the standard deviation of the feature. Standardization centers the feature distribution around 0 and scales it by the standard deviation. It helps in making features comparable and ensures that they have a similar scale.

Standardization is useful when the data is normally distributed or when dealing with algorithms that assume Gaussian distribution or are sensitive to different scales. It handles outliers better than normalization because it uses the mean and standard deviation, which are robust to extreme values. However, standardization changes the range and can make interpretation of the scaled features more challenging.

The choice between normalization and standardization depends on the specific problem and the characteristics of the data. Normalization is often used when the distribution of the data is not necessarily Gaussian and we want to preserve the original range of values. Standardization is useful when we assume a Gaussian distribution or when dealing with algorithms that are sensitive to different scales.

By scaling the features, we ensure that they contribute equally during the learning process, prevent certain features from dominating based on their scale, and help the learning algorithm converge more effectively.

Choice of Learning Rate

The learning rate is a hyperparameter that determines the step size taken in each iteration of the gradient descent algorithm. It plays a crucial role in the convergence and performance of the model. Choosing an appropriate learning rate is essential to ensure effective learning and prevent issues such as slow convergence or overshooting the optimal solution.

Selecting the optimal learning rate is often an iterative process. Here are some guidelines to consider when choosing a learning rate:

- **Start with a small learning rate:** It is generally recommended to start with a small learning rate, such as 0.01 or 0.001. This helps ensure stability and prevents large updates that might cause the algorithm to diverge.
- **Gradually increase the learning rate:** If the initial learning rate is too small, the convergence might be slow. In such cases, you can try gradually increasing the learning rate to speed up convergence. However, it's important to monitor the performance and check for any signs of overshooting or instability.
- **Use learning rate schedules:** Instead of using a fixed learning rate throughout the training process, you can employ learning rate schedules that adapt the learning rate over time. Common approaches include reducing the learning rate after a certain number of iterations or based on a validation metric.

- **Monitor the training progress:** Keep an eye on the training progress and observe how the cost function decreases over iterations. If the cost function is not decreasing or fluctuating significantly, it might indicate that the learning rate is too high or too low. Adjust the learning rate accordingly.
- **Cross-validation:** Perform cross-validation experiments with different learning rates to evaluate the model's performance. This can help identify the learning rate that leads to the best generalization performance on unseen data.
- **Use optimization algorithms:** Instead of manually tuning the learning rate, you can utilize optimization algorithms that adaptively adjust the learning rate based on the gradients. Popular algorithms like Adam, RMSprop, or AdaGrad automatically adjust the learning rate during training.

It's important to note that the optimal learning rate can vary depending on the dataset, model complexity, and problem domain. Therefore, experimentation and fine-tuning are often necessary to find the best learning rate for a specific task.

The learning rate (denoted as α) determines the step size taken in each iteration of the gradient descent algorithm. It is multiplied by the gradient of the cost function with respect to the model parameters to update the parameter values. The general update equation for a parameter θ in gradient descent is:

In the gradient descent, the parameters are updated as

$$\theta_j = \theta_j - \alpha \frac{\partial}{\partial \theta_j} J(\theta)$$

The learning rate determines the size of the step taken in the direction of steepest descent. If the learning rate is too small, the updates will be too conservative, and the algorithm may converge slowly. On the other hand, if the learning rate is too large, the updates can overshoot the optimal solution, causing the algorithm to diverge.

Therefore, selecting an appropriate learning rate is crucial for efficient convergence. It should strike a balance between convergence speed and stability. If the learning rate is too high, the algorithm may fail to converge or oscillate around the optimal solution. If the learning rate is too low, the algorithm may converge very slowly.

The choice of the learning rate depends on various factors such as the problem domain, the characteristics of the data, and the complexity of the model. It often requires experimentation and tuning to find the optimal learning rate for a specific problem. Techniques like learning rate schedules, which adjust the learning rate over time, or adaptive optimization algorithms can help automatically adapt the learning rate during training.

The learning rate (α) is a hyperparameter that determines the step size in each iteration of gradient descent. Choosing an appropriate learning rate is crucial for the success of the optimization algorithm. To ensure that the cost function ($J(\theta)$) decreases after every iteration, we can plot the cost function against the number of iterations. This plot helps us assess whether gradient descent is working correctly. If the plot shows a gradual decrease in the cost function over iterations, it indicates that the algorithm is converging effectively. This is typically what we want to see, as shown in Fig. 6. However, if the plot exhibits oscillations or erratic behaviour, it suggests that the learning rate might be too large. In such cases, the cost function may not consistently decrease with each iteration, or it may fail to converge. This scenario is illustrated in Fig. 7(b) or (c). On the other hand, if the plot shows a very slow convergence or no significant decrease in the cost function, it indicates that the learning rate might be too small. In this case, the algorithm takes longer to converge, as shown in Fig. 7(a).To select a good learning rate value (α), it is common practice to try different values such as 0.001, 0.01, 0.1, 1, and so on. For each value, we plot the cost function versus the number of iterations and observe the shape of the plots. Based on these plots, we can identify a learning rate value that results in a smooth and consistent decrease in the cost function over iterations, indicating effective convergence.

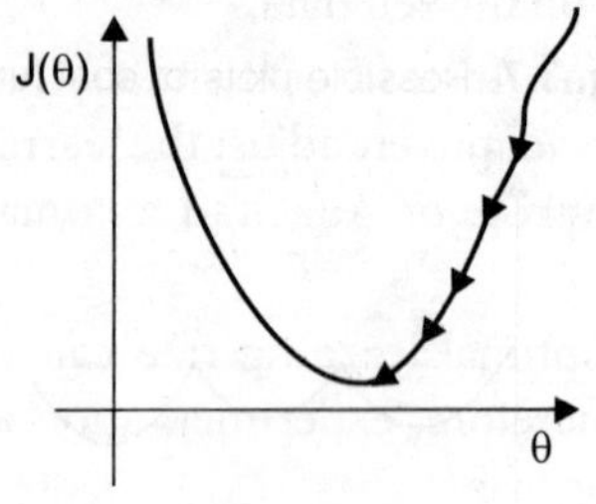

Fig. 3.4. An appropriate value for α, converge path

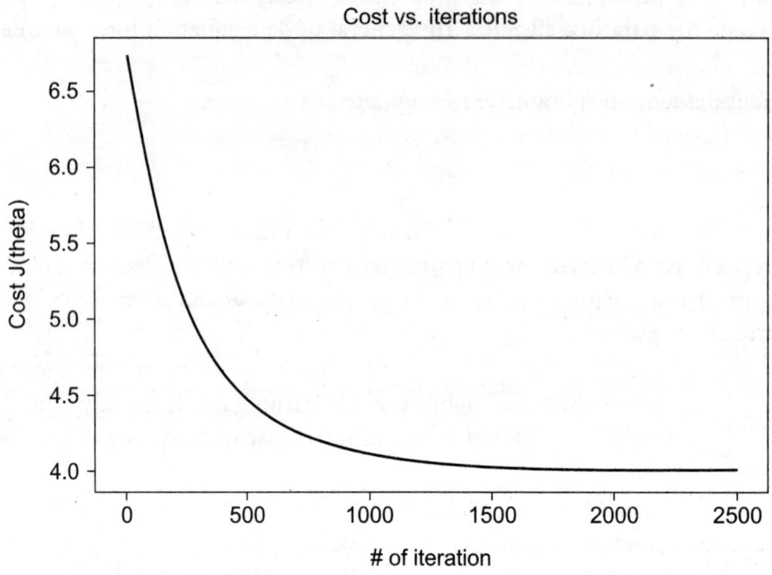

Fig. 3.5. Cost function vs no. of interations

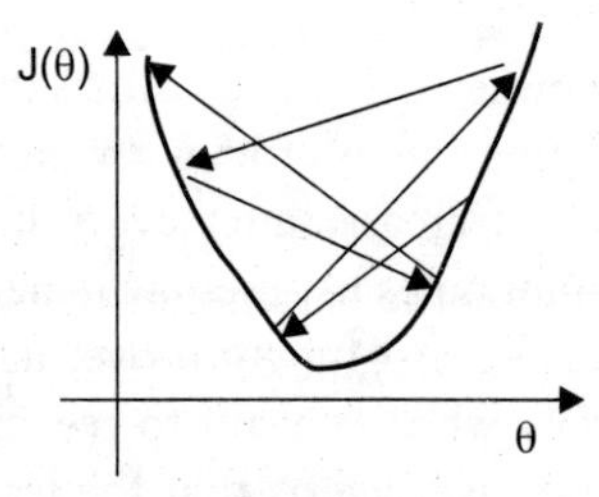

Fig. 3.6. Value of α is too large path does not converge

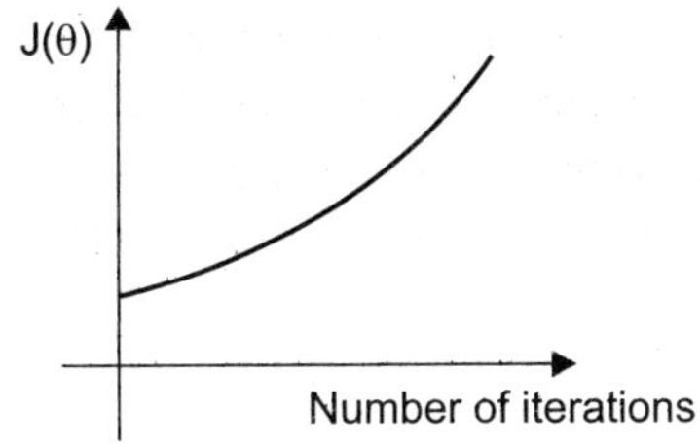

Fig. 3.7. Possible plots of cost function

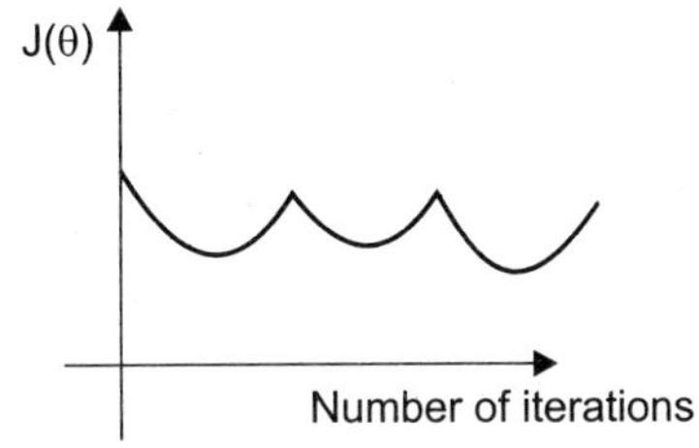

Fig. 3.8. Possible plots of cost function

In summary, choosing an appropriate learning rate is crucial for gradient descent. A too small learning rate leads to slow convergence, while a too large learning rate may prevent convergence or cause erratic behavior in the cost function. By experimenting with different learning rate values and observing the cost function versus the number of iterations plots, we can determine a suitable learning rate for our optimization task.

Implementation of Linear Regression in Python

Linear regression on a single feature

A step-by-step implementation of linear regression on a single feature in Python:

Load the dataset: Read the dataset containing the feature values (X) and the target values (y) into your program. You can use the pandas library to load the dataset from a CSV file. Use a library like pandas to read the dataset from a CSV file. Assume the dataset contains two columns: 'feature' and 'target'. Store the feature values in an array X and the target values in an array y for example:

Code:

```
import pandas as pd

data = pd.read_csv('your_dataset.csv')
X = data['feature'].values
y = data['target'].values
```

Initialize the model parameters: Initialize the parameters theta0 and theta1 with some random values. These parameters represent the intercept and slope of the linear regression line, respectively.

Code:

```
theta0 = 0.0
theta1 = 0.0
```

Define the cost function: Implement the cost function that calculates the mean squared error (MSE) between the predicted values and the actual values. The cost function measures the error between the predicted values and the actual values. In this case, we'll use the mean squared error (MSE) as the cost function. The formula for MSE is (1/2m) *

Code:

```
def compute_cost(X, y, theta0, theta1):
    m = len(X) # Number of training examples
    y_pred = theta0 + theta1 * X
    cost = np.sum((y_pred – y) ** 2)/(2 * m)
    return cost
```

Define the gradient descent algorithm: Implement the gradient descent algorithm to update the parameters theta0 and theta1 iteratively. Gradient descent is an optimization algorithm used to update the parameters theta0 and theta1 iteratively. In each iteration, the parameters are updated using the gradient of the cost function. The update equations are:

theta0 = theta0 – alpha * (1/m) * sum(y_pred – y)

theta1 = theta1 – alpha * (1/m) * sum((y_pred – y) * X)

Here, alpha is the learning rate, which controls the step size during parameter updates, and m is the number of training examples. The update equations are as follows:

Code:

```
def gradient_descent(X, y, theta0, theta1, alpha, num_iterations):
    m = len(X) # Number of training examples
    costs = [] # List to store the cost values

    for _ in range(num_iterations):
        y_pred = theta0 + theta1 * X
        theta0 = alpha * np.sum(y_pred – y)/m
        theta1 = alpha * np.sum((y_pred – y) * X)/m
        cost = compute_cost(X, y, theta0, theta1)
        costs.append(cost)

    return theta0, theta1, costs
```

Specify the hyperparameters: Choose the hyperparameters for the gradient descent algorithm, such as the learning rate (alpha) and the number of iterations. Choose the hyperparameters for the gradient descent algorithm. The learning rate (alpha) determines how fast the algorithm converges, and the number of iterations determines how many times the algorithm updates the parameters.

Code:

```
alpha = 0.01
num_iterations = 1000
```

Run the gradient descent algorithm: Call the gradient_descent function with the dataset, initial parameters, and hyperparameters to obtain the optimized values of theta0, theta1, and the cost values at each iteration. The function iterates over the specified number of iterations, updating the parameters and calculating the cost at each step.

Code:

```
theta0, theta1, costs = gradient_descent(X, y, theta0, theta1, alpha, num_iterations)
```

Plot the cost function: Plot the cost values against the number of iterations to visualize the convergence of the gradient descent algorithm. Visualize the convergence of the gradient descent algorithm by plotting the cost values against the number of iterations. This plot shows how the cost decreases over time, indicating the progress of the optimization process. If the cost decreases steadily, it suggests that the algorithm is working correctly.

Code:

```
plt.plot(range(num_iterations), costs)
plt.xlabel('Number of Iterations')
plt.ylabel('Cost')
plt.title('Cost vs. Number of Iterations')
plt.show()
```

Plot the linear regression line: Finally, plot the scatter plot of the data points and overlay the linear regression line represented by the parameters theta0 and theta1. Finally, plot the scatter plot of the data points to visualize the relationship between the feature and the target. Overlay the linear regression line on the scatter plot using the optimized values of theta0 and theta1. The line represents the best fit line that minimizes the overall error between the predicted and actual values.

Code:

```
plt.scatter(X, y)
plt.plot(X, theta0 + theta1 * X, color='red')
plt.xlabel('Feature')
plt.ylabel('Target')
plt.title('Linear Regression')
plt.show()
```

Linear Regression on Multiple Features

Load the dataset: Use a library like pandas to read the dataset from a CSV file. Assume the dataset contains multiple columns, including the features and the target variable. Store the feature values in a matrix X and the target values in an array y.

Code:

```
import pandas as pd

# Load the dataset from a CSV file
data = pd.read_csv('dataset.csv')

# Extract the feature matrix X and target variable y
X = data.drop('target', axis=1).values
y = data['target'].values
```

Feature scaling: It is often beneficial to scale the features to ensure they are on a similar scale. This can be done using techniques like standardization (subtracting the mean and dividing by the standard deviation) or normalization (scaling the values between a specified range). Scaling helps in achieving faster convergence during gradient descent.

Code:

```
from sklearn.preprocessing import StandardScaler

# Initialize the StandardScaler
scaler = StandardScaler()

# Scale the feature matrix X
X_scaled = scaler.fit_transform(X)
```

Initialize the model parameters: Initialize the parameter vector theta with initial values. The parameter vector represents the coefficients for each feature in the linear regression equation.

Code:

```
import numpy as np

# Initialize the parameter vector theta
theta = np.zeros(X_scaled.shape[1] + 1)  # Add one for the intercept term
```

Define the cost function: The cost function measures the error between the predicted values and the actual values. In the case of multiple features, the cost function is usually the mean squared error (MSE) or the mean squared error with regularization (MSE with L1 or L2 regularization). The cost function formula is (1/2m) * sum((X.dot(theta) - y)^2), where X is the feature matrix, theta is the parameter vector, y is the target values, and m is the number of training examples.

Code:

```
def cost_function(X, y, theta):
    m = len(y)  # Number of training examples
    predictions = X.dot(theta)
    error = predictions - y
    cost = (1/(2 * m)) * np.sum(error ** 2)
    return cost
```

Define the gradient descent algorithm: Gradient descent is an optimization algorithm used to update the parameters theta iteratively. In each iteration, the parameters are updated using the gradient of the cost function. The update equation is: theta = theta - alpha * (1/m) * X.T.dot(X.dot(theta) - y), where alpha is the learning rate, m is the number of training examples, X.T is the transpose of the feature matrix X, X.dot(theta) represents the predicted values, and X.dot(theta) - y represents the error.

Code:

```
def gradient_descent(X, y, theta, alpha, num_iterations):
    m = len(y)  # Number of training examples
    costs = []  # To store the cost values at each iteration
```

```
for i in range(num_iterations):
    predictions = X.dot(theta)
    error = predictions - y
    gradient = (1/m) * X.T.dot(error)
    theta = theta – alpha * gradient
    cost = cost_function(X, y, theta)
    costs.append(cost)

return theta, costs
```

Specify the hyperparameters: Choose the hyperparameters for the gradient descent algorithm. The learning rate (alpha) determines how fast the algorithm converges, and the number of iterations determines how many times the algorithm updates the parameters.

Code:

```
learning_rate = 0.01
num_iterations = 1000
```

Run the gradient descent algorithm: Call the gradient_descent function with the feature matrix X, target values y, initial parameters theta, and hyperparameters to obtain the optimized values of theta and the cost values at each iteration. The function iterates over the specified number of iterations, updating the parameters and calculating the cost at each step.

Code:

```
# Add a column of ones for the intercept term
X_scaled_with_intercept = np.column_stack((np.ones(X_scaled.shape[0]), X_scaled))

# Run gradient descent to obtain optimized theta and cost values
theta_optimized, cost_values = gradient_descent(X_scaled_with_intercept, y, theta, learning_rate,
num_iterations)
```

Plot the cost function: Visualize the convergence of the gradient descent algorithm by plotting the cost values against the number of iterations. This plot shows how the cost decreases over time, indicating the progress of the optimization process. If the cost decreases steadily, it suggests that the algorithm is working correctly.

Code:

```
import matplotlib.pyplot as plt

# Plot the cost values against the number of iterations
plt.plot(range(num_iterations), cost_values)
plt.xlabel('Number of Iterations')
plt.ylabel('Cost Function')
plt.title('Cost Function vs. Number of Iterations')
plt.show()
```

Make predictions: Once the parameters theta are optimized, you can use them to make predictions on new, unseen data. Multiply the feature matrix of the new data by the optimized theta to obtain the predicted target values.

Code:

```
# Example prediction on new, unseen data
new_data = np.array([[1, 2, 3], [4, 5, 6]]) # Replace with your own data
new_data_scaled = scaler.transform(new_data)
new_data_scaled_with_intercept = np.column_stack((np.ones(new_data_scaled.shape[0]), new_
data_scaled))
predictions = new_data_scaled_with_intercept.dot(theta_optimized)
```

By following these steps, you can implement linear regression on multiple features using gradient descent. Adjusting the learning rate, the number of iterations, and considering feature scaling can help improve the performance of the algorithm and find the optimal values of the parameters for your dataset.

Review Questions

Multiple Choice Questions

Q.1. What is the primary objective of linear regression?

(*a*) Minimize the sum of squared errors
(*b*) Maximize the sum of squared errors
(*c*) Minimize the sum of absolute errors
(*d*) Maximize the sum of absolute errors

Q.2. Which of the following techniques is used to find the best-fitting line in linear regression?

(*a*) Least squares method
(*b*) Gradient descent
(*c*) Normal equation
(*d*) All of the above

Q.3. In a simple linear regression model, if the coefficient of determination (R-squared) is 0.75, what does it indicate?

(*a*) 75% of the variability in the dependent variable is explained by the independent variable.
(*b*) 25% of the variability in the dependent variable is explained by the independent variable.
(*c*) The model is overfitting.
(*d*) The model is underfitting.

Q.4. Which of the following is the equation of a simple linear regression model?

(*a*) y = mx + b
(*b*) y = mx2 + b
(*c*) y = ax + b
(*d*) y = ax2 + b

Q.5. What does the slope coefficient (m) represent in a linear regression model?

(*a*) Intercept of the line
(*b*) Angle of inclination of the line
(*c*) Rate of change in the dependent variable for a one-unit change in the independent variable
(*d*) Rate of change in the independent variable for a one-unit change in the dependent variable

Q.6. In linear regression, what is the purpose of residual analysis?

(*a*) To determine the coefficients of the model
(*b*) To check the linearity assumption
(*c*) To assess the goodness of fit of the model
(*d*) To identify influential data points and outliers

Q.7. Which of the following assumptions is not required for linear regression?

(*a*) Linearity
(*b*) Independence of errors
(*c*) Homoscedasticity
(*d*) Multicollinearity

Q.8. Which method is used to evaluate the performance of a linear regression model on unseen data?

(*a*) R-squared
(*b*) Mean absolute error (MAE)
(*c*) Root mean squared error (RMSE)
(*d*) All of the above

Q.9. In multiple linear regression, what does the coefficient of determination (R-squared) measure?

(*a*) The proportion of variability explained by the model
(*b*) The correlation between independent variables
(*c*) The significance of coefficients
(*d*) The standard error of the regression coefficients

Q.10. Which technique can be used to deal with multicollinearity in linear regression?

(*a*) Feature scaling
(*b*) Principal component analysis (PCA)
(*c*) Regularization methods like Ridge or Lasso regression
(*d*) Residual analysis

Answers

1. (*a*) 2. (*d*) 3. (*a*) 4. (*c*) 5. (*c*) 6. (*d*) 7. (*d*) 8. (*d*) 9. (*a*)
10. (*c*)

Unsolved Questions

1. Define linear regression and explain its primary objective in the context of machine learning.
2. What are the assumptions of linear regression, and why is it important to validate these assumptions?
3. Describe the difference between simple linear regression and multiple linear regression.
4. Provide an example scenario where simple linear regression would be an appropriate modeling choice.
5. Discuss the metrics used for evaluating the performance of a linear regression model.
6. Explain the significance of the coefficient of determination (R-squared) in model evaluation.
7. Why might feature scaling be important in linear regression, and what are common methods for feature scaling?
8. Discuss the impact of outliers on linear regression models and potential strategies for handling them.

Fill in the Blanks

1. Linear regression aims to establish a __________ relationship between one or more independent variables and a dependent variable.
2. In the equation y=mx+b, the term m represents the __________ of the regression line.
3. The coefficient of determination, also known as R-squared, measures the proportion of the variance in the dependent variable that is __________ by the independent variables.
4. Feature scaling methods, such as __________, can be applied to ensure that all variables contribute equally to the linear regression model.
5. Simple linear regression involves predicting a dependent variable using only __________ independent variable.

EXERCISE

1. You run gradient descent for 30 iterations with $\alpha = 0.1$ and compute $j(\theta)$ for each iteration. You find that the value of $j(\theta)$ decreases slowly and is still decreasing after 15 iterations. Based on this, which of the following conclusions seems most plausible?
   (a) $\alpha = 0.1$ is an effective choice of learning rate.
   (b) It would be more promising to try a larger value of α (say $\alpha = 0.5$)
   (c) Rather than use the current value of α, it would be more promising to try a smaller value of α (say $\alpha = 0.05$)
2. Suppose you have m = 100 training examples with n = 5 features and would learn a linear regression

model to directly fit the dataset. According to the notations in this chapter, what are the dimensions of θ, X, and Y?

3. In this exercise, you are asked to generate an artificial dataset based on a linear model, and then learn the model using gradient descent. Specifically,
    1. Generate 100 data examples (x(i), y(i)), i = 1, 2, ..., 100, which are randomly drawn from the model y = a + bx + N(0, 1) where a and b are constants (say a = 1, b = 2), $0 \le x \le 2$, N(0, 1) is a random number of Gaussian distribution with mean = 0 and variance = 1. Plot a 2D scatterplot for your generated data examples. Please note that sampling on x should be randomly rather than uniformly.
    2. Learn a linear regression model y = θ0 + θ1x to fit the generated examples. Compare the results (θ0, θ1) with the pre-defined model parameters (a, b). Plot the fitted line along with the data examples, and the cost function versus iteration index.
4. In this exercise, you are asked to generate an artificial dataset based on a nonlinear model, and then learn the model using gradient descent. Specifically,
    1. Generate 100 data examples (x(i), y(i)), i = 1, 2, ..., 100, which are randomly drawn from the model $y = a + bx + cx^2 + dx^3 + ex^4 + 0.5\,N(0, 1)$ where a, b, c, d, and e are constants (say a = 1, b = 2, c = 1.5, d = 3, e = 1), $0 \le x \le 1$, N(0,1) is a random number of Gaussian distribution with mean=0 and variance=1. Plot a 2D scatterplot for your generated data examples. Please note that sampling on x should be randomly rather than uniformly.
    2. Learn a linear regression model y = θ0 + θ1x + θ2x2 + θ3x3 + θ4x4 to fit the generated examples. Compare the results (θ0, θ1, θ2, θ3, θ4) with the pre-defined model parameters (a, b, c, d, e). Plot the fitted line along with the data examples, and the cost function versus iteration index.

❑❑❑

4

(Logistic Regression)

CLASSIFICATION

In classification tasks, the target variable is qualitative or categorical, meaning it takes on discrete values representing different classes or categories. The goal of classification is to assign an input vector x to one of the K discrete categories or classes, denoted as Ck, where k = 1, 2, ..., K. The classification function maps the input data examples to these categories based on their common characteristics. When dealing with binary classification, where there are only two classes (C1 and C2), the label variable y can be encoded as binary values, such as $y \in \{0, 1\}$. For example, y = 0 can represent class C1, and y = 1 can represent class C2.

In multi-class classification tasks, the label variable y is typically represented using integers or an m-bit one-hot code. For m-class classification, the label y can take on m different values, each representing a distinct class. One-hot encoding is a common approach where each class is represented by a binary vector of length m, with a value of 1 in the corresponding class index and 0s elsewhere. This one-hot encoding allows for efficient representation and handling of categorical labels in machine learning algorithms. The classification process involves dividing the input space into decision regions, where each region corresponds to a specific class. The decision boundaries or decision surfaces separate these regions and determine how the input vectors are assigned to different classes. For instance, if we have K=5 classes, then the label y for class 3 would be y = [0, 0, 1, 0, 0]T.

In summary, classification is the task of assigning input vectors to discrete categories or classes, with the label variable y representing the class membership. Binary classification uses binary encoding (0 or 1) for representing the classes, while multi-class classification often employs integer labels or one-hot encoding for representing multiple classes.

Input (X)	Categorical label or class (y)
Email	y = 0 (not spam), y = 1 (spam)
Online Transaction	y = 0 (not fraudulent), y = 1 (fraudulent)
Tumor	y = 0 (benign), y = 1 (malignant)

Logistic Regression

Logistic regression is indeed a classification algorithm used to assign observations to discrete classes. While linear regression is used for predicting continuous numerical values, logistic regression is specifically designed for binary or multi-class classification problems. Logistic regression is a type of regression analysis used to model the probability of a binary outcome. It is commonly used for classification tasks in machine learning. Logistic regression is widely used in various fields, including the social and natural sciences, as well as in natural language processing (NLP) and machine learning. In the context of NLP, logistic regression serves as a fundamental and commonly used supervised machine learning algorithm for classification tasks. It is often used as a baseline model for text classification, sentiment analysis, spam detection, and other NLP tasks. The simplicity and interpretability of logistic regression make it a popular choice for these applications.

Logistic regression also has a close relationship with neural networks, particularly with single-layer neural networks known as perceptron's. In fact, logistic regression can be viewed as a simplified version of a neural network with a single sigmoid activation function. This connection highlights the underlying principles and concepts shared between logistic regression and neural networks.

Furthermore, logistic regression can serve as a building block or component within more complex machine learning models. For example, in deep learning architectures, logistic regression may be used as an output layer for binary or multi-class classification tasks. It provides a probabilistic interpretation of the model's predictions and can be trained using gradient-based optimization algorithms.

The main difference between linear regression and logistic regression lies in the nature of the predictions they make.

Linear regression is used for predicting a continuous numerical value, such as predicting the test score of a student on a scale of 0 to 100. The model learns a linear relationship between the input variables (e.g., time spent studying) and the output variable (e.g., test score) and provides a continuous range of predictions. Linear regression aims to minimize the difference between the predicted values and the actual values by fitting a straight line to the data. linear regression is suitable for predicting continuous numerical values.

On the other hand, logistic regression is used for predicting a categorical outcome or making binary classifications, such as determining whether a student passed or failed the exam. The model learns the probability of belonging to a certain class based on the input variables. Logistic regression uses the logistic sigmoid function to map the output of the linear equation to a probability value between 0 and 1. If the probability is above a certain threshold (e.g., 0.5), the observation is classified as one class (e.g., passed), and if it is below the threshold, it is classified as the other class (e.g., failed). Logistic regression allows us to interpret the predicted probabilities as the likelihood of belonging to a particular class. logistic regression is more appropriate for binary classification tasks and providing probability scores for categorical outcomes.

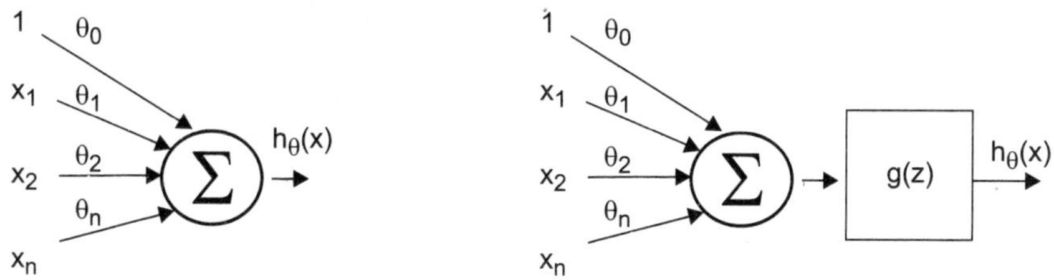

(a) Linear regression (b) Logistic regression

Fig. 4.1. Comparison between linear regression and logistic regression

Overall, logistic regression plays a crucial role in both traditional statistical analysis and modern machine learning, serving as a fundamental technique for classification problems and establishing connections to more advanced models like neural networks.

The key difference lies in the transformation of the output. In logistic regression, the output of the linear combination of input features and model parameters is passed through the logistic sigmoid function (also known as the logistic function). This sigmoid function maps the continuous output to a probability value between 0 and 1, representing the likelihood of belonging to a certain class.

For binary classification, the logistic regression model predicts the probability of belonging to the positive class (e.g., class 1), and the probability of belonging to the negative class (e.g., class 0) can be obtained as 1 minus the predicted probability. By applying a threshold (usually 0.5), observations with predicted probabilities above the threshold are classified as the positive class, and those below the threshold are classified as the negative class.

For multi-class classification, logistic regression can be extended using techniques such as one-vs-rest or softmax regression. One-vs-rest creates multiple binary logistic regression models, each trained to distinguish one class from the rest. Softmax regression, on the other hand, generalizes logistic regression to handle multiple classes directly by applying the softmax function to calculate the probabilities for each class.

Logistic regression is named for the function used at the core of the method, the logistic function. The logistic function, also called the sigmoid function was developed by statisticians to describe properties of population growth in ecology, rising quickly and maxing out at the carrying capacity of the environment. It's an S-shaped curve that can take any real-valued number and map it into a value between 0 and 1, but never exactly at those limits.

$$\frac{1}{1+e^{-\text{value}}} \quad \text{...(1)}$$

where e is the base of the natural logarithms (Euler's number or the EXP () function in your spreadsheet) and value is the actual numerical value that you want to transform. Below is a plot of the numbers between –5 and 5 transformed into the range 0 and 1 using the logistic function.

Now that we know what the logistic function is, let's see how it is used in logistic regression.

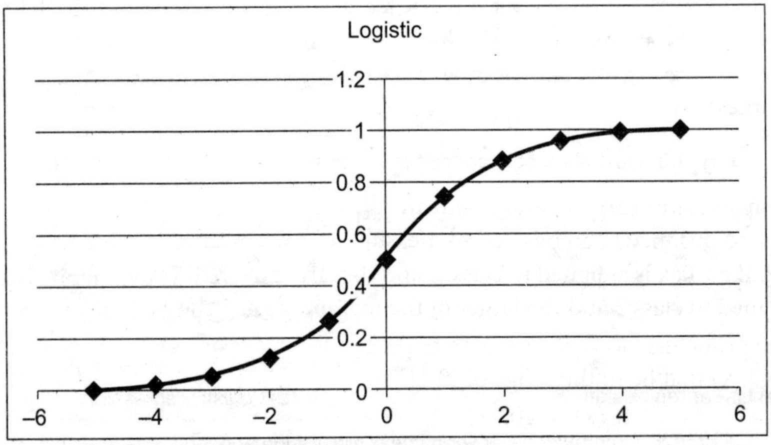

Fig. 4.2. Logistic Function

The sigmoid function has a characteristic S-shaped curve that maps any real-valued number to a value between 0 and 1. As the input value of z increases, the sigmoid function approaches 1, indicating a higher probability of the positive class. Conversely, as the input value of z decreases, the sigmoid function approaches 0, indicating a higher probability of the negative class.

In logistic regression, the goal is to find the optimal weights that maximize the likelihood of the observed data. This is achieved by minimizing the logistic loss function, which quantifies the difference between the predicted probabilities and the actual class labels. The logistic loss function is derived from the sigmoid function and is specifically designed for binary classification tasks.

Logistic Regression Model

If the input vector space in a 2-class classification problem is linearly separable, there exists a linear decision boundary $\theta^T x = 0$, where θ and x are the column vectors, defined as

$$\theta = \begin{bmatrix} \theta_0 \\ \theta_1 \\ \vdots \\ \theta_n \end{bmatrix} \in R^{(n+1)\times 1}, \qquad x = \begin{bmatrix} 1 \\ x_1 \\ \vdots \\ x_n \end{bmatrix} \in R^{(n+1)\times 1}$$

where x_j, j = 1, 2, ..., n is the jth feature. We can define a dummy feature $x_0 = 1$. θ is the parameter vector.

We consider n = 2, and let $q^T x = 0$ be the decision boundary, shown in Fig. 3. An input vector x is assigned to one class (say class 2) if $\theta^T x \geq 0$ and to another class (say class1) otherwise. It can be proven that the value of $\theta^T x$ gives a signed measure of the perpendicular distance r of any point x from the decision boundary

$$r = \frac{\theta^T x}{\sqrt{\theta_1^2 + 0_2^2}} \qquad ...(2)$$

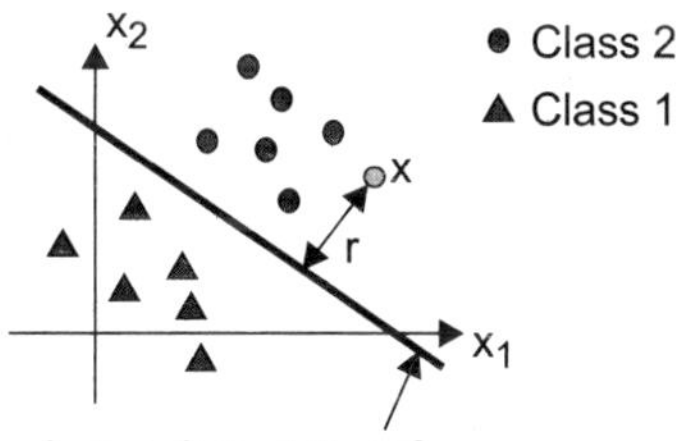

Fig. 4.3. Illustration of linear decision boundary in two class classification.

If data examples are linearly separable and an optimal decision boundary has been found, illustrated in Fig. 3, the signed distance r can be used to measure or predict how likely a data example comes from class 1 or class 2. If r > 0, x is assigned to class 2, and the larger the r, the more likely x comes from class 2. If r < 0, x is assigned to class 1 and the larger of the magnitude of r, the more likely x comes from class 1. For classification problems, however, we wish to predict discrete class labels, or more generally posterior probabilities p(Ck|x) that lie in the range of [0,1].

$$h_\theta(x) = g(\theta^T x) \qquad ...(3)$$

to map the signed distance r to a probabilistic space [0, 1], and thus $h_\theta(x)$ can be interpreted as the probability of x belonging to a class. It is known as an activation function. For example, one of the good candidates of activation function is sigmoid function equation 1.

$$g(z) = \frac{1}{1+e^{-z}} \quad ...(4)$$

When z = 0, g(z) is equal to 0.5. When z departures from zero to the positive side, g(z) quickly approaches 1. When z moves from zero to the negative side, g(z) will quickly approach 0.

Thus, based on the model (3), x would be predicted as class 1 if $h_\theta(x) < 0.5$ (i.e., $\theta^T x < 0$), and as class 2 if $h_\theta(x) \geq 0.5$ (i.e., $\theta^T x > 0$). The decision boundary is defined by $h_\theta(x) = 0.5$, i.e.,

$$\theta^T x = g^{-1}(0.5) = 0. \quad ...(5)$$

The hypothesis $h_\theta(x) = g(\theta^T x)$ can be interpreted as the probability of x belonging to one of the classes (say class 2), and thus the probability of x belonging to another class (say class 1) is $1 - h_\theta(x)$.

Form the figure 1 the output of the linear combination is

$$z = \theta_0 + \theta_1 x_1 + \theta_2 x_2 + ... + \theta_n xn = \theta^T x \quad ...(6)$$

Given x and θ, the hypothesis for the logistic regression, which is the output of logistic regression, is

$$h_\theta(x) = g(z) = g(\theta^T x) = \frac{1}{1+e^{-\theta^T x}} \quad ...(7)$$

$h_\theta(x)$ can be interpreted as the estimated probability of y = 1, denoted by P[y = 1 | x; θ]. Class 1 is indicated by y = 0, and class 2 is indicated by y = 1. Thus, the posterior probability $p(C2|x) = h_\theta(x)$ and $p(C1|x) = 1 - h_\theta(x)$.

Intuitively, the prediction of y can be performed as

$$\hat{y} = \{1 h_\theta(x) \geq 0.5, 0\ h_\theta(x) < 0.5 \quad ...(8)$$

The decision boundary separating the two classes can be determined by setting the weighted sum of inputs to 0, i.e., $\theta^T x = 0$. If the input vector space is nonlinear separable (Fig.5(b) and (c) in Example 3.2), we can generalize (4.5) to a nonlinear function of x.

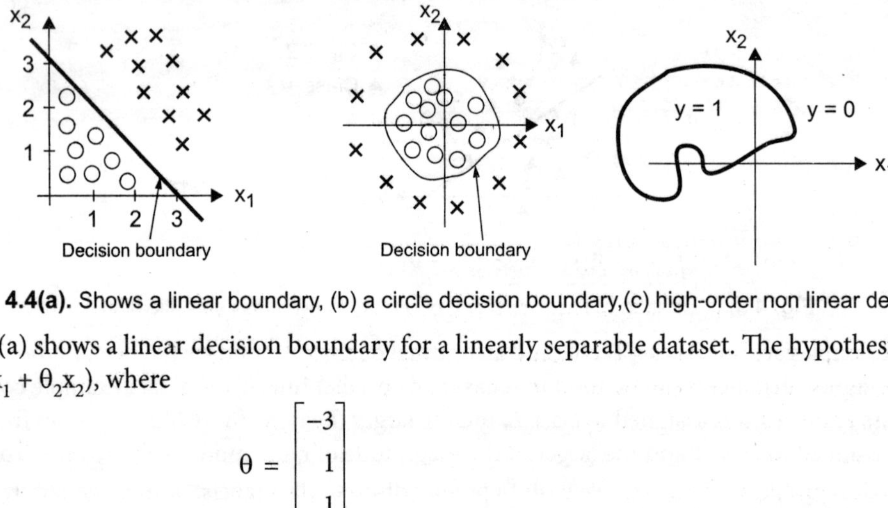

Fig. 4.4(a). Shows a linear boundary, (b) a circle decision boundary,(c) high-order non linear decision

Fig.4(a) shows a linear decision boundary for a linearly separable dataset. The hypothesis is $h_\theta(x) = g(\theta_0 + \theta_1 x_1 + \theta_2 x_2)$, where

$$\theta = \begin{bmatrix} -3 \\ 1 \\ 1 \end{bmatrix}$$

We will predict y = 1 if $\theta_0 + \theta_1 x_1 + \theta_2 x_2 \geq 0$, and predict y = 0 if $\theta_0 + \theta_1 x_1 + \theta_2 x_2 < 0$. Thus, the decision boundary is the line $\theta_0 + \theta_1 x_1 + \theta_2 x_2 = 0$, i.e., $-3 + x_1 + x_2 = 0$ for this case. Any point located right-up the line will be classified as y=1, and a point below the line will be classified as y=0. The hypothesis values on the decision boundary is equal to 0.5.

Fig.4(b) shows a non-linear decision boundary when the data set is not linearly separable. The hypothesis $h_\theta(x) = g(\theta_0 + \theta_1 x_1 + \theta_2 x_2 + \theta_3 x_1^2 + \theta_4 x_2^2)$, with $\theta = [-1, 0, 0, 1, 1]T$. The decision boundary is $\theta_0 + \theta_1 x_1 + \theta_2 x_2 + \theta_3 x_1^2 + \theta_4 x_2^2 = 0$, i.e., $x_1^2 + x_2^2 = 1$. The model predicts $y = 1$ if $x_1^2 + x_2^2 \geq 1$, and predicts $y = 0$ if otherwise.

Fig.4(c) shows a more complicated decision boundary, based on the hypothesis $h_\theta(x) = g(\theta_0 + \theta_1 x_1 + \theta_2 x_2 + \theta_3 x_1^2 + \theta_4 x_2^2 + \theta_5 x_1 x_2^2 + \theta_6 x_1^2 x_2 + \ldots)$ with higher-order polynomial features involved.

Cost Function

The cost function for logistic regression, for a single data example (x, y), is defined as the Binary Cross-Entropy Loss or Log Loss. The purpose of this cost function is to measure the discrepancy between the predicted probability and the true binary label.

$$J(h_\theta(x), y)) = \begin{cases} -\ln(h_\theta(x)) & \text{if } y = 1 \\ -\ln(1 - h_\theta(x)) & \text{if } y = 0 \end{cases} \quad \ldots(9)$$

where y is the value of the label. We can understand the cost function in this way: if the label y is 1, the hypothesis $h_\theta(x)$ is expected to be close 1. In other words, the value of $h_\theta(x)$ near 0 will result in a larger penalty than $h_\theta(x)$ near 1. The function, $-\ln(h_\theta(x))$, has this characteristic, shown in Fig.5(a). On the other hand, if the label y is 0, the hypothesis $h_\theta(x)$ is expected to be close 0 with a smaller penalty. The function, $-\ln(1 - h_\theta(x))$, has this characteristic, shown in Fig.5(b).

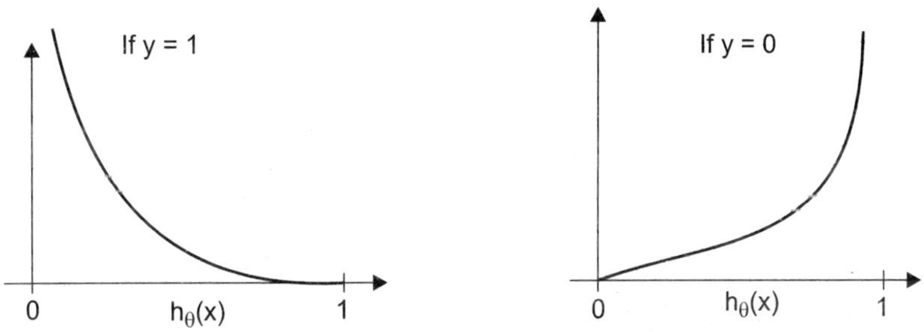

Fig. 4.5. Cost function $J(h_\theta(x), y)$, (a) y = 1, (b) y = 0

The cost function in (9) can be equivalently represented by a more compact format

$$J(h_\theta(x), y) = -y \ln(h_\theta(x)) - (1 - y) \ln(1 - h_\theta(x)) \quad \ldots(10)$$

The cost function for m examples, $(x^{(1)}, y^{(1)}), (x^{(2)}, y^{(2)}), \ldots, (x^{(m)}, y^{(m)})$, will be

$$\begin{aligned} J(\theta) &= (1/m) \Sigma J(h_\theta(x^{(i)}), y^{(i)}) \\ &= -1/m\, \Sigma[y^{(i)} \ln (h_\theta(x^{(i)})) + (1 - y^{(i)}) \ln(1 - h_\theta(x^{(i)}))] \end{aligned} \quad \ldots(11)$$

where $h_\theta(x) = g(z) = g(\theta^T x) = 1/1 + e - \theta^T x$

To fit parameters, we minimize the cost function with respect to θ, i.e., $\theta* = \arg\min \theta J(\theta)$.

To predict, given a new value of x, the label can be predicted as

$$\hat{y} = \{1 h_\theta * (x) \geq 0.5, 0\ h_\theta * (x) < 0.5 \quad \ldots(12)$$

Logistic Regression: Maximum Likelihood

In logistic regression, the maximum likelihood estimation (MLE) is commonly used to estimate the parameters of the logistic regression model. The MLE aims to find the values of the model parameters that maximize the likelihood of the observed data.

The likelihood function represents the probability of observing the given data given the model parameters. In logistic regression, the likelihood function is derived from the assumption that the target variable follows a Bernoulli distribution. The likelihood function is defined as the product of the probabilities of observing the actual class labels for each data point.

Consider the problem of two-class classification with the following assumptions:

(1) The probability $p(y = 1|x; \theta) = h_\theta(x)$ and $p(y = 0|x; \theta) = 1 - h_\theta(x)$, where $h_\theta(x)$ defined by 7 is the output of activation function and is interpreted/treated as the posterior probability of class;

(2) All examples in the training dataset are independently drawn from the same probability distribution. The first assumption can be represented by a compact form

$$p(y|x; \theta) = h_\theta(x)^y \cdot (1 - h_\theta(x))^{1-y} \quad ...(13)$$

The likelihood function for m examples can be defined as the m-dimensional joint posterior probability of vector y given a matrix of features X

$$L(\theta) = p(y|X; \theta) = \prod_{i=1}^{m} p(y^{(i)} | x^{(i)}; \theta)$$

$$= \prod_{i=1}^{m} h_\theta(x^{(i)})^{y^{(i)}} \cdot (1 - h_\theta(x^{(i)}))^{1-y^{(i)}} \quad ...(14)$$

The logarithm likelihood function can be obtained by applying ln(.) operation to (14)

$$l(\theta) = \sum_{i=1}^{m} [y^{(i)} \ln(h_\theta(x^{(i)})) + (1 - y^{(i)}) \ln(1 - h_\theta(x^{(i)}))] \quad ...(15)$$

By comparing (15) with (11), we have

$$J(\theta) = -\frac{1}{m} l(\theta) \quad ...(16)$$

Equation 16 implies that minimizing the cost function $J(\theta)$ is equivalent to maximizing the likelihood function $l(\theta)$, i.e.,

$$\theta^* = \arg\min_\theta J(\theta) = \arg\max_\theta l(\theta) \quad ...(17)$$

Gradient Descent Algorithms

To learn the parameter θ, we will use gradient descent algorithm to minimize the cost function (11) and thus equivalently to maximize the likelihood function (17). To calculate the partial derivative of $J(\theta)$ with respect to θ_j, we need to use the chain rule and the following derivative equations,

$$\frac{d}{dz} g(z) = g(z)(1 - g(z)), \quad g(z) \text{ is the sigmoid function} \quad ...(18)$$

$$\frac{d}{du} \ln(u) = \frac{1}{u}, \quad \ln(u) \text{ is the nature logarithm function} \quad ...(19)$$

It can be shown that the partial derivative of $J(\theta)$ is

$$\frac{\partial J(\theta)}{\partial \theta_j} = \frac{1}{m} \sum_{i=1}^{m} [(h_\theta(x^{(i)} - y^{(i)} \cdot x_j^{(i)}] \quad ...(20)$$

where $j = 0, 1, 2, ..., n$, $xj^{(i)}$ is the jth feature of th i^{th} example and $x_0^{(i)} = 1$. Please note that (20) has the same form as that was used for linear regression with a different definition of hypothesis function $h_\theta(x)$.

If we format the above derivatives as a gradient vector

$$\text{grad} = \frac{\partial J(\theta)}{\partial \theta} = \begin{bmatrix} \frac{\partial J(\theta)}{\partial \theta_0} \\ \frac{\partial J(\theta)}{\partial \theta_1} \\ \vdots \\ \frac{\partial J(\theta)}{\partial \theta_n} \end{bmatrix} \qquad ...(21)$$

Then it is easy to verify that the gradient vector can be represented in vectorized format

$$\text{grad} = \frac{1}{m} X^T (g(X \cdot \theta) - Y)$$

where, $$X = \begin{bmatrix} -- x^{(1)^T} -- \\ -- x^{(2)^T} -- \\ \vdots \\ -- x^{(m)^T} -- \end{bmatrix} = \begin{bmatrix} 1 & x_1^{(1)} & \cdots & x_n^{(1)} \\ 1 & x_1^{(2)} & \cdots & x_n^{(2)} \\ \vdots & \vdots & & \vdots \\ 1 & x_1^{(m)} & \cdots & x_n^{(m)} \end{bmatrix} \in R^{m \times (n+1)}, \quad Y = \begin{bmatrix} y^{(1)} \\ y^{(2)} \\ \vdots \\ y^{(m)} \end{bmatrix} \qquad ...(22)$$

X^T is the transpose of X. In matrix X, each row represents a data example while each column corresponds to a feature. Y is the label vector. Like the gradient decent algorithm for linear regression.

Step-by-Step Instructions for the Gradient Descent Algorithm in Logistic Regression

Step 1: Initialize the parameters:

Initialize the parameter vector θ with zeros or random small values.

Step 2: Define the sigmoid function:

The sigmoid function is defined as: σ(z) = 1/(1 + e^(-z)), where z is the linear combination of the input features and parameters: z = θ^T * X.

Step 3: Perform the gradient descent iterations:

Set the number of iterations (num_iterations) and the learning rate (alpha) for the algorithm.

For each iteration:

Compute the linear combination of the input features and parameters: z = θ^T * X.

Apply the sigmoid function to obtain the predicted probabilities: h = σ(z).

Compute the error between the predicted probabilities and the true labels: error = h - y.

Update the parameters using the gradient descent update rule: θ = θ – (alpha/m) * X^T * error, where m is the number of training examples and X^T is the transpose of the input feature matrix X.

Compute the cost function using the negative log-likelihood: J(θ) = (–1/m) * Σ[y * log(h) + (1 – y) * log(1 – h)].

Step 4: Repeat Step 3 for the specified number of iterations.

Step 5: Return the optimized parameters θ.

Here are the formulas used in the gradient descent algorithm for logistic regression:

Sigmoid function:

σ(z) = 1/(1 + e^(–z))

Linear combination:

$z = \theta^T * X$, where θ is the parameter vector and X is the input feature matrix.

Gradient Descent Update Rule

θ = θ – (alpha/m) * X^T * error, where α is the learning rate, m is the number of training examples, X^T is the transpose of X, and error is the difference between the predicted probabilities and the true labels.

Cost Function (Negative Log-likelihood)

J(θ) = (–1/m) * Σ[y * log(h) + (1 – y) * log(1 – h)], where y is the true label, h is the predicted probability, and the summation is over all training examples.

Besides gradient descent, there are some advanced optimization algorithms available to fit parameters θ. These advanced algorithms include Conjugate gradient, BFGS, and L_BFGS. Let's go through each optimization algorithm and explain them in more detail:

Conjugate Gradient

The Conjugate Gradient method is an iterative algorithm used for solving large sparse systems of linear equations. It is particularly useful in optimization problems, neural network training, and image restoration tasks. The main advantage of the Conjugate Gradient method is its efficiency in solving high-dimensional problems.

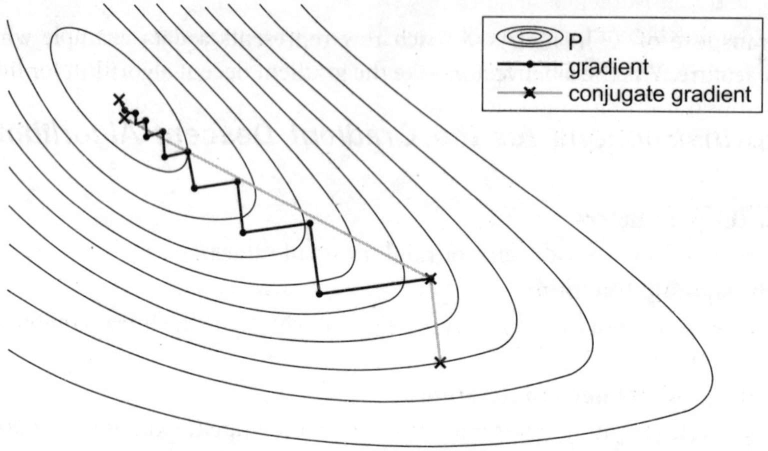

The Conjugate Gradient method aims to find the exact solution to the linear system of equations Ax = b, where A is a symmetric positive-definite matrix, x is the unknown variable, and b is the right-hand side vector.

The Conjugate Gradient algorithm is an optimization algorithm commonly used in logistic regression to find the optimal parameters that minimize the cost function. It is an iterative method that avoids the need to store and compute the Hessian matrix. Here are the step-by-step instructions for applying the Conjugate Gradient algorithm:

Step 1: Initialize the parameters:

Initialize the parameter vector θ with zeros or random small values.

Step 2: Define the cost function and its partial derivatives:

Define the cost function J(θ) that measures the mismatch between the predicted probabilities and the true labels.

Compute the partial derivatives of the cost function with respect to each parameter θ_j, denoted as ∂J(θ)/∂θ_j.

Step 3: Set the initial search direction and gradient:

Set the initial search direction d = -∂J(θ) / ∂θ (negative gradient).

Set the initial gradient g = d.

Step 4: Perform the Conjugate Gradient iterations:

For each iteration:

Compute the step size α using a line search method or by solving a one-dimensional optimization problem.

Update the parameter vector: θ = θ + α * d.

Compute the new gradient: g_new = −∂J(θ)/∂θ.

Compute the conjugate direction: β = (g_new^T * g_new)/(g^T * g).

Update the search direction: d = g_new + β * d.

Update the gradient: g = g_new.

Step 5: Repeat Step 4 until convergence or a maximum number of iterations is reached.

Step 6: Return the optimized parameters θ.

The Conjugate Gradient algorithm iteratively updates the parameters by moving in conjugate directions, which helps accelerate convergence. It does not require the computation and storage of the Hessian matrix, making it more efficient for large-scale logistic regression problems.

It's worth noting that the exact implementation of the Conjugate Gradient algorithm may vary depending on the programming language or software library being used. The specific details of the line search method and convergence criteria may also differ.

Implementation

```
import numpy as np
from scipy.optimize import minimize

# Define the function to optimize
def objective_func(x):
    return x[0]**2 + 2 * x[1]**2 + 3 * x[2]**2 + 2 * x[0] * x[1] – 2 * x[1] * x[2]

# Define the gradient of the function
def gradient_func(x):
    return np.array([2 * x[0] + 2 * x[1], 4 * x[1] – 2 * x[0] – 2 * x[2], 6 * x[2] – 2 * x[1]])

# Define the initial guess
x0 = np.array([1, −1, 2])

# Initialize a list to store intermediate solutions
allvecs = []
```

```
# Define a callback function to store intermediate solutions
def callback(x):
    allvecs.append(x)

# Use the Conjugate Gradient method to minimize the function
result = minimize(objective_func, x0, method='CG', jac=gradient_func, callback=callback, options={'disp': True})

# Print the optimized parameters
print("Optimized Parameters:")
print(result.x)


# Plot the convergence graph
import matplotlib.pyplot as plt


iterations = len(allvecs)
objective_values = [objective_func(x) for x in allvecs]
plt.plot(range(iterations), objective_values)
plt.xlabel("Iteration")
plt.ylabel("Objective Function Value")
plt.title("Conjugate Gradient Optimization")
plt.show()
```

Output:

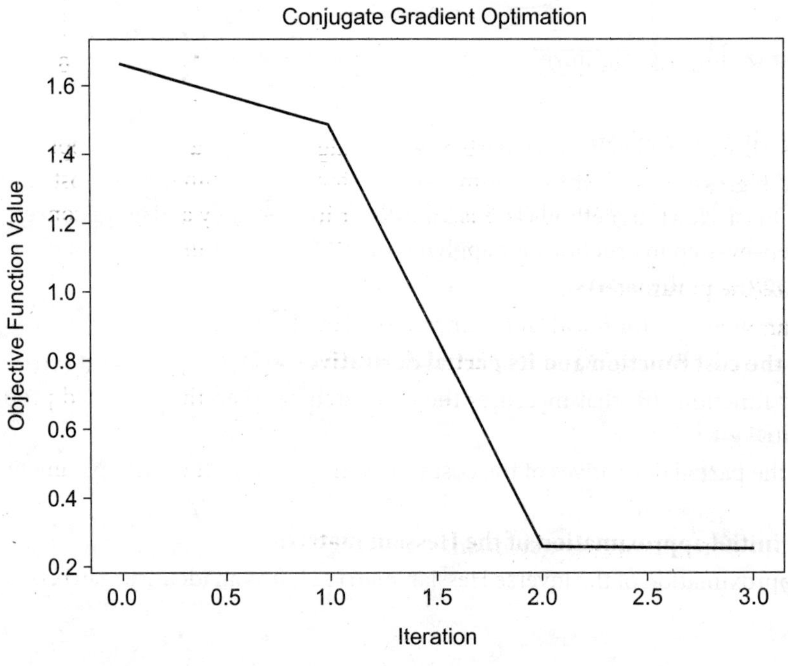

Explanation

BFGS (Broyden-Fletcher-Goldfarb-Shanno):

The BFGS (Broyden-Fletcher-Goldfarb-Shanno) algorithm is an iterative algorithm used for solving unconstrained non-linear optimization problems. It is a popular method for finding the minimum of a function without any constraints.

The BFGS algorithm belongs to the class of Quasi-Newton methods, which aim to determine the descent direction by approximating the Hessian matrix of the loss function. It combines both the gradient information and curvature information of the objective function to iteratively update the solution.

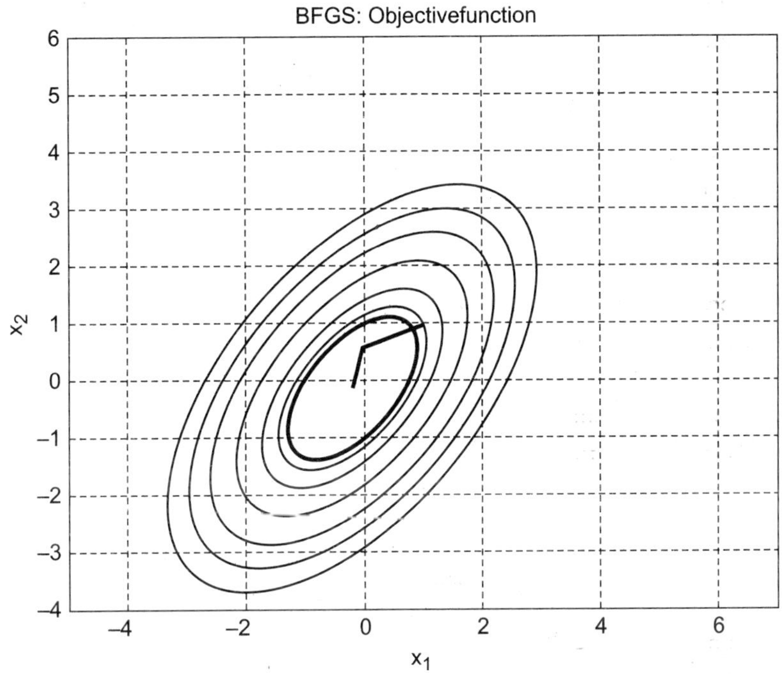

The BFGS (Broyden-Fletcher-Goldfarb-Shanno) algorithm is a popular optimization algorithm used in logistic regression to find the optimal parameters that minimize the cost function. It belongs to the class of Quasi-Newton methods and is known for its efficiency and good convergence properties. Here are the step-by-step instructions for applying the BFGS algorithm:

Step 1: Initialize the parameters:

Initialize the parameter vector θ with zeros or random small values.

Step 2: Define the cost function and its partial derivatives:

Define the cost function J(θ) that measures the mismatch between the predicted probabilities and the true labels.

Compute the partial derivatives of the cost function with respect to each parameter θ_j, denoted as ∂J(θ)/∂θ_j.

Step 3: Set the initial approximation of the Hessian matrix:

Initialize the approximation of the inverse Hessian matrix H_0 as an identity matrix or a positive definite matrix.

Step 4: Perform the BFGS iterations:

For each iteration:

Compute the gradient vector: g = ∂J(θ)/∂θ.

Update the parameter vector: θ = θ – H * g, where H is the current approximation of the inverse Hessian matrix.

Compute the new gradient vector: g_new = ∂J(θ)/∂θ.

Compute the difference vectors: s = θ – θ_old and y = g_new – g.

Update the approximation of the inverse Hessian matrix:

Compute the scalar rho = 1/(y^T * s).

Update the matrix H as H = (I – rho * s * y^T) * H * (I – rho * y * s^T) + rho * s * s^T.

Step 5: Repeat Step 4 until convergence or a maximum number of iterations is reached.

Step 6: Return the optimized parameters θ.

The BFGS algorithm approximates the inverse Hessian matrix using the information from previous iterations. This approximation helps in determining the search direction and step size for parameter updates. The BFGS algorithm typically converges quickly and is computationally efficient for logistic regression problems.

It's important to note that the exact implementation of the BFGS algorithm may vary depending on the programming language or software library being used. The specific details of the convergence criteria and line search method may also differ.

Implementation

```
import numpy as np
import matplotlib.pyplot as plt
from scipy.optimize import minimize

# Define the logistic regression cost function
def logistic_cost(theta, X, y):
    m = len(y)
    h = sigmoid(X.dot(theta))
    cost = (-y * np.log(h) - (1 - y) * np.log(1 - h)).mean()
    grad = (X.T.dot(h - y))/m
    return cost, grad

# Define the sigmoid function
def sigmoid(z):
    return 1/(1 + np.exp(-z))

# Define the BFGS optimization algorithm
def bfgs(X, y, initial_theta):
    result=minimize(logistic_cost,initial_theta,args=(X,y),method='BFGS',jac=True,options={'maxiter':
    400})
    return result.x, result.fun
```

```
# Generate some example data
np.random.seed(0)
X1 = np.random.multivariate_normal([0, 2], [[1, 0.5], [0.5, 1]], 100)
X2 = np.random.multivariate_normal([2, 0], [[1, 0.5], [0.5, 1]], 100)
X = np.vstack((X1, X2))
y = np.hstack((np.zeros(100), np.ones(100)))

# Add intercept term to X
X = np.hstack((np.ones((X.shape[0], 1)), X))

# Initialize parameters
initial_theta = np.zeros(X.shape[1])

# Run BFGS optimization algorithm
theta, cost = bfgs(X, y, initial_theta)

# Plot the decision boundary
x1_min, x1_max = X[:, 1].min() – 1, X[:, 1].max() + 1
x2_min, x2_max = X[:, 2].min() – 1, X[:, 2].max() + 1
xx1, xx2 = np.meshgrid(np.linspace(x1_min, x1_max, 100), np.linspace(x2_min, x2_max, 100))
X_grid = np.c_[np.ones((xx1.ravel().shape[0], 1)), xx1.ravel(), xx2.ravel()]
Z = sigmoid(X_grid.dot(theta))
Z = Z.reshape(xx1.shape)

# Plot the data points
plt.scatter(X[:, 1], X[:, 2], c=y, cmap=plt.cm.Paired, edgecolors='k')
plt.contourf(xx1, xx2, Z, cmap=plt.cm.Paired, alpha=0.6)

# Set plot labels and title
plt.xlabel('Feature 1')
plt.ylabel('Feature 2')
plt.title('BFGS Logistic Regression')

# Show the plot
plt.show()
```

Output

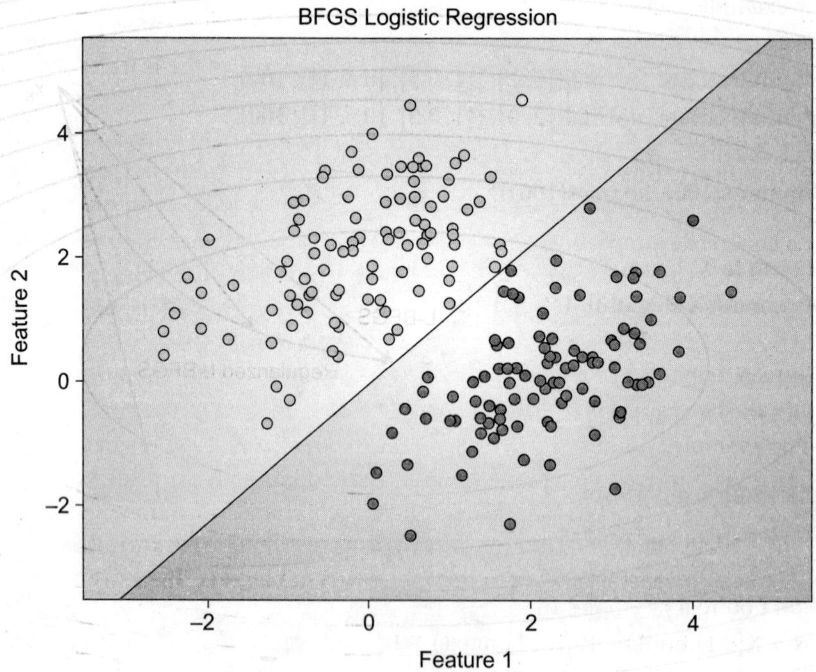

Explanation

This code generates some example data with two classes and applies the BFGS algorithm to perform logistic regression. The resulting decision boundary is then plotted using the contourf function.

L-BFGS (Limited-memory BFGS):

L-BFGS (Limited-memory BFGS) is a variant of the BFGS algorithm that is specifically designed for solving optimization problems with a large number of variables, typically more than 1000. It addresses the memory limitations of the standard BFGS algorithm by using a limited amount of memory to approximate the Hessian matrix.

The L-BFGS algorithm is particularly useful for problems with a low-dimensional parameter space, where the number of variables is relatively small compared to the number of data points or parameters.

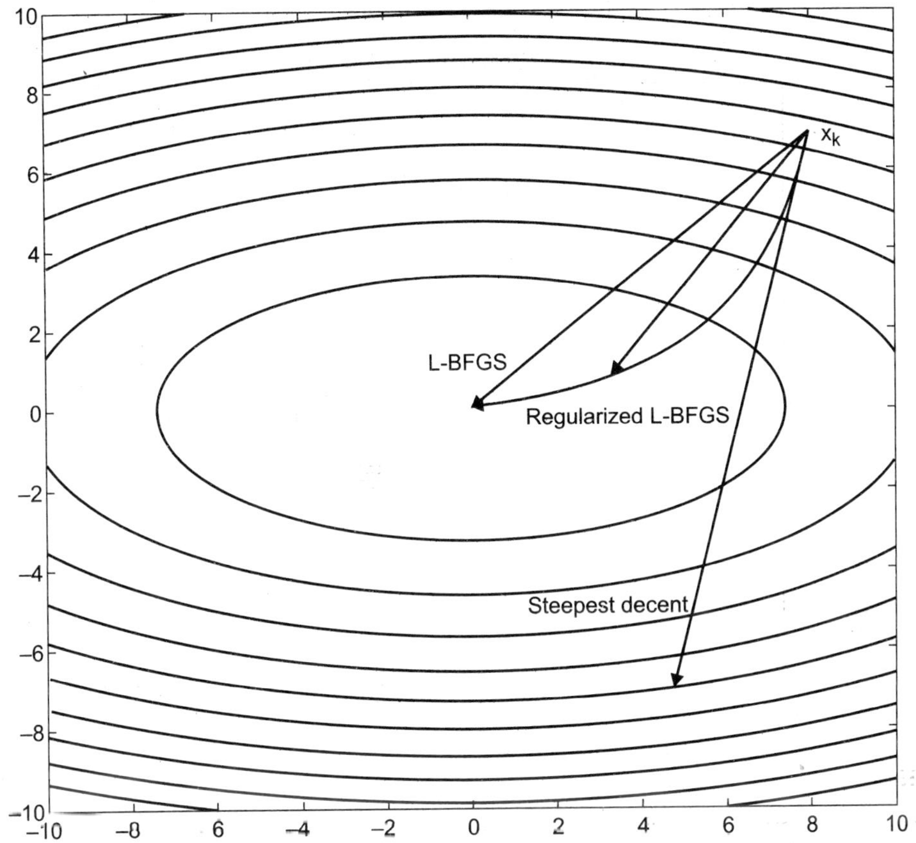

The L-BFGS (Limited-memory BFGS) algorithm is a variant of the BFGS algorithm that addresses memory and computational efficiency concerns when dealing with large-scale optimization problems. It is particularly useful when the number of parameters is very large and storing the full Hessian matrix becomes impractical. L-BFGS approximates the inverse Hessian matrix using limited memory, resulting in a more memory-efficient algorithm. Here are the step-by-step instructions for applying the L-BFGS algorithm:

Step 1: Initialize the parameters:

Initialize the parameter vector θ with zeros or random small values.

Step 2: Define the cost function and its partial derivatives:

Define the cost function J(θ) that measures the mismatch between the predicted probabilities and the true labels.

Compute the partial derivatives of the cost function with respect to each parameter θ_j, denoted as ∂J(θ)/∂θ_j.

Step 3: Set the initial approximation of the inverse Hessian matrix:

Initialize the approximation of the inverse Hessian matrix H_0 as an identity matrix or a positive definite matrix.

Step 4: Set up the limited memory storage:

Choose the number of previous iterations to store in memory, denoted as m.

Initialize the memory variables s and y with m empty lists.

Step 5: Perform the L-BFGS iterations:

For each iteration:

Compute the gradient vector g = ∂J(θ) / ∂θ.

Update the parameter vector: θ = θ – H * g, where H is the current approximation of the inverse Hessian matrix.

Compute the new gradient vector g_new = ∂J(θ)/∂θ.

Compute the difference vectors: s = θ – θ_old and y = g_new – g.

Update the memory variables:

Append the latest s and y vectors to the respective memory lists.

If the number of stored iterations exceeds m, remove the oldest stored vectors from the memory lists.

Perform the L-BFGS two-loop recursion to update the approximation of the inverse Hessian matrix:

Initialize the variables alpha and rho.

Iterate from the most recent stored iteration to the oldest stored iteration:

Compute the scalar rho = 1/(y_i^T * s_i).

Compute the scalar alpha = rho * s_i^T * q.

Update the vector q as q = q – alpha * y_i.

Update the vector r as r = r + (alpha – rho * y_i^T * r) * s_i.

Compute the scalar gamma = s_m^T * y_m / (y_m^T * y_m).

Update the vector z as z = gamma * r.

Iterate from the oldest stored iteration to the most recent stored iteration:

Compute the scalar beta = rho * y_i^T * z.

Update the vector z as z = z + (alpha - beta) * s_i.

Step 6: Repeat Step 5 until convergence or a maximum number of iterations is reached.

Step 7: Return the optimized parameters θ.

The L-BFGS algorithm provides an efficient way to approximate the inverse Hessian matrix using limited memory, making it suitable for large-scale optimization problems. It strikes a balance between memory requirements and computational efficiency, making it a popular choice for logistic regression and other optimization tasks.

Note that the exact implementation of the L-BFGS algorithm may vary depending on the programming language or software library being used. The specific details of the convergence criteria, memory management, and line search method may also differ.

Implementation

```
import numpy as np
import matplotlib.pyplot as plt
from scipy.optimize import minimize

# Define the logistic regression cost function
def logistic_cost(theta, X, y):
    m = len(y)
```

```
    h = sigmoid(X.dot(theta))
    cost = -(1/m) * (y.T.dot(np.log(h)) + (1-y).T.dot(np.log(1-h)))
    grad = (1/m) * X.T.dot(h-y)
    return cost, grad

# Define the sigmoid function
def sigmoid(z):
    return 1 / (1 + np.exp(-z))

# Generate synthetic data for demonstration
np.random.seed(0)
X = np.random.randn(100, 2)
y = np.random.randint(0, 2, size=100)

# Add intercept term to the feature matrix
X = np.column_stack((np.ones(len(X)), X))

# Define the initial parameters
initial_theta = np.zeros(X.shape[1])

# Define the callback function to collect cost values
cost_history = []
def callback(theta):
    cost, _ = logistic_cost(theta, X, y)
    cost_history.append(cost)

# Apply L-BFGS optimization using Scipy's minimize function
result = minimize(logistic_cost, initial_theta, args=(X, y), method='L-BFGS-B', jac=True,
callback=callback)

# Extract the optimized parameters
optimized_theta = result.x

# Plot the graph of the cost function over iterations
plt.plot(cost_history)
plt.xlabel('Iterations')
plt.ylabel('Cost')
plt.title('Cost Function Convergence')
plt.show()
```

Output:

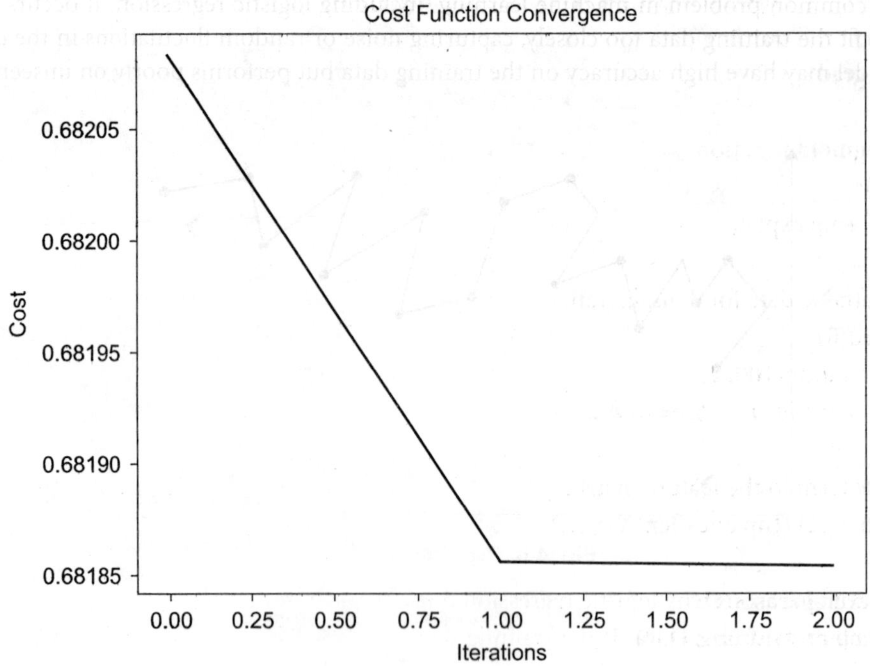

Explanation

In this example, we first define the logistic_cost function that computes the cost function and its gradient for logistic regression. The sigmoid function is also defined to calculate the sigmoid of a given input.

Next, we generate synthetic data for demonstration purposes. The feature matrix X is augmented with an intercept term, and the initial parameters are set to zeros.

The callback function is defined to collect the cost values at each iteration during the optimization process. The cost_history list is used to store these values.

The L-BFGS optimization algorithm is applied using the Scipy library's minimize function. The logistic_cost function is passed as the objective function, along with the initial parameters, feature matrix, and labels. The method is set to 'L-BFGS-B', which indicates the L-BFGS algorithm with bounded constraints. The jac parameter is set to True to indicate that the gradient is provided by the logistic_cost function. The callback function is also specified to collect the cost values at each iteration.

Finally, the optimized parameters are extracted from the result, and the graph of the cost function over iterations is plotted using matplotlib.

Note that you may need to install the necessary libraries (NumPy, matplotlib, and Scipy) if you haven't already.

These optimization algorithms aim to find the optimal values for the parameters (theta) by iteratively updating them based on the cost function and its derivatives. The goal is to minimize the cost function and find the best-fit parameters that yield the most accurate predictions. By using these advanced optimization algorithms, you can improve the efficiency and accuracy of your classification model by finding the optimal parameters for the given dataset.

Overfitting in Logistic Regression

Overfitting is a common problem in machine learning, including logistic regression. It occurs when a model learns to fit the training data too closely, capturing noise or random fluctuations in the data. As a result, the model may have high accuracy on the training data but performs poorly on unseen or test data.

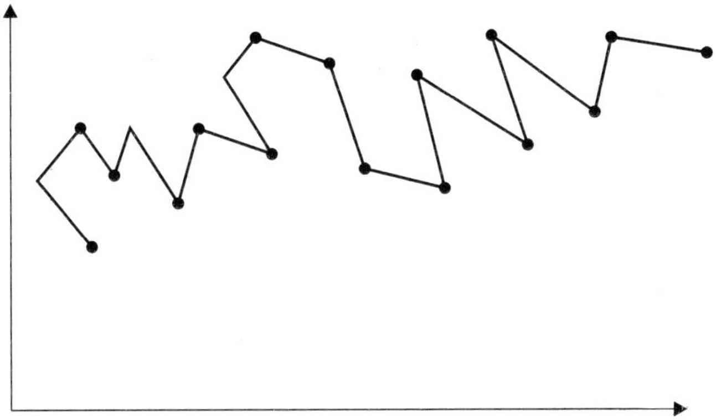

Fig. 4.6. Overfitted data

There are several reasons why logistic regression models can suffer from overfitting:

1. **Insufficient Training Data:** If the training dataset is small, the model may not have enough diverse examples to learn general patterns and instead memorize specific instances, leading to overfitting.
2. **Complex Model:** Logistic regression models with a large number of parameters or high polynomial degrees are more prone to overfitting. A complex model can capture noise or irrelevant features in the data, resulting in poor generalization.
3. **Feature Overload:** Including too many irrelevant or redundant features in the model can increase the risk of overfitting. It is important to select informative and relevant features that truly contribute to the target variable.
4. **Lack of Regularization:** Logistic regression models without regularization techniques, such as L1 or L2 regularization, are more susceptible to overfitting. Regularization adds a penalty term to the cost function, discouraging overly complex models and promoting generalization.

To mitigate the problem of overfitting in logistic regression, several techniques can be employed:

1. **Cross-validation:** Splitting the dataset into training and validation sets and using techniques like k-fold cross-validation helps assess the model's performance on unseen data and prevents overfitting.

   Example: Let's consider an example of using k-fold cross-validation to prevent overfitting in logistic regression.

   Suppose we have a dataset with 1000 samples and we want to train a logistic regression model to classify the data. To avoid overfitting, we can use k-fold cross-validation, where the dataset is divided into k subsets or folds. Here's how the process works:

   (*i*) **Splitting the Data:** First, we randomly divide the dataset into k equal-sized folds. For example, let's assume we choose k = 5, so we have 5 folds, each containing 200 samples.

(*ii*) **Training and Validation:** We then iterate through k iterations, where each iteration uses one fold as the validation set and the remaining k-1 folds as the training set. In the first iteration, we use fold 1 as the validation set and folds 2-5 as the training set. In the second iteration, we use fold 2 as the validation set and folds 1, 3, 4, and 5 as the training set, and so on.

(*iii*) **Model Training and Evaluation:** In each iteration, we train the logistic regression model on the training set and evaluate its performance on the validation set. We compute the accuracy, precision, recall, or any other desired metric to assess the model's performance.

(*iv*) **Average Performance:** After completing all k iterations, we obtain k performance metrics (e.g., k accuracy values). We can then calculate the average performance metric across all iterations to get a more reliable estimate of the model's performance on unseen data.

By using k-fold cross-validation, we can assess how well the logistic regression model generalizes to unseen data. It helps to identify if the model is overfitting by evaluating its performance on multiple validation sets. If the model consistently performs well across all folds, it indicates a good generalization capability. On the other hand, if the performance varies significantly across folds, it suggests overfitting.

By adjusting the value of k, such as using 5-fold, 10-fold, or even leave-one-out cross-validation (k = number of samples), we can control the trade-off between the size of the training set and the number of evaluation iterations. The larger the value of k, the smaller the training set in each iteration, but the more reliable the estimation of the model's performance.

Overall, cross-validation provides a robust technique to prevent overfitting in logistic regression and helps in the selection of hyperparameters or assessing the model's generalization performance.

Sample Code:

```
import numpy as np
from sklearn.model_selection import cross_val_score
from sklearn.linear_model import LogisticRegression
from sklearn.datasets import make_classification

# Generate synthetic dataset
X, y = make_classification(n_samples=1000, n_features=10, n_informative=5, random_
state=42)

# Create logistic regression model
model = LogisticRegression()

# Perform k-fold cross-validation
k = 5
scores = cross_val_score(model, X, y, cv=k, scoring='accuracy')
```

```
# Print the accuracy scores for each fold
for i, score in enumerate(scores):
    print(f"Fold {i+1}: Accuracy = {score:.4f}")

# Calculate and print the average accuracy across all folds
avg_score = np.mean(scores)
print(f"Average Accuracy: {avg_score:.4f}")
```

2. **Regularization:** Applying regularization techniques, such as L1 or L2 regularization, adds a penalty term to the cost function. This encourages the model to simplify and avoids overfitting by reducing the impact of irrelevant features or reducing parameter magnitudes.

   (i) **L 1 Regularization or Lasso**

   L1 regularization, also known as Lasso regularization, is another technique used to prevent overfitting in logistic regression (and other models). It adds a penalty term to the cost function that encourages the model to select only a subset of relevant features by promoting sparsity in the parameter values.

   The regularized cost function with L1 regularization is given by:

   $J(\theta) = -1/m * [\Sigma(y*\log(h(x)) + (1-y)*\log(1-h(x)))] + \lambda * \Sigma(|\theta|)$

   Where:

   $J(\theta)$ is the regularized cost function.

   m is the number of training examples.

   y is the true label (0 or 1) of a training example.

   h(x) is the sigmoid function output (predicted probability) given input x.

   θ is the vector of model parameters (weights).

   λ is the regularization parameter.

   The L1 regularization term is the sum of the absolute values of the model parameters ($\Sigma(|\theta|)$). By adding this term to the cost function, the model is encouraged to set many parameter values to zero, effectively performing feature selection.

   Here's an example of how to apply L1 regularization (Lasso) in logistic regression using Python and scikit-learn:

```
from sklearn.datasets import load_iris
from sklearn.model_selection import train_test_split
from sklearn.linear_model import LogisticRegression
from sklearn.metrics import accuracy_score

# Load the Iris dataset
iris = load_iris()
X = iris.data
y = iris.target
```

```
# Split the dataset into training and test sets
X_train, X_test, y_train, y_test = train_test_split(X, y, test_size=0.2, random_state=42)

# Create a Logistic Regression model with L1 regularization (Lasso)
model = LogisticRegression(penalty='l1', solver='liblinear')

# Train the model using the training data
model.fit(X_train, y_train)

# Make predictions on the test set
y_pred = model.predict(X_test)

# Calculate the accuracy of the model
accuracy = accuracy_score(y_test, y_pred)
print("Accuracy:", accuracy)
```

We start by loading the Iris dataset using load_iris() from scikit-learn. Then, we split the dataset into training and test sets using train_test_split(). Next, we create a Logistic Regression model with L1 regularization by setting penalty='l1' and solver='liblinear'. The solver parameter is set to 'liblinear' because it supports L1 regularization.

After creating the model, we train it using the training data with the fit() method. Then, we use the trained model to make predictions on the test set using the predict() method. Finally, we calculate the accuracy of the model's predictions using the true labels of the test set and accuracy_score().

Note that the example uses the Iris dataset for demonstration purposes. You can replace it with your own dataset by loading the data and labels into the X and y variables, respectively.

Make sure to have scikit-learn installed (pip install scikit-learn) before running this code.

(ii) **L 2 Regularization or Ridge**

L2 regularization, also known as Ridge regularization, is a technique used in machine learning to prevent overfitting by adding a penalty term to the cost function. It helps to reduce the magnitude of the model's coefficients, encouraging them to be small and avoiding large fluctuations in the parameter values.

The L2 regularization term is calculated as the squared sum of the coefficients multiplied by a regularization parameter, often denoted as λ (lambda). The regularization term is added to the original cost function, and by minimizing the combined objective, the model finds a balance between fitting the training data and keeping the coefficients small. The L2 regularization term can be expressed mathematically as:

L2 regularization term = λ * ||w||^2

where w represents the model's coefficients.

By introducing the L2 regularization term, the model is encouraged to distribute the weightage across all the features, as opposed to focusing on a few dominant features. This helps to avoid overemphasis on particular features that may lead to overfitting.

In practical terms, when training a model with L2 regularization, the regularization parameter λ needs to be tuned. Higher values of λ result in stronger regularization, leading to smaller coefficient values and increased bias. On the other hand, lower values of λ reduce the regularization effect, allowing the model to fit the training data more closely.

Applying L2 regularization in logistic regression is straightforward using scikit-learn. You can use the LogisticRegression class and set the penalty parameter to 'l2'.

Sample Code:

```
from sklearn.datasets import load_iris
from sklearn.model_selection import train_test_split
from sklearn.linear_model import LogisticRegression
from sklearn.metrics import accuracy_score

# Load the Iris dataset
iris = load_iris()
X = iris.data
y = iris.target

# Split the dataset into training and test sets
X_train, X_test, y_train, y_test = train_test_split(X, y, test_size=0.2, random_state=42)

# Create a Logistic Regression model with L2 regularization (Ridge)
model = LogisticRegression(penalty='l2')

# Train the model using the training data
model.fit(X_train, y_train)

# Make predictions on the test set
y_pred = model.predict(X_test)

# Calculate the accuracy of the model
accuracy = accuracy_score(y_test, y_pred)
print("Accuracy:", accuracy)
```

We load the Iris dataset, split it into training and test sets, and create a Logistic Regression model with L2 regularization by setting penalty='l2' (which is the default value). Then, we train the model, make predictions on the test set, and calculate the accuracy of the model's predictions.

Remember to have scikit-learn installed (pip install scikit-learn) before running this code.

3. **Feature Selection:** Carefully selecting relevant features can improve the model's generalization. Removing irrelevant or redundant features reduces the complexity of the model and reduces the risk of overfitting.

   Sample Code:

```
from sklearn.ensemble import RandomForestClassifier
from sklearn.datasets import load_iris
from sklearn.feature_selection import SelectFromModel

# Load the dataset
iris = load_iris()
X, y = iris.data, iris.target

# Create a Random Forest classifier
rf = RandomForestClassifier()

# Perform feature selection
feature_selector = SelectFromModel(rf)
X_selected = feature_selector.fit_transform(X, y)

# Get the selected feature indices
selected_indices = feature_selector.get_support(indices=True)

# Print the selected feature names
selected_features = [iris.feature_names[i] for i in selected_indices]
print("Selected features:", selected_features)
```

   I've used the load_iris function from the sklearn.datasets module to load the Iris dataset as a sample dataset. You can replace it with the appropriate code or function to load your specific dataset.

   The rest of the code remains the same, performing feature selection using the Random Forest algorithm and printing the selected feature names.

   Remember to replace the dataset loading code (load_iris in this case) with your actual dataset loading code in order to use this example with your own dataset.

4. **Early Stopping:** Monitoring the performance of the model during training and stopping the training process when the performance on the validation set starts to deteriorate can prevent overfitting. This is known as early stopping.

   Early stopping is a technique used to prevent overfitting by monitoring the performance of the model during training and stopping the training process when the performance on the validation set starts to deteriorate. This helps to find the optimal point where the model generalizes well without overfitting to the training data.

The basic idea behind early stopping is to divide the available data into a training set and a validation set. The model is trained on the training set and evaluated on the validation set after each training iteration or epoch. The performance metric on the validation set, such as the validation loss or accuracy, is monitored over time.

The training process is typically stopped when the performance on the validation set stops improving or starts to worsen consistently. This is an indication that the model has started to overfit the training data and is not generalizing well to new, unseen data. By stopping the training at this point, we can avoid further overfitting and select a model that performs well on unseen data.

Here's a high-level overview of how early stopping works:

(*i*) Split the dataset into a training set and a validation set.

(*ii*) Initialize the model and set the hyperparameters.

(*iii*) Iterate over the training set for a fixed number of epochs or until a stopping criterion is met.

(*iv*) After each epoch, evaluate the model's performance on the validation set.

(*v*) Track the performance metric (e.g., validation loss or accuracy) over time.

(*vi*) If the performance on the validation set starts to deteriorate, stop the training process.

(*vii*) Select the model with the best performance on the validation set as the final model.

It's important to note that early stopping should be used in conjunction with other regularization techniques, such as regularization, to achieve better generalization and prevent overfitting.

The implementation of early stopping depends on the specific machine learning framework or library you are using. Most frameworks provide built-in functionality or callbacks to implement early stopping during training.

Remember to tune the parameters, such as the stopping criterion and the number of epochs, based on the specific problem and dataset to find the optimal trade-off between model performance and training time.

5. **Data Augmentation:** Increasing the size of the training dataset through techniques like data augmentation or synthetic data generation can provide more diverse examples for the model to learn from, reducing the risk of overfitting.

Data augmentation is a technique used to increase the size and diversity of the training dataset by applying various transformations to the existing data. This helps to provide more varied examples for the model to learn from, reducing the risk of overfitting and improving generalization.

The basic idea behind data augmentation is to create new training examples by applying random transformations to the original data samples. These transformations are typically designed to preserve the class labels or target values while introducing variations in the input data.

Some common data augmentation techniques include:

(*i*) **Image data augmentation:** For image classification tasks, transformations such as random rotations, translations, flips, zooms, and color distortions can be applied to the images.

(*ii*) **Text data augmentation:** For text classification or natural language processing tasks, techniques like word replacement, synonym substitution, random insertion or deletion of words, and sentence paraphrasing can be used to generate new textual variations.

(*iii*) **Audio data augmentation:** For audio classification or speech recognition tasks, transformations such as time stretching, pitch shifting, background noise addition, and speed variation can be applied to the audio signals.

By applying these transformations, the augmented data introduces new variations and perturbations into the training set, making the model more robust and less prone to overfitting. It helps the model to learn to generalize across different variations of the input data.

Here's a high-level overview of how data augmentation works:

(*i*) Prepare the original training dataset.

(*ii*) Define the desired data augmentation techniques and parameters.

(*iii*) Iterate over the original training samples.

(*iv*) Apply random transformations to each sample to create augmented samples.

(*v*) Add the augmented samples to the training dataset.

(*vi*) Repeat the process until the desired size of the augmented dataset is reached.

(*vii*) Train the model using the augmented dataset.

It's important to note that data augmentation should be used judiciously and in a way that is relevant to the problem domain. The choice of augmentation techniques and parameters should align with the nature of the data and the specific task at hand. Additionally, data augmentation is typically applied during the training phase and not during the evaluation or testing phase.

The implementation of data augmentation depends on the specific machine learning framework or library you are using. Many popular frameworks, such as TensorFlow and PyTorch, provide built-in functions or libraries for data augmentation.

Remember to strike a balance between the amount of augmentation applied and the diversity of the augmented data. Too much augmentation may introduce unrealistic or irrelevant variations, while too little augmentation may not provide enough diversity to improve generalization.

It is important to find the right balance between model complexity and the amount of available data to avoid overfitting. Regularization and proper evaluation techniques can help in achieving a well-generalized logistic regression model.

Multi-class Classification: One vs All

In multi-class classification, we aim to assign a label or category to each input data instance from a set of multiple class labels. The process involves training a model using labeled data where each data instance is associated with one of the class labels. The model learns the patterns and relationships in the training data to make predictions on new, unseen data. There are various approaches to tackle multi-class classification, and one commonly used technique is the "One-vs-All" (also known as "One-vs-Rest") approach. This approach transforms the multi-class problem into multiple binary classification problems.

In multi-class classification, we have a target variable that can take on more than two classes. For example, let's consider a problem where we want to classify images of animals into three classes: cat, dog, and bird. Each input example (image) is associated with one of these classes. To perform multi-class classification, we need a model that can assign a probability or score to each class for a given input example. The class with the highest probability or score is then predicted as the output class.

Binary classification vs. Multi-class classification

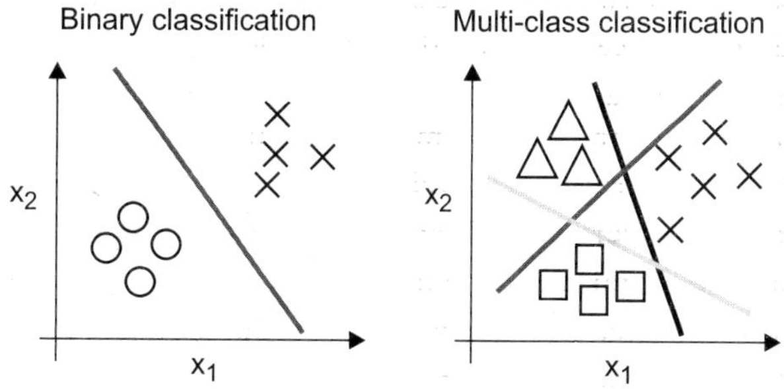

Binary Classification

If you have a dataset with only two class instances, then you indeed have a binary classification problem. In that case, you can directly use a binary classifier model to classify the instances into the two classes. Since you have only two class instances, you can train a single binary classifier model using any suitable algorithm such as logistic regression, support vector machine, or decision tree. The classifier will learn to distinguish between the two classes based on the available features or input variables.

Once the model is trained, you can use it to make predictions on new, unseen data. The predicted class labels will fall into one of the two classes. To evaluate the performance of the binary classifier, you can calculate a confusion matrix. A confusion matrix provides a tabular representation of the predicted class labels against the actual class labels. It allows you to assess the accuracy of the classifier's predictions and determine metrics such as true positives, true negatives, false positives, and false negatives.

With a confusion matrix, you can derive various performance metrics such as accuracy, precision, recall, and F1 score. These metrics provide insights into the classifier's ability to correctly classify instances and can help you assess its effectiveness. In summary, for a binary classification problem with two class instances, you can use a single binary classifier model and evaluate its performance using a confusion matrix.

Example: Check email is spam or not, predicting gender based on height and weight.

Multi-Class Classification

When dealing with a dataset that has multiple class labels, the number of classifier models required depends on the classification technique used. In the One-vs-All (also known as One-vs-Rest) approach, if there are N class instances, N binary classifier models are trained. Each model is trained to distinguish between one class and the rest of the classes. This means that for N class instances, N binary classifiers are created, resulting in N separate models. In the One-vs-One approach, if there are N class instances, N * (N-1)/2 binary classifier models are trained. Each model is trained to differentiate between two individual classes. This approach involves pairwise comparisons between classes, creating separate binary classifiers for each pair. The total number of classifiers is given by the combination formula C(N, 2) = N * (N-1)/2.

Regarding the confusion matrix, it is a useful tool to evaluate the performance of a classification model in the multi-class setting. However, it can become more complex to interpret compared to binary classification. In a multi-class confusion matrix, the rows represent the true class labels, and the columns represent the predicted class labels. Each entry in the matrix represents the number of instances that belong to a particular true class and were predicted to be in a specific class. The diagonal elements represent the instances that were correctly classified for each class, while the off-diagonal elements represent misclassifications. Understanding the confusion matrix in a multi-class scenario involves considering not only overall accuracy but also individual class performance. Metrics such as precision, recall, and F1 score can be calculated for each class to assess how well the classifier performs for that particular class.

Interpreting a multi-class confusion matrix requires considering the relationships between classes and analyzing patterns of misclassifications. It can provide insights into potential biases or difficulties the classifier may have in distinguishing certain classes. While the confusion matrix in a multi-class setting may be more complex to understand, it remains an essential tool for evaluating the performance of a classifier and gaining insights into its strengths and weaknesses across different classes.

Example: Check whether the fruit is apple, banana, or orange.

One vs. All (One-vs-Rest)

In the One-vs-All (One-vs-Rest) approach for N-class instances, we generate N binary classifier models, where N is equal to the number of class labels present in the dataset. For each class label, we train a binary classifier to distinguish that particular class from the rest of the classes. This means that for N class labels, we create N separate binary classifiers.

During training, each binary classifier is trained on a subset of the data, where the positive class consists of instances from the corresponding class label and the negative class consists of instances from all the other classes. After training, the binary classifiers can be used to classify new instances by assigning them to the class with the highest predicted probability or confidence score among all the binary classifiers. By utilizing N binary classifiers, the One-vs-All approach allows us to handle multi-class classification problems effectively. Each classifier focuses on distinguishing one class from the rest, enabling us to classify instances into multiple classes.

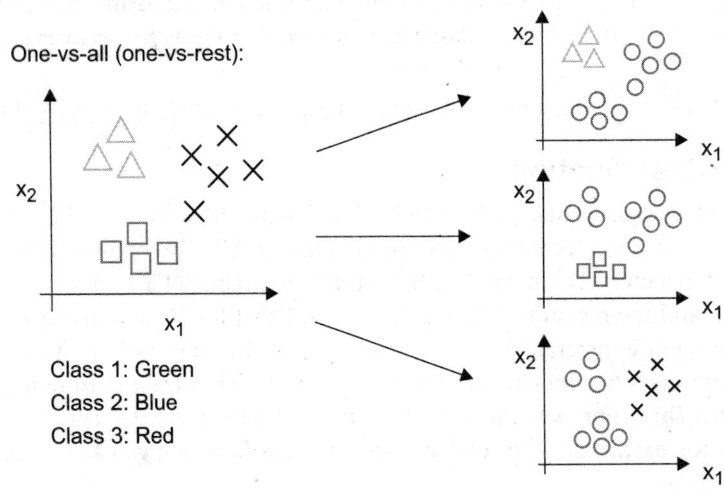

In the context of the above image, let's consider a classification problem with three classes: Green (type 1), Blue (type 2), and Red (type 3).

In the One-vs-All (One-vs-Rest) approach for multi-class classification, we indeed need to generate a binary classifier for each class label present in the dataset. In the case of the three classes (Green, Blue, Red), we would create three binary classifiers as follows:

Classifier 1: Green vs. Rest

- Positive class: Green
- Negative classes: Blue, Red

Classifier 2: Blue vs. Rest

- Positive class: Blue
- Negative classes: Green, Red

Classifier 3: Red vs. Rest

- Positive class: Red
- Negative classes: Green, Blue

Each binary classifier is trained independently to distinguish its respective positive class from the rest of the classes. During prediction, each classifier will output a probability or score for its positive class, and the class with the highest score will be assigned as the final prediction.

Now to train these three classifiers, we need to create three training datasets. So let's consider our primary dataset is as follows,

Features			Classes
x1	x2	x3	G
x4	x5	x6	B
x7	x8	x9	R
x10	x11	x12	G
x13	x14	x15	B
x16	x17	x18	R
Class 1: Green Class 2: Blue Class 3: Red			

You can see that there are three class labels Green, Blue, and Red present in the dataset. Now we have to create a training dataset for each class.

In the One-vs-All approach, the training dataset for each binary classifier is constructed as follows:

For each class label:

Assign a positive label (+1) to the instances that belong to that class.

Assign a negative label (–1) to the instances that do not belong to that class.

For example, let's consider the three classes (Green, Blue, Red) again:

Classifier 1: Green vs. Rest

- **Positive class:** Green (+1)
- **Negative classes:** Blue (–1), Red (–1)

Classifier 2: Blue vs. Rest

- **Positive class:** Blue (+1)
- **Negative classes:** Green (–1), Red (–1)

Classifier 3: Red vs. Rest

- **Positive class:** Red (+1)
- **Negative classes:** Green (–1), Blue (–1)

So, the training dataset for each classifier will have the class labels set to +1 for the positive class and −1 for the negative classes, while the remaining features are left unchanged. Its looks like that.

Main Dataset			
Features			Classes
x1	x2	x3	G
x4	x5	x6	B
x7	x8	x9	R
x10	x11	x12	G
x13	x14	x15	B
x16	x17	x18	R

Training Dataset 1 Class: Green			
Features			Green
x1	x2	x3	+1
x4	x5	x6	−1
x7	x8	x9	−1
x10	x11	x12	+1
x13	x14	x15	−1
x16	x17	x18	−1

Class 1: Green Class 2: Blue Class 3: Red

Fig. 4.7. Training dataset for Green class

Training Dataset 2 Class: Blue			
Features			Blue
x1	x2	x3	−1
x4	x5	x6	+1
x7	x8	x9	−1
x10	x11	x12	−1
x13	x14	x15	+1
x16	x17	x18	−1

Training Dataset 3 Class: Red			
Features			Red
x1	x2	x3	−1
x4	x5	x6	−1
x7	x8	x9	+1
x10	x11	x12	−1
x13	x14	x15	−1
x16	x17	x18	+1

Fig. 4.8. Traning dataset for Blue class and Red class

Let's understand it by an example,

- Consider the primary dataset, in the first row; we have x1, x2, x3 feature values, and the corresponding class value is G, which means these feature values belong to G class. So we put +1 value in the class column for the correspondence of green type. Then we applied the same for the x10, x11, x12 input train data.
- For the rest of the values of the features which are not in correspondence with the Green class, we put -1 in their class column.

After constructing the training dataset for each binary classifier, the next step is to train the classifier models using the provided data. You can apply an appropriate classification algorithm to train each binary classifier. Some common classification algorithms used in multi-class classification include logistic regression, support vector machines (SVM), random forests, and neural networks. The specific algorithm choice depends on various factors such as the nature of the data, the complexity of the problem, and the desired performance.

For each binary classifier, you would feed its respective training dataset into the chosen algorithm. The classifier model will learn the patterns and relationships between the input features and the class labels based on the training data. The goal is to optimize the model's parameters to accurately classify instances into the positive class (+1) and negative class (-1) for that particular class. Once the training process is complete, each binary classifier will have learned its own decision boundaries or rules specific to its class. These decision boundaries collectively define the boundaries for the multi-class classification problem.

After training, you can use the trained classifiers to predict the class labels for new unseen instances by applying them individually to the input data. The class label predicted by the classifier with the highest confidence or probability is considered the final predicted class label for that instance in the multi-class classification problem.

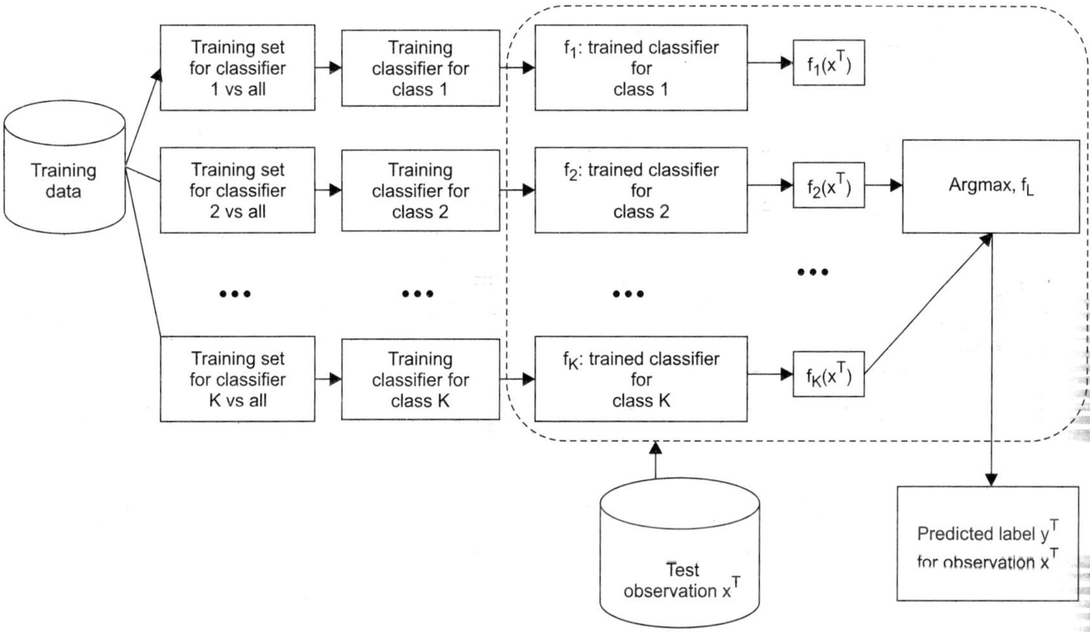

After the training model, when we pass input test data to the model, then that data is considered as input for all generated classifiers. If there is any possibility that our input test data belongs to a particular class, then the classifier created for that class gives a positive response in the form of +1, and all other classifier models provide an adverse reaction in the way of -1. Similarly, binary classifier models predict the probability of correspondence with concerning classes.

By analyzing the probability scores, we predict the result as the class index having a maximum probability score.

- Let's understand with one example by taking three test features values as y1, y2, and y3, respectively.
- We passed test data to the classifier models. We got the outcome in the form of a positive rating derived from the Green class classifier with a probability score of (0.9).
- Again We got a positive rating from the Blue class with a probability score of (0.4) along with a negative classification score from the remaining Red classifier.
- Hence, based on the positive responses and decisive probability score, we can say that our test input belongs to the Green class.

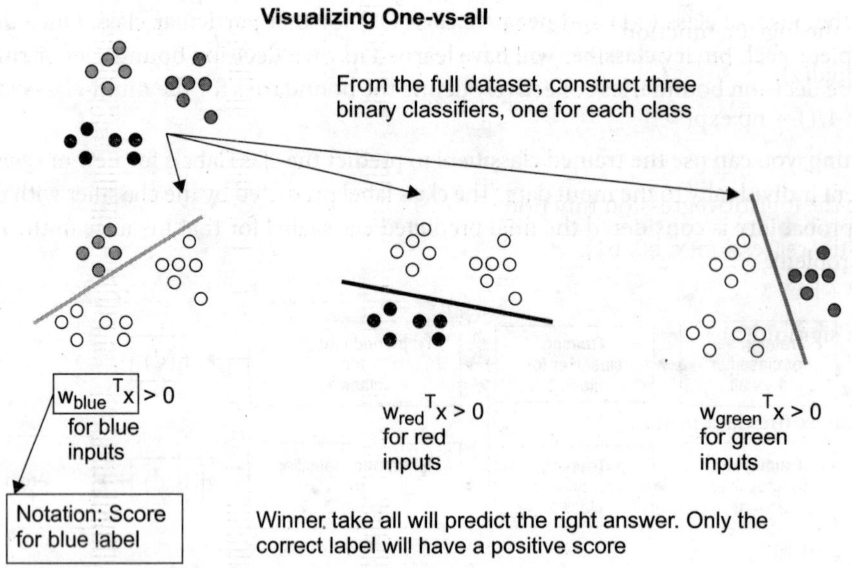

Fig. 4.9. Visualizing One -vs- all

Types of Logistic Regression

Binary Logistic Regression: This is the most basic form of logistic regression where the dependent variable has only two categories or classes. The goal is to predict the probability of an observation belonging to one of the two classes. In binary logistic regression, we have a binary dependent variable with two classes, usually represented as 0 and 1. The logistic regression model uses the logistic or sigmoid function to model the probability of an observation belonging to class 1.

The logistic function is defined as:

$$\text{sigmoid}(z) = 1/\ 1 + e^\wedge(-z)) \qquad \text{...(2)}$$

Here, z is the linear combination of the predictors and their corresponding coefficients. The logistic function maps the linear combination to a value between 0 and 1, representing the probability of the observation belonging to class 1. The logistic regression model estimates the coefficients that maximize the likelihood of observing the given data, given the predicted probabilities.

Example: Let's plot the binary logistic regression function. In this example, we will use a simple case with one predictor variable.

First, let's define the logistic function or sigmoid function:

$$\text{sigmoid}(z) = 1/(1 + e^\wedge(-z))$$

Now, let's plot the logistic regression function with the following equation:

$$p(y = 1 \mid x) = \text{sigmoid}(b0 + b1{*}x)$$

Where b0 and b1 are the coefficients of the logistic regression model, and x is the predictor variable.

Code:

```
import numpy as np
import matplotlib.pyplot as plt
```

```
# Define the logistic function
def sigmoid(z):
    return 1/(1 + np.exp(-z))

# Define the logistic regression function
def logistic_regression(x, b0, b1):
    z = b0 + b1 * x
    return sigmoid(z)

# Generate some data points
np.random.seed(0)
x = np.linspace(-10, 10, 100)
b0 = -2  # Intercept
b1 = 0.5  # Coefficient for the predictor variable
noise = np.random.normal(0, 0.1, 100)
y_true = np.where(x < 0, 0, 1)
y = y_true + noise

# Compute the probabilities using the logistic regression function
y_proba = logistic_regression(x, b0, b1)

# Plot the data points
plt.scatter(x, y, c=y_true, cmap='bwr', label='Data')
plt.colorbar(ticks=[0, 1], label='Class')
plt.xlabel('x')
plt.ylabel('y')
plt.title('Binary Logistic Regression')
plt.grid(True)

# Plot the logistic regression curve
plt.plot(x, y_proba, color='black', label='Logistic Regression')

plt.legend()
plt.show()
```

Output:

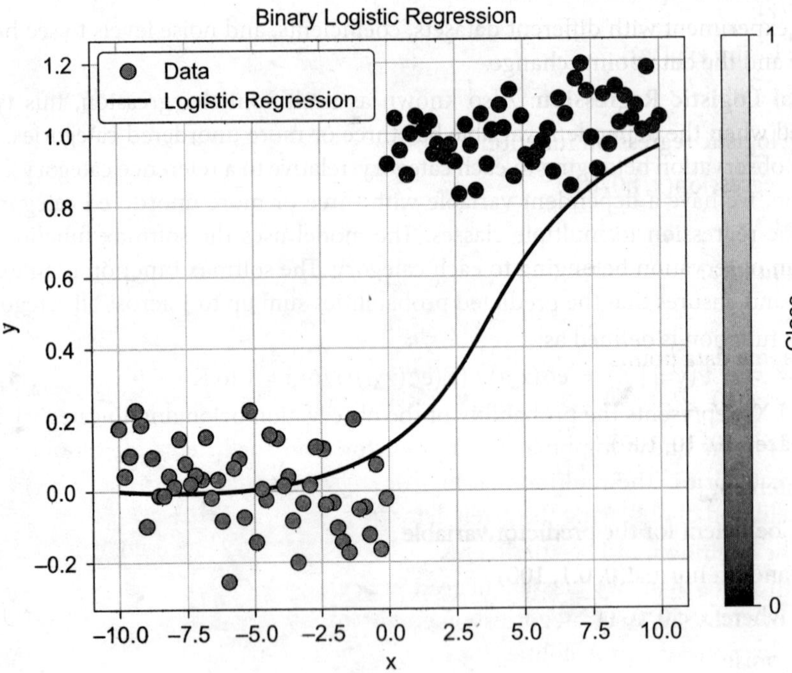

Explanation

The plot shows a scatter plot of data points along with the binary logistic regression curve. Let's break down the components of the plot:

1. **Data Points:** The scatter plot displays the data points as individual dots. Each dot represents an observation with its corresponding x and y values. In this example, the x-axis represents the predictor variable, and the y-axis represents the response variable. The color of the dots represents the true class of each data point. Blue dots indicate class 0, and red dots indicate class 1.
2. **Colorbar:** The colorbar on the right side of the plot corresponds to the class labels. It shows a color mapping where blue represents class 0, and red represents class 1. This helps in understanding the color coding of the data points.
3. **Logistic Regression Curve:** The black curve represents the binary logistic regression curve. It is obtained by applying the logistic regression function to the predictor variable (x) using the estimated coefficients (b0 and b1). The curve separates the data points into two regions based on their predicted probabilities of belonging to class 1. The curve serves as the decision boundary for the logistic regression model.

The plot provides a visual representation of how the logistic regression model separates the data points into different classes based on their positions and the logistic function. The curve's shape and position are determined by the coefficients of the logistic regression equation, which can be adjusted to fit the data and find the optimal decision boundary. By analyzing the plot, you can observe how the logistic regression model assigns probabilities to each class based on the predictor variable and predicts the class labels accordingly. The goal is to find the decision boundary that best separates the two classes and maximizes the model's predictive performance.

Feel free to experiment with different datasets, coefficients, and noise levels to see how the logistic regression curve and the data points change.

Multinomial Logistic Regression: Also known as multinomial regression, this type of logistic regression is used when the dependent variable has three or more unordered categories. It predicts the probability of an observation belonging to each category, relative to a reference category. In multinomial logistic regression, we have a dependent variable with three or more unordered categories. It extends the binary logistic regression to multiple classes. The model uses the softmax function to model the probabilities of an observation belonging to each category. The softmax function is an extension of the logistic function and ensures that the predicted probabilities sum up to 1 across all categories.

The softmax function is defined as:

$$P(y=j \mid X) = e^\wedge(z\_j) / (\Sigma(e^\wedge(z\_i))) \text{ for } i = 1 \text{ to } K \quad ...(3)$$

Here, P(y=j | X) represents the probability of the observation belonging to category j, X represents the predictors, z_j is the linear combination of predictors and coefficients for category j, and K is the total number of categories. The multinomial logistic regression model estimates the coefficients that maximize the likelihood of observing the given data, given the predicted probabilities for each category.

Example: The Multinomial Logistic Regression is an extension of the Binary Logistic Regression for problems with more than two classes. Instead of predicting a binary outcome, it aims to predict the probabilities of each class in a categorical outcome. In Multinomial Logistic Regression, we use the softmax function to model the probabilities for each class. The softmax function takes a vector of inputs and transforms it into a vector of probabilities that sum up to 1. The formula for the softmax function is as follows:

$$P(y=j|X) = \text{exp}(WjX)/\text{sum}(\text{exp}(WkX)) \text{ for } j = 1, 2, ..., K$$

Here:

P(y=j|X) is the probability of the j-th class given the input X.

X is the input vector of features.

Wj is the weight vector associated with the j-th class.

To fit the Multinomial Logistic Regression model, we use the maximum likelihood estimation (MLE) approach to estimate the parameters (weights). The objective is to maximize the log-likelihood of the observed data. The formula for the log-likelihood is as follows:

$$L(W) = \text{sum}(\text{sum}(Yij*\log(P(y=j|X))))$$

Here:

Yij is the indicator variable that takes a value of 1 if the observation belongs to the j-th class, and 0 otherwise.

P(y=j|X) is the predicted probability of the j-th class given the input X.

To optimize the log-likelihood, various optimization algorithms such as gradient descent or Newton's method can be used.

Once the model is trained, we can make predictions by computing the probabilities for each class using the softmax function. The predicted class for a given observation is the one with the highest probability.

In summary, Multinomial Logistic Regression extends Binary Logistic Regression to handle problems with multiple classes. It uses the softmax function to model the class probabilities and maximizes the log-likelihood to estimate the weights. By predicting the class with the highest probability, we can assign observations to their respective classes.

Code:

```
import numpy as np
import matplotlib.pyplot as plt
from sklearn.datasets import make_blobs
from sklearn.linear_model import LogisticRegression

# Generate synthetic data with three classes
X, y = make_blobs(n_samples=150, centers=3, random_state=42)

# Create an instance of Multinomial Logistic Regression model
logreg = LogisticRegression(multi_class='multinomial', solver='lbfgs')

# Fit the model to the data
logreg.fit(X, y)

# Create a meshgrid to plot the decision boundaries
x_min, x_max = X[:, 0].min() - 1, X[:, 0].max() + 1
y_min, y_max = X[:, 1].min() - 1, X[:, 1].max() + 1
xx, yy = np.meshgrid(np.arange(x_min, x_max, 0.02),
                     np.arange(y_min, y_max, 0.02))

# Predict the class labels for each point on the meshgrid
Z = logreg.predict(np.c_[xx.ravel(), yy.ravel()])
Z = Z.reshape(xx.shape)

# Plot the data points and decision boundaries
plt.figure(figsize=(8, 6))
plt.contourf(xx, yy, Z, alpha=0.8)
plt.scatter(X[:, 0], X[:, 1], c=y, edgecolors='k')
plt.xlabel('X1')
plt.ylabel('X2')
plt.title('Multinomial Logistic Regression')
plt.colorbar()
plt.show()
```

Output:

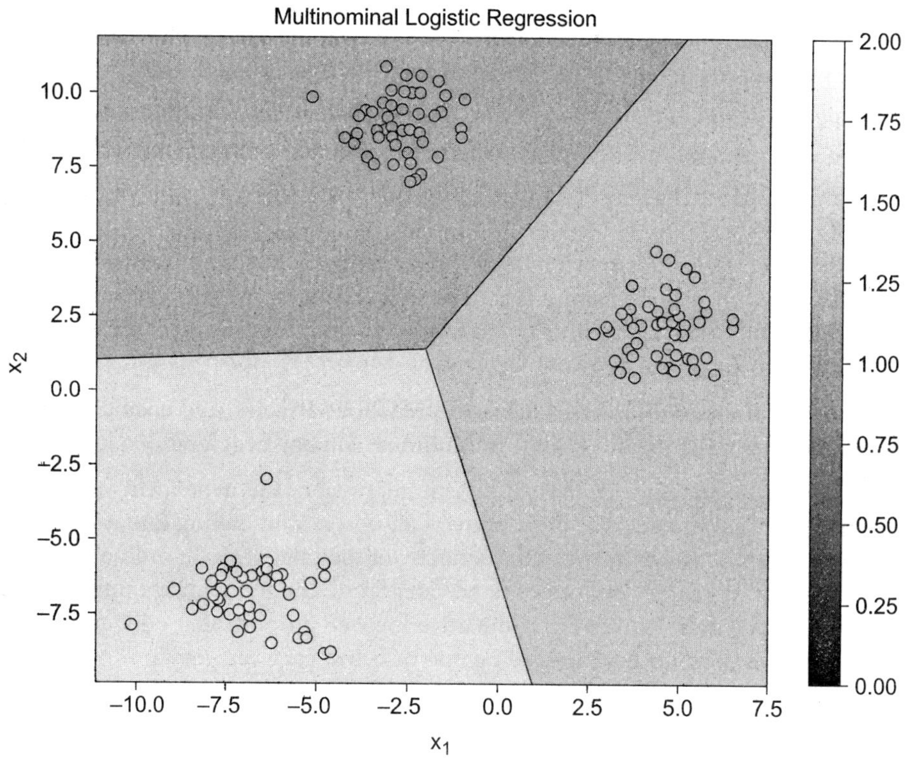

Explanation

In Multinomial Logistic Regression, we have more than two classes to predict. Let's consider an example where we have three classes: Class A, Class B, and Class C. The goal is to predict the class label based on two predictor variables, X1 and X2.

Here's an explanation of the plot components:

Data Points: The scatter plot displays the data points in a two-dimensional space. Each data point represents an observation with its corresponding values of X1 and X2. The color of the data points represents the true class labels. For example, blue dots indicate Class A, red dots indicate Class B, and green dots indicate Class C.

Decision Boundaries: The decision boundaries are the curves or lines that separate the different classes in the plot. In Multinomial Logistic Regression, these decision boundaries are nonlinear and can take various shapes. The decision boundaries are determined by the estimated coefficients of the logistic regression equation for each class.

Color Regions: The plot is divided into different color regions, each corresponding to a specific class. These regions are defined by the decision boundaries and indicate the areas where the logistic regression model predicts a particular class. For example, within the blue region, the model predicts Class A, within the red region, the model predicts Class B, and within the green region, the model predicts Class C.

The plot helps visualize how the Multinomial Logistic Regression model assigns probabilities to each class based on the predictor variables X1 and X2. The decision boundaries separate the feature space into different regions, and each region corresponds to a different predicted class. The goal is to find the decision boundaries that maximize the likelihood of correctly classifying the observations.

By analyzing the plot, you can observe how the model's decision boundaries and color regions adapt to the data distribution and the relationships between the predictor variables and the classes. Adjusting the coefficients and adding more predictor variables can lead to different decision boundaries and classification outcomes.

Remember that the plot represents a two-dimensional space, but Multinomial Logistic Regression can work with higher-dimensional feature spaces as well. The plot provides a visual understanding of the model's classification behavior, but it may not capture the full complexity of the underlying decision function in high-dimensional spaces.

Feel free to experiment with different datasets, predictor variables, and coefficients to see how the decision boundaries and color regions change in Multinomial Logistic Regression.

Ordinal Logistic Regression: In ordinal logistic regression, the dependent variable has three or more ordered categories. It predicts the probability of an observation falling into each category relative to the others, taking into account the order or hierarchy of the categories. In ordinal logistic regression, the dependent variable has three or more ordered categories. The model takes into account the order or hierarchy of the categories. It uses the cumulative logit or proportional odds model to model the cumulative probabilities of an observation falling into or below each category.

The cumulative logit model is defined as:

$$\text{logit}\ (P\ (y \leq j \mid X)) = \alpha\_j - \beta\text{\^{}}T{*}X \qquad \text{...(4\_}$$

Here, logit (P (y≤j | X)) represents the log-odds of the observation falling into or below category j, α_j represents the threshold or cutpoint for category j, β^T*X is the linear combination of predictors and coefficients, and P (y≤j | X) represents the cumulative probability of the observation falling into or below category j. The ordinal logistic regression model estimates the coefficients and thresholds that maximize the likelihood of observing the given data, given the predicted cumulative probabilities.

Example: In the given example, we are using ordinal logistic regression to model the relationship between the number of hours studied (predictor variable) and the academic performance category (ordinal target variable).

We generate example data using the NumPy library. The predictor variable, X, is generated as an array of random numbers drawn from a standard normal distribution. Each value represents the number of hours studied by a student. The target variable, y, is generated as an array of random integers between 0 and 2, representing the ordinal categories (low, medium, high) of academic performance.

Code:

```
import numpy as np
import matplotlib.pyplot as plt
import statsmodels.api as sm
```

```
# Generate example data
np.random.seed(0)
X = np.random.randn(100, 1)  # Predictor variable (number of hours studied)
y = np.random.randint(0, 3, 100)  # Ordinal target variable (academic performance category)

# Add constant column to the predictor variable
X = sm.add_constant(X)

# Fit ordinal logistic regression model
model = sm.MNLogit(y, X)
result = model.fit()

# Generate points on x-axis for plotting
x_vals = np.linspace(X[:, 1].min(), X[:, 1].max(), 100)

# Calculate cumulative probabilities for each category
cum_probs = result.predict(sm.add_constant(x_vals))

# Plot cumulative probabilities for each category
plt.plot(x_vals, cum_probs[:, 0], label='Low')
plt.plot(x_vals, cum_probs[:, 1], label='Medium')
plt.plot(x_vals, cum_probs[:, 2], label='High')

# Add labels and legend
plt.xlabel('Number of Hours Studied')
plt.ylabel('Cumulative Probability')
plt.legend()

# Show the plot
plt.show()
```

Output:

Optimization terminated successfully.

Current function value: 1.087302

Iterations: 4

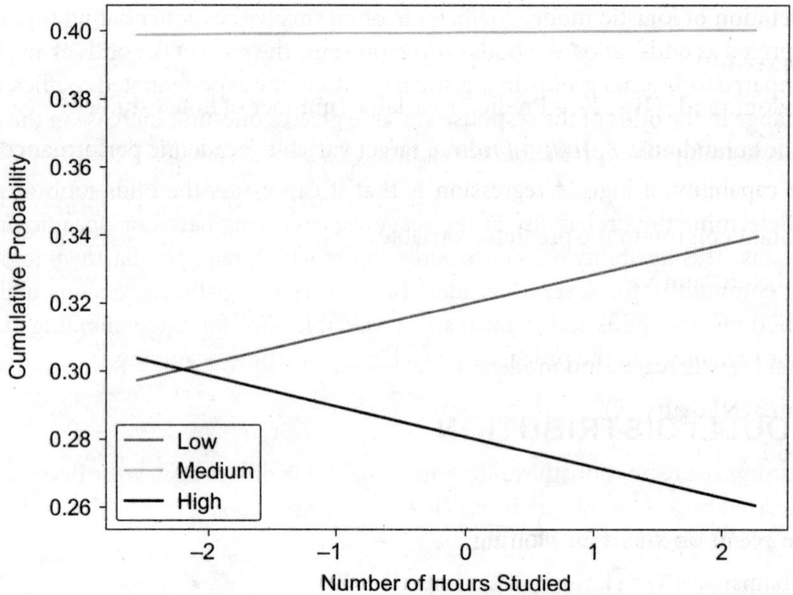

Explanation

The plot generated by the code shows the cumulative probabilities for each category (low, medium, high) as a function of the number of hours studied. Here's an explanation of the plot:

X-axis: Represents the number of hours studied, which is the predictor variable in this example.

Y-axis: Represents the cumulative probability. It shows the likelihood that an individual's academic performance category falls within or below a specific category.

Lines: Three lines are plotted, each representing the cumulative probability for a specific category (low, medium, high).

The blue line represents the cumulative probability for the "Low" category.

The orange line represents the cumulative probability for the "Medium" category.

The green line represents the cumulative probability for the "High" category.

Interpretation: As you move along the x-axis (number of hours studied), the lines depict how the cumulative probabilities change for each category. For example, the higher the number of hours studied, the higher the cumulative probability of achieving a higher performance category (e.g., medium or high). Conversely, a lower number of hours studied would result in a higher cumulative probability for the "Low" category.

Legend: The legend at the top right of the plot indicates the color corresponding to each category.

This plot provides insights into how the cumulative probabilities change as the predictor variable (number of hours studied) varies, allowing for a visual understanding of the relationship between the predictor variable and the ordinal target variable.

Basic of Logistic Model

Indeed, logistic regression is a powerful tool because it provides predictions in the form of probabilities that are bounded between 0 and 1. The logistic regression model predicts the probability that the response variable takes a value of 1, given a specific set of predictor values.

The interpretation of logistic model coefficients often involves exponentiating them, which allows them to be interpreted as odds ratios. An odds ratio represents the ratio of the odds of an event occurring in one group compared to another group. In logistic regression, the exponentiated coefficients provide the multiplicative change in the odds of the response variable given a one-unit increase in the corresponding predictor variable, holding other predictors constant.

The unique capability of logistic regression is that it can assess the odds ratio of predictors and simultaneously determine the probability of the response occurring based on specific predictor values or covariate patterns. This flexibility has contributed to the widespread popularity of logistic regression in the statistical community for several decades. In summary, logistic regression's ability to provide probability predictions and odds ratios makes it a valuable tool for understanding the relationship between predictor variables and the probability of a binary outcome occurring.

THE BERNOULLI DISTRIBUTION

In binary response logistic regression, the underlying probability distribution is the Bernoulli distribution, which is characterized by a set of observations that can take the values 1 or 0. The probability function for a random sample in logistic regression can be expressed as follows:

$$f(y, p) = \prod_{i=1}^{n} p_i^{y_i}(1-p_i)^{1-y_i} \qquad ...(1)$$

where the joint PDF is the product, Π, of each observation in the data being modeled, symbolized by the subscript i. Usually the product term is dropped as being understood since all joint probability functions are products across the independent components of their respective distributions. We may then characterize the Bernoulli distribution for a single observation as

$$f(y_i; p_i) = p_i^{y_i}(1-p_i)^{1-y_i} \qquad ...(2)$$

where y is the response variable being modeled and p is the probability that y has the value of 1. Again, 1 generally indicates a success, or that the event of interest has occurred. y only has values of 1 or 0, whereas p has values ranging from 0 to 1. p is many times symbolized as π or as μ. In fact, we shall be using the μ symbolization for the predicted mean or fit throughout most of the book. A probability function generates or produces data on the basis of known parameters. That's the meaning of f(y; p). What is needed in order to estimate the true parameters of the population data is to estimate the parameters on the basis of known data. After all we are modeling known data—and attempting to estimate parameter(s). We do this by inverting the order of y and p in the PDF. We attempt to calculate p on the basis of y. This relationship is called the likelihood function.

Statisticians may characterize the likelihood function as

$$L(p_i; y_i) = p_i^{y_i}(1-p_i)1-y_i \qquad ...(3)$$

But usually parameterize the structure of the likelihood function by putting it into what is called exponential family form. Mathematically it is identical to Equation 3 above.

$$L(p; y) = \prod_{i=1}^{n} \exp\left\{y_i \ln\left(\frac{p_i}{1-p_i}\right) + \ln(1-p_i)\right\} \qquad ...(4)$$

Note that "ln" is a symbol for the natural log of an expression. It is also symbolized as "log." Keep in mind that it differs from "log to the base 10," or "log10." The exponentiation of a logged value is the value itself; that is, exp(ln(x)) = x, or $e^{\ln(x)} = x$.

Statisticians usually take the log of both sides of the likelihood function, creating what is called the log-likelihood function. Doing this allows a summation across observations rather than multiplication. This makes it much easier for the algorithms used to estimate distribution parameters to converge; that is, to solve for the estimates. The Bernoulli log-likelihood function can be displayed as

$$L(p; y) = \sum_{i=1}^{n} \left\{ y_i \ln\left(\frac{p_i}{1-p_i}\right) + \ln(1-p_i) \right\} \qquad ...(5)$$

The model parameters may be determined by simple calculus. Take the derivative of the log-likelihood function, set to 0, and solve. The problem is that the solution must be obtained iteratively, but for most all modeling situations, the solution takes only a few iterations to find the appropriate parameter estimates. The details of estimation can be found in Hilbe (2009). We need not worry about them in this discussion.

One of the nice features of presenting the log-likelihood function in exponential form is that we may abstract from it a link function as well as the mean and variance functions of the underlying Bernoulli distribution. The link function, which I'll discuss shortly, is whatever follows the y of the first term of the right-hand side of Equation 1.5. Here it is log(p/(1 – p)). The mean of the distribution can be obtained as the derivative of the negative of the second term with respect to the link. The second derivative yields the variance. For the Bernoulli distribution, these values are

$$\text{Mean} = \mu = p$$
$$\text{Variance} = V(\mu) = p(1-p) = \mu(1-\mu)$$

In the case of Bernoulli-based logistic regression, the mean is symbolized as μ (mu) and variance as μ(1 – μ). The above link and log-likelihood functions are many times expressed in terms of μ as well. It is important to note that strictly speaking the estimated p or μ should be symbolized as $\hat{p}$ and $\hat{\propto}$, respectively. p and μ are typically reserved for the true population values. However, for ease of interpretation, I will use the symbol μ in place of $\hat{\propto}$ throughout the book.

I should also mention that for grouped logistic regression, which we address in Chapter 5, μ and p are not the same, with μ defined as n · p. But I'll delay making this distinction until we begin discussing grouped models.

Let us look at a logistic regression and how it differs from normal or ordinary linear regression. Recall that a regression attempts to understand a response variable on the basis of one of more predictors or explanatory variables. This is usually symbolized as

$$\hat{y}_i = \beta_0 + \beta_1 x_{i1} + \beta_2 x_{i2} + ... + \beta_p x_{ip} \qquad ...(6\_$$

where y-hat, or $\hat{y}$, is the sum of the terms in the regression. The sum of regression terms is also referred to as the linear predictor, or xb. Each βx is a term indicating the value of a predictor, x, and its coefficient, β. In linear regression, which is based in matrix form on the Gaussian or normal probability distribution, $\hat{y}$ is the predicted value of the regression model as well as the linear predictor. j indicates the number of predictors in a model. There is a linear relationship between the predicted or fitted values of the model and the terms on the right-hand side of Equation 6—the linear predictor. $y\hat{x} = b$. This is not the case for logistic regression.

The linear predictor of the logistic model is

$$x_i b = \beta_0 + \beta_1 x_{i1} + + \beta_2 x_{i2} + ... + \beta_p x_{ip} \qquad ...(7)$$

However, the fitted or predicted value of the logistic model is based on the link function, log(μ/(1 – μ)). In order to establish a linear relationship of the predicted value, μ, and the linear predictor, we have the following relationship:

$$\ln\left(\frac{\mu_i}{1-\mu_i}\right) = x_i b = \beta_0 + \beta_1 x_{i1} + \beta_2 x_{i2} + \ldots + \beta_p x_{ip} \quad \ldots(8\_$$

where μ, like p, is the probability that the response value y is equal to 1. It can also be thought of as the probability of the presence or occurrence of some characteristic, while 1 – p can be thought of as the probability of the absence of that characteristic. Notice that μ/(1 – μ), or p/(1 – p), is the formula for odds. The odds of something occurring is the probability of its success or presence divided by the probability of its failure or absence, 1 – p. If μ = 0.7, (1 – μ) = 0.3μ + (1 – μ) always equals 1. The log of the odds has been called by statisticians the logit function, from which the term logistic regression derives.

In order to determine μ on the basis of the linear predictor, xb, we solve the logit function for μ, without displaying subscripts, as

$$\mu = \frac{\exp(xb)}{1+\exp(xb)} = \frac{1}{1+\exp(-xb)} \quad \ldots(9)$$

The equations in (1.9) above are very important, and will be frequently used in our later discussion. Once a logistic model is solved, we may calculate the linear predictor, xb, and then apply either equation to determine the predicted value, μ for each observation in the model.

Evaluating Hypotheses

In various scenarios, it is crucial to accurately evaluate the performance of learned hypotheses. There are two main reasons for this. Firstly, it helps determine whether the hypothesis should be used or not. For instance, when dealing with a limited-size database that assesses the effectiveness of different medical treatments, it is essential to have a precise understanding of the accuracy of the learned hypotheses. This knowledge guides decision-making regarding the adoption or rejection of the hypothesis. Secondly, evaluating hypotheses plays a vital role in many learning methods. For example, in the process of post-pruning decision trees to avoid overfitting, it is necessary to assess the impact of potential pruning steps on the accuracy of the resulting decision tree. By understanding the likely errors associated with estimating the accuracy of both the pruned and unpruned trees, one can make informed decisions about the effectiveness of the pruning process.

In summary, accurate evaluation of learned hypotheses is important for both determining their usability and assessing their impact within learning algorithms. It helps avoid erroneous conclusions and guides decision-making in various domains and tasks.

Estimating the accuracy of a hypothesis becomes more challenging when the available data is limited. In such cases, two main difficulties arise:

Bias in the estimate. When evaluating the accuracy of a learned hypothesis, relying solely on its performance on the training examples can lead to an optimistic bias. This is because the hypothesis is specifically designed to fit the training data, potentially resulting in overfitting. The overfitted hypothesis may perform well on the training examples but may not generalize well to unseen data.

To obtain an unbiased estimate of the hypothesis's accuracy on future examples, it is common practice to evaluate it on a separate set of test examples. These test examples should be chosen independently of the training data and the hypothesis itself. By using a separate test set, we can assess how well the hypothesis performs on new, unseen examples and obtain a more reliable estimate of its future accuracy.

By testing the hypothesis on an independent test set, we can gauge its ability to generalize beyond the training data and gain a better understanding of its performance in real-world scenarios. This helps mitigate the impact of overfitting and provides a more objective measure of the hypothesis's accuracy.

Variance in the estimate. Another challenge in estimating the accuracy of a hypothesis arises from the composition of the test examples used for evaluation. Even when the test examples are chosen independently and unbiasedly from the training examples, the measured accuracy can still differ from the true accuracy of the hypothesis.

The variability in the measured accuracy is influenced by the specific makeup of the test examples. If the test set is relatively small, there is a higher likelihood of experiencing greater variance in the measured accuracy. This means that different subsets of test examples may yield slightly different accuracy measurements.

The reason for this variability is that the performance of a hypothesis can be influenced by the specific characteristics and distribution of the test examples. If the test set is not representative of the overall data distribution, the measured accuracy may not accurately reflect the hypothesis's performance on unseen examples.

To mitigate this issue, it is advisable to use larger test sets whenever possible. By increasing the number of test examples, we can reduce the impact of sample variability and obtain a more reliable estimate of the hypothesis's true accuracy.

ESTIMATING HYPOTHESIS ACCURACY

During the evaluation of a learned hypothesis, our primary goal is to estimate its accuracy in classifying future instances. Simultaneously, we also aim to determine the likely error associated with this accuracy estimate. In other words, we want to quantify the uncertainty or variability in the estimated accuracy and establish confidence intervals or error bars to accompany the estimate. Estimating the probable error in the accuracy estimate is crucial for understanding the reliability and generalizability of the learned hypothesis. It allows us to gauge the level of confidence we can place in the accuracy estimate and provides valuable insights into the performance of the hypothesis on unseen data. By assessing the error bars associated with the accuracy estimate, we can gain a better understanding of the potential range within which the true accuracy of the hypothesis is expected to lie. This information helps in making informed decisions about the suitability and effectiveness of the learned hypothesis for real-world applications.

Various statistical techniques and evaluation methods can be employed to estimate the error and establish confidence intervals for the accuracy estimate. These techniques take into account factors such as the size of the evaluation set, the variability of the data, and the assumptions made during the learning process.

In this chapter, we examine a specific setting for the learning problem. We start with a space of possible instances, denoted as X, which represents a broad range of objects or entities (e.g., all people in a population). Within this space, there exist various target functions that we are interested in learning (e.g., identifying individuals who are likely to purchase new skis this year).

We assume that different instances within the space X may occur with different frequencies or probabilities. To capture this, we introduce an unknown probability distribution, denoted as D, which defines the likelihood of encountering each instance in X. For example, the distribution D might assign a higher probability to encountering 19-year-old people compared to 109-year-old people. Importantly, this probability distribution D does not specify whether a given instance is a positive or negative example; it solely determines the probability of encountering the instance. The learning task at hand is to learn the target concept or target function, denoted as f. To accomplish this, we consider a space of possible hypotheses, denoted as H, which represents different possible explanations or models for the target concept. The learner receives training examples of the target function f from a trainer. The trainer selects instances independently from the distribution D and provides the learner with each instance x along with its correct target value f(x).

The goal of the learner is to use the provided training examples to infer and learn the underlying target concept or function f. This involves finding the most suitable hypothesis from the hypothesis space H that accurately captures the relationship between instances and their corresponding target values.

To provide a concrete example, let's consider the learning task of predicting whether a person plans to purchase new skis this year. We collect a sample of training data by surveying people as they arrive at a ski resort. In this scenario, the instance space X represents the space of all people, and each person can be characterized by various attributes such as their age, occupation, frequency of skiing last year, and so on. The probability distribution D is defined over this instance space X. It assigns a probability to each person, indicating the likelihood that the person will be encountered as the next individual arriving at the ski resort. For example, younger individuals who frequently visit ski resorts might have a higher probability of being encountered compared to older individuals with no prior skiing experience. The target function f : X + {O,1), denoted as f, takes an instance x from the instance space X and assigns it a binary label {0, 1} based on whether or not the person plans to purchase new skis this year. The function f essentially classifies each person according to their intention to buy skis. The learning task is to learn the target function f using the training data collected from the survey. Each training example consists of an instance x, representing a person, and its corresponding target value f(x) indicating whether the person plans to purchase skis. By analyzing the collected training data and considering different hypotheses from the hypothesis space H, the learner aims to find the best-fitting hypothesis that accurately predicts whether an individual intends to buy skis based on their attributes.

In summary, in this specific example, the instance space X represents all people, the probability distribution D determines the likelihood of encountering each person, and the target function f classifies individuals as either planning to purchase skis or not. The learning task is to learn the target function f by leveraging the training data obtained through surveys conducted at the ski resort.

Within this general setting we are interested in the following two questions:

1. Given a hypothesis h and a data sample containing n examples drawn at random according to the distribution D, what is the best estimate of the accuracy of h over future instances drawn from the same distribution?
2. What is the probable error in this accuracy estimate?

Sample Error and True Error

To answer these questions, we need to distinguish carefully between two notions of accuracy or, equivalently, error. One is the error rate of the hypothesis over the sample of data that is available. The other is the error rate of the hypothesis over the entire unknown distribution D of examples. We will call these the sample error and the true error respectively.

The sample error of a hypothesis with respect to some sample S of instances drawn from X is the fraction of S that it misclassifies:

Definition: The sample error (denoted $error_s(h)$) of hypothesis h with respect to target function f and data sample S is

$$error_s(h) = \frac{1}{n}\sum_{x \in S} \delta(f(x), h(x))$$

Where n is the number of examples in S, and the quantity $S(f(x), h(x))$ is 1 if $f(x) \neq h(x)$, and 0 otherwise.

The true error of a hypothesis is the probability that it will misclassify a single randomly drawn instance from the distribution D.

Definition: The true error (denoted $error_D(h)$) of hypothesis h with respect to target function f and distribution D, is the probability that h will misclassify an instance drawn at random according to D.

$$error_D(h) = \Pr_{x \in D}[f(x) \neq h(x)]$$

Here the notation denotes that the probability is taken over the instance distribution D.

What we usually wish to know is the true error $error_D(h)$ of the hypothesis, because this is the error we can expect when applying the hypothesis to future examples. All we can measure, however, is the sample error $error_s(h)$ of the hypothesis for the data sample S that we happen to have in hand. The main question considered in this section is "How good an estimate of $error_D(h)$ is provided by $error_s(h)$?"

Confidence Intervals for Discrete-Valued Hypotheses

Here we give an answer to the question "How good an estimate of $error_D(h)$ is provided by $error_s(h)$?' for the case in which h is a discrete-valued hypothesis. More specifically, suppose we wish to estimate the true error for some discrete valued hypothesis h, based on its observed sample error over a sample S, where

- the sample S contains n examples drawn independent of one another, and independent of h, according to the probability distribution D
- n>=30
- hypothesis h commits r errors over these n examples (i.e., errors(h) = r/n).

Under these conditions, statistical theory allows us to make the following assertions:

1. Given no other information, the most probable value of $error_D(h)$ is errors(h)
2. With approximately 95% probability, the true error $error_D(h)$ lies in the interval

$$erros_s(h) \pm 1.96\sqrt{\frac{error_s(h)(1 - error_s(h))}{n}}$$

BASICS OF SAMPLING THEORY

In this section, we will cover fundamental concepts from statistics and sampling theory that are essential for understanding the principles of hypothesis testing and estimation. These concepts include probability distributions, expected value, variance, as well as specific distributions such as the Binomial and Normal distributions. We will also explore the notion of confidence intervals, both two-sided and one-sided. To grasp the concepts presented in this section, it is beneficial to have a foundational understanding of these statistical concepts. Probability distributions describe the likelihood of different outcomes occurring, while expected value represents the average value we would expect to obtain from a random variable. Variance, on the other hand, measures the spread or variability of a distribution.

- A random variable represents the outcome of a probabilistic experiment and can be viewed as a variable that takes on different values based on the result of the experiment. In other words, it is a numerical quantity that is associated with the uncertain outcomes of the experiment.

  For example, consider the experiment of flipping a fair coin. We can define a random variable, let's say X, to represent the outcome of this experiment. X can take two possible values: "Heads" or "Tails," corresponding to the two possible outcomes of the coin flip. The value of X depends on the actual outcome of the experiment, and it provides a way to assign a numerical representation to the different outcomes.

  Random variables can be classified as either discrete or continuous. Discrete random variables have a countable number of possible values, such as the number of heads obtained in multiple coin flips. Continuous random variables, on the other hand, can take on any value within a certain range, such as the height of individuals or the time it takes to complete a task.
- A probability distribution for a random variable Y describes the likelihood or probability of each possible value that Y can take on. It specifies the probabilities associated with each value of Y, denoted as Pr(Y = yi), where yi represents a specific outcome or value that Y can assume.
- The expected value, also known as the mean, of a random variable Y is a measure of the average or central tendency of its possible values. It represents the weighted sum of the values of Y, where each value is weighted by its corresponding probability. The expected value of Y, denoted as E[Y] or sometimes represented by the symbol μ, is calculated by multiplying each possible value yi of Y by its corresponding probability Pr(Y = yi), and then summing up these products for all possible values of Y:

  $$E[Y] = \Sigma\, yi * Pr(Y = yi)$$

  In this formula, Ci represents a constant that is often omitted for simplicity. The expected value, or mean, of a random variable Y is E[Y] = Ci yi Pr(Y = yi). The symbol μy is commonly used to represent E[Y].
- The variance of a random variable Y measures the spread or dispersion of its possible values around the expected value or mean (μy). It quantifies the average squared deviation of Y from its mean.

  The variance of Y, denoted as Var(Y), is calculated by taking the expected value of the squared difference between Y and its mean:

  $$Var(Y) = E[(Y - \mu y)^2]$$

  In this formula, (Y - μy) represents the deviation of each value of Y from its mean, squared to eliminate the effect of negative deviations. The expected value operator E[] is then applied to obtain the average of these squared deviations. The variance provides a measure of the variability or spread of the random variable Y. A smaller variance indicates that the values of Y tend to be close to the mean, while a larger variance indicates greater variability or dispersion. The square root of the variance, known as the standard deviation, is often used as a more interpretable measure of the spread of the distribution. It has the same units as the random variable Y and provides a measure of the average deviation from the mean.
- The standard deviation of a random variable Y is a measure of the dispersion or spread of its possible values around the mean (μy). It provides a more interpretable measure of variability than the variance. The standard deviation of Y, denoted as σy, is calculated as the square root of the variance:

  $$\sigma y = \sqrt{Var(Y)}$$

In other words, it is the positive square root of the variance. By taking the square root, the standard deviation is returned to the original units of the random variable Y, making it easier to interpret.

The standard deviation quantifies the average amount by which individual values of Y deviate from the mean. A smaller standard deviation indicates that the values of Y tend to be closer to the mean, while a larger standard deviation indicates greater variability or dispersion of values. The standard deviation is widely used in statistics and probability theory to describe the spread of data or the uncertainty associated with a random variable. It helps in understanding the range of values that can be expected for Y and allows for comparisons between different datasets or distributions.

- The Binomial distribution is a discrete probability distribution that models the number of successes (e.g., heads) in a fixed number of independent Bernoulli trials (e.g., coin tosses), where each trial has the same probability of success (e.g., probability of heads) denoted as p.

  The probability mass function (PMF) of the Binomial distribution is given by:

  $$P(X = r) = C(n, r) * p^r * (1 - p)^(n - r)$$

  where:

  X is the random variable representing the number of successes (r heads),
  n is the number of trials (coin tosses),
  r is the number of successes (heads) we want to observe,
  C(n, r) is the binomial coefficient, also known as "n choose r" and represents the number of ways to choose r successes from n trials,
  p is the probability of success (probability of heads in a single toss),
  (1 – p) is the probability of failure (probability of tails in a single toss).

- The Normal distribution, also known as the Gaussian distribution or bell curve, is a continuous probability distribution that is widely used to model and describe various natural phenomena and measurements in fields such as statistics, physics, finance, and social sciences.

  The Normal distribution is characterized by its bell-shaped curve, which is symmetric and centered around its mean, denoted by μ (mu). The shape of the curve is determined by two parameters: the mean μ and the standard deviation σ (sigma). The mean represents the central tendency or average of the distribution, while the standard deviation represents the spread or dispersion of the data points around the mean.

  The probability density function (PDF) of the Normal distribution is given by the formula:

  $$f(x) = (1/\sqrt{}(2\pi\sigma^2)) * e^(-(x - \mu)^2/(2\sigma^2))$$

  where:

  x is the random variable representing the observed values,
  μ is the mean of the distribution,
  σ is the standard deviation of the distribution,
  π is the mathematical constant pi,
  e is the mathematical constant approximately equal to 2.71828.

- The Central Limit Theorem (CLT) is a fundamental result in probability theory and statistics. It states that under certain conditions, the sum (or average) of a large number of independent and identically distributed (i.i.d.) random variables will be approximately normally distributed, regardless of the shape of the original distribution.

The key idea behind the Central Limit Theorem is that as the sample size increases, the distribution of the sample mean becomes increasingly close to a Normal distribution. This holds true even if the individual random variables are not normally distributed themselves. This makes the Normal distribution a useful approximation for many real-world phenomena, as it often emerges as the limiting distribution of the sample mean.

- An estimator is a statistical concept that refers to a random variable or a function of random variables used to estimate an unknown parameter of interest in a population. The estimator provides an estimate or approximation of the parameter based on observed data.

  Let's denote the estimator as Y, and the parameter being estimated as p. The estimator Y takes on different values depending on the sample data it is calculated from. Each value of the estimator Y corresponds to a specific estimate of the parameter p. The estimator Y is considered a random variable because its value is subject to variation due to sampling variability. The goal of using an estimator is to obtain an estimate of the parameter that is as close to the true value as possible. The quality of an estimator is typically assessed based on its accuracy, precision, bias, and efficiency.

- The estimation bias of an estimator Y for a parameter p is defined as the difference between the expected value of the estimator, E[Y], and the true value of the parameter, p. Mathematically, the bias is calculated as (E[Y] – p).

  If the bias of an estimator is zero, it means that, on average, the estimator provides estimates that are equal to the true parameter value. In other words, the estimator does not systematically overestimate or underestimate the parameter.

  An unbiased estimator is desirable because it provides estimates that are, on average, accurate representations of the true parameter value. However, it's important to note that unbiasedness does not guarantee that individual estimates will always be close to the true value. Unbiasedness only implies that, on average, the estimator is not systematically biased in one direction.

- A N% confidence interval estimate for a parameter p is a range of values calculated from sample data that is expected to include the true value of the parameter with a probability of N%. This means that if we were to repeatedly sample from the same population and construct N% confidence intervals, approximately N% of those intervals would contain the true parameter value.

Error Estimation and Estimating Binomial Proportions

Error estimation refers to the process of estimating the error or uncertainty associated with a statistical estimate or prediction. In various fields, including statistics and machine learning, error estimation plays a crucial role in assessing the reliability and accuracy of models and predictions.

When it comes to estimating binomial proportions, which involves estimating the probability of success in a binary outcome (e.g., the proportion of successes in a series of trials), error estimation is particularly important. Estimating binomial proportions is commonly encountered in areas such as quality control, public opinion polling, and medical research. To estimate the error or uncertainty associated with a binomial proportion estimate, several methods can be employed. One commonly used approach is based on the properties of the binomial distribution and the concept of confidence intervals. A confidence interval provides a range of plausible values for the unknown binomial proportion, along with an associated level of confidence. The width of the interval reflects the uncertainty in the estimate. The most widely used method for constructing confidence intervals for binomial proportions is the

Wald method, which relies on approximations using the normal distribution. Other methods, such as the Wilson score interval or the Agresti-Coull interval, provide improved performance for small sample sizes or extreme proportions.

In addition to confidence intervals, other error estimation techniques for binomial proportions include hypothesis testing, where the null hypothesis assumes a specific proportion value, and the p-value is used to assess the evidence against the null hypothesis. Resampling methods, such as bootstrapping, can also be employed to estimate the sampling distribution and derive confidence intervals.

Overall, error estimation is essential in estimating binomial proportions to quantify the uncertainty in the estimated proportions and provide a measure of the reliability of the results. It allows researchers and practitioners to make informed decisions and draw valid conclusions based on the estimated proportions and their associated uncertainties.

The Binomial Distribution

The binomial distribution is a probability distribution that models the number of successes in a fixed number of independent Bernoulli trials. It is characterized by two parameters: the number of trials (n) and the probability of success in each trial (p).

The probability mass function (PMF) of the binomial distribution is given by the formula:

$$P(X = k) = C(n, k) * p^k * (1 - p)^(n - k)$$

where:

X is the random variable representing the number of successes

k is the number of successes we are interested in

C(n, k) is the binomial coefficient, also known as "n choose k," which represents the number of ways to choose k successes out of n trials

p is the probability of success in a single trial

(1 – p) is the probability of failure in a single trial

n is the total number of trials

The mean (μ) and variance (σ^2) of the binomial distribution are given by:

$$\mu = n * p$$

$$\sigma^2 = n * p * (1 - p)$$

These formulas provide information about the expected number of successes and the spread or variability of the distribution.

The binomial distribution is commonly used in various applications, such as analyzing survey responses, modeling the success rate of a manufacturing process, or studying the occurrence of events with two possible outcomes (success or failure). It is particularly useful when dealing with discrete data and a fixed number of trials.

By understanding the binomial distribution, we can calculate probabilities, make predictions, and analyze the behavior of random variables associated with binomial processes.

For example, let's say we have a dataset of 100 customers, and 70 of them made a purchase. We can model this using the binomial distribution with n = 100 and the estimated probability p = 0.7. With this distribution, we can make predictions on the likelihood of future customers making a purchase based on their characteristics or features.

Example: We set the parameters n to 10 (number of trials) and p to 0.5 (probability of success). We calculate the binomial probabilities using the formula P(X=k) = C(n, k) * p^k * (1-p)^(n-k), where C(n,

k) is the binomial coefficient. We then plot the probabilities using a bar plot, with the x-axis representing the number of successes and the y-axis representing the probability.

The resulting plot will show the distribution of the number of successes in n trials with a probability of success p.

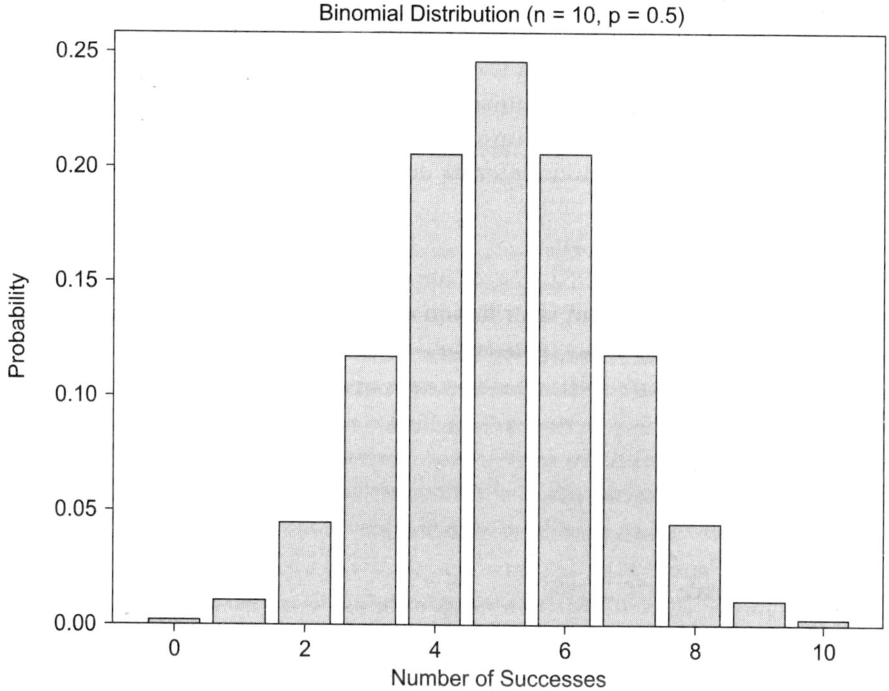

In summary, the binomial distribution provides a mathematical framework to model and analyze scenarios with a fixed number of independent trials and two possible outcomes. In machine learning, it is commonly used to estimate probabilities and make predictions in binary classification problems.

Mean and Variance

The expected value, also known as the mean value or average, is a measure of the central tendency of a random variable. It represents the average value that would be obtained if the random variable were repeatedly sampled.

Mathematically, the expected value of a discrete random variable X is denoted as E[X] or μ and is calculated by summing the product of each possible value of X and its corresponding probability.

$$E[X] = \Sigma (x * P(X = x))$$

In simpler terms, it is the weighted average of all possible values of X, where the weights are given by the probabilities of each value occurring.

The variance of a random variable measures the spread or variability of its values around the expected value. It quantifies the average squared deviation of the random variable from its mean.

Mathematically, the variance of a random variable X is denoted as Var(X) or σ^2 and is calculated by taking the sum of the squared differences between each value of X and its expected value, weighted by their corresponding probabilities.

$$Var(X) = \Sigma ((x - E[X])^2 * P(X = x))$$

The variance provides information about the dispersion of the random variable's values. A smaller variance indicates that the values are closer to the expected value, while a larger variance indicates greater variability.

These properties, the expected value and variance, are fundamental in understanding the behavior and characteristics of random variables. They provide insights into the central tendency and spread of the variable's values, which are crucial for various statistical analyses and decision-making processes.

The standard deviation is a measure of the dispersion or spread of a random variable's values around its mean or expected value. It is the square root of the variance and provides a more intuitive understanding of the variability of the random variable.

Mathematically, the standard deviation of a random variable X is denoted as σ and is calculated as the square root of the variance:

$$\sigma = \sqrt{\text{Var}(X)}$$

The standard deviation represents the typical amount by which individual values deviate from the mean. A smaller standard deviation indicates that the values are closely clustered around the mean, while a larger standard deviation indicates greater variability or dispersion of the values.

In practical terms, the standard deviation allows us to quantify the typical range within which most of the random variable's values lie. It is widely used in statistics to compare the variability of different datasets, assess the precision of estimates, and make inferences about the population from a sample.

By understanding the standard deviation of a random variable, we gain insights into the spread and consistency of its values, enabling us to better interpret and analyze the data.

Estimators, Bias, and Variance

In statistics, estimators are used to estimate unknown parameters of a population based on sample data. Estimators are random variables themselves, and their properties, such as bias and variance, are important in assessing their quality and reliability.

Bias: The bias of an estimator measures the systematic deviation between the expected value of the estimator and the true value of the parameter being estimated. An estimator is unbiased if, on average, it produces estimates that are equal to the true value of the parameter. Mathematically, the bias of an estimator $E[\hat{\theta}] - \theta$, where $E[\hat{\theta}]$ represents the expected value of the estimator and θ represents the true value of the parameter. A biased estimator consistently overestimates or underestimates the true parameter value.

The bias of an estimator is defined as the difference between the expected value of the estimator and the true value of the parameter:

$$\text{Bias}(\hat{\theta}) = E[\hat{\theta}] - \theta$$

where $E[\hat{\theta}]$ represents the expected value of the estimator $\hat{\theta}$ and θ represents the true value of the parameter being estimated.

Variance: The variance of an estimator quantifies the variability or spread of the estimator's values around its expected value. It measures how much the estimates of the parameter differ from one another when obtained from different samples. A high variance indicates that the estimator's values are widely scattered, while a low variance indicates that they are more tightly clustered. Mathematically, the variance of an estimator is denoted as $\text{Var}(\hat{\theta})$.

The variance of an estimator measures the spread or variability of the estimator's values around its expected value:

$$\mathrm{Var}(\hat{\theta}) = E[(\hat{\theta} - E[\hat{\theta}])^2]$$

where $\mathrm{Var}(\hat{\theta})$ represents the variance of the estimator $\hat{\theta}$.

Bias-Variance Tradeoff: There is often a tradeoff between bias and variance in estimators. An estimator with low bias tends to provide estimates close to the true parameter value, but it may have a higher variability (higher variance) across different samples. On the other hand, an estimator with low variance produces more consistent estimates but may have a systematic deviation from the true parameter value (bias). Achieving an optimal balance between bias and variance depends on the specific context and goals of the estimation.

Minimizing Mean Squared Error: In many cases, the quality of an estimator is evaluated based on its mean squared error (MSE), which is the average of the squared differences between the estimator's values and the true parameter value. The MSE can be decomposed into the sum of the bias squared and the variance of the estimator:

$$\mathrm{MSE}(\hat{\theta}) = \mathrm{Bias}(\hat{\theta})^2 + \mathrm{Var}(\hat{\theta})$$

Minimizing the MSE involves finding an estimator that strikes a balance between low bias and low variance. However, reducing bias often increases variance and vice versa, so careful consideration is needed to select an appropriate estimator for a given problem.

Understanding the bias and variance of estimators helps in assessing their reliability, comparing different estimation methods, and making informed decisions in statistical analyses.

Confidence Intervals

A confidence interval is a range of values that is constructed based on the sample data and is expected to contain the true value of a parameter with a certain level of confidence. More precisely:

An N% confidence interval for a parameter p is an interval estimate calculated from the sample data, such that if we were to repeat the sampling process many times and construct N% confidence intervals, approximately N% of those intervals would contain the true value of the parameter.

For example, if we have a 95% confidence interval for a population mean, it means that if we were to repeat the sampling process many times and calculate 95% confidence intervals, approximately 95% of those intervals would include the true population mean. The level of confidence, denoted as N%, represents the desired probability of capturing the true parameter value within the interval. Common levels of confidence include 90%, 95%, and 99%, among others.

The construction of a confidence interval involves using statistical methods and formulas, typically based on the sample data and assuming certain distributional assumptions. The width of the interval is influenced by factors such as the sample size, variability of the data, and the desired level of confidence. Confidence intervals are widely used in statistical inference to provide a range of plausible values for an unknown parameter based on limited sample data. They help quantify the uncertainty associated with the estimation process and provide a measure of the precision of the estimate.

Let's consider an **example** of estimating the population mean μ based on a sample from a normally distributed population.

Suppose we have a random sample of size n from the population, denoted as $X_1, X_2, \ldots, X_n$, where each Xi follows a normal distribution with mean μ and variance σ^2.

The sample mean, denoted as $\bar{X}$ (X-bar), is an estimator of the population mean μ. Its mathematical formula is:

$$\bar{X} = (X_1 + X_2 + ... + X_n)/n$$

The expected value (mean) of the sample mean is equal to the population mean:

$$E[\bar{X}] = E[(X_1 + X_2 + ... + X_n)/n] = (E[X_1] + E[X_2] + ... + E[X_n])/n = \mu$$

This means that, on average, the sample mean ⊠X will be equal to the population mean μ.

The variance of the sample mean, denoted as Var(⊠X), is calculated as:

$$\begin{aligned} Var(\bar{X}) &= Var[(X_1 + X_2 + ... + X_n)/n] \\ &= (1/n^2) * (Var(X_1) + Var(X_2) + ... + Var(X_n)) = (\sigma^2/n) \end{aligned}$$

The standard deviation of the sample mean, denoted as σ(⊠X), is the square root of the variance:

$$\sigma(\bar{X}) = \sqrt{(\sigma^2/n)}$$

Now, let's say we want to construct a 95% confidence interval for the population mean μ. We can use the formula:

$$\bar{X} \pm Z * (\sigma(\bar{X}))$$

Here, Z is the critical value from the standard normal distribution that corresponds to the desired level of confidence. For a 95% confidence interval, Z is approximately 1.96.

For example, if we have a sample of size n = 100, and the sample mean is $\bar{X}$ = 50, and the sample standard deviation is s = 10, then the confidence interval would be:

$$50 \pm 1.96 * (10/\sqrt{100}) = 50 \pm 1.96$$

Thus, the 95% confidence interval for the population mean μ would be (48.04, 51.96).

This means that we are 95% confident that the true population mean falls within this interval. In repeated sampling, approximately 95% of the calculated confidence intervals will contain the true population mean.

The confidence interval provides a range of plausible values for the population mean based on the sample data, taking into account the uncertainty associated with the estimation process.

A Normal distribution (also called a Gaussian distribution) is a bell-shaped distribution defined by

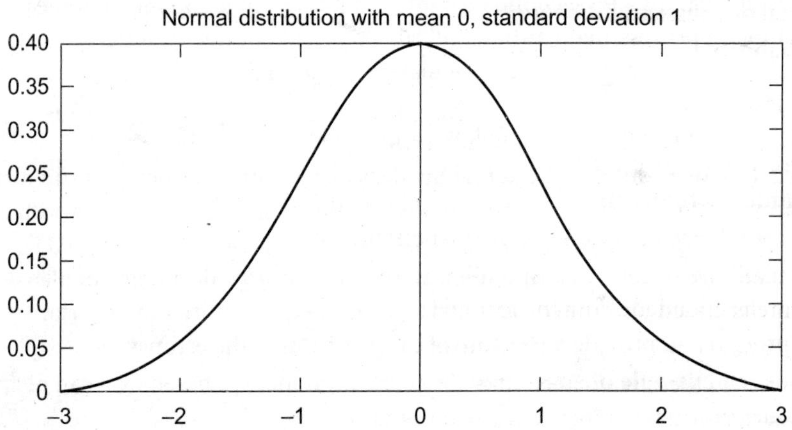

the probability density function

$$p(x) = \frac{1}{\sqrt{2\pi\sigma^2}} e^{-\frac{1}{2}\left(\frac{x-\mu}{\sigma}\right)^2}$$

A Normal distribution is fully determined by two parameters in the above formula: μ and σ.

If the random variable X follows a normal distribution, then:

The probability that X will fall into the interval (a, b) is given by

$$\equiv_{a}^{b} p(x)dx$$

The expected, or mean value of X, E[X], is

$$E[X] = \mu$$

The variance of X, Var(X), is

$$Var(X) = \sigma^2$$

The standard deviation of X, σx, is

$$\sigma x = \sigma$$

The Central Limit Theorem states that the sum of a large number of independent, identically distributed random variables follows a distribution that is approximately Normal.

mean μ and standard deviation σ. For large n, any Binomial distribution is very closely approximated by a Normal distribution with the same mean and variance.

One reason that we prefer to work with the Normal distribution is that most statistics references give tables specifying the size of the interval about the mean that contains N% of the probability mass under the Normal distribution. This is precisely the information needed to calculate our N% confidence interval.

To summarize, if a random variable Y obeys a Normal distribution with mean μ and standard deviation σ, then the measured random value y of Y will fall into the following interval N% of the time

$$\mu \pm z_N\sigma$$

Equivalently, the mean μ will fall into the following interval N% of the time

$$y \pm z_N\sigma$$

The normal or gaussian distribution

1. **Probability Density Function (PDF):**

   The PDF of the Normal distribution is given by the formula:

   PDF(x) = (1/sqrt(2πσ^2)) * exp(–(x – μ)^2/(2σ^2))

   where x is the variable, μ is the mean of the distribution, and σ is the standard deviation.

2. **Confidence Interval:**

   The confidence interval for a Normal distribution is calculated as follows:

   Calculate the z-score corresponding to the desired confidence level. For a two-tailed test, the z-score is obtained using the formula:

   z = invNorm(1 – (1 – α)/2)

   where α is the significance level (1-confidence level), and invNorm() is the inverse of the standard Normal cumulative distribution function.

   Calculate the margin of error:

   Margin of Error = z * σ

where z is the z-score and σ is the standard deviation.

Calculate the lower bound of the confidence interval:

$$\text{Lower Bound} = \mu - \text{Margin of Error}$$

Calculate the upper bound of the confidence interval:

$$\text{Upper Bound} = \mu + \text{Margin of Error}$$

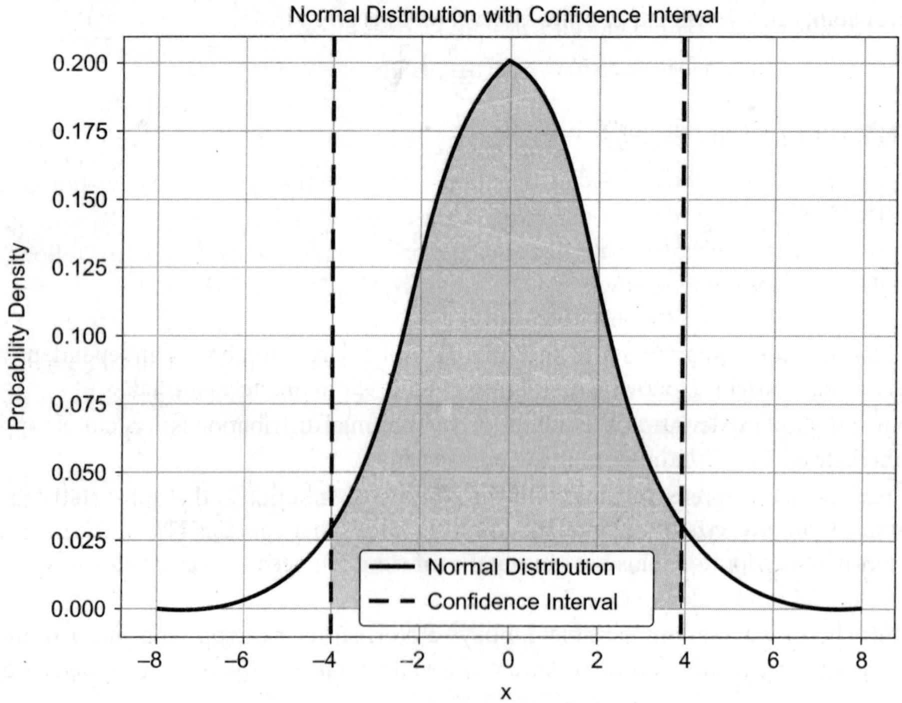

A GENERAL APPROACH FOR DERIVING CONFIDENCE INTERVALS

The approach described there illustrates a general approach followed in many estima6on problems. In particular, we can see this as a problem of estimating the mean (expected value) of a population based on the mean of a randomly drawn sample of size n.

The general process includes the following steps:

Identify the underlying population parameter p to be estimated, for example, $error_D(h)$.

Define the estimator Y (e.g., $error_s(h)$). It is desirable to choose a minimum variance, unbiased estimator.

Define the probability distribution Dy that governs the estimator Y, including its mean and variance.

Determine the N% confidence interval by finding thresholds L and U such that N% of the mass in the probability distribution Dy falls between L and U.

Central Limit Theorem

The Central Limit Theorem (CLT) is a fundamental theorem in probability theory and statistics. It states that, under certain conditions, the sum or average of a large number of independent and identically distributed random variables will follow an approximately Normal distribution, regardless of the shape of the original distribution.

Let X1, X2, ..., Xn be a sequence of independent and identically distributed random variables with a common mean μ and standard deviation σ. The CLT states that as n (the sample size) approaches infinity, the distribution of the sample mean (X-bar) approaches a Normal distribution with mean μ and standard deviation σ/sqrt(n).

Mathematically, we can express the CLT as:

$$(1)\ \text{X-bar} \sim N(\mu, \sigma/\text{sqrt}(n))$$

Where:

X-bar represents the sample mean,

N(μ, σ/sqrt(n)) denotes the Normal distribution with mean μ and standard deviation σ/sqrt(n).

The CLT tells us that regardless of the shape of the original distribution of the Xi variables, as long as they are independent and identically distributed, their sample mean will tend to follow a Normal distribution as the sample size increases

The standard deviation of the sample mean, σ/sqrt(n), represents the standard error of the mean. It quantifies the variability or dispersion of the sample means around the population mean μ. As the sample size increases (larger n), the standard error decreases, indicating that the sample mean becomes a more precise estimate of the population mean.

In practical terms, the CLT allows us to make statistical inferences about population parameters based on sample data. It justifies the use of Normal distribution-based techniques, such as confidence intervals and hypothesis tests, by providing a mathematical basis for their validity even when the underlying population distribution is not Normal.

Overall, the CLT is a fundamental concept in statistics that underpins many statistical methods and provides a basis for understanding the behavior of sample means in relation to population parameters.

DIFFERENCE IN ERROR OF TWO HYPOTHESES

In the given scenario, where we have two hypotheses h1 and h2 tested on independent samples S1 and S2, we wish to estimate the difference d between the true errors of these hypotheses. We will follow the four-step procedure described earlier to derive a confidence interval estimate for d.

Step 1: Define the estimator

The estimator for d is the difference between the sample errors, denoted as 2:

$$d = \text{errors(h1)} - \text{errors(h2)}$$

Step 2: Determine the probability distribution of the estimator

For large sample sizes n1 and n2 (e.g., both > 30), the errors(h1) and errors(h2) follow approximately Normal distributions. As the difference of two Normal distributions is also a Normal distribution, the estimator 2 will also follow an approximately Normal distribution with mean d. Additionally, the variance of this distribution is the sum of the variances of errors(h1) and errors(h2), which can be approximated using as:

$$\text{variance} = \text{errors(h1)}(1 - \text{errors(h1)})/n1 + \text{errors(h2)}(1 - \text{errors(h2)})/n2$$

Step 3: Derive the confidence interval estimate for d

Using the Normal distribution properties, we can derive a two-sided confidence interval for estimating the difference d:

$$\text{confidence interval} = d \pm z * \text{sqrt(variance)}$$

where z is the value corresponding to the desired confidence level N% from the Normal distribution (e.g., z0.95 for 95% confidence).

Step 4: Modify for one-sided confidence intervals (if needed)

If one-sided bounds are desired, either for the largest possible difference or the smallest, the above expression can be modified accordingly.

It is worth noting that the analysis mentioned above assumes independent testing on separate samples S1 and S2. However, in some cases, it is acceptable to use the confidence interval equation when both hypotheses h1 and h2 are tested on a single sample S (as long as S is still independent of h1 and h2). In this case, the variance calculation will be different, but the confidence interval given by equation will still provide a valid estimate.

COMPARING LEARNING ALGORITHMS

An appropriate test for comparing learning algorithms is the statistical hypothesis test. The goal is to determine whether an observed difference between the algorithms is statistically significant, indicating that the difference is not due to random chance. A discussion of alternative methods is given by Dietterich (1996).

As usual, we begin by specifying the parameter we wish to estimate. Suppose we wish to determine which of L_A and L_B is the better learning method on average for learning some particular target function f. A reasonable way to define "on average" is to consider the relative performance of these two algorithms averaged over all the training sets of size n that might be drawn from the underlying instance distribution D. In other words, we wish to estimate the expected value of the difference in their errors

$$\underset{S \subset D}{E}\,[error_D(L_A(S)) - error_D(L_B(S))] \qquad ...(1)$$

where L(S) denotes the hypothesis output by learning method L when given the sample S of training data and where the subscript S c D indicates that the expected value is taken over samples S drawn according to the underlying instance distribution D. The above expression describes the expected value of the difference in errors between learning methods L_A and L_B.

Of course in practice we have only a limited sample Do of data when comparing learning methods. In such cases, one obvious approach to estimating the above quantity is to divide Do into a training set So and a disjoint test set T0. The training data can be used to train both L_A and L_B, and the test data can be used to compare the accuracy of the two learned hypotheses. In other words, we measure the quantity

$$error_{T_0}(L_A(S_0)) - error_{T_0}(L_B(S_0)) \qquad ...(2)$$

Notice two key differences between this estimator and the quantity in Equation 1. First, we are using $error_{To}(h)$ to approximate errorD(h). Second, we are only measuring the difference in errors for one training set So rather than taking the expected value of this difference over all samples S that might be drawn from the distribution D.

One way to improve on the estimator given by Equation 2 is to repeatedly partition the data Do into disjoint training and test sets and to take the mean of the test set errors for these different experiments. This leads to the procedure shown in Table 1 for estimating the difference between errors of two learning methods, based on a fixed sample Do of available data. This procedure first partitions the data into k disjoint subsets of equal size, where this size is at least 30. It then trains and tests the learning algorithms k times, using each of the k subsets in turn as the test set, and using all remaining data as the training set. In this way, the learning algorithms are tested on k independent test sets, 'and the mean difference in errors δ is returned as an estimate of the difference between the two learning algorithms.

The quantity δ returned by the procedure of Table 1 can be taken as an estimate of the desired quantity from Equation 1 More appropriately, we can view δ as an estimate of the quantity

$$\underset{S \subset D_0}{E}\left[\text{error}_D(L_A(S)) - \text{error}_D(L_B(S))\right] \qquad ...(3)$$

where S represents a random sample of size $\frac{k-1}{k}|D_0|$ drawn uniformly from Do. The only difference between this expression and our original expression in Equation 1 is that this new expression takes the expected value over subsets of the available data Do, rather than over subsets drawn from the full instance distribution D.

1. Partition the available data D_0 into k disjoint subsets T_1, T_2, ... T_k of equal size, where this size is at least 30.
2. For i from 1 to k, do

   Use T_i for the test set, and the remaining data for training set S_i
   - ❑ $S_i \leftarrow \{D_0 - T_i\}$
   - ❑ $h_A \leftarrow L_A(S_i)$
   - ❑ $h_B \leftarrow L_B(S_i)$
   - ❑ $\delta_i \leftarrow \text{error}_{Ti}(h_A) - \text{error}_{Ti}(h_B)$
3. Return the value δ, where

$$\delta = \frac{1}{k}\sum_{i=1}^{k}\delta_i$$

Table 1: A procedure to estimate the difference in error between two learning methods L_A and L_B. Approximate confidence intervals for this estimate are given in the text.

The approximate N% confidence interval for estimating the quantity in Equation 3 using δ is given by

$$\bar{\delta} \pm t_{N.k-1}\, s_{\bar{g}} \qquad ...(4)$$

where tN, k–l is a constant that plays a role analogous to that of Z_N in our earlier confidence interval expressions, and where $s_{\bar{g}}$, is an estimate of the standard deviation of the distribution governing δ. In particular, s_g is defined as

$$s_{\bar{g}} \equiv \sqrt{\frac{1}{k(k-1)}\sum_{i=1}^{k}(\delta_i - \bar{\delta})^2} \qquad ...(5)$$

Note the procedure described here for comparing two learning methods involves testing the two learned hypotheses on identical test sets. This contrasts with the method described in above section for comparing hypotheses that have been evaluated using two independent test sets.

Review Questions

Multiple Choice Questions

Q.1. What is the primary objective of logistic regression?

(*a*) Minimize the sum of squared errors
(*b*) Maximize the likelihood function
(*c*) Minimize the cross-entropy loss
(*d*) Maximize the sum of squared errors

Q.2. In logistic regression, what type of variable is the dependent variable?

(*a*) Continuous (*b*) Categorical (*c*) Ordinal (*d*) Nominal

Q.3. Which activation function is commonly used at the output layer of logistic regression?

(*a*) ReLU (*b*) Sigmoid (*c*) Tanh (*d*) Linear

Q.4. Logistic regression is used for:

(*a*) Regression problems (*b*) Classification problems
(*c*) Clustering problems (*d*) Dimensionality reduction

Q.5. What is the purpose of the sigmoid function in logistic regression?

(*a*) To map the output to the range [0, 1] (*b*) To transform the input features
(*c*) To normalize the data (*d*) To reduce the dimensionality of the data

Q.6. Which optimization algorithm is commonly used to train logistic regression models?

(*a*) Gradient descent (*b*) Random search (*c*) Hill climbing (*d*) Genetic algorithm

Q.7. What is the cost function used in logistic regression?

(*a*) Mean squared error (MSE) (*b*) Mean absolute error (MAE)
(*c*) Cross-entropy loss (*d*) Hinge loss

Q.8. In logistic regression, how is the probability of the positive class calculated?

(*a*) Using the softmax function (*b*) Using the sigmoid function
(*c*) Using the ReLU function (*d*) Using the Tanh function

Q.9. What does the odds ratio represent in logistic regression?

(*a*) The change in the log-odds of the dependent variable for a one-unit change in the independent variable
(*b*) The change in the probability of the dependent variable for a one-unit change in the independent variable
(*c*) The correlation between independent variables
(*d*) The standard error of the regression coefficients

Q.10. In logistic regression, how is the decision boundary determined?

(*a*) By fitting a straight line to the data
(*b*) By minimizing the sum of squared errors
(*c*) By maximizing the likelihood function
(*d*) By setting a threshold on the predicted probabilities

Q.11. In statistical hypothesis testing, the null hypothesis (H0) represents:

(*a*) The hypothesis that the researcher wants to prove
(*b*) The hypothesis that there is no significant difference or effect
(*c*) The hypothesis that there is a significant difference or effect
(*d*) The hypothesis that there is a positive relationship between variables

Q.12. The alternative hypothesis (Ha) in hypothesis testing:

(*a*) Supports the null hypothesis
(*b*) Is always rejected in favor of the null hypothesis
(*c*) Represents the claim or theory that the researcher wants to prove
(*d*) Is the same as the null hypothesis

Q.13. A two-tailed test is appropriate when:

(*a*) The researcher wants to test for a difference or effect in a specific direction
(*b*) The researcher wants to test for a difference or effect in any direction
(*c*) The sample size is small
(*d*) The data are not normally distributed

Q.14. When should you reject the null hypothesis in hypothesis testing?

(*a*) When the p-value is greater than the significance level
(*b*) When the p-value is less than the significance level
(*c*) When the p-value is equal to the significance level
(*d*) When the sample size is large

Answers

1. (*c*)	2. (*b*)	3. (*b*)	4. (*b*)	5. (*a*)	6. (*a*)	7. (*c*)	8. (*b*)	9. (*a*)
10. (*d*)	11. (*b*)	12. (*c*)	13. (*b*)	14. (*b*)				

Unsolved Questions

1. Define logistic regression and explain its primary use in classification problems.
2. How does logistic regression handle binary and multiclass classification tasks?
3. Describe the logistic function (sigmoid) and its role in logistic regression.
4. Explain why the logistic function is preferred over a linear function for binary classification.
5. Discuss the training process of a logistic regression model and the optimization algorithms commonly used.
6. What are common evaluation metrics for assessing the performance of a logistic regression classifier?
7. Compare and contrast binary logistic regression with multinomial logistic regression.

8. Provide an example scenario where multinomial logistic regression would be applicable.
9. Identify a real-world application where logistic regression could be applied for classification.
10. Discuss potential challenges and considerations for implementing logistic regression in that context.
11. Experiment with different hyperparameter values (e.g., learning rate, regularization) in your logistic regression model.
12. Compare the model's performance under various hyperparameter configurations.

Fill in the Blanks

1. Logistic regression is a type of __________ algorithm used for binary and multiclass classification tasks.
2. The logistic function, also known as the __________ function, transforms the output of the linear combination of features into a range between 0 and 1.
3. The logistic regression model predicts the __________ of an instance belonging to a particular class.
4. The __________ is a common optimization algorithm used during the training of logistic regression models.
5. Multinomial logistic regression extends binary logistic regression to handle __________ classification problems.
6. In logistic regression, the coefficients represent the __________ in the log-odds of the dependent variable for a one-unit change in the predictor variable.
7. The decision boundary in logistic regression is a hyperplane that separates the feature space into regions corresponding to different __________.
8. Receiver Operating Characteristic (ROC) curves are used to visualize the __________ of a logistic regression model across different probability thresholds.

EXERCISE

1. A multiclass logistic regression, as in Eq. 12.13, has parameters β(c) 0 and β(c) for each class c. Show that we can always get the same predicted probabilities by setting β(c) 0 = 0, β(c) = 0 for any one class c, and adjusting the parameters for the other classes appropriately.
2. Find the first and second derivatives of the log-likelihood for logistic regression with one predictor variable. Explicitly write out the formula for doing one step of Newton's method. Explain how this relates to re-weighted least squares.

❑❑❑

5

(Discussion on clustering)

INTRODUCTION

What are Clusters?

The term "cluster" originates from the Old English word "clyster," which referred to a collection or grouping. A cluster represents a collection of alike entities or individuals that are situated closely or in close proximity. Typically, every element within a cluster shares common attributes, making it possible to employ machine learning techniques for recognizing patterns and distinguishing these groups. This forms the foundation for numerous machine learning applications that address data-related challenges across various sectors.

Machine Learning (ML) is indeed considered a subfield of Artificial Intelligence (AI). It focuses on the development of algorithms and models that enable systems to learn and make predictions or decisions based on data, without being explicitly programmed. ML algorithms are the fundamental building blocks of ML systems. These algorithms are designed to learn from data and improve their performance over time. They analyze patterns, relationships, and dependencies within the data to identify trends and make predictions or decisions. One of the key advantages of ML is its ability to generate predictions or decisions based on data-driven models. Instead of relying solely on human-designed rules and logic, ML systems leverage historical data to discover patterns and relationships. These patterns are then used to make predictions about future or unseen data instances.

The process of ML involves several steps, including data collection, preprocessing, model training, evaluation, and prediction. During the training phase, the ML model learns from labeled or unlabeled data to identify patterns and make predictions. The model is evaluated using performance metrics to assess its accuracy and generalization capabilities. Once trained, the model can be deployed to make predictions or decisions on new data instances. ML has revolutionized various industries and applications, such as image and speech recognition, natural language processing, recommendation systems, fraud detection, and autonomous vehicles. It enables systems to adapt and improve their performance based on the available data, leading to more intelligent and accurate behavior. In summary, ML is a subfield of AI that focuses on developing algorithms and models to enable systems to learn from data and make predictions or decisions. By leveraging historical data, ML systems can generate data-driven predictions and improve their performance over time.

The general architecture of ML is depicted in figure 1 and consists of several steps: business understanding (understanding and knowledge of the domain), data acquisition and understanding (gathering and understanding data), modeling (which entails feature engineering, model training, and evaluation), and deployment (deploy the model on the cloud).

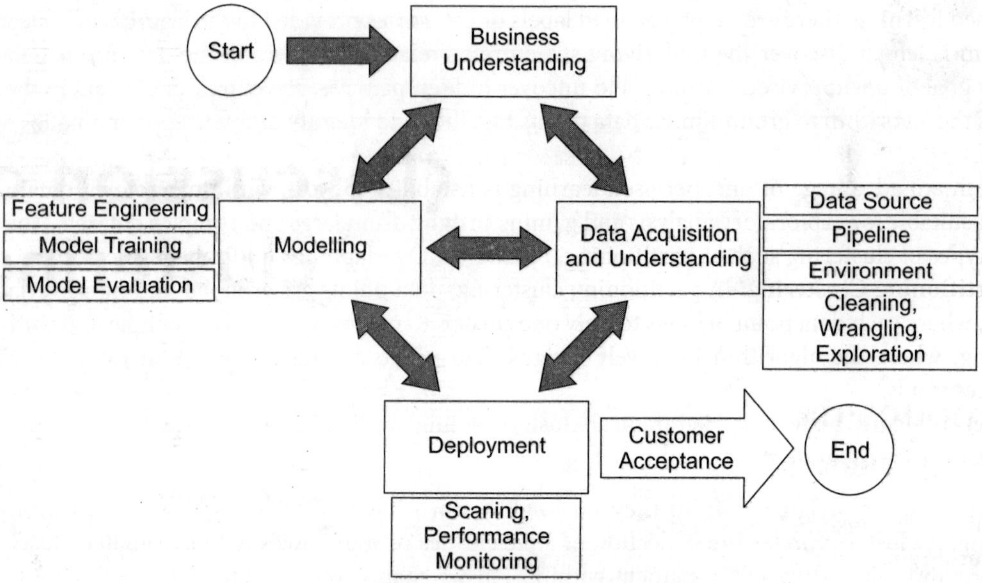

Fig. 5.1. Basis Architecture of ML

Supervised Learning, Unsupervised Learning, and Reinforcement Learning are the three major categories of ML.

Supervised Learning: In Supervised Learning, the model is trained on labeled data, where each data point is associated with a corresponding target or label. The model learns from this labeled data to understand the relationship between the input features and the corresponding output. Once trained, the model can make predictions on new, unseen data by mapping the input features to the learned output labels. Examples of Supervised Learning algorithms include linear regression, decision trees, and neural networks.

Unsupervised Learning: In Unsupervised Learning, the model is trained on unlabeled data, where no specific target or label is provided. The goal of Unsupervised Learning is to discover patterns, structures, or relationships in the data without prior knowledge. The model automatically learns from the data by extracting meaningful features, grouping similar data points, or reducing the dimensionality of the data. Unsupervised Learning techniques include clustering algorithms, dimensionality reduction methods like Principal Component Analysis (PCA), and generative models like Gaussian Mixture Models (GMM) or Autoencoders.

Reinforcement Learning: Reinforcement Learning involves an agent learning through interaction with an environment. The agent takes actions in the environment and receives feedback in the form of rewards or penalties based on its actions. The objective of the agent is to learn the optimal policy that maximizes its cumulative rewards over time. Reinforcement Learning algorithms employ trial-and-error learning, where the agent explores the environment, takes actions, and updates its policy based on the received rewards. Q-learning and Deep Q-Networks (DQN) are examples of Reinforcement Learning algorithms.

These three categories of Machine Learning provide different approaches for learning from data, depending on the availability of labeled or unlabeled data and the nature of the learning task. Each category has its own set of algorithms and techniques tailored to specific learning scenarios.

Unsupervised Learning

Unsupervised learning refers to algorithms that analyze and identify patterns in unlabeled data. Unlike supervised learning, there are no pre-defined labels or categories provided to the algorithm. Instead, the algorithm is left to discover the underlying structure or relationships within the data on its own. The primary goal of unsupervised learning is to uncover hidden patterns, structures, or clusters in the data. It allows the algorithm to group similar data points together and identify differences or anomalies within the data.

The main advantage of unsupervised learning is its ability to work with unannotated data, which makes it suitable for exploratory analysis and gaining insights from large and complex datasets. There are several types of clustering such as partitioning, hierarchal, Overlapping and Probabilistic.

Partitioning Clustering: In partitioning clustering, data points are grouped into non-overlapping clusters, where each data point belongs to only one cluster. K-means is a popular example of partitioning clustering, where the algorithm iteratively assigns data points to clusters based on the proximity to cluster centroids.

Hierarchical Clustering: Hierarchical clustering builds a hierarchy of clusters, where each data point starts as a separate cluster, and then clusters are iteratively merged or divided based on their similarity or distance. This process forms a tree-like structure known as a dendrogram, representing the hierarchical relationships between clusters.

Overlapping Clustering: Overlapping clustering allows data points to belong to multiple clusters simultaneously with varying degrees of membership. Fuzzy clustering techniques, such as Fuzzy C-Means, are commonly used for this purpose. Each data point is assigned membership values indicating the degree of belonging to different clusters.

Probabilistic Clustering: Probabilistic clustering algorithms utilize probability distributions to create clusters. Gaussian Mixture Models (GMM) is a popular probabilistic clustering technique where data points are modeled as a mixture of Gaussian distributions. The algorithm estimates the parameters of these distributions to determine the cluster assignments.

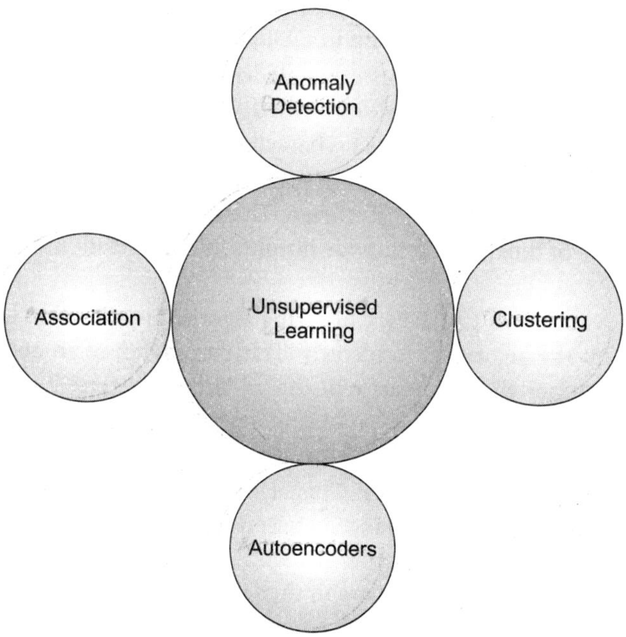

Fig. 5.2. Types of Unsupervised Learning

There are four types of unsupervised tasks: Clustering, Principal component analysis, Anomaly detection, and Autoencoders.

Clustering: Clustering algorithms aim to group similar data points together based on their intrinsic properties or similarity measures. Clustering is indeed a fundamental concept in unsupervised learning. It involves grouping similar data points together to identify underlying patterns or structures within a dataset. Clustering algorithms analyze the data and automatically assign data points to different clusters based on their similarity or proximity to each other.

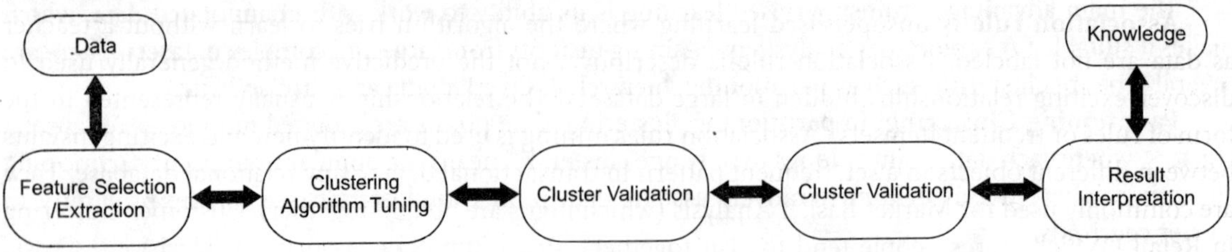

Fig. 5.3. Workflow of clustering in unsupervised ML

The output of clustering can be visualized in graphical form, as shown in figure ??. The groups are formed based on similarities among them.

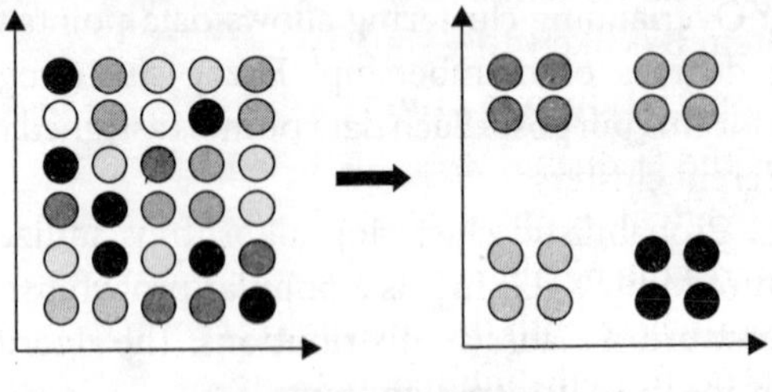

Fig. 5.4. Clustering

Here are some key points about clustering in unsupervised learning:

- **Finding Structure or Patterns:** Clustering algorithms aim to discover inherent structures or patterns in the data without any prior knowledge or labels. The goal is to identify groups or clusters of data points that share similar characteristics or properties.
- **Natural Clusters:** Clustering algorithms can identify natural clusters in the data, which represent meaningful groups or categories. These clusters can help in understanding the inherent structure of the data and provide insights into the relationships between different data points.
- **Adjusting the Number of Clusters:** Clustering algorithms allow you to specify the number of clusters you want the algorithm to identify. This parameter, often denoted as "k" in k-means clustering, determines the granularity of the resulting clusters. By adjusting the number of clusters, you can explore different levels of detail in the data and obtain a suitable representation of the underlying structure.
- **Similarity and Proximity Measures:** Clustering algorithms rely on similarity or proximity measures to determine the resemblance between data points. Common distance metrics used include Euclidean distance, Manhattan distance, or cosine similarity. These measures define how close or similar two data points are in the feature space.

- **Cluster Validation:** Evaluating the quality of the obtained clusters is an important aspect of clustering. Various methods, such as silhouette score or within-cluster sum of squares, can be used to assess the compactness and separation of the clusters.

Clustering algorithms, such as k-means, hierarchical clustering, DBSCAN (Density-Based Spatial Clustering of Applications with Noise), or Gaussian Mixture Models, are commonly used in unsupervised learning to identify and analyze the underlying structure in datasets. By applying clustering techniques, you can gain insights into the relationships between data points and potentially discover new patterns or segments within your data.

Association rule is unsupervised learning where the algorithm tries to learn without a teacher as data are not labeled. Association rule is descriptive, not the predictive method generally used to discover exciting relationships hidden in large datasets. The relationship is usually represented in the form of rules or frequent itemsets . Association rules mining is used to identify new and exciting insights between different objects in a set, frequent pattern in transactional data or any relational database. They are commonly used for Market Basket Analysis (which items are bought together), Customer clustering in Retail (Which stores people tend to visit together), Price Bundling, Assortment Decisions, Cross-Selling, and others. This can be considered an advanced form of what-if scenario; if this, then that.

Association rule mining is a data mining technique used to discover interesting relationships or associations among items in a dataset. It aims to find patterns in large datasets, particularly in transactional databases or datasets with categorical variables. These patterns are expressed in the form of rules, such as "if item A is purchased, then item B is likely to be purchased."

The primary concept in association rule mining is the support and confidence of a rule:

1. **Support:** It indicates the frequency of an itemset (a combination of items) in the dataset. It measures how often the items in the itemset co-occur together.
2. **Confidence:** It measures the reliability or strength of an association rule. It is the ratio of the number of transactions where both the antecedent (left-hand side) and the consequent (right-hand side) of the rule occur to the number of transactions where only the antecedent occurs.

Association rules are typically written in the form:

Antecedent => Consequent (Support, Confidence)

Example: Suppose you have a dataset of customer transactions in a grocery store. Here's a simplified dataset:

Transaction	Items
1	Bread, Milk
2	Bread, Diapers, Beer, Eggs
3	Milk, Diapers, Beer, Coke
4	Bread, Milk, Diapers, Beer
5	Bread, Milk, Diapers, Coke

Let's say we want to find association rules that describe purchasing behavior. We might be interested in finding rules with high support and confidence, such as:

- {Milk} ⇒ {Bread} (Support: 3/5, Confidence: 3/3)
- {Beer} ⇒ {Diapers} (Support: 2/5, Confidence: 2/2)
- {Diapers, Milk} ⇒ {Beer} (Support: 2/5, Confidence: 2/3)

In these rules, the antecedent represents items that are likely to be purchased together (e.g., {Milk}, {Beer}), and the consequent represents items that are frequently purchased together with the antecedent items (e.g., {Bread}, {Diapers}, {Beer}).

Association rule mining can provide valuable insights into customer behavior, product placement, and cross-selling opportunities. However, it's important to note that the discovered associations might not always be meaningful or actionable, and domain knowledge is often required to interpret and use the results effectively.

Principal Component Analysis (PCA): PCA is a dimensionality reduction technique that aims to identify the most important features or dimensions in the data. It transforms the data into a new set of uncorrelated variables called principal components, which capture the maximum variance in the original data.

Principal Component Analysis (PCA) is a dimensionality reduction technique commonly used in statistics and machine learning to transform high-dimensional data into a lower-dimensional representation while retaining as much of the original variance as possible. The primary goal of PCA is to find the orthogonal axes, called principal components, along which the data varies the most. These principal components help capture the most important information within the data.

PCA works by identifying the directions of maximum variance in the data and projecting the data points onto these directions to obtain a new set of coordinates. This new representation often reduces the dimensionality of the data while preserving the most significant patterns.

Here's a step-by-step explanation of how PCA works:

1. **Standardize the Data:** First, the data is centered by subtracting the mean of each feature from the corresponding data points. This step ensures that the data has zero mean.
2. **Compute the Covariance Matrix:** The covariance matrix is computed to capture the relationships between different features. It shows how much two features vary together. The covariance matrix is symmetric and positive semi-definite.
3. **Compute Eigenvectors and Eigenvalues:** Eigenvectors and eigenvalues are calculated from the covariance matrix. Eigenvectors represent the directions of maximum variance, while eigenvalues quantify the amount of variance along each eigenvector.
4. **Sort Eigenvectors by Eigenvalues:** Eigenvectors are ranked based on their corresponding eigenvalues in descending order. The eigenvector with the highest eigenvalue represents the primary axis of variance, and subsequent eigenvectors capture diminishing variances.
5. **Choose Principal Components:** The top k eigenvectors, where k is the desired number of dimensions in the reduced space, are selected as the principal components. These components form the new basis for projecting the data.
6. **Project Data onto Principal Components:** The original data is projected onto the selected principal components to obtain the lower-dimensional representation. Each data point is transformed into a new set of coordinates defined by the principal components.

PCA has various applications, such as:

- Dimensionality reduction to enhance data visualization and analysis.
- Noise reduction and data compression.
- Feature extraction to identify the most important patterns in the data.
- Data preprocessing before applying machine learning algorithms.

Overall, PCA is a valuable technique for reducing the complexity of high-dimensional data while retaining its essential structure and patterns.

Example: Let's consider an example to better understand Principal Component Analysis (PCA). Imagine we have a dataset containing information about the height and weight of individuals. This dataset has two features: "Height" and "Weight."

Original Data (Height vs. Weight):

Height (inches)	Weight (pounds)
60	120
65	150
72	180
63	135
68	160
70	170

Standardize the Data: Subtract the mean of each feature from its corresponding values to center the data:

Height (inches)	Weight (pounds)
-5	-20
0	10
7	40
-3	–15
2	10
4	20

Compute the Covariance Matrix: Calculate the covariance matrix based on the centered data:

Cov(Height, Height)	Cov(Height, Weight)
15.33	31.67
31.67	66.67

1. **Compute Eigenvectors and Eigenvalues:**
   Calculate the eigenvectors and eigenvalues of the covariance matrix:
   Eigenvalues: 82.33, -0.33
   Eigenvectors: [0.93, 0.36], [-0.36, 0.93]
2. **Sort Eigenvectors by Eigenvalues:**
   Sort the eigenvectors based on their corresponding eigenvalues:
   Eigenvectors: [0.36, 0.93], [0.93, -0.36]
3. **Choose Principal Components:**
   Choose the top eigenvector [0.36, 0.93] as the principal component for dimensionality reduction.

4. **Project Data onto Principal Component:**
Project the original data onto the principal component to obtain the lower-dimensional representation:

Principal Component
-20.87
2.47
44.07
-12.29
6.99
11.63

In this example, PCA transformed the original data into a lower-dimensional representation using the first principal component. This reduced the dataset from two features (Height and Weight) to one feature (Principal Component), while retaining the maximum variance in the data.

Note that in practice, PCA is often used on larger datasets with more features to achieve meaningful dimensionality reduction and visualization.

Anomaly Detection: Anomaly detection algorithms identify unusual or anomalous data points that deviate significantly from the expected behavior or patterns in the data. These algorithms are useful for detecting fraud, detecting outliers, or identifying rare events.

Anomaly detection is any process that finds the outliers of a dataset. These anomalies might point to unusual network traffic, uncover a sensor on the fritz, or identify data for cleaning before analysis. It is called an anomaly when the data patterns are beyond the normal patterns or deviate from the normal patterns. For example, the anomalous traffic pattern in a network means the hacked system is sending sensitive content to the unauthorized host. In order to detect anomalies is to identify or predict those data points that are deviated from the normal pattern

Autoencoders: Autoencoders are neural network models that are trained to reconstruct the input data. They consist of an encoder that compresses the data into a lower-dimensional representation and a decoder that reconstructs the original input from the compressed representation. Autoencoders can be used for tasks such as feature extraction, data denoising, or anomaly detection.

Autoencoders are an unsupervised learning technique that leverages the capabilities of neural networks for the task of representation learning. Autoencoders are a specific type of feedforward neural network where the input is the same as the output. They compress the input into a lower-dimensional code and then reconstruct the output from this representation. The code is a compact "summary" or "compression" of the input, also called the latent-space representation. An autoencoder consists of 3 components: encoder, code, and decoder. The encoder compresses the input and produces the code, and the decoder then reconstructs the input using this code. To build an autoencoder, three components are needed: an encoding method, decoding method, and a loss function to compare the output with the target. Autoencoders are mainly a dimensionality reduction (or compression) algorithm.

Fig. 5.6. Autoencoder Components

The unsupervised learning process involves allowing the algorithm to learn and extract meaningful information from the data without explicit guidance or predefined labels. It is a powerful technique for uncovering patterns and insights in large and unlabeled datasets.

There are several types of clustering such as partitioning, hierarchal, Overlapping and Probabilistic.

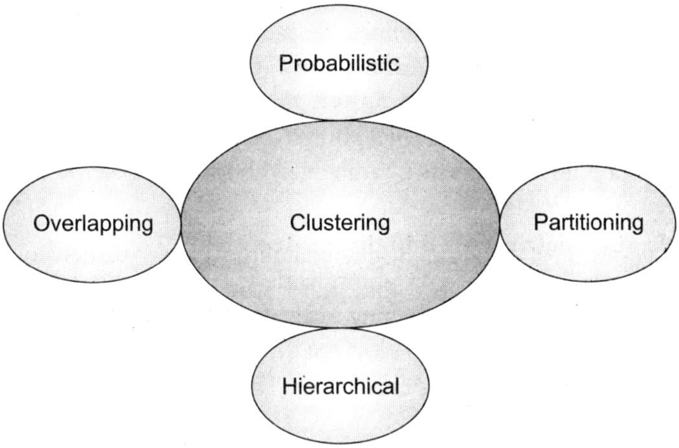

Fig. 5.7. Types of Clustering

1. **Partitioning Clustering:** This type of clustering aims to partition the data points into non-overlapping clusters, where each data point belongs to only one cluster. The well-known k-means algorithm falls into this category. K-means starts by randomly assigning cluster centroids and then iteratively updates the centroids to minimize the distance between data points and their assigned centroids.
2. **Hierarchical Clustering:** In hierarchical clustering, each data point starts as a separate cluster, and then pairs of clusters are iteratively merged based on their similarity or distance. This process continues until all data points belong to a single cluster, forming a hierarchical structure of clusters. Hierarchical clustering can be agglomerative (bottom-up) or divisive (top-down) depending on the direction of merging or splitting clusters.
3. **Overlapping Clustering:** Overlapping clustering allows data points to belong to multiple clusters simultaneously with varying degrees of membership. Fuzzy clustering is an example of this type, where each data point is assigned a membership value representing its degree of belonging to each cluster. Fuzzy C-means is a popular algorithm used for fuzzy clustering.
4. **Probabilistic Clustering:** Probabilistic clustering utilizes probability distributions to create clusters. Gaussian Mixture Models (GMM) is a well-known algorithm in this category. GMM assumes that the data points are generated from a mixture of Gaussian distributions, and it estimates the parameters of these distributions to determine the cluster assignments.
5. **DBSCAN (Density-Based Spatial Clustering of Applications with Noise):** DBSCAN is a density-based clustering algorithm that identifies clusters based on the density of data points. It groups together data points that are close to each other and have sufficient nearby neighbors, while distinguishing noise points.

   DBSCAN is a density-based clustering algorithm that identifies clusters of data points based on their density distribution in the feature space. Unlike some other clustering algorithms,

DBSCAN does not assume that clusters have a specific shape or size. Instead, it focuses on identifying regions of high density separated by regions of lower density, which allows it to handle clusters of varying shapes and handle noise points effectively.

The main idea behind DBSCAN is to define clusters as areas of the data space where there is a sufficient density of data points. This is achieved by considering two important parameters: epsilon (ε) and minimum points (MinPts).

- **Epsilon (ε):** This parameter defines the radius around each data point within which the algorithm searches for neighboring points. It determines the distance within which points are considered part of the same cluster.
- **Minimum Points (MinPts):** For a point to be considered a core point, it must have at least MinPts data points within its ε-radius neighborhood. Core points are central to forming clusters.

DBSCAN classifies data points into three categories:

1. **Core Points:** These are data points with at least MinPts points within their ε-radius neighborhood. Core points belong to clusters and help expand clusters.
2. **Border Points:** Border points are not core points themselves, but they are within the ε-radius neighborhood of a core point. They can belong to a cluster, but they are not central to it.
3. **Noise Points:** Noise points do not have enough data points within their ε-radius neighborhood to be considered core points or belong to any cluster.

The DBSCAN algorithm proceeds as follows:

1. Select a data point randomly and check if it has at least MinPts points within its ε-radius neighborhood.
2. If it does, expand the cluster by adding all directly reachable points (core points) to the cluster.
3. Repeat this process for all core points in the cluster until no more points can be added.
4. Move to the next unvisited point and repeat the process.
5. If a point is not part of any cluster, mark it as a noise point.

DBSCAN has several advantages, such as its ability to handle clusters of varying shapes, robustness to noise, and not requiring the user to specify the number of clusters beforehand. However, it might struggle with clusters of significantly different densities and can be sensitive to the choice of ε and MinPts parameters.

In summary, DBSCAN is a powerful clustering algorithm for identifying dense regions in data space and is particularly useful for applications where clusters might have irregular shapes and noise points need to be handled effectively.

Example: Suppose we have the following set of data points in a 2D feature space:

Data Points:

(1, 1), (1.5, 2), (2, 2), (8, 8), (8.5, 9), (9, 9),
(1, 10), (10, 1), (10, 10)

Let's use DBSCAN to cluster these data points. For this example, we'll set ε = 2 and MinPts = 3.

1. Start with the first data point (1, 1). It has two neighboring points within ε-distance: (1.5, 2) and (2, 2). Since both of them have at least MinPts neighbors, they form a cluster. The cluster includes: (1, 1), (1.5, 2), and (2, 2).

2. Move to the next data point (8, 8). It has two neighboring points within ε-distance: (8.5, 9) and (9, 9). Similar to the first cluster, they form a new cluster: (8, 8), (8.5, 9), and (9, 9).
3. The remaining data points (1, 10), (10, 1), and (10, 10) are considered noise points since they do not have enough neighbors within ε-distance to be core points.

The resulting clusters and noise points are:

Cluster 1: (1, 1), (1.5, 2), (2, 2)

Cluster 2: (8, 8), (8.5, 9), (9, 9)

Noise Points: (1, 10), (10, 1), (10, 10)

In this example, DBSCAN successfully identified two clusters based on the density of data points. The clusters have varying shapes and sizes, demonstrating DBSCAN's ability to handle such scenarios effectively. The noise points are also correctly identified.

Keep in mind that the choice of ε and MinPts can impact the clustering results. Experimenting with different parameter values may lead to different cluster assignments.

6. **Agglomerative Clustering:**

Agglomerative clustering starts with individual data points as clusters and recursively merges the closest clusters based on a linkage criterion (e.g., single linkage, complete linkage, average linkage) until a desired number of clusters is reached

Agglomerative Clustering is a hierarchical clustering technique that starts by considering each data point as an individual cluster and then iteratively merges clusters based on certain criteria until a stopping condition is met. The process continues until all data points are part of a single cluster, forming a hierarchy of clusters.

Here's how Agglomerative Clustering works:

1. **Initialization:** Begin by treating each data point as an individual cluster.
2. **Merge Step:** In each iteration, identify the two closest clusters based on a distance metric. This distance can be measured using various methods such as Euclidean distance, Manhattan distance, etc. The distance between clusters can be computed using different linkage criteria like single linkage, complete linkage, average linkage, and more.
3. **Merge Clusters:** Merge the two closest clusters into a single cluster. Update the distance matrix to reflect the distances between the newly formed cluster and the remaining clusters.
4. **Repeat:** Repeat the merge step until a stopping condition is met. This can be a specified number of clusters or a desired level of similarity.
5. **Hierarchy:** The merging process forms a dendrogram, which is a tree-like structure representing the hierarchy of clusters. The y-axis in the dendrogram represents the distance or similarity, and the x-axis represents the data points or clusters.
6. **Cutting the Dendrogram:** To obtain a specific number of clusters, you can cut the dendrogram at a certain threshold distance. The horizontal line drawn at this threshold corresponds to the desired number of clusters.

Here's a simple example with data points and Euclidean distance:

Data Points:

A(1, 2), B(2, 3), C(3, 8), D(4, 9), E(9, 10), F(10, 11)

Initialization:

Individual clusters: A, B, C, D, E, F

Iteration 1:

Merge A and B -> AB(1.41), C(3, 8), D(4, 9), E(9, 10), F(10, 11)

Iteration 2:

Merge AB and C -> ABC(4.24), D(4, 9), E(9, 10), F(10, 11)

Iteration 3:

Merge D and E -> DE(1.41), ABC(4.24), F(10, 11)

Iteration 4:

Merge DE and F -> DEF(2.24), ABC(4.24)

Final Clusters: DEF, ABC

Dendrogram:

```
          |---DEF(2.24)
          |
---ABC(4.24)---|
          |
          |---C(3.00)
```

In this example, the agglomerative clustering process merges the data points into two clusters, DEF and ABC. The dendrogram visually represents the hierarchy of clusters and the distances at which they were merged.

Agglomerative Clustering is flexible and can work with various distance metrics and linkage criteria, making it suitable for a wide range of applications.

7. **Spectral Clustering:**

Spectral clustering transforms the data into a lower-dimensional space using graph theory techniques and then applies traditional clustering methods. It's effective for capturing complex relationships between data points.

Spectral Clustering is a clustering technique that utilizes the eigenvalues and eigenvectors of a similarity matrix derived from the data to partition it into clusters. Unlike some traditional methods that rely on distance metrics, Spectral Clustering focuses on the underlying structure of the data in a transformed space. It is particularly effective for data that might not exhibit clear spherical or convex structures.

Here's an overview of how Spectral Clustering works:

1. **Similarity Matrix:** Construct a similarity matrix that captures the pairwise similarities between data points. This can be achieved using various similarity measures such as Gaussian similarity, k-nearest neighbors, or affinity matrix based on data attributes.
2. **Graph Construction:** Treat the similarity matrix as an adjacency matrix of a graph, where each data point corresponds to a node, and the similarity values determine the edge weights between nodes. This creates a graph representation of the data.
3. **Graph Laplacian:** Compute the graph Laplacian matrix, which is derived from the adjacency matrix and reflects the relationships between nodes in the graph.

4. **Eigenvalue Decomposition:** Compute the eigenvalues and eigenvectors of the graph Laplacian matrix. The eigenvectors are arranged in ascending order of their corresponding eigenvalues.
5. **Dimension Reduction:** Select a subset of the eigenvectors corresponding to the smallest eigenvalues. These eigenvectors form a lower-dimensional representation of the data.
6. **Clustering**: Apply a traditional clustering algorithm, such as k-means, to the reduced-dimensional eigenvector space. The number of clusters, k, is typically determined beforehand or through techniques like the eigengap method.

Spectral Clustering is powerful because it can discover clusters that might have complex shapes or are not linearly separable in the original feature space. It can capture both global and local structures in the data, making it suitable for various applications like image segmentation, community detection in networks, and more.

Example: Consider a dataset of points in a 2D space with some points forming circular clusters and others forming linear clusters. Traditional distance-based methods might struggle to cluster such data. Spectral Clustering can uncover the circular and linear structures more effectively by exploiting the eigenvalues and eigenvectors.

In this example, Spectral Clustering would involve creating the similarity matrix, constructing the graph Laplacian, computing eigenvalues and eigenvectors, and finally applying a clustering algorithm on the eigenvector space.

Keep in mind that Spectral Clustering involves several matrix computations, and the choice of parameters such as the number of clusters (k) and the similarity metric can impact the results.

It's important to note that each type of clustering algorithm has its strengths and limitations, and the choice of algorithm depends on the specific characteristics of the data and the goals of the analysis.

Clustering is divided into two groups – hard clustering and soft clustering. In hard clustering, the data point is assigned to one of the clusters only whereas in soft clustering, it provides a probability likelihood of a data point to be in each of the clusters.

K-means Clustering

It initializes a pre-defined number of k clusters and uses distance metrics to calculate the distance of each data point from the centroid of each cluster. It assigns the data points into one of the k clusters based on its distance. K-means is a partitional clustering algorithm. In partitional clustering, the algorithm aims to partition the data into a pre-defined number of clusters, where each data point belongs to exactly one cluster.

Partitional clustering algorithms like K-means are suitable for datasets where the number of clusters is known or can be estimated. They are efficient and scalable for large datasets, but they may struggle with finding clusters of complex shapes or handling outliers. Other examples of partitional clustering algorithms include K-medoids, Gaussian Mixture Models (GMM), and DBSCAN (Density-Based Spatial Clustering of Applications with Noise). Each algorithm has its own characteristics, advantages, and limitations, making them suitable for different types of data and clustering scenarios.

- Let the set of data points (or instances) D be
  {x1 , x2 , …, xn },
  where xi = (xi1 , xi2 , …, xir) is a vector in a real valued space $X \subseteq R^r$, and r is the number of attributes (dimensions) in the data.

The k-means algorithm partitions the given data into k clusters.
– Each cluster has a cluster center, called centroid.
– k is specified by the user

The basic steps of the K-means clustering algorithm. Here is a more detailed explanation of the algorithm:

- **Initialization:** Choose the number of clusters, k, and randomly initialize k cluster centroids.
- **Assignment:** For each data point, calculate the distance between the data point and each cluster centroid using a distance metric such as Euclidean distance. Assign the data point to the cluster with the nearest centroid.
- **Update:** After all data points have been assigned to clusters, calculate the new centroids for each cluster by taking the mean of all the data points assigned to that cluster.
- **Iteration:** Repeat steps 2 and 3 until convergence, which occurs when the cluster assignments no longer change significantly or a maximum number of iterations is reached.
- **Output:** The final cluster assignments and centroids represent the result of the K-means clustering algorithm.

K-means Algorithm

Algorithm k-means(k, D)

```
Choose k data points as the initial centroids (cluster centers)
repeat
for each data point x ∈ D do
compute the distance from x to each centroid;
assign x to the closest centroid // a centroid represents a cluster
endfor
re-compute the centroids using the current cluster memberships
until the stopping criterion is met
```

Stopping/convergence Criterion

The convergence criterion for the K-means algorithm is typically based on the stability of the cluster assignments and the centroids. The algorithm iteratively updates the cluster assignments and the centroids until a certain condition is met, indicating that the algorithm has converged to a stable solution.

The most commonly used stopping criteria for K-means include:

No (or minimum) re-assignments of data points to different clusters:

- If, during an iteration, no data point is reassigned to a different cluster, or if the number of reassignments falls below a certain threshold, the algorithm is considered to have converged.

No (or minimum) change of centroids:

- Calculate the movement of centroids as the Euclidean distance between the old centroid mj and the new centroid mj' for each cluster: movement = dist(mj, mj')
- If the movement of all centroids falls below a certain threshold, the algorithm is considered to have converged.

Minimum decrease in the sum of squared error (SSE):

- The SSE is calculated as the sum of the squared distances between each data point x and its assigned centroid mj: SSE = Σ dist(x, mj)^2 for all data points x
- Track the SSE for each iteration and check for a minimum decrease in SSE between consecutive iterations. If the decrease in SSE falls below a certain threshold, the algorithm is considered to have converged.

In summary, the convergence criterion for the K-means algorithm can be based on the stability of cluster assignments, centroids, or the decrease in SSE. The specific criterion used depends on the desired behavior and characteristics of the clustering algorithm in a given context.

Example Code:

```
import numpy as np
import matplotlib.pyplot as plt


def k_means(X, k, max_iters=100):
    centroids = X[np.random.choice(range(len(X)), size=k, replace=False)]

    for _ in range(max_iters):
        clusters = [[] for _ in range(k)]
        for point in X:
            distances = [np.linalg.norm(point - centroid) for centroid in centroids]
            cluster_idx = np.argmin(distances)
            clusters[cluster_idx].append(point)

        new_centroids = []
        for cluster in clusters:
            new_centroids.append(np.mean(cluster, axis=0))
        new_centroids = np.array(new_centroids)

        if np.all(centroids == new_centroids):
            break

        centroids = new_centroids

    return centroids, clusters

X = np.array([[2, 10], [2, 5], [8, 4], [5, 8], [7, 5], [6, 4], [1, 2], [4, 9]])
k = 3
```

```
centroids, clusters = k_means(X, k)
print("Final centroids:")
print(centroids)

print("Final clusters:")
for i, cluster in enumerate(clusters):
  print(f"Cluster {i+1}:")
  print(cluster)

# Plotting the data points and clusters
colors = ['r', 'g', 'b']
for i, cluster in enumerate(clusters):
  cluster_points = np.array(cluster)
  plt.scatter(cluster_points[:, 0], cluster_points[:, 1], c=colors[i], label=f"Cluster {i+1}")

plt.scatter(centroids[:, 0], centroids[:, 1], c='k', marker='x', label='Centroids')
plt.xlabel('X')
plt.ylabel('Y')
plt.title('K-means Clustering')
plt.legend()
plt.show()
```

Output:

```
Final centroids:
[[7.          4.33333333]
 [1.5         3.5       ]
 [3.66666667  9.        ]]
Final clusters:
Cluster 1:
[array([8, 4]), array([7, 5]), array([6, 4])]
Cluster 2:
[array([2, 5]), array([1, 2])]
Cluster 3:
[array([2, 10]), array([5, 8]), array([4, 9])]
```

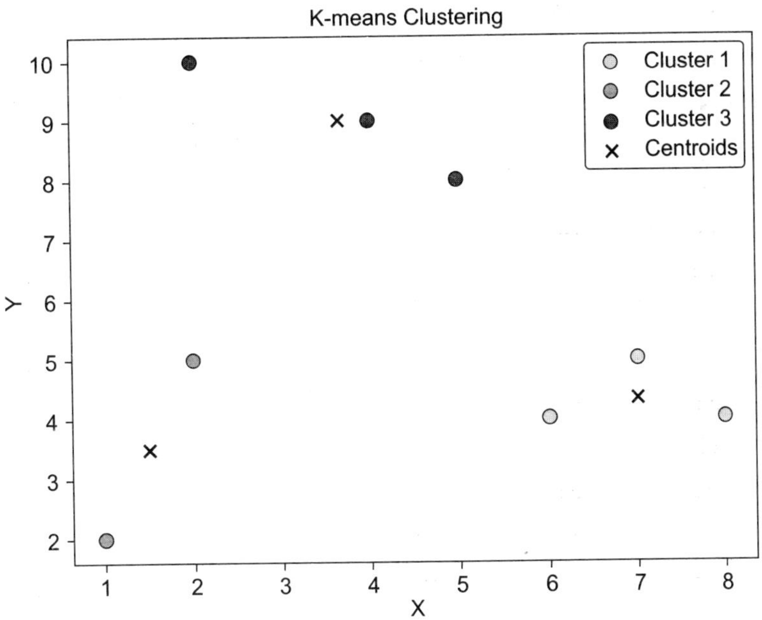

Explanation Code

1. First, we import the necessary libraries: numpy for numerical operations and matplotlib.pyplot for plotting.
2. We define the k_means function, which takes three arguments: X (the data points), k (the number of clusters), and max_iters (the maximum number of iterations). This function performs the k-means clustering algorithm.
3. Inside the k_means function, we initialize the centroids randomly by selecting k data points from X without replacement.
4. We start the main loop that iterates max_iters times. In each iteration, we assign each data point to the nearest centroid by calculating the Euclidean distance between the data point and each centroid. We group the data points into clusters based on their assignments.
5. After assigning all data points to clusters, we update the centroids by calculating the mean of the data points in each cluster. These new centroids become the updated centroids for the next iteration.
6. We check if the centroids have converged by comparing them with the updated centroids. If they are the same, we break out of the loop and return the final centroids and clusters.
7. Outside the function, we define the data points X and the number of clusters k.
8. We call the k_means function with X and k as arguments, and store the returned centroids and clusters in variables.
9. We print the final centroids and clusters to the console.
10. We use matplotlib.pyplot to plot the data points and clusters. We iterate over each cluster, assigning a different color to each cluster, and plot the data points within each cluster. We also plot the centroids as black 'x' markers.

11. We add labels, title, and a legend to the plot.
12. Finally, we display the plot using plt.show().

The code demonstrates how to perform k-means clustering and visualize the results using matplotlib. It can be customized by changing the data points, the number of clusters, or the maximum number of iterations.

Output Explanation

1. Final Centroids:
2. The final centroids represent the coordinates of the centroids after the k-means algorithm has converged. These centroids are calculated by taking the mean of the data points within each cluster. In the code, the final centroids are printed to the console. They represent the center points of the clusters.
3. Cluster Assignments:
4. The cluster assignments indicate which cluster each data point belongs to. In the code, the cluster assignments are stored in the clusters variable. Each data point is assigned a cluster label, which is an integer value from 0 to k-1 (where k is the number of clusters). The cluster assignments can be used to analyze the grouping of the data points and understand how they are divided into clusters.

Visualization

The code also includes a plot that visually represents the data points and their clusters. The data points are scattered on the plot, and each cluster is represented by a different color. The centroids are plotted as black 'x' markers. This plot helps in visualizing the clustering results and understanding the separation of the data points into different clusters.

Overall, the output provides information about the final centroids (representing the cluster centers) and the cluster assignments of the data points, allowing you to analyze and interpret the results of the k-means clustering algorithm.

An Example Distance Function

The k-means algorithm can be used for any application data set where the mean can be defined and computed. In the **Euclidean space**, the mean of a cluster is computed with:

$$m_f = \frac{1}{|C_f|} \sum_{x_i \in C_f} x_i \qquad ...(2)$$

where $|C_f|$ is the number of data points in cluster C_j. The distance from one data point x_i to a mean (centroid) m_j is computed with

$$\begin{aligned} dist(x_i, m_j) &= ||x_i - m_j|| \qquad ...(3) \\ &= \sqrt{(x_{i1} - m_{i1})^2 + (x_{i2} - m_{i2})^2 + ... + (x_{ie} - m_{ie})^2} \end{aligned}$$

In K-means clustering, the algorithm aims to minimize the within-cluster sum of squares, which is the sum of the squared distances between each data point and its assigned cluster centroid. The algorithm iteratively adjusts the cluster assignments and centroid positions to find a configuration that minimizes this objective function.

Note that K-means is sensitive to the initial placement of cluster centroids, and different initializations can lead to different results. To mitigate this, the algorithm is often run multiple times with different initializations, and the best clustering solution is selected based on a criterion such as the lowest within-cluster sum of squares. Overall, K-means clustering is a simple and widely used algorithm for partitioning data into k clusters based on distance. It is computationally efficient and can handle large datasets, but it may struggle with finding clusters of non-spherical shapes or handling outliers effectively.

Strengths of k-means

K-means algorithm has several strengths that make it widely used in clustering tasks:

1. **Simplicity:** K-means is a simple and easy-to-understand clustering algorithm. It is straightforward to implement and interpret, making it accessible even to beginners.
2. **Scalability:** K-means can handle large datasets efficiently, making it suitable for clustering tasks with a large number of data points.
3. **Speed:** K-means algorithm is computationally efficient and converges relatively quickly, especially for low-dimensional data. It is an iterative algorithm that converges to a solution in a finite number of steps.
4. **Efficient:** Time complexity: O(tkn), where n is the number of data points, k is the number of clusters, and t is the number of iterations. – Since both k and t are small. k-means is considered a linear algorithm.
5. **Flexibility:** K-means allows flexibility in choosing the number of clusters (k) based on domain knowledge or by using techniques like the elbow method or silhouette analysis. It can adapt to different data distributions and can handle both spherical and non-spherical clusters.
6. **Cluster Interpretability:** K-means produces well-defined clusters with clear boundaries. The resulting clusters are easy to interpret and analyze, especially when visualized.
7. **Robustness:** K-means is robust to noise and outliers in the dataset. Outliers may have a minimal effect on the centroid calculation and cluster assignments, allowing the algorithm to handle noisy data reasonably well.
8. **Versatility:** K-means can be applied to various types of data, including numerical and continuous variables. It can also handle high-dimensional data, although the curse of dimensionality can affect its performance.

Weaknesses of k-means

While the k-means algorithm has many strengths, it also has several weaknesses that should be taken into consideration:

1. **Sensitive to Initialization:** K-means is sensitive to the initial selection of cluster centroids. Different initializations can lead to different final cluster assignments and results. It is possible to get stuck in local optima, resulting in suboptimal clustering solutions. Multiple runs with different initializations or using more advanced initialization techniques can help mitigate this issue.
    - The algorithm is sensitive to initial seeds.

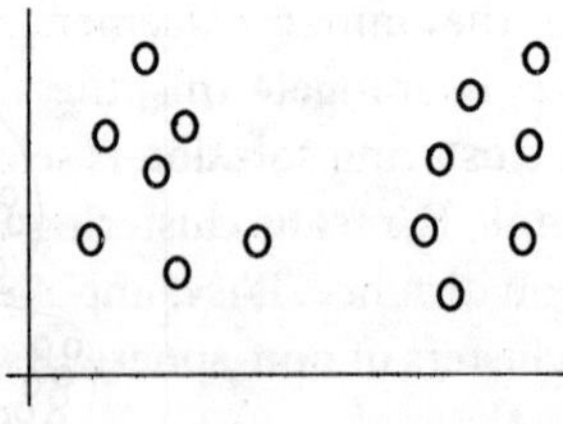

(A) Random selection of seeds (centroids)

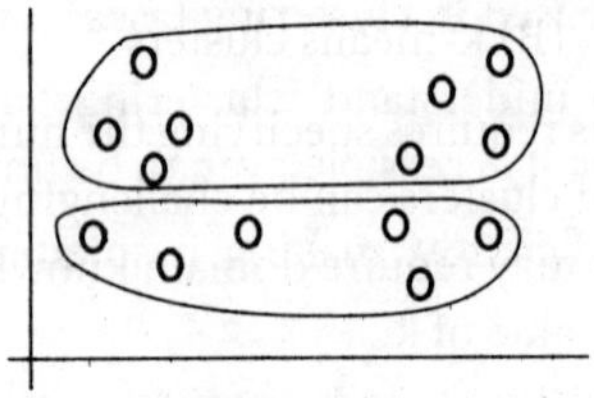

(B) Iteration 1

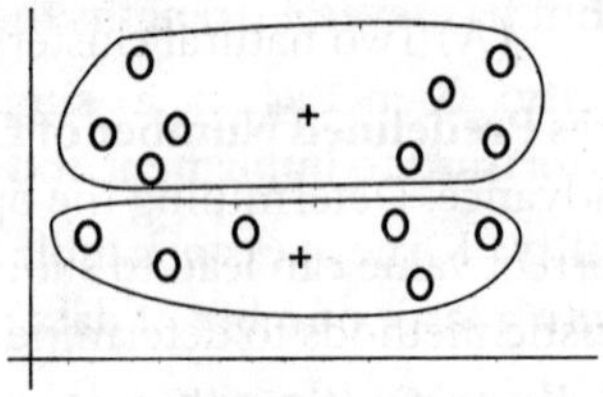

(C) Iteration 2

- If we use different seeds: good results

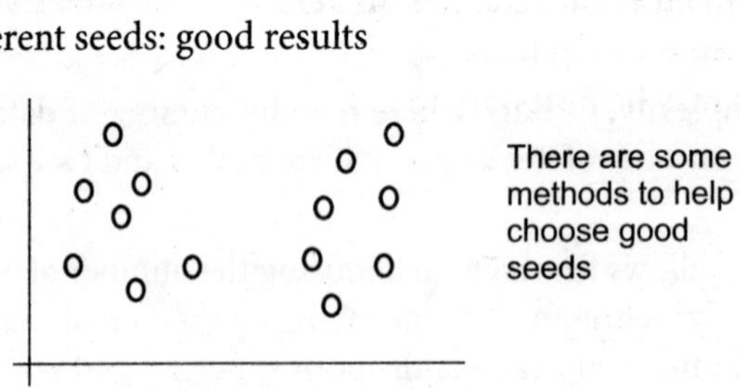

(A) Random selection of k seeds (centroids)

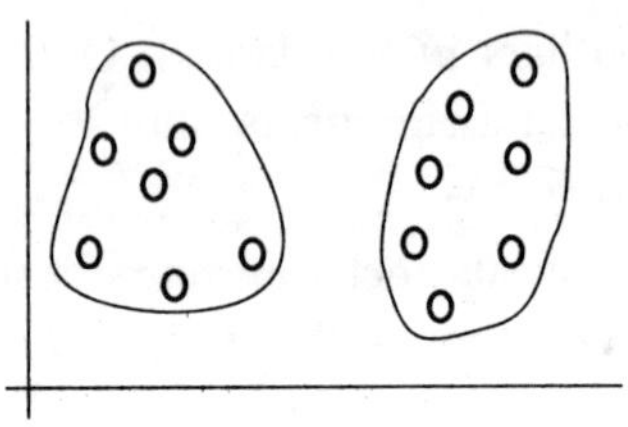

(B) Iteration 1

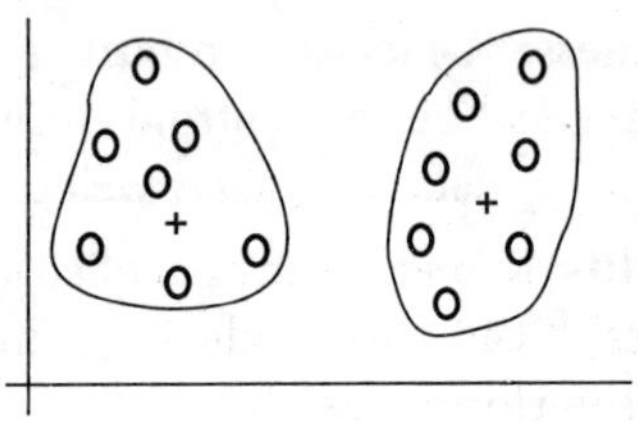

(C) Iteration 2

2. **Assumes Spherical Clusters:** K-means assumes that clusters are spherical, isotropic, and of equal size. It calculates the centroid based on the mean of the data points within each cluster. This assumption may not hold for datasets with clusters of different shapes, densities, or sizes, leading to poor clustering results.
   - The k-means algorithm is not suitable for discovering clusters that are not hyper-ellipsoids (or hyper-spheres).

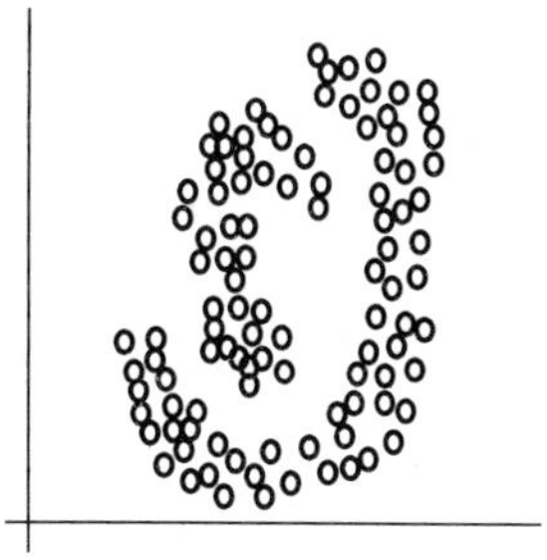

(A) Two natural clusters

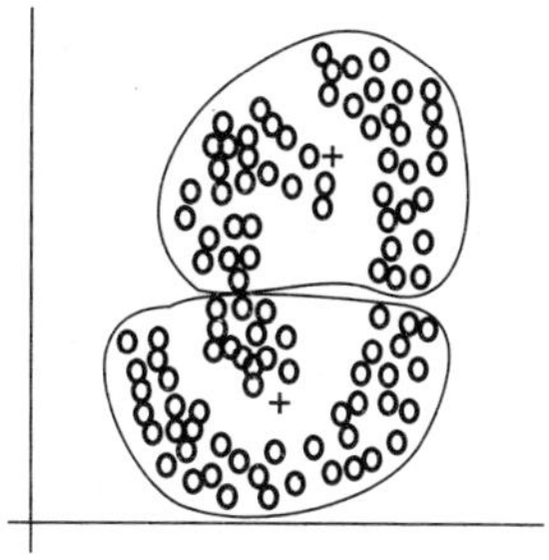

(B) k-means clusters

3. **Requires Predefined Number of Clusters:** K-means requires specifying the number of clusters (k) in advance. Determining the optimal number of clusters can be challenging, and choosing an incorrect value can lead to suboptimal results. It may require domain knowledge or the use of heuristic methods to determine the appropriate value of k.
4. **Sensitivity to Outliers:** K-means is sensitive to outliers, as they can significantly affect the centroid calculation and cluster assignments. Outliers can distort the clustering results and lead to less accurate or meaningful clusters. Preprocessing techniques like outlier detection or data transformation may be necessary to handle outliers effectively.

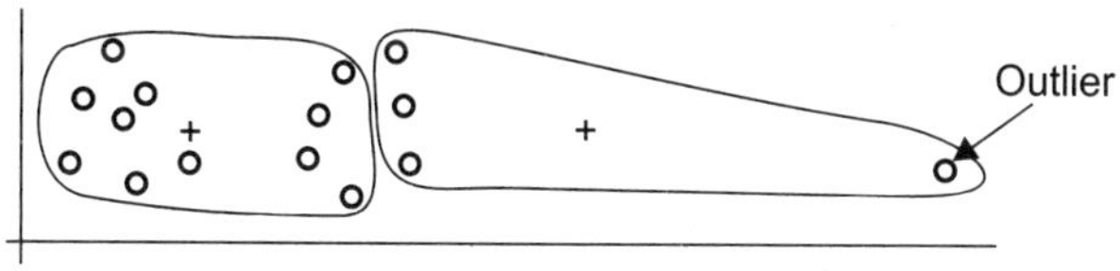

(A) Undesirable clusters

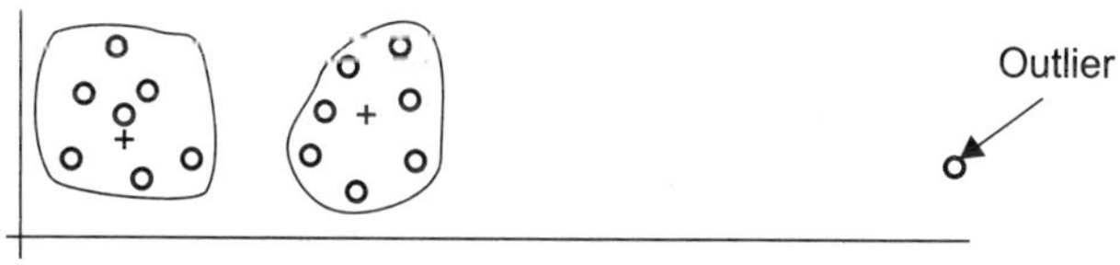

(B) Ideal clusters

To deal with outliers

Address the issue of outliers in the k-means clustering process:

1. **Removing Outliers:** One approach is to identify and remove data points that are significantly further away from the cluster centroids compared to other data points. This can be done by calculating the distance between each data point and its assigned centroid. Points that have distances above a certain threshold can be considered outliers and removed from the clustering process. Monitoring these potential outliers over multiple iterations can provide a more robust assessment before deciding to remove them.
2. **Random Sampling:** Another method is to perform random sampling. Instead of using the entire dataset, a smaller subset of data points is selected for clustering. By using a smaller sample, the likelihood of selecting outliers is reduced. The remaining data points can then be assigned to clusters based on distance or similarity comparisons, or by employing classification techniques.

Both methods aim to mitigate the impact of outliers on the clustering process. However, it's important to note that removing outliers or using random sampling may introduce biases or result in a loss of valuable information. The selection of appropriate thresholds or sample sizes should be carefully considered based on the specific dataset and domain knowledge.

3. **Limited Handling of Non-Linear Data:** K-means assumes that clusters are convex and linearly separable. It may struggle to identify clusters with complex shapes or clusters that are not well-separated by hyperplanes. Non-linear data may require the use of more advanced clustering algorithms, such as density-based or hierarchical clustering.
4. **Requires Feature Scaling:** K-means is influenced by the scale and range of the features. If the features have different scales, variables with larger values can dominate the clustering process. It is often necessary to perform feature scaling or normalization before applying k-means to ensure that all features contribute equally to the clustering.
5. **Lack of Probabilistic Cluster Assignment:** K-means provides hard cluster assignments, where each data point belongs to only one cluster. In reality, some data points may have ambiguous or uncertain cluster memberships. Probabilistic clustering algorithms, such as Gaussian Mixture Models, offer more flexible and probabilistic cluster assignments.

It is important to consider these weaknesses and assess whether k-means is suitable for the specific dataset and clustering task at hand. In some cases, alternative clustering algorithms may be more appropriate to overcome these limitations.

Hierarchical Clustering

Hierarchical clustering is a popular method for grouping data objects into clusters based on their similarities. It is an unsupervised learning technique that builds a hierarchy of clusters, starting with individual data points and progressively merging them into larger clusters.

The key idea behind hierarchical clustering is to create a dendrogram, which is a tree-like structure representing the relationships between data points or clusters. The dendrogram can be visualized as a hierarchical arrangement of nested clusters, where the leaves of the tree represent individual data points, and the branches represent the merging of clusters at different levels.

Produce a nested sequence of clusters, a tree, also called Dendrogram.

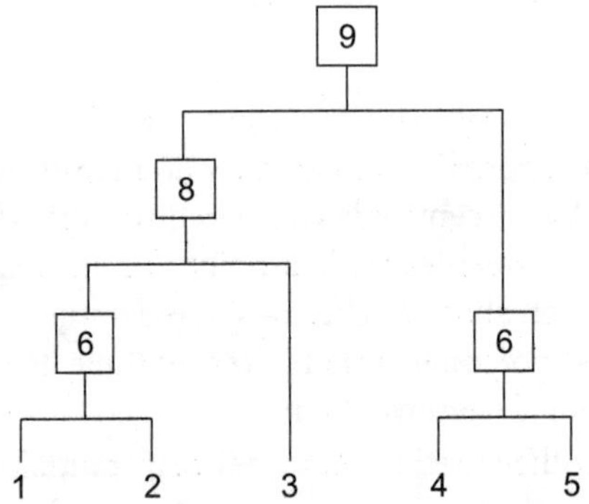

There are two main types of hierarchical clustering:

1. **Agglomerative Hierarchical Clustering:** This approach starts by considering each data point as a separate cluster and then iteratively merges the closest pairs of clusters based on a specified

similarity measure. The process continues until all data points are merged into a single cluster. The resulting dendrogram provides insights into the hierarchical structure of the data.

In agglomerative hierarchical clustering, the algorithm starts with each data point as a separate cluster and progressively merges the most similar (or nearest) pairs of clusters until all data points are merged into a single cluster, forming a dendrogram from the bottom level.

The merging process in agglomerative hierarchical clustering can be summarized as follows:

1. Start with each data point as an individual cluster.
2. Calculate the similarity or distance between all pairs of clusters.
3. Merge the two clusters with the highest similarity or smallest distance, creating a new cluster.
4. Update the similarity or distance matrix to reflect the newly formed cluster.
5. Repeat steps 2-4 until all data points are merged into a single cluster.

This bottom-up approach gradually builds the dendrogram, where each level of the dendrogram represents a different stage of clustering. The merging decisions are based on a similarity measure, such as Euclidean distance, Manhattan distance, or correlation coefficient, depending on the chosen linkage criterion.

The dendrogram provides a visual representation of the clustering process, with the height of the branches indicating the dissimilarity between clusters. The height at which clusters merge represents the similarity threshold at which they are combined.

Agglomerative hierarchical clustering offers a hierarchical view of the data, allowing for different levels of granularity in clustering. By cutting the dendrogram at a certain height, clusters of varying sizes and similarity can be obtained.

Overall, agglomerative hierarchical clustering is a versatile and widely used clustering technique that provides insights into the hierarchical structure of the data and allows for flexible interpretations at different levels of clustering.

Agglomerative clustering algorithm

1. Make each data point in the data set D a cluster,
2. Compute all pair-wise distances of $x_1, x_2, ..., x_n \in D$;
2. repeat
3. find two clusters that are nearest to each other;
4. merge the two clusters from a new cluster c;
5. compute the distance from c to all other clusters;
12. until there is only one cluster left

2. **Divisive Hierarchical Clustering:** This approach takes the opposite approach by considering all data points as one large cluster and then recursively splitting it into smaller clusters until each cluster contains a single data point. The process continues until a stopping criterion is met. Divisive hierarchical clustering provides a top-down view of the data's structure.

   In divisive hierarchical clustering, the algorithm starts with all data points in a single cluster, which is referred to as the root cluster. It then recursively splits the root cluster into a set of child clusters until each cluster consists of only a single data point, forming singleton clusters.

   The divisive clustering process can be summarized as follows:

   1. Start with all data points belonging to a single cluster (root cluster).

2. Select a cluster and apply a splitting criterion to divide it into two or more child clusters.
3. Repeat step 2 for each child cluster, recursively splitting them further until singleton clusters are formed (clusters with only one data point).
4. The resulting cluster hierarchy forms a tree-like structure, with the root cluster at the top and the singleton clusters as the leaves.

The splitting criterion used in divisive clustering determines how to partition a cluster into child clusters. Various criteria can be employed, such as distance-based measures, variance reduction, or other statistical techniques. The choice of the splitting criterion depends on the specific algorithm and the nature of the data.

Divisive hierarchical clustering provides a hierarchical decomposition of the data, where each level of the tree represents a different stage of clustering. The resulting cluster hierarchy can be visualized using dendrograms, similar to agglomerative clustering, which show the order and sequence of the splitting process.

One advantage of divisive clustering is that it allows for a top-down exploration of the data, providing insights into the relationships between clusters at different levels of granularity. However, divisive clustering can be computationally expensive, especially when dealing with large datasets, as it involves recursively partitioning clusters until singleton clusters are obtained.

Measuring the Distance of Two Clusters

When measuring the distance between two clusters in hierarchical clustering, there are several approaches that can be used. When performing clustering algorithms, measuring the distance between two clusters is essential to determine their similarity or dissimilarity. Various distance metrics can be used for this purpose, depending on the nature of the data and the specific requirements of the clustering algorithm. These approaches result in different variations of the algorithm and can impact the clustering results. Here are a few commonly used methods:

Single Link: Also known as the nearest neighbor method, this approach measures the distance between the closest pair of data points from different clusters. It considers the smallest distance between any two points from the two clusters. The distance between two clusters is the distance between two closest data points in the two clusters, one data point from each cluster.

In single-link hierarchical clustering, the distance between two clusters is defined as the shortest distance between any two points belonging to different clusters. It considers the closest pair of data points from each cluster when calculating the distance.

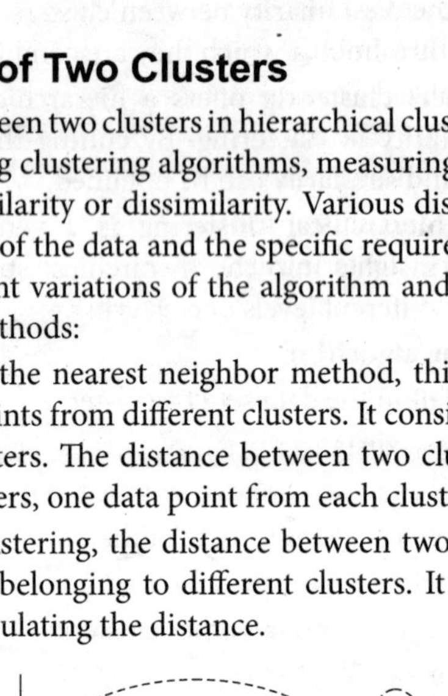

Two natural clusters are split into two

Here's how the single-link method works:

1. Calculate the pairwise distances between all data points in different clusters.

2. Initially, each data point is treated as a separate cluster.
3. Find the two clusters with the smallest distance between their closest points.
4. Merge these two clusters into a new cluster.
5. Update the distance matrix to reflect the distances between the new cluster and the remaining clusters.
6. Repeat steps 3-5 until all data points are merged into a single cluster.

The resulting dendrogram, which represents the hierarchical structure of the clusters, can be visualized as a tree-like structure. The height at which two clusters are merged in the dendrogram indicates their dissimilarity or distance.

Single-link clustering tends to produce elongated, chaining clusters. It has a tendency to form clusters based on local connections rather than global structure. It can be sensitive to outliers and noise in the data since a single outlier can connect distant points and influence the clustering results.

Despite its limitations, single-link clustering can be useful in scenarios where clusters are expected to have a chain-like structure or when dealing with non-convex shapes in the data.

Example: In this example, we have four data points denoted as P1, P2, P3, and P4. The clusters A, B, and C are formed during the single-link hierarchical clustering process.

Initially, each data point is treated as a separate cluster. The algorithm starts by merging the two closest points, P1 and P2, into cluster A. Then, the next closest pair, P3 and P4, are merged into cluster B. Finally, clusters A and B are merged into the final cluster C.

The dendrogram can be visualized as a tree structure, where the height of the branches represents the distance between clusters. In this case, the distance between A and B is greater than the distances within each cluster, indicating their dissimilarity.

Please note that the distances and cluster formations in the dendrogram are based on the specific data and distance metric used in the clustering algorithm.

```
                |-------+
                |   C   |
                +-------+
                  /   \
                 /     \
         +-------+     +-------+
         |   A   |     |   B   |
         +-------+     +-------+
           /   \         /   \
          /     \       /     \
+-------+ +-------+ +-------+ +-------+
|  P1   || P2    || P3    || P4    |
+-------+ +-------+ +-------+ +-------+
```

Here's a step-by-step explanation of the example:

1. Initially, we have four data points: P1, P2, P3, and P4.
2. The algorithm starts by considering each point as a separate cluster: A = {P1}, B = {P2}, C = {P3}, and D = {P4}.

3. It calculates the pairwise distances between clusters using a distance metric (e.g., Euclidean distance).
4. The two closest clusters based on the shortest distance are A and B. They are merged into a new cluster, denoted as AB = {P1, P2}.
5. Next, the algorithm calculates the distances between AB and the remaining clusters.
6. The closest clusters based on the shortest distance are C and AB. They are merged into a new cluster, denoted as ABC = {P1, P2, P3}.
7. Finally, the last remaining cluster D is merged with ABC to form the final cluster, denoted as ABCD = {P1, P2, P3, P4}.

The resulting dendrogram represents the merging process. The height of the branches in the dendrogram indicates the dissimilarity or distance between clusters. In this case, the distance between clusters A and B is smaller compared to the distances within each cluster, indicating their similarity. On the other hand, the distance between clusters A/B and C is greater, indicating their dissimilarity.

Overall, single-link clustering favors merging clusters that have at least one pair of points with a small distance between them, resulting in long, elongated clusters. It can be useful when dealing with elongated or irregularly shaped clusters in the data.

Complete Link: Also known as the farthest neighbor method, this approach measures the distance between the farthest pair of data points from different clusters. It considers the largest distance between any two points from the two clusters.

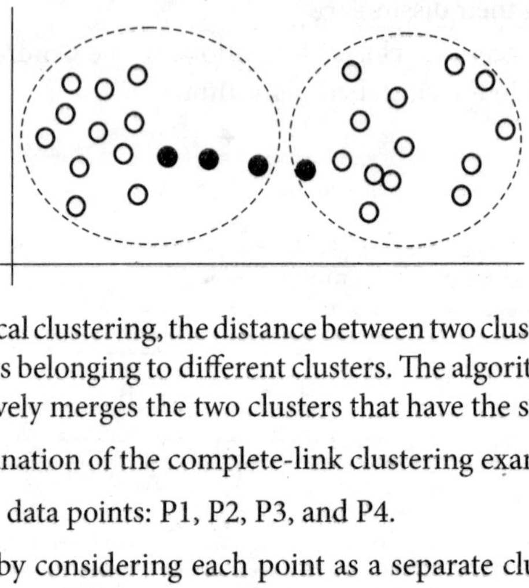

In complete-link hierarchical clustering, the distance between two clusters is defined as the maximum distance between any two points belonging to different clusters. The algorithm starts with each data point as a separate cluster and iteratively merges the two clusters that have the smallest maximum distance.

Here's a step-by-step explanation of the complete-link clustering example:

1. Initially, we have four data points: P1, P2, P3, and P4.
2. The algorithm starts by considering each point as a separate cluster: A = {P1}, B = {P2}, C = {P3}, and D = {P4}.
3. It calculates the pairwise distances between clusters using a distance metric (e.g., Euclidean distance).
4. The two clusters with the smallest maximum distance are A and B. They are merged into a new cluster, denoted as AB = {P1, P2}.
5. Next, the algorithm calculates the distances between AB and the remaining clusters.

6. The cluster with the smallest maximum distance to AB is C. AB and C are merged into a new cluster, denoted as ABC = {P1, P2, P3}.
7. Finally, the last remaining cluster D is merged with ABC to form the final cluster, denoted as ABCD = {P1, P2, P3, P4}.

The resulting dendrogram represents the merging process. The height of the branches in the dendrogram indicates the dissimilarity or distance between clusters. In this case, the distance between clusters A and B is small compared to the distances within each cluster, indicating their similarity. The distance between clusters A/B and C is also small, indicating their similarity. However, the distance between clusters A/B/C and D is greater, indicating their dissimilarity.

Complete-link clustering tends to form compact clusters that have small maximum distances within each cluster. It can be useful when dealing with compact and well-separated clusters in the data.

Average Link: This approach calculates the average distance between all pairs of data points from different clusters. It considers the average of the distances between all possible pairs of points.

In average-link clustering, the distance between two clusters is calculated as the average of all pairwise distances between the data points in the two clusters. This method aims to find a compromise between the sensitivity of complete-link clustering to outliers and the tendency of single-link clustering to form long chains.

The average-link method considers the average distance between all pairs of data points in two clusters as the measure of similarity or dissimilarity between the clusters. This approach helps to overcome the limitations of single-link clustering, where long chains of clusters can be formed due to the consideration of only the closest data points. At the same time, it mitigates the sensitivity to outliers that can occur in complete-link clustering, which considers the maximum distance between data points.

By calculating the average distance, the average-link method provides a more balanced measure of similarity that takes into account the overall distribution of distances between the data points in the clusters. This can lead to the formation of more compact and spherical clusters that align with the intuitive notion of clusters as cohesive and well-defined groups.

Overall, the average-link clustering method offers a compromise between the extreme behaviors of single-link and complete-link clustering, resulting in more robust and meaningful cluster formations.

In average-link hierarchical clustering, the distance between two clusters is calculated as the average of all pairwise distances between data points from the two clusters. This distance measure provides a representation of the average similarity between the data points in the clusters.

Here is a description of the graphical representation of average-link hierarchical clustering in a dendrogram:

1. Each data point is represented by a vertical line or a leaf at the bottom of the dendrogram.
2. As the clustering algorithm progresses, clusters are merged based on their average linkage distances.
3. The merging process is shown by branches connecting the clusters.
4. The height or length of the branches represents the average distance between the merged clusters.
5. The height of the branches is calculated by taking the average of all pairwise distances between the data points in the clusters being merged.

```
   |---------|
   |         |
 --|    A    |
   |         |
 --|---------|
        |
  ------|------
   |         |
 --|    B    |
   |         |
 --|---------|
        |
  ------|------
   |         |
 --|   C,D   |
   |         |
  -------------
```

In this representation, the vertical lines represent the individual data points (A, B, C, D), and the branches show the merging of clusters. The height of the branches indicates the average distance between the data points in the merged clusters.

It's important to note that this is a simplified representation, and the actual dendrogram may vary depending on the specific data and the average distances between clusters.

Centroids: This approach calculates the distance between the centroids (mean vectors) of the two clusters. It considers the distance between the centroids as a measure of dissimilarity.

In this method, the distance between two clusters is the distance between their centroids

Centroids in clustering refer to the central points or representative points of clusters. The centroid of a cluster is computed as the mean or average of the feature values of all data points within that cluster. It is used as a reference point to represent the cluster in a multi-dimensional feature space.

The centroid represents the central tendency of the data points in a cluster and is often considered as the "center" of the cluster. It is calculated by taking the mean of the feature values across all data points in the cluster. For example, if we have a cluster with two-dimensional data points (x, y), the centroid would be the average of the x-coordinates and y-coordinates of all the points in that cluster.

The use of centroids in clustering algorithms, such as k-means, allows for efficient computation and comparison of distances between clusters. By comparing the distances between centroids, clusters can be merged or split during the clustering process.

Centroids are important in clustering because they provide a compact representation of the cluster and can be used for various purposes, such as cluster visualization, cluster analysis, and prediction. They serve as reference points for understanding the characteristics and properties of clusters and can be useful for interpreting and analyzing the results of clustering algorithms.

It's important to note that the use of centroids assumes that the data within a cluster is distributed around a central point. In some cases, where the data distribution is non-linear or irregular, other techniques like medoids or representative points may be used instead of centroids.

The complexity

- All the algorithms are at least $O(n^2)$. n is the number of data points.
- Single link can be done in $O(n^2)$.
- Complete and average links can be done in $O(n^2 \log n)$.
- Due the complexity, hard to use for large data sets.
  - Sampling
  - Scale-up methods (e.g., BIRCH).

Distance Function

A distance function, also known as a similarity measure or dissimilarity measure, is a mathematical function that quantifies the similarity or dissimilarity between two data points or objects. It is a fundamental concept used in various fields, including machine learning, data mining, and pattern recognition, to compare and analyze the relationships between data points.

The distance function takes two data points as input and calculates a numerical value that represents the distance or dissimilarity between them. The choice of distance function depends on the type of data and the specific problem domain. Different distance functions have different properties and capture different aspects of similarity or dissimilarity.

Minkowski Distance:

Minkowski distance is a generalization of different distance measures, including the Euclidean distance and the Manhattan distance. It is a distance measure that can be used to calculate the dissimilarity between two data points in a multi-dimensional space. Suppose X is a vector space then a norm on X is a real valued function $||x||$which satisfies below conditions -

- Zero Vector- Zero vector will have zero length.
- Scalar Factor- The direction of vector doesn't change when you multiply it with a positive number though its length will be changed.
- Triangle Inequality- If distance is a norm then the calculated distance between two points will always be a straight line.

The Minkowski distance between two points x and y in a d-dimensional space is defined as:

$$d(x, y) = (\Sigma|xi - yi|^p)^(1/p)$$

Here, xi and yi are the coordinates of the two points in each dimension, and p is a parameter that determines the type of Minkowski distance. When $p = 1$, it becomes the Manhattan distance, and when $p = 2$, it becomes the Euclidean distance.

The Minkowski distance allows for adjusting the level of emphasis on different dimensions and provides flexibility in measuring dissimilarity based on the specific requirements of the problem. For example, when p is set to a larger value, it places more weight on larger differences between coordinate values and may be more sensitive to outliers.

The Minkowski distance can be used in various applications, including clustering, classification, and nearest neighbor search, where the goal is to identify similar or dissimilar data points based on their feature values. By adjusting the value of the parameter p, the Minkowski distance can be tailored to the specific needs of the problem at hand.

Euclidean distance: This is the most common distance metric used in many applications. It calculates the straight-line distance between two points in Euclidean space. It is suitable for continuous data and is based on the Pythagorean theorem.

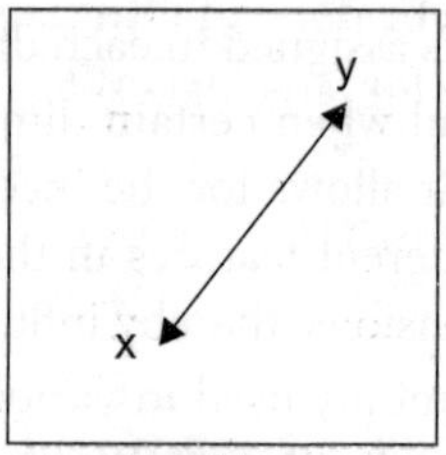

Euclidean

Euclidean distance is a popular distance metric used to measure the straight-line distance between two points in Euclidean space. It is named after the Greek mathematician Euclid, who introduced the concept of Euclidean geometry.

The Euclidean distance between two points, denoted as p and q, is calculated as the square root of the sum of the squared differences between their coordinates. In other words, it measures the length of the straight line connecting the two points.

Mathematically, the Euclidean distance between two points (p1, p2, ..., pn) and (q1, q2, ..., qn) in n-dimensional space can be calculated using the following formula:

d = sqrt((p1 – q1)^2 + (p2 – q2)^2 + ... + (pn – qn)^2)

where sqrt denotes the square root and ^2 denotes squaring.

Euclidean distance is widely used in various fields, including machine learning, data analysis, and pattern recognition. It is particularly useful when dealing with continuous data or numerical features. For example, it can be used to measure the similarity or dissimilarity between two data points in clustering algorithms, such as k-means, or in distance-based classification algorithms, such as k-nearest neighbors (KNN).

It is important to note that Euclidean distance assumes that all dimensions or features are equally important and contributes equally to the overall distance. In some cases, when dealing with high-dimensional data or data with different scales, it may be necessary to normalize or standardize the features before calculating the Euclidean distance to avoid bias towards certain dimensions.

Overall, Euclidean distance provides a straightforward and intuitive measure of distance between points in Euclidean space and serves as a fundamental tool in many data analysis and machine learning tasks.

Weighted Euclidean distance is a variant of the Euclidean distance where each dimension or feature is assigned a weight that reflects its relative importance in the distance calculation. Unlike the traditional Euclidean distance, where all dimensions are considered equally important, weighted Euclidean distance allows for the customization of the distance calculation based on the specific requirements of the problem.

In weighted Euclidean distance, each dimension is multiplied by its corresponding weight before calculating the squared difference. The weights can be positive or negative, indicating the direction and magnitude of the impact on the distance calculation. A positive weight amplifies the contribution of the corresponding dimension, while a negative weight diminishes it.

The formula for weighted Euclidean distance between two points (p1, p2, ..., pn) and (q1, q2, ..., qn) in n-dimensional space is as follows:

$$d = sqrt(w1 * (p1 - q1)^2 + w2 * (p2 - q2)^2 + ... + wn * (pn - qn)^2)$$

where w1, w2, ..., wn represent the weights assigned to each dimension.

Weighted Euclidean distance is useful when certain dimensions are more relevant or informative for the distance calculation than others. It allows for the incorporation of domain knowledge or prior assumptions about the importance of different features in the data. By adjusting the weights, one can emphasize or de-emphasize specific dimensions, thereby influencing the overall distance measurement.

Weighted Euclidean distance is commonly used in various fields such as pattern recognition, data mining, and multi-objective optimization. It offers a flexible way to tailor the distance calculation to the specific needs of the problem at hand and can lead to more meaningful and accurate results by considering the varying importance of different features.

Squared Distance and Chebychev Distance

Squared Distance

Squared distance is a distance metric commonly used in various algorithms and applications. It is calculated by taking the square of the Euclidean distance between two points. The squared distance between two points (p1, p2, ..., pn) and (q1, q2, ..., qn) in n-dimensional space is given by:

$$d^2 = (p1 - q1)^2 + (p2 - q2)^2 + ... + (pn - qn)^2$$

Squared distance is often used because it is computationally efficient and avoids the square root operation, which can be costly in some scenarios. However, squared distance does not preserve the exact magnitude of the distances and can lead to biased results, particularly when comparing distances across different scales or when interpreting the distances in their original units.

Chebyshev Distance

Chebyshev distance, also known as the maximum or $L\infty$ distance, is a metric that measures the maximum absolute difference between corresponding coordinates of two points. It is named after the mathematician Pafnuty Chebyshev. The Chebyshev distance between two points (p1, p2, ..., pn) and (q1, q2, ..., qn) in n-dimensional space is given by:

$$d = max(|p1 - q1|, |p2 - q2|, ..., |pn - qn|)$$

Chebyshev distance is useful when considering the worst-case scenario or maximum discrepancy between the coordinates of two points. It is commonly used in problems involving spatial planning, routing, and optimization, where the goal is to find the shortest path or the most efficient route based on the maximum difference in coordinates.

Both squared distance and Chebyshev distance are distance metrics used to quantify the dissimilarity or similarity between data points. The choice between these metrics depends on the specific problem at hand and the characteristics of the data.

Manhattan distance: Also known as city block distance or L1 norm, it calculates the sum of the absolute differences between the coordinates of two points. It is often used for discrete or categorical data.

Manhattan distance, also known as city block distance or L1 distance, is a distance metric commonly used in machine learning and data analysis. It measures the distance between two points in a grid-like space by summing the absolute differences of their coordinates.

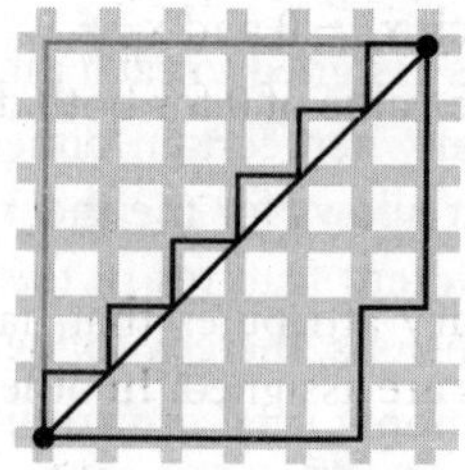

The Manhattan distance between two points (p1, p2, ..., pn) and (q1, q2, ..., qn) in n-dimensional space is calculated by summing the absolute differences of their coordinates:

$$d = |p1 - q1| + |p2 - q2| + ... + |pn - qn|$$

The term "Manhattan distance" is derived from the analogy of measuring distances in a grid-like city where one can only travel along horizontal and vertical paths, without diagonal movements.

Manhattan distance is commonly used when working with grid-based or lattice-like structures, such as image processing, board games, and route planning in urban environments. It is particularly useful in situations where movements are constrained to specific directions and diagonal movements are not allowed.

Compared to other distance metrics like Euclidean distance, Manhattan distance tends to give more weight to differences in individual dimensions rather than considering their overall magnitude. It is also less sensitive to outliers and can be more interpretable in certain scenarios.

Overall, Manhattan distance provides a straightforward and intuitive measure of dissimilarity between points based on their grid-like distance in each dimension. It is a versatile distance metric that finds applications in various fields.

Distance Functions for Binary Attributes

Binary Attribute

In the context of distance functions, a binary attribute refers to an attribute that takes on one of two possible values, typically represented as 0 or 1. Binary attributes are commonly used to represent yes/no or true/false conditions. has two values or states but no ordering relationships, e.g., – Gender: male and female.

- We use a confusion matrix to introduce the distance functions/measures.
- Let the ith and jth data points be x_i and x_j (vectors)

Confusion Matrix

		Data point j: 1	Data point j: 0	
Data point i	1	a	b	a + b
	0	c	d	c + d
		a + c	b + d	a + b + c + d

a: the number of attributes with the value of 1 for bot data points.

b: the number of attributes for which $x_{if} = 1$ and $x_{jf} = 0$, where $x_{if}(x_{if})$ is the value of the fth attribute of the data point $x_i(x_j)$.

c: the number of attributes for which $x_{if} = 0$ and $x_{jf} = 1$.

d: the number of attributes with the value of 0 for both data points.

Symmetric Binary Attributes

Symmetric binary attributes refer to binary attributes that have the same meaning or interpretation regardless of the order in which the values are assigned. In other words, the attribute values do not have an inherent order or preference.

A binary attribute is symmetric if both of its states (0 and 1) have equal importance, and carry the same weights, e.g., male and female of the attribute Gender

- **Distance function:** Simple Matching Coefficient, proportion of mismatches of their values

$$\text{dist}(x_i, x_j) = \frac{b+c}{a+b+c+d}$$

Symmetric binary attributes: example

x_1	1	1	1	0	1	0	0
x_2	0	1	1	0	0	1	0

$$\text{dist}(x_i, x_f) = \frac{2+1}{2+2+1+2} = \frac{3}{7} = 0.429$$

Asymmetric binary attributes refer to binary attributes where the order or assignment of the attribute values carries significance or meaning. In other words, the attribute values have an inherent order or preference.

When dealing with asymmetric binary attributes, different distance measures can be used depending on the specific context and requirements of the analysis.

if one of the states is more important or more valuable than the other. – By convention, state 1 represents the more important state, which is typically the rare or infrequent state.

Jaccard Coefficient

The Jaccard coefficient, also known as the Jaccard similarity coefficient, is a measure of similarity between two sets. It is often used in data analysis and information retrieval to compare the similarity of two binary attribute sets.

The Jaccard coefficient is calculated as the size of the intersection of the two sets divided by the size of their union. In terms of binary attributes, it measures the proportion of shared attribute values between two objects.

The formula for calculating the Jaccard coefficient is as follows:

$$J(A, B) = |A \cap B| / |A \cup B|$$

where A and B are two sets representing binary attributes, $|A \cap B|$ denotes the size of the intersection of sets A and B (i.e., the count of common attribute values), and $|A \cup B|$ denotes the size of the union of sets A and B (i.e., the count of unique attribute values in both sets).

The Jaccard coefficient ranges from 0 to 1, where 0 indicates no shared attribute values and 1 indicates that the two sets have identical attribute values. A higher Jaccard coefficient indicates a greater similarity between the sets.

The Jaccard coefficient is useful in various applications, such as measuring document similarity, evaluating clustering algorithms, and assessing the performance of recommendation systems.

Let's consider an example to illustrate the Jaccard coefficient for binary attributes.

Suppose we have two sets A and B representing binary attributes:

$$A = \{0, 1, 1, 0, 1\}$$

$$B = \{1, 1, 0, 0, 0\}$$

To calculate the Jaccard coefficient, we need to determine the size of the intersection and the size of the union of the two sets.

Intersection ($A \cap B$): This is the set of attribute values that are common to both sets A and B.

$A \cap B = \{0, 1, 0, 0, 0\}$ (only the positions where both A and B have a value of 1)

Union ($A \cup B$): This is the set of all unique attribute values from both sets A and B.

$$A \cup B = \{0, 1, 1, 0, 1\}$$

Next, we calculate the sizes of the intersection and union:

$|A \cap B| = 3$ (count of common attribute values)

$|A \cup B| = 4$ (count of unique attribute values)

Finally, we calculate the Jaccard coefficient:

$$J(A, B) = |A \cap B|/|A \cup B| = 3/4 = 0.75$$

So, in this example, the Jaccard coefficient between sets A and B is 0.75. This indicates a relatively high similarity between the two sets, as they share 75% of their attribute values.

The Jaccard coefficient is a useful measure for comparing the similarity of binary attribute sets, particularly in cases where the presence or absence of specific attributes is important.

Nominal Attributes

When working with nominal attributes, such as categorical variables, different distance measures can be used to quantify the dissimilarity between attribute values. Here are a few commonly used distance measures for nominal attributes:

Hamming Distance: This distance measure is used for attributes that have a fixed number of categories. It calculates the number of positions at which two attribute values differ. For example, if we have two nominal attributes "red" and "blue," the Hamming distance would be 1 since they differ in one position.

Let A and B be two nominal attributes of the same length.

The Hamming distance is calculated as:

Hamming_distance(A, B) = (Number of positions where A and B differ) / (Total number of positions)

Simple Matching Coefficient: This coefficient measures the proportion of matches between two attribute values. It counts the number of positions at which two attribute values are the same and divides it by the total number of positions. It ranges from 0 (no matches) to 1 (complete match).

Let A and B be two nominal attributes of the same length.

The Simple Matching Coefficient is calculated as:

SMC(A, B) = (Number of matching positions between A and B) / (Total number of positions)

Jaccard Distance: This distance measure is also applicable to nominal attributes. It is calculated as the complement of the Jaccard coefficient we discussed earlier. It measures the dissimilarity between two attribute values as the ratio of the number of different positions to the total number of positions.

Overlap Coefficient: This coefficient is similar to the Jaccard coefficient but only considers the positions where both attribute values are non-zero. It calculates the ratio of the number of matches to the number of non-zero positions.

Let A and B be two nominal attributes of the same length.

The Overlap coefficient is calculated as:

Overlap_coefficient(A, B) = (Number of matching positions between A and B) / (Number of non-zero positions)

These distance measures provide a way to quantify the dissimilarity between nominal attributes and are useful in clustering, classification, and other data analysis tasks. The choice of the appropriate distance measure depends on the specific characteristics and requirements of the data.

Example:

A = {red, green, blue, blue, yellow}

B = {red, blue, green, green, red}

Hamming Distance:

- Number of positions where A and B differ: 2 (at index 2 and index 4)
- Total number of positions: 5
- Hamming_distance(A, B) = 2/5 = 0.4

Simple Matching Coefficient:

- Number of matching positions between A and B: 3 (at index 1, index 3, and index 5)
- Total number of positions: 5
- SMC(A, B) = 3/5 = 0.6

Jaccard Distance:

- Number of matching positions between A and B: 3 (at index 1, index 3, and index 5)
- Total number of positions: 5
- Jaccard_coefficient(A, B) = 3/5 = 0.6
- Jaccard_distance(A, B) = 1 – Jaccard_coefficient(A, B) = 1 - 0.6 = 0.4

Overlap Coefficient:

- Number of matching positions between A and B: 3 (at index 1, index 3, and index 5)
- Number of non-zero positions: 5
- Overlap_coefficient(A, B) = 3/5 = 0.6

These values illustrate the dissimilarity between the nominal attributes A and B using different distance measures.

Data Standardization

In the Euclidean space, standardization of attributes is recommended to ensure that all attributes have equal impact on the computation of distances. This is because Euclidean distance is sensitive to the scale of the variables.

When the attributes in a dataset have different scales, variables with larger magnitudes can dominate the computation of Euclidean distance. This can lead to biased results and inaccurate comparisons between data points.

By standardizing the attributes, all variables are transformed to have a mean of zero and a standard deviation of one. This brings them to a similar scale and ensures that each attribute contributes equally to the computation of distances. It allows for fair and meaningful comparisons between data points, regardless of the original scale of the variables.

Standardization is particularly important in cases where the attributes have different units or measurement scales. It helps to eliminate the impact of scale-related biases and allows for more reliable analysis and modeling in the Euclidean space.

Overall, standardization of attributes is a valuable preprocessing step when working with Euclidean distance to ensure fair and accurate comparisons between data points.

Consider the following pair of data points

– xi: (0.1, 20) and xj: (0.9, 720).

The distance is almost completely dominated by (720 – 20) = 700.

Standardize Attributes

To standardize the attributes, we need to calculate the mean and standard deviation for each attribute in the dataset. Let's assume that the dataset consists of the following pairs of data points:

xi: (0.1, 20)

xj: (0.9, 720)

To standardize the first attribute (0.1 and 0.9), we calculate the mean and standard deviation as follows:

Mean (μ1) = (0.1 + 0.9)/2 = 0.5

Standard Deviation (σ1) = sqrt(((0.1 – 0.5)^2 + (0.9 – 0.5)^2)/2) = 0.4

To standardize the second attribute (20 and 720), we calculate the mean and standard deviation as follows:

Mean (μ2) = (20 + 720)/2 = 370

Standard Deviation (σ2) = sqrt(((20 – 370)^2 + (720 – 370)^2)/2) = 344.21

Now, we can apply the standardization formula to each attribute of the data points:

Standardized xi: ((0.1 – 0.5)/0.4, (20 – 370)/344.21) = (–1, –1.08)

Standardized xj: ((0.9 – 0.5)/0.4, (720 – 370)/344.21) = (1, 1.08)

By standardizing the attributes, we bring them to a common value range and ensure that they have equal impact in the computation of distances. In this case, the standardized attributes are (-1, -1.08) for xi and (1, 1.08) for xj, which allows for a more balanced distance calculation.

Interval-scaled Attributes

Interval-scaled attributes are numerical attributes that have a meaningful zero point but do not have a natural ratio between their values. These attributes can be standardized using the following formula:

Standardized value = (Value – Mean)/Standard Deviation

Where,

Value: The original value of the attribute

Mean: The mean value of the attribute in the dataset

Standard Deviation: The standard deviation of the attribute in the dataset

By applying this formula, we can transform the interval-scaled attribute values to have a mean of 0 and a standard deviation of 1. This allows for a more consistent and comparable representation of the attribute values.

For example, consider a dataset with the following interval-scaled attribute values:

Values: [10, 20, 30, 40, 50]

To standardize these values, we first calculate the mean and standard deviation:

$$\begin{aligned}\text{Mean} &= (10 + 20 + 30 + 40 + 50)/5 = 30 \\ \text{Standard Deviation} &= \text{sqrt}(((10 - 30)\text{^}2 + (20 - 30)\text{^}2 + (30 - 30)\text{^}2 + (40 - 30)\text{^}2 \\ &\quad + (50 - 30)\text{^}2)/5) \\ &= 14.14\end{aligned}$$

Now, we can apply the standardization formula to each value:

Standardized values:

$$\begin{aligned}(10 - 30)/14.14 &\approx -1.41 \\ (20 - 30)/14.14 &\approx -0.71 \\ (30 - 30)/14.14 &= 0 \\ (40 - 30)/14.14 &\approx 0.71 \\ (50 - 30)/14.14 &\approx 1.41\end{aligned}$$

The standardized values have a mean of 0 and a standard deviation of 1, allowing for easier comparison and analysis of the attribute values.

Approaches to Standardize Interval Scaled Attributes

There are several approaches to standardize interval-scaled attributes, depending on the specific requirements and characteristics of the dataset. Here are two commonly used approaches:

Z-score Standardization (or Standard Score)

This approach transforms the attribute values to have a mean of 0 and a standard deviation of 1.

The formula for z-score standardization is:

Standardized value = (Value - Mean) / Standard Deviation

This method is useful when the attribute values are normally distributed and there are no extreme outliers.

Transforms the attribute values so that they have a mean of zero and a mean absolute deviation of 1. The mean absolute deviation of attribute f, denoted by sf , is computed as follows

$$s_f = \frac{1}{n}(|x_{if} - m_f| + |x_{2f} - m_f| + \ldots + |x_{nf} - m_f|)$$

$$m_f = \frac{1}{n}(x_{1f} + x_{2f} + \ldots + x_{nf})$$

Z-score: $$z(x_{if}) = \frac{x_{if} - m_f}{s_f}$$

Min-Max Scaling

This approach scales the attribute values to a specific range, typically between 0 and 1.

The formula for min-max scaling is:

Standardized value = (Value – Min)/(Max – Min)

This method is useful when you want to preserve the relative relationships between the attribute values and when the distribution of the values is not necessarily normal.

It's important to note that the choice of standardization method depends on the nature of the data and the specific analysis or modeling task at hand. It's also important to consider the potential impact of outliers on the standardization process and whether any data transformations are necessary to handle them appropriately.

Ratio-scaled Attributes

Ratio-scaled attributes are variables that have a natural zero point and can be compared in terms of ratios. Examples of ratio-scaled attributes include age, weight, height, and income.

When standardizing ratio-scaled attributes, there are a few approaches that can be used:

Min-max Scaling

This approach scales the attribute values to a specific range, typically between 0 and 1.

The formula to calculate the standardized value using min-max scaling is:

$$X\_scaled = (X - X\_min)/(X\_max - X\_min)$$

where X is the original value, X_min is the minimum value of the attribute, and X_max is the maximum value of the attribute.

Decimal Scaling

This approach scales the attribute values by shifting the decimal point of each value to the left or right.

The number of decimal places to shift depends on the maximum absolute value of the attribute.

For example, if the maximum absolute value is 1000, you can scale the values by dividing them by 1000, resulting in a range of –1 to 1.

Log Transformation

This approach applies a logarithmic transformation to the attribute values.

The formula to calculate the standardized value using log transformation is:

$$X\_log = \log(X)$$

where X is the original value.

Log transformation can be useful when the attribute values span a large range and have a skewed distribution.

The choice of standardization method depends on the specific characteristics of the data and the requirements of the analysis. It is important to consider the distribution of the attribute values and the intended use of the standardized data when selecting the appropriate approach.

Nominal Attributes

Nominal attributes are categorical variables that represent qualitative characteristics or categories. They do not have an inherent order or numerical value associated with them. Examples of nominal attributes include gender (male/female), color (red/blue/green), and occupation (doctor/teacher/engineer).

When working with nominal attributes, standardization is not typically applicable because there is no meaningful numerical scale to measure the differences between categories. However, nominal attributes can be encoded or transformed into numerical representations to facilitate analysis or machine learning algorithms.

One common approach is one-hot encoding, also known as dummy coding. In one-hot encoding, each category in a nominal attribute is represented as a binary indicator variable. For example, if we have a nominal attribute "color" with categories "red," "blue," and "green," we can create three separate binary variables: "red" (1 if the color is red, 0 otherwise), "blue" (1 if the color is blue, 0 otherwise), and "green" (1 if the color is green, 0 otherwise). This transformation allows us to use numerical values for further analysis or modeling.

Other encoding techniques for nominal attributes include ordinal encoding (assigning numerical values to categories based on a predefined order) and label encoding (assigning a unique numerical label to each category). The choice of encoding method depends on the specific requirements and characteristics of the data and the analysis task at hand.

It's important to note that the choice of encoding should be carefully considered, as different encoding approaches may introduce different levels of bias or assumptions into the analysis.

Ordinal Attributes

Ordinal attributes are categorical variables that have a natural order or ranking associated with them. The categories of ordinal attributes represent different levels or positions in a hierarchical or ordered scale. Examples of ordinal attributes include educational attainment (elementary school, high school, college), satisfaction level (low, medium, high), and income level (low, medium, high).

When working with ordinal attributes, standardization is not typically applicable because the numerical values assigned to the categories already represent their inherent order or ranking. However, similar to nominal attributes, ordinal attributes can be encoded or transformed into numerical representations to facilitate analysis or modeling.

One common approach is ordinal encoding, where each category is assigned a unique numerical value based on its position in the order or scale. For example, if we have an ordinal attribute "education level" with categories "elementary school," "high school," and "college," we can assign numerical values such as 1, 2, and 3, respectively, to represent their order.

It's important to note that when using ordinal encoding, the numerical values assigned to the categories should reflect their relative order accurately. Care should be taken to avoid introducing any misleading assumptions or biases into the analysis based on the chosen encoding scheme.

Other encoding techniques for ordinal attributes include label encoding (assigning a unique numerical label to each category without considering their order) and custom encoding methods that take into account specific domain knowledge or expert judgment.

The choice of encoding method for ordinal attributes depends on the specific requirements of the analysis and the nature of the data. It's essential to consider the meaning and interpretation of the ordinal scale when selecting an appropriate encoding strategy.

Mixed Attributes

Mixed attributes refer to datasets or variables that contain a combination of different types of attributes, such as numerical, categorical, ordinal, or nominal. These datasets pose unique challenges in terms of data analysis and modeling because different attribute types require different approaches for handling and processing.

When working with mixed attribute datasets, it is important to consider the nature of each attribute type and select appropriate techniques for data preprocessing, analysis, and modeling. Here are some approaches commonly used for handling mixed attributes:

1. **Data preprocessing:** Before analyzing the data, it is essential to preprocess the mixed attribute dataset to ensure compatibility and consistency across the different attribute types. This may involve steps such as handling missing values, encoding categorical or nominal attributes, scaling or standardizing numerical attributes, and transforming ordinal attributes into a meaningful numerical representation.
2. **Feature engineering:** Feature engineering involves creating new features or transforming existing features to enhance the predictive power of the model. This can be especially useful for mixed attribute datasets. For example, numerical attributes can be transformed into categorical bins or ordinal ranks, categorical attributes can be one-hot encoded or transformed into numerical representations, and ordinal attributes can be encoded based on their relative order.
3. **Model selection:** The choice of the modeling technique depends on the specific task and the types of attributes in the dataset. For example, regression models may be suitable for predicting numerical outcomes, while classification models may be more appropriate for categorical or nominal attributes. Ensemble methods or hybrid models that combine different algorithms can also be used to handle mixed attribute datasets effectively.
4. **Feature selection:** In the presence of mixed attributes, it is important to identify the most relevant features for the modeling task. Feature selection techniques can help identify the subset of attributes that contribute the most to the predictive power of the model. This can improve model performance, reduce overfitting, and simplify the interpretation of results.
5. **Evaluation and interpretation:** When analyzing mixed attribute datasets, it is important to consider the interpretability of the results. Different attribute types may have different impacts on the model's predictions and their interpretation. Visualizations, statistical tests, and domain knowledge can aid in interpreting and understanding the relationships between different attributes and the target variable.

Overall, handling mixed attribute datasets requires a thoughtful approach that considers the characteristics of each attribute type and employs appropriate techniques for data preprocessing, feature engineering, model selection, and interpretation. By carefully addressing the challenges posed by mixed attributes, meaningful insights can be derived and accurate models can be built.

Convert to a Single Type

When dealing with mixed attribute datasets, it may sometimes be necessary or beneficial to convert all attributes to a single type to simplify the analysis or modeling process. This conversion can be done by transforming the attributes into a common representation that is suitable for the specific task at hand. Here are a few approaches for converting mixed attributes to a single type:

1. **Numerical representation:** One approach is to convert all attributes to a numerical representation. This can be done by assigning numerical values to categorical or nominal attributes using techniques like one-hot encoding, label encoding, or ordinal encoding. For ordinal attributes, the numerical representation can be based on the order or rank of the categories. For example, we can encode the "Name" attribute using label encoding, where each unique name is assigned a unique numerical value. The "Favorite Subject" attribute can also be encoded using one-hot encoding, where each category becomes a binary attribute. The "Age" attribute, being numerical, remains unchanged.
2. **Categorical representation:** Conversely, you can convert all attributes to a categorical representation. This can be useful when the specific values of the attributes are important for the analysis. In this case, numerical attributes can be discretized into categorical bins or ranges based on certain criteria. In this case, the "Age" attribute can be discretized into age ranges or bins, such as "Child", "Teenager", "Adult", etc. The "Grade" attribute can also be treated as a categorical attribute, with categories like "1st Grade", "2nd Grade", and so on.
3. **Feature extraction:** Another approach is to perform feature extraction to derive a new set of attributes that capture the underlying patterns or relationships in the data. This can involve techniques like principal component analysis (PCA), which extracts orthogonal features that explain the maximum variance in the data. These extracted features can then be treated as a single type of attribute. For example, we can use PCA to extract principal components that represent the overall variation in the dataset. These extracted features can then be treated as a single type of attribute.
4. **Domain-specific conversion:** Depending on the domain or the specific task, you may have domain-specific knowledge or rules that allow you to convert the attributes into a single type. For example, if you are working with textual data, you can convert all attributes to text and apply natural language processing techniques. For example, if we know that certain favorite subjects are related to specific grades, we can create a new attribute called "Subject-Grade" that combines the information from both attributes.

It is important to note that the choice of conversion method should be guided by the nature of the data, the specific analysis or modeling task, and the insights you want to derive from the data. Consider the trade-offs between the loss of information and the simplification gained by converting to a single type, and choose the most appropriate approach for your particular situation.

Combining Individual Distances

Combining individual distances refers to the process of aggregating or combining multiple distances or dissimilarities between pairs of objects into a single measure that represents the overall similarity or dissimilarity between the objects. This is commonly done in clustering and classification tasks, where the goal is to group similar objects together or make decisions based on their similarity.

There are several methods for combining individual distances, and the choice of method depends on the specific problem and the nature of the distances being considered. Here are a few common approaches:

1. **Average:** In this method, the individual distances are averaged or summed up to obtain an average distance. This approach assumes that all distances contribute equally to the overall similarity or dissimilarity.

2. **Weighted average:** Similar to the average method, but with different weights assigned to each individual distance. The weights reflect the relative importance or relevance of each distance measure.
3. **Maximum or minimum:** The maximum or minimum distance among the individual distances is taken as the overall distance. This approach considers the most extreme dissimilarity between the objects.
4. **Mahalanobis distance:** This distance measure takes into account the correlation structure of the variables. It calculates the distance by considering the covariance matrix of the variables.
5. **Similarity-based measures:** Instead of combining distances, similarity-based measures can be used to quantify the similarity between objects. Common methods include cosine similarity, Jaccard similarity, and Pearson correlation coefficient.

It's important to note that the choice of combining method should align with the problem at hand and the characteristics of the data. Some methods may be more suitable for certain types of data or specific analysis goals. Experimentation and evaluation of different methods are often necessary to determine the most effective approach for a particular task.

How to Choose a Clustering Algorithm

Choosing a clustering algorithm depends on various factors such as the nature of the data, the goal of the clustering task, and the specific requirements of the problem at hand. Here are some considerations to keep in mind when selecting a clustering algorithm. Let's consider an example scenario where we want to cluster a dataset of customer demographics for market segmentation. We have information about customers' age, income, and purchase history. Here's how the considerations mentioned earlier can guide our choice of a clustering algorithm:

1. **Data characteristics:** Consider the type of data you are working with. Some clustering algorithms work well with numerical data, while others are suitable for categorical or text data. Additionally, consider the dimensionality of the data and whether the algorithm can handle high-dimensional data effectively. he data consists of numerical attributes (age, income) and possibly categorical attributes (purchase history). We need an algorithm that can handle numerical data and potentially categorical data as well.
2. **Algorithm scalability:** Consider the scalability of the algorithm, especially if you are working with large datasets. Some algorithms are computationally expensive and may not be suitable for big data scenarios. Ensure that the chosen algorithm can handle the size of your dataset within acceptable time and resource constraints. The dataset contains thousands of customers. We need an algorithm that can handle large datasets efficiently.
3. **Cluster shape and density:** Different clustering algorithms make different assumptions about the shape and density of clusters. Some algorithms, like k-means, assume spherical or convex clusters, while others, like DBSCAN, can handle clusters of arbitrary shape and density. Assess the shape and density characteristics of your data and choose an algorithm that aligns with those characteristics. We don't have any specific assumptions about the shape or density of the clusters. We want an algorithm that can identify clusters of varying shapes and densities.
4. **Interpretability:** Depending on your goal, you may need clusters that are easily interpretable and meaningful. Some algorithms, such as hierarchical clustering, provide hierarchical structures that can be easily visualized and understood. Other algorithms, like Gaussian Mixture Models,

provide probabilistic cluster assignments that can capture uncertainty. We want clusters that are easily interpretable and provide meaningful insights for market segmentation.

5. **Scalability of interpretability:** If interpretability is important to you, consider the scalability of the interpretability of the clustering algorithm. Some algorithms, like k-means, provide straightforward interpretations of clusters, while others, like agglomerative hierarchical clustering, become less interpretable as the number of data points increases. As the number of customers increases, we want the interpretability of the clusters to remain manageable.
6. **Robustness to noise and outliers:** Consider the presence of noise or outliers in your data. Some algorithms, like DBSCAN, can handle noisy data and automatically identify outliers as noise points. Others, like k-means, are sensitive to outliers and may assign them to clusters. There might be noisy data points or outliers in the dataset. We want an algorithm that can handle such cases effectively.
7. **Prior knowledge:** If you have prior knowledge or assumptions about the underlying structure of the data, consider whether the algorithm can incorporate that knowledge. For example, if you have domain-specific knowledge that certain attributes should be more important than others, you may want to choose an algorithm that allows for custom weightings or constraints. We don't have any prior knowledge or assumptions about the data. We are open to exploring the inherent patterns in the dataset.
8. **Evaluation metrics:** Determine the evaluation metrics that are appropriate for your clustering task. Different algorithms may optimize different objective functions, and it's important to select an algorithm that aligns with your evaluation criteria. Common evaluation metrics include silhouette coefficient, cohesion, separation, and internal validity indices. We will evaluate the quality of the clusters using metrics like silhouette coefficient, cohesion, separation, and possibly external validity indices if we have ground truth labels.
9. **Implementation and availability:** Consider the availability and ease of implementation of the algorithm. Many clustering algorithms are readily available in popular libraries and software packages, making them easier to use. Consider the programming language you are comfortable with and the availability of suitable implementations. We prefer using a widely available implementation in a popular library, such as scikit-learn in Python.

It's often a good idea to experiment with multiple clustering algorithms and compare their results to choose the one that best meets your requirements and produces meaningful and interpretable clusters for your specific problem.

Based on these considerations, a suitable clustering algorithm for this example could be DBSCAN (Density-Based Spatial Clustering of Applications with Noise). DBSCAN can handle numerical data, is scalable, can discover clusters of arbitrary shapes and densities, and is robust to noise and outliers. It also provides meaningful interpretations of clusters based on density and can handle large datasets efficiently. Additionally, it is readily available in the scikit-learn library.

However, it's important to note that the choice of clustering algorithm ultimately depends on the specific requirements and characteristics of your dataset and problem domain. It's always recommended to experiment with multiple algorithms and evaluate their results based on your specific evaluation criteria before finalizing the choice of clustering algorithm.

Cluster Evaluation

Cluster evaluation is the process of assessing the quality and effectiveness of clustering algorithms in identifying meaningful and useful clusters in a dataset. Evaluating clusters is important to determine the reliability of the clustering results and to gain insights into the structure and patterns present in the data.

After clustering, a confusion matrix is constructed to evaluate the performance of the clustering algorithm. While confusion matrices are commonly used in supervised learning for classification tasks, they can also be adapted for cluster evaluation by comparing the clustering results with known ground truth or external criteria.

The confusion matrix is a square matrix that shows the counts of data points that are assigned to each cluster by the clustering algorithm. The rows represent the true labels or ground truth, while the columns represent the assigned clusters. Each cell in the matrix represents the count of data points that belong to a specific combination of true label and assigned cluster.

From the confusion matrix, several measurements can be computed to assess the quality of the clustering results:

Entropy: Entropy measures the uncertainty or disorder in the clustering results. It is calculated based on the distribution of data points across different clusters. Lower entropy indicates a more homogeneous and well-separated clustering.

Entropy: For each cluster, we can measure its entropy as follows:

$$\text{entropy}(D_i) = -\sum_{j=1}^{k} \Pr_i(c_j)\log_2 \Pr_i(c_j) \quad \text{...(1)}$$

where $\Pr_i(c_j)$ is the proportion of class c_j data points in cluster i or D_i. The total entropy of the whole clustering (which considers all clusters) is

$$\text{entropy}_{total}(D) = \sum_{i=1}^{k} \frac{|D_i|}{|D|} \times \text{entropy}(D_i) \quad \text{...(2)}$$

Suppose we have a clustering result with 100 data points and 3 clusters. The distribution of data points across clusters is as follows:

- **Cluster 1:** 40 data points
- **Cluster 2:** 30 data points
- **Cluster 3:** 30 data points

To calculate entropy, we first compute the probability of each cluster by dividing the count of data points in each cluster by the total number of data points:

- Cluster 1 probability = 40/100 = 0.4
- Cluster 2 probability = 30/100 = 0.3
- Cluster 3 probability = 30/100 = 0.3

Next, we calculate the entropy using the formula:

$$\text{Entropy} = -(p1 * \log2(p1) + p2 * \log2(p2) + p3 * \log2(p3))$$

$$\text{Entropy} = -(0.4 * \log2(0.4) + 0.3 * \log2(0.3) + 0.3 * \log2(0.3))$$

Purity: Purity measures the degree of cluster purity, i.e., how well the clusters correspond to the true labels or ground truth. It is calculated based on the majority class within each cluster. Higher purity indicates a higher correspondence between clusters and true labels.

Purity: This again measures the extent that a cluster contains only one class of data. The purity of each cluster is computed with

$$\text{purity}(D_i) = \max_j (\Pr_i(c_j)) \quad \text{...(3)}$$

The total purity of the whole clustering (considering all clusters) is

$$\text{purity}_{total}(D) = \sum_{i=1}^{k} \frac{|D_i|}{|D|} \times \text{purity}(D_i) \quad \text{...(4)}$$

Consider the same clustering result as above. Additionally, we have the ground truth labels for each data point. Let's assume there are 5 different true labels in the dataset.

To calculate purity, we evaluate each cluster and find the majority class within that cluster. Suppose the majority classes in each cluster are as follows:

- **Cluster 1 majority class:** True Label A
- **Cluster 2 majority class:** True Label B
- **Cluster 3 majority class:** True Label C

Purity is calculated by summing up the counts of the majority classes in each cluster and dividing it by the total number of data points:

Purity = (count of majority class in Cluster 1 + count of majority class in Cluster 2 + count of majority class in Cluster 3) / 100

Precision: Precision measures the proportion of data points correctly assigned to a cluster out of all the data points assigned to that cluster. It focuses on the correctness of cluster assignments and is computed for each individual cluster.

Let's consider a binary clustering problem with two clusters: Cluster A and Cluster B. We have a set of true positives (TP), false positives (FP), true negatives (TN), and false negatives (FN) based on the ground truth.

Precision for Cluster A is calculated as TP_A / (TP_A + FP_A), where TP_A is the count of true positives in Cluster A and FP_A is the count of false positives in Cluster A.

Recall: Recall measures the proportion of data points correctly assigned to a cluster out of all the data points that belong to the true label. It focuses on the completeness of cluster assignments and is computed for each individual true label.

Similarly, recall for Cluster A is calculated as TP_A/(TP_A + FN_A), where TP_A is the count of true positives in Cluster A and FN_A is the count of false negatives in Cluster A.

F-score: The F-score combines precision and recall into a single measure that balances both precision and recall. It is the harmonic mean of precision and recall and provides a single metric to evaluate the overall performance of the clustering algorithm.

The F-score combines precision and recall into a single measure. It is calculated as the harmonic mean of precision and recall:

F-score = 2 * (Precision * Recall)/(Precision + Recall)

These measurements provide insights into the accuracy, completeness, and quality of the clustering results. They can help in comparing different clustering algorithms or parameter settings and in understanding the strengths and weaknesses of the clustering approach.

It's important to note that these measurements are based on the availability of ground truth or external criteria. In unsupervised clustering, where ground truth labels are not available, alternative evaluation metrics such as silhouette coefficient or clustering indices may be used.

There are various evaluation metrics and techniques that can be used to assess the quality of clusters. Here are some commonly used approaches for cluster evaluation:

Internal evaluation: Internal evaluation metrics assess the quality of clusters based on the data and the clustering algorithm itself, without using any external information. Some popular internal evaluation metrics include:

- **Silhouette coefficient:** Measures the cohesion and separation of clusters. The silhouette coefficient measures the cohesion and separation of clusters. It calculates the average silhouette coefficient for all data points, where a higher value indicates better clustering. For example, if we have three clusters and their silhouette coefficients are 0.7, 0.6, and 0.8, it indicates that the third cluster has the highest cohesion and separation, making it the most well-defined cluster.

  Silhouette Coefficient (s) = (b – a)/max(a, b)

  Where:

  a: Average distance between a sample and all other points in the same cluster.

  b: Average distance between a sample and all other points in the nearest neighboring cluster.

  Higher values of the silhouette coefficient indicate better clustering quality, with a range of [–1, 1]. Values close to 1 indicate well-separated clusters, values close to 0 indicate overlapping clusters, and negative values suggest that samples may be assigned to the wrong cluster.
- **Davies-Bouldin index:** Evaluates the compactness and separation of clusters. The Davies-Bouldin index evaluates the compactness and separation of clusters. A lower index value indicates better clustering. For instance, if we have two clusters and their Davies-Bouldin index values are 0.5 and 0.3, the second cluster is more compact and well-separated, indicating better clustering quality.

  Davies-Bouldin Index = (1/n) * Σ (max(R(i) + R(j))/d(c(i), c(j)))

  Where:

  n: Number of clusters.

  R(i): Average distance between points within cluster i.

  d(c(i), c(j)): Distance between cluster centroids i and j.

  Lower values of the Davies-Bouldin index indicate better clustering quality, with values closer to 0 indicating well-separated clusters.
- **Dunn index:** Quantifies the compactness and separation of clusters. The Dunn index quantifies the compactness and separation of clusters. It measures the minimum distance between clusters and the maximum diameter of clusters. A higher Dunn index indicates better clustering. For example, if we have three clusters and their Dunn index values are 0.9, 1.2, and 1.1, the second cluster has the highest compactness and separation, indicating better clustering quality.

  Dunn Index = min_inter-cluster_distance/max_intra-cluster_distance

  Where:

  min_inter-cluster_distance: The minimum distance between any two clusters.

  max_intra-cluster_distance: The maximum diameter of any cluster.

  A higher Dunn index indicates better clustering quality, with larger values indicating better separation and compactness of clusters.

- **Calinski-Harabasz index:** Measures the ratio of between-cluster and within-cluster dispersion. he Calinski-Harabasz index measures the ratio of between-cluster and within-cluster dispersion. A higher index value indicates better clustering. For instance, if we have four clusters and their Calinski-Harabasz index values are 150, 200, 180, and 160, the second cluster has the highest between-cluster dispersion relative to within-cluster dispersion, indicating better clustering quality.

  Calinski-Harabasz Index = (BSS/WSS) * (n – k)/(k – 1)

  Where:

  BSS: Between-cluster sum of squares.

  WSS: Within-cluster sum of squares.

  n: Total number of data points.

  k: Number of clusters.

  Higher values of the Calinski-Harabasz index indicate better clustering quality, with larger values indicating better separation and compactness of clusters.

  External evaluation: External evaluation metrics assess the quality of clusters by comparing them to a known ground truth or external criteria. This is applicable when there are pre-defined class labels or expert knowledge available for comparison. Some commonly used external evaluation metrics include:

- **Rand index:** Measures the similarity between two data partitions. The Rand index measures the similarity between two data partitions, such as the clustering result and the ground truth. It compares the pairs of data points and calculates the number of agreements and disagreements. A higher Rand index indicates better clustering agreement with the ground truth.

  The Rand Index measures the similarity between two data partitions, taking into account both the true positive (TP) and true negative (TN) pairs.

  RI = (TP + TN)/(TP + TN + FP + FN)

  Where:

  TP: Number of true positive pairs (pairs of data points that belong to the same cluster in both the predicted and ground truth partitions).

  TN: Number of true negative pairs (pairs of data points that belong to different clusters in both the predicted and ground truth partitions).

  FP: Number of false positive pairs (pairs of data points that belong to the same cluster in the predicted partition but different clusters in the ground truth partition).

  FN: Number of false negative pairs (pairs of data points that belong to different clusters in the predicted partition but the same cluster in the ground truth partition).

  The Rand Index yields a value between 0 and 1, where a higher value indicates better agreement between the predicted and ground truth partitions.

- **Adjusted Rand index:** Adjusts the Rand index for chance agreement. The Adjusted Rand index adjusts the Rand index for chance agreement. It takes into account the expected random agreement between partitions. Similar to the Rand index, a higher Adjusted Rand index indicates better clustering agreement with the ground truth.

  The Adjusted Rand Index adjusts the Rand Index for chance agreement, providing a measure of the similarity between two partitions that accounts for random clustering.

  ARI = (RI – Expected_RI)/(max(RI) – Expected_RI)

Where:

Expected_RI: The expected Rand Index for random clustering.

The Adjusted Rand Index ranges from –1 to 1, where 1 indicates perfect agreement, 0 indicates random clustering, and negative values indicate disagreement.

- **Fowlkes-Mallows index:** Evaluates the similarity between two clusterings. The Fowlkes-Mallows index evaluates the similarity between two clusterings. It calculates the geometric mean of the pairwise precision and recall of the clusters. A higher Fowlkes-Mallows index indicates better similarity between the two clusterings.

  The Fowlkes-Mallows Index computes the geometric mean of the pairwise precision and recall between the predicted and ground truth clusters.

  FMI = sqrt(Precision * Recall)

  Where:

  Precision: Ratio of true positive pairs to the sum of true positive and false positive pairs.

  Recall: Ratio of true positive pairs to the sum of true positive and false negative pairs.

  The Fowlkes-Mallows Index ranges from 0 to 1, with 1 indicating perfect agreement between the predicted and ground truth clusters.

- **Jaccard index:** Measures the similarity of two sets. The Jaccard index measures the similarity of two sets. In the context of cluster evaluation, it compares the pairs of data points and calculates the number of pairs that are in the same cluster in both clusterings. A higher Jaccard index indicates better similarity between the two clusterings.

  The Jaccard Index is a similarity coefficient that measures the similarity between two sets by calculating the ratio of the intersection of the sets to the union of the sets. In the context of clustering evaluation, it is often used to assess the similarity between the predicted clusters and the ground truth clusters.

  The formula for the Jaccard Index is as follows:

  Jaccard Index = (Number of common elements)/(Number of total unique elements)

  Let's consider an example to illustrate the calculation of the Jaccard Index. Suppose we have the following clustering results and ground truth labels:

  Predicted Clusters:

  Cluster 1: {A, B, C}

  Cluster 2: {D, E, F}

  Cluster 3: {G, H}

  Ground Truth Clusters:

  Cluster 1: {A, C, D}

  Cluster 2: {B, E, F, G}

  Cluster 3: {H}

  To calculate the Jaccard Index for each cluster, we compare the intersection and union of the predicted and ground truth clusters:

  Jaccard Index for Cluster 1 = $|\{A, C\} \cap \{A, C, D\}|/|\{A, B, C\} \cup \{A, C, D\}|$ = 2/4 = 0.5

  Jaccard Index for Cluster 2 = $|\{B, E, F\} \cap \{B, E, F, G\}|/|\{B, E, F\} \cup \{B, E, F, G\}|$ = 3/4 = 0.75

  Jaccard Index for Cluster 3 = $|\{H\} \cap \{H\}|/|\{G, H\} \cup \{H\}|$ = 1/2 = 0.5

To obtain an overall evaluation, you can calculate the average Jaccard Index across all clusters.

Overall Jaccard Index = (Jaccard Index Cluster 1 + Jaccard Index Cluster 2 + Jaccard Index Cluster 3)/Number of Clusters

= (0.5 + 0.75 + 0.5)/3 = 0.5833

The Jaccard Index ranges from 0 to 1, with 1 indicating perfect agreement between the predicted and ground truth clusters. A higher Jaccard Index value indicates a higher degree of similarity between the clusters.

Visual evaluation: Visual inspection of the clustering results can also provide valuable insights into the quality and meaningfulness of the clusters. Visual evaluation involves plotting the data and the clusters in a low-dimensional space to visually assess the separation and cohesion of the clusters.

Domain-specific evaluation: In some cases, domain-specific evaluation measures may be used to assess the usefulness of the clusters in a specific application or domain. These measures are tailored to the specific requirements and objectives of the problem at hand.

It's important to note that no single evaluation metric can provide a definitive measure of cluster quality. Different metrics have different strengths and limitations, and the choice of metric depends on the specific goals, characteristics of the data, and domain knowledge.

In practice, it is often recommended to use a combination of evaluation metrics and techniques to gain a comprehensive understanding of the clustering results and make informed decisions. Additionally, comparing the results of different clustering algorithms and parameter settings can provide further insights into the effectiveness of the clustering process.

An example

Assume we have a text collection D of 900 documents from three topics (or three classes), Science, Sports, and Politics. Each class has 300 documents. Each document in D is labeled with one of the topics (classes). We use this collection to perform clustering to find three clusters. Note that class/topic labels are not used in clustering. After clustering, we want to measure the effectiveness of the clustering algorithm.

Cluster	Science	Sports	Politics	Entropy	Purity
1	250	20	10	0.589	0.893
2	20	180	80	1.198	0.643
3	30	100	210	1.257	0.617
Total	300	300	300	1.031	0.711

A Remark about Ground Truth Evaluation

In clustering evaluation, external evaluation methods are commonly used to compare different clustering algorithms. These methods rely on the availability of external information, such as class labels or ground truth, to assess the quality of the clustering results.

The rationale behind external evaluation is that even though a clustering algorithm may perform well on labeled data sets (where the ground truth is known), there is no guarantee that it will perform equally well on real-life data sets where class labels are not available. However, if an algorithm consistently performs well on labeled data sets, it can provide some confidence in the algorithm's quality and effectiveness.

External evaluation methods are considered to be based on external data or information because they rely on external criteria, such as class labels, to evaluate the clustering results. These methods typically involve comparing the clusters produced by the algorithm with the known ground truth or class labels. Common external evaluation measures include the Jaccard Index, Rand Index, Fowlkes-Mallows Index, and Adjusted Rand Index.

By using external evaluation methods, researchers and practitioners can assess and compare the performance of different clustering algorithms, understand their strengths and weaknesses, and make informed decisions about which algorithm may be suitable for a particular application or data set.

Evaluation Based on Internal Information

Intra-cluster cohesion (compactness) and inter-cluster separation (isolation) are two important aspects of evaluating the quality of clustering results.

Intra-cluster cohesion measures how close the data points within a cluster are to the cluster centroid. It is a measure of how compact and tightly packed the cluster is. A commonly used measure of intra-cluster cohesion is the Sum of Squared Error (SSE). SSE calculates the sum of the squared distances between each data point in the cluster and the centroid of that cluster. Lower SSE values indicate that the data points are closer to the centroid, suggesting a more compact and cohesive cluster.

Inter-cluster separation measures the distance between different cluster centroids. It is a measure of how well-separated the clusters are from each other. The goal is to have distinct clusters with centroids that are far away from each other. This indicates that the clusters are well-isolated and distinct. Measures like the distance between cluster centroids or the variance between clusters are commonly used to assess inter-cluster separation.

In summary, a good clustering algorithm should produce clusters with high intra-cluster cohesion, meaning that the data points within a cluster are close to each other, and high inter-cluster separation, indicating that the clusters are well-separated and distinct from each other. By considering both intra-cluster cohesion and inter-cluster separation, clustering algorithms can be evaluated in terms of their ability to produce compact and well-separated clusters.

Indirect Evaluation

Indirect evaluation is a method of evaluating clustering results that involves using some external information or ground truth to assess the quality of the clustering. In this approach, the clustering results are compared to a known reference or benchmark, such as true class labels or expert-defined clusters, to evaluate the clustering performance.

There are several indirect evaluation measures that can be used:

1. **Adjusted Rand Index (ARI):** ARI is a measure of the similarity between the clustering results and the ground truth, taking into account all pairs of data points and their cluster assignments. It ranges from -1 to 1, where a higher value indicates better agreement between the clustering and the ground truth.
2. **Normalized Mutual Information (NMI):** NMI is a measure of the mutual information between the clustering and the ground truth, normalized by the entropy of the clustering and the ground truth. It ranges from 0 to 1, with higher values indicating better clustering performance.

3. **Fowlkes-Mallows Index (FMI):** FMI measures the geometric mean of precision and recall of the clustering results compared to the ground truth. It ranges from 0 to 1, where 1 indicates perfect clustering.
4. **Homogeneity, Completeness, and V-measure:** These are measures that evaluate different aspects of the clustering performance, including the purity of each cluster (homogeneity), the extent to which each true class is assigned to the same cluster (completeness), and the harmonic mean of homogeneity and completeness (V-measure).

Indirect evaluation is useful when the ground truth or external information is available, such as in cases where data points are labeled or clustered by experts. It provides a quantitative assessment of the clustering quality by comparing it to a known reference, making it a valuable method for assessing the performance of clustering algorithms. However, it is important to note that the quality of the evaluation heavily depends on the quality and appropriateness of the ground truth or external information used.

Holes in Data Space

Holes in data space refer to regions in the data distribution where there is little or no data available. These regions may have sparse or missing data points, making them "holes" in the overall data representation. Holes in data space, also known as sparse regions or missing data, can significantly impact the performance and accuracy of clustering algorithms. Addressing this issue requires a thoughtful and comprehensive approach to ensure that the clustering results are meaningful and representative of the underlying data distribution. The presence of holes in data space can have significant implications for data analysis and machine learning tasks, including clustering.

The existence of holes in data space can lead to several challenges:

1. **Bias in clustering:** Holes in data space can introduce bias in clustering results. If a clustering algorithm encounters regions with sparse data points, it may not be able to identify meaningful clusters in those areas. This can lead to skewed clustering results and affect the overall accuracy of the clustering solution.
2. **Overfitting:** In the presence of holes, clustering algorithms may overfit the data and create clusters that do not accurately represent the underlying data distribution. This can result in clusters that are sensitive to noise and outliers, reducing the generalization capability of the clustering model.
3. **Inaccurate cluster boundaries:** Holes in data space can lead to poorly defined cluster boundaries. Clustering algorithms may struggle to differentiate between different clusters in regions with sparse data, leading to inaccurately identified cluster boundaries.
4. **Data bias:** The presence of holes in data space can be an indication of data bias. If certain regions of the data space have less representation, it may indicate an uneven distribution of data, which can bias the clustering results towards more densely populated regions.

To address the issue of holes in data space during clustering, several strategies can be employed:

1. **Data imputation:** Missing data points in regions with holes can be imputed using various imputation techniques. This can help fill the gaps in the data distribution and make the clustering process more robust. Data imputation involves filling in the missing values in sparse regions with estimated or imputed values. There are various imputation techniques, such as mean imputation, median imputation, k-nearest neighbor imputation, and regression-based imputation. By imputing missing data, the clustering algorithm can better understand the structure of the data and identify meaningful clusters.

2. **Density-based clustering:** Density-based clustering algorithms, such as DBSCAN, are more resilient to holes in data space. They can identify clusters based on local density rather than relying on distance-based measures, making them suitable for handling sparse regions. Density-based clustering algorithms, like Density-Based Spatial Clustering of Applications with Noise (DBSCAN), are well-suited to handle sparse regions. These algorithms rely on the density of data points rather than distance measures to form clusters. They can detect dense regions as clusters and leave sparse regions as outliers or noise, thus avoiding the creation of spurious clusters in data holes.
3. **Feature engineering:** By carefully selecting or engineering relevant features, it may be possible to mitigate the impact of holes in data space and improve the clustering performance. Feature engineering plays a crucial role in mitigating the impact of data holes. By carefully selecting or engineering relevant features, one can highlight patterns and information that might otherwise be obscured by sparse regions. Domain knowledge and data analysis can help identify meaningful features that provide better insights into the data distribution.
4. **Ensemble clustering:** Combining multiple clustering algorithms or running the same algorithm with different parameters can help reduce the impact of holes and provide more reliable clustering results. Ensemble clustering involves combining the results of multiple clustering algorithms to achieve more robust and stable cluster assignments. Ensemble techniques can help overcome the variability introduced by sparse regions and improve the overall clustering performance.

Handling holes in data space is a crucial aspect of clustering and requires careful consideration to ensure accurate and meaningful results.

Data Regions and Empty Regions

Data regions and empty regions refer to different areas in the data space when performing clustering. Let's define each of these regions:

1. **Data Regions:** Data regions are areas in the data space that contain a significant concentration of data points. These regions represent clusters where data points are close to each other, indicating similar characteristics or patterns. In data regions, the density of data points is high, and they are usually well-defined and easily distinguishable from other regions.
2. **Empty Regions (Sparse Regions):** Empty regions, also known as sparse regions or holes in data space, are areas that have a low concentration or even no data points. These regions indicate data points' absence, which may be due to missing data or data points that do not belong to any existing clusters. Empty regions pose a challenge in clustering because they might create artificial clusters or affect the clustering algorithm's performance.

Handling empty regions is crucial in clustering tasks to ensure that the algorithm does not produce spurious clusters or overlook important patterns. Various techniques, as discussed in the previous response, can be used to address empty regions, such as data imputation, density-based clustering, feature selection, ensemble clustering, and incorporating domain knowledge.

In summary, data regions represent well-defined clusters in the data space with a high density of data points, while empty regions or sparse regions indicate areas with a low or no concentration of data points, requiring careful handling during clustering to obtain meaningful and accurate results.

Review Questions

Multiple Choice Questions

Q.1. Which of the following is a goal of clustering analysis?

(*a*) Classification (*b*) Prediction (*c*) Summarization (*d*) All of the above

Q.2. Which clustering algorithm is sensitive to the order of data points and initialization?

(*a*) K-means (*b*) Hierarchical clustering
(*c*) DBSCAN (*d*) Mean Shift

Q.3. Which of the following distance metrics is commonly used in clustering?

(*a*) Manhattan distance (*b*) Euclidean distance
(*c*) Cosine similarity (*d*) All of the above

Q.4. What is the main drawback of the K-means clustering algorithm?

(*a*) Sensitivity to outliers (*b*) Computationally expensive
(*c*) Requires predefined number of clusters (*d*) Not suitable for high-dimensional data

Q.5. Which clustering algorithm is capable of identifying clusters of arbitrary shapes?

(*a*) K-means (*b*) Agglomerative clustering
(*c*) DBSCAN (*d*) Gaussian Mixture Model (GMM)

Q.6. What is the purpose of the elbow method in K-means clustering?

(*a*) To find the optimal number of clusters (*b*) To initialize centroids
(*c*) To compute cluster distances (*d*) To determine cluster membership

Q.7. In hierarchical clustering, which linkage criterion measures the distance between the closest points in two clusters?

(*a*) Single linkage (*b*) Complete linkage (*c*) Average linkage (*d*) Ward linkage

Q.8. Which clustering algorithm does not require the number of clusters to be specified beforehand?

(*a*) K-means (*b*) Hierarchical clustering
(*c*) DBSCAN (*d*) Gaussian Mixture Model (GMM)

Q.9. Which clustering algorithm is based on density connectivity?

(*a*) K-means (*b*) Hierarchical clustering
(*c*) DBSCAN (*d*) Mean Shift

Q.10. Which clustering algorithm assigns each data point to the cluster whose mean is closest?

(*a*) K-means (*b*) Agglomerative clustering
(*c*) DBSCAN (*d*) Mean Shift

Q.11. Which distance metric is commonly used to measure the similarity between two vectors in Euclidean space?

(*a*) Euclidean distance
(*b*) Manhattan distance
(*c*) Cosine similarity
(*d*) Mahalanobis distance

Q.12. Which distance metric is also known as the "city block" or "taxicab" distance?

(*a*) Euclidean distance
(*b*) Manhattan distance
(*c*) Chebyshev distance
(*d*) Minkowski distance

Q.13. In which scenario is the cosine similarity most appropriate?

(*a*) When the magnitude of the vectors is significant
(*b*) When the direction of the vectors is significant
(*c*) When both magnitude and direction of the vectors are significant
(*d*) When the vectors have high dimensionality

Q.14. Which distance metric is more sensitive to outliers?

(*a*) Euclidean distance
(*b*) Manhattan distance
(*c*) Chebyshev distance
(*d*) Mahalanobis distance

Q.15. Which distance metric is used to measure the dissimilarity between two probability distributions?

(*a*) Euclidean distance
(*b*) Manhattan distance
(*c*) Mahalanobis distance
(*d*) Kullback-Leibler divergence

Answers

1. (*d*)	2. (*a*)	3. (*d*)	4. (*c*)	5. (*c*)	6. (*a*)	7. (*a*)	8. (*c*)	9. (*c*)
10. (*a*)	11. (*a*)	12. (*b*)	13. (*b*)	14. (*b*)	15. (*d*)			

Fill in the Blanks

1. __________ is a technique in unsupervised learning that involves grouping similar data points together based on certain criteria.
2. A __________ is a specific method or approach used to group data points into clusters based on their similarities.
3. A __________ measures the dissimilarity or similarity between two data points in a feature space.
4. When choosing a clustering algorithm, it's important to consider factors such as the algorithm's __________, scalability, and suitability for the specific dataset.
5. __________ is a process that involves assessing the quality and effectiveness of the clusters produced by a clustering algorithm.
6. Holes in data space, where certain regions lack data points, can pose challenges for __________ algorithms.
7. The __________ algorithm is a popular hierarchical clustering method that forms clusters by iteratively merging or splitting them based on proximity.
8. In __________ clustering, the number of clusters needs to be specified beforehand, while in __________ clustering, the algorithm determines the optimal number of clusters.

9. A __________ is a visual representation that illustrates the relationships and distances between data points in a multidimensional space.
10. Density-based clustering algorithms, such as DBSCAN, can identify clusters as regions of __________ data points separated by areas of lower density.

Unsolved Questions

1. Discuss common metrics used for evaluating the quality of clusters in clustering algorithms.
2. How does the choice of evaluation metric depend on the nature of the data and the clustering task?
3. Describe the concept of centroid-based clustering and provide an example of a centroid-based clustering algorithm.
4. How does the choice of distance metric impact the results of a clustering algorithm?
5. Discuss scenarios where external validation metrics, such as Adjusted Rand Index, are more suitable for cluster evaluation.
6. What are the limitations of using internal validation metrics like the Davies-Bouldin Index?
7. Explain the role of a distance function in clustering algorithms.
8. Compare and contrast different distance functions commonly used in clustering.
9. What factors should be considered when deciding which clustering algorithm to use for a particular dataset?
10. Provide examples of scenarios where hierarchical clustering might be more suitable than k-means clustering.
11. Explore the concept of "holes" in data space and discuss strategies for addressing this challenge in clustering.
12. How do outliers impact the performance of clustering algorithms, and what techniques can be used to handle outliers?

❑❑❑

Question Bank

CHAPTER 1

1. Who is considered the "father of Artificial Intelligence"?

(*a*) Alan Turing (*b*) John McCarthy (*c*) Herbert Simon (*d*) Marvin Minsky

2. Which year saw the coining of the term "Artificial Intelligence"?

(*a*) 1943 (*b*) 1956 (*c*) 1965 (*d*) 1972

3. What landmark event is associated with the "AI Winter"?

(*a*) The development of expert systems

(*b*) The victory of IBM's Deep Blue over Garry Kasparov

(*c*) The failure to deliver on early promises of AI, leading to reduced funding and interest

(*d*) The emergence of neural networks

4. What significant milestone marked the beginning of modern AI research?

(*a*) IBM's Watson winning Jeopardy!

(*b*) The development of the first chess-playing computer

(*c*) The publication of the Dartmouth Conference proposal in 1956

(*d*) The creation of the first artificial neural network

5. Which type of AI aims to simulate human cognitive abilities and understanding?

(*a*) Weak AI (*b*) Narrow AI (*c*) Strong AI (*d*) Superintelligent AI

6. What distinguishes Weak AI from Strong AI?

(*a*) Weak AI can perform tasks within a limited domain, while Strong AI aims to replicate human-like intelligence across a wide range of tasks.

(*b*) Weak AI is programmed to follow specific instructions, while Strong AI can learn and adapt independently.

(*c*) Weak AI has limited computational power compared to Strong AI.

(*d*) Weak AI is only capable of mimicking human behavior superficially, while Strong AI can achieve genuine understanding and consciousness.

7. In the context of problem-solving, what does a "problem space" refer to?

(*a*) The physical environment in which a problem occurs

(*b*) The set of all possible solutions to a problem

(*c*) The representation of a problem and all possible states and actions to solve it

(*d*) The time it takes to solve a problem

8. Which algorithm guarantees finding the optimal solution to a problem, provided enough time and memory?

(*a*) Depth-First Search (DFS) (*b*) Breadth-First Search (BFS)

(*c*) A* search algorithm (*d*) Hill Climbing

9. **Which search algorithm is more likely to find a solution quickly but may not necessarily find the optimal solution?**
   (*a*) Depth-First Search (DFS)
   (*b*) Uniform Cost Search (UCS)
   (*c*) A* search algorithm
   (*d*) Best-First Search

10. **Which heuristic function is used in the A* search algorithm?**
   (*a*) f(n) = g(n) + h(n)
   (*b*) f(n) = g(n) - h(n)
   (*c*) f(n) = g(n) * h(n)
   (*d*) f(n) = g(n) / h(n)

11. **Which search algorithm is likely to be more efficient when memory usage is a concern?**
   (*a*) Depth-First Search (DFS)
   (*b*) Breadth-First Search (BFS)
   (*c*) Iterative Deepening Depth-First Search (IDDFS)
   (*d*) A* search algorithm

12. **What is the primary function of a knowledge-based system?**
   (*a*) Storing and retrieving data
   (*b*) Performing calculations and numerical analysis
   (*c*) Mimicking human reasoning and decision-making processes using stored knowledge
   (*d*) Controlling hardware components in a computer system

13. **Which component of a knowledge-based system is responsible for storing and organizing domain-specific knowledge?**
   (*a*) Inference engine
   (*b*) User interface
   (*c*) Knowledge base
   (*d*) Database management system

14. **In a rule-based expert system, what are rules composed of?**
   (*a*) Data structures
   (*b*) Procedural code
   (*c*) Heuristic functions
   (*d*) Condition-action pairs

15. **What is the purpose of the inference engine in a knowledge-based system?**
   (*a*) To acquire knowledge from external sources
   (*b*) To represent knowledge using a formal language
   (*c*) To reason with the knowledge stored in the knowledge base to derive new information or make decisions
   (*d*) To present the system's findings to the user in a human-readable format

16. **Which type of knowledge representation is most suitable for expressing factual information and relationships between entities?**
   (*a*) Semantic networks
   (*b*) Frames
   (*c*) Production rules
   (*d*) Predicate logic

17. **Which of the following is a declarative knowledge representation language often used in artificial intelligence?**
   (*a*) Procedural language
   (*b*) Functional language
   (*c*) Predicate logic
   (*d*) Assembly language

18. **What is the primary advantage of using frames for knowledge representation?**
   (*a*) Frames are more efficient for storing large amounts of data.

(*b*) Frames allow for hierarchical organization of knowledge.
(*c*) Frames facilitate inference and reasoning.
(*d*) Frames are easier to implement compared to other representation methods.

19. Which knowledge representation technique uses nodes and arcs to represent concepts and their relationships?
(*a*) Semantic networks (*b*) Frames
(*c*) Production systems (*d*) Predicate logic

20. In which type of knowledge representation are facts and rules represented as conditional statements?
(*a*) Semantic networks (*b*) Frames
(*c*) Production systems (*d*) Predicate logic

21. Which of the following is a limitation of using propositional logic for knowledge representation?
(*a*) It cannot represent uncertainty or ambiguity.
(*b*) It is not suitable for representing rules or procedures.
(*c*) It is computationally expensive for large knowledge bases.
(*d*) It cannot represent relationships between entities.

22. What are conceptual graphs primarily used for in artificial intelligence?
(*a*) Representing knowledge using a formal graphical notation
(*b*) Processing natural language text (*c*) Performing numerical computations
(*d*) Simulating neural networks

23. Which of the following best describes the structure of a conceptual graph?
(*a*) A directed graph with nodes representing concepts and arcs representing relationships between them
(*b*) A tree-like structure with a root node and multiple branches
(*c*) A linear sequence of symbols representing logical statements
(*d*) A matrix representation of propositional logic formulas

24. In conceptual graphs, what do the labeled arcs between nodes represent?
(*a*) Logical operators connecting propositions
(*b*) Semantic relationships between concepts
(*c*) Numerical values associated with concepts
(*d*) Procedural instructions for performing computations

25. Which of the following is a benefit of using conceptual graphs for knowledge representation?
(*a*) They provide a standardized notation for representing knowledge across different domains.
(*b*) They are particularly efficient for representing numerical data.
(*c*) They can only represent simple, binary relationships between concepts.
(*d*) They require specialized hardware for efficient processing.

26. How are existential and universal quantifiers represented in conceptual graphs?
(*a*) By attaching special symbols to nodes and arcs

(*b*) By using different colors for nodes and arcs
(*c*) By including explicit labels indicating quantification
(*d*) By using specific shapes for nodes

27. In artificial intelligence, what is the role of quantifiers in knowledge representation?
(*a*) Quantifiers are used to define relationships between entities.
(*b*) Quantifiers determine the scope of variables in logical expressions.
(*c*) Quantifiers represent uncertainty in probabilistic reasoning.
(*d*) Quantifiers define the degree of membership in fuzzy logic systems.

28. Which of the following is an example of a universal quantifier in logical statements?
(*a*) There exists (∃) (*b*) For all (∀) (*c*) Not (~) (*d*) If-then (→)

29. What does the statement "∀x P(x)" mean in logical expressions?
(*a*) There exists an x such that P(x) is true. (*b*) For all x, P(x) is true.
(*c*) There exists an x such that P(x) is false. (*d*) Not all x satisfy P(x).

30. In predicate logic, how is existential quantification represented?
(*a*) ∀ (For all) (*b*) ∃ (There exists) (*c*) ~ (Not) (*d*) ↔ (If and only if)

31. Which of the following statements correctly represents the negation of "∀x P(x)"?
(*a*) ∀x ~P(x) (*b*) ∃x ~P(x) (*c*) ~∀x P(x) (*d*) ~∃x P(x)

32. In artificial intelligence, what does the concept of equality primarily refer to?
(*a*) Equivalence of logical statements (*b*) Similarity between objects or entities
(*c*) Identity of values or objects (*d*) Balance in decision-making processes

33. Which property of equality states that if two objects are equal, then they can be substituted for each other in any expression without changing the truth value?
(*a*) Reflexivity (*b*) Symmetry (*c*) Transitivity (*d*) Substitution

34. What is the formal notation used to represent equality between two objects or values in predicate logic?
(*a*) ≈ (*b*) ≡ (*c*) = (*d*) ==

35. Which property of equality states that if two objects are equal, then their properties or attributes are also equal?
(*a*) Reflexivity (*b*) Symmetry (*c*) Transitivity (*d*) Substitution

36. In AI systems, why is the property of transitivity important in reasoning?
(*a*) It ensures that two objects with equal properties are considered equivalent.
(*b*) It allows for the substitution of equal objects in logical expressions.
(*c*) It ensures that equal objects remain equal under any transformation.
(*d*) It establishes a symmetric relationship between equal objects.

37. In the Wumpus World environment, what is the primary objective of the agent?
(*a*) To collect treasures scattered throughout the world
(*b*) To avoid encountering the Wumpus monster

(*c*) To navigate to the exit of the cave
(*d*) To find and kill the Wumpus monster

38. What hazard exists in the Wumpus World besides the Wumpus monster?
(*a*) Bottomless pits (*b*) Giant spiders
(*c*) Poisonous gas clouds (*d*) Treacherous traps

39. Which percept indicates the presence of a breeze in an adjacent square in the Wumpus World?
(*a*) Stench (*b*) Glitter (*c*) Bump (*d*) None

40. What action does the agent take in the Wumpus World if it perceives a stench?
(*a*) Shoot an arrow (*b*) Move forward (*c*) Turn left (*d*) Turn right

41. How does the agent determine the location of the Wumpus monster in the Wumpus World?
(*a*) By following the direction of the breeze (*b*) By shooting arrows randomly
(*c*) By following the direction of the stench (*d*) By observing glitter in adjacent squares

42. What is variance?
(*a*) A measure of the spread of a dataset around its mean
(*b*) The average absolute deviation from the mean
(*c*) The square root of the sum of squared differences from the mean
(*d*) The difference between the largest and smallest values in a dataset

43. What does standard deviation measure?
(*a*) The absolute spread of a dataset (*b*) The average deviation from the mean
(*c*) The square root of variance
(*d*) The difference between the largest and smallest values in a dataset

44. Which of the following statements about standard deviation is true?
(*a*) Standard deviation is always positive.
(*b*) Standard deviation is a measure of central tendency.
(*c*) Larger standard deviation indicates a narrower spread of data.
(*d*) Standard deviation is insensitive to outliers.

45. If a dataset has a high standard deviation, what does it indicate about the data?
(*a*) The data points are closely clustered around the mean.
(*b*) The data points are widely spread out from the mean.
(*c*) The data points are evenly distributed.
(*d*) The data points are symmetrically distributed.

46. What does skewness measure in a dataset?
(*a*) The spread of the data around the mean (*b*) The symmetry of the data distribution
(*c*) The presence of outliers in the data
(*d*) The degree of asymmetry in the data distribution

47. Which of the following statements is true regarding skewness?
(*a*) A positively skewed distribution has a longer left tail.

(*b*) Skewness is always zero in a symmetric distribution.
(*c*) A negatively skewed distribution has a longer right tail.
(*d*) Skewness measures the concentration of data around the mean.

48. What is kurtosis?
(*a*) A measure of the spread of the data around the mean
(*b*) A measure of the symmetry of the data distribution
(*c*) A measure of the concentration of data around the mean
(*d*) A measure of the peakedness or flatness of the data distribution

49. Which of the following indicates a leptokurtic distribution?
(*a*) Positive kurtosis
(*b*) Negative kurtosis
(*c*) Excess kurtosis of zero
(*d*) Excess kurtosis greater than zero

50. If a dataset has a positive kurtosis, what does it imply about the distribution?
(*a*) The distribution is platykurtic.
(*b*) The distribution is mesokurtic.
(*c*) The distribution has a heavy tail.
(*d*) The distribution is symmetric.

Answers

1. (*b*)	2. (*b*)	3. (*c*)	4. (*c*)	5. (*c*)	6. (*a*)	7. (*c*)	8. (*b*)	9. (*a*)
10. (*a*)	11. (*c*)	12. (*c*)	13. (*c*)	14. (*d*)	15. (*c*)	16. (*d*)	17. (*c*)	18. (*b*)
19. (*a*)	20. (*c*)	21. (*a*)	22. (*a*)	23. (*a*)	24. (*b*)	25. (*a*)	26. (*c*)	27. (*b*)
28. (*b*)	29. (*b*)	30. (*b*)	31. (*d*)	32. (*c*)	33. (*d*)	34. (*c*)	35. (*d*)	36. (*c*)
37. (*d*)	38. (*a*)	39. (*d*)	40. (*a*)	41. (*c*)	42. (*a*)	43. (*c*)	44. (*a*)	45. (*b*)
46. (*d*)	47. (*c*)	48. (*d*)	49. (*d*)	50. (*c*)				

❑❑❑

CHAPTER 2

1. **What is machine learning?**
   (*a*) The process of designing algorithms to perform a specific task without explicit programming.
   (*b*) The study of human cognition and decision-making processes.
   (*c*) The development of hardware systems capable of autonomous decision-making.
   (*d*) The application of mechanical engineering principles to software development.

2. **What is supervised learning?**
   (*a*) Learning from labeled data with predefined input-output pairs.
   (*b*) Learning from unstructured data without any guidance.
   (*c*) Learning from rewards or punishments in a dynamic environment.
   (*d*) Learning from human demonstrations and examples.

3. **Which algorithm is commonly used for regression tasks in machine learning?**
   (*a*) Support Vector Machine (SVM) (*b*) K-means clustering
   (*c*) Decision Tree (*d*) Linear Regression

4. **What is the primary goal of unsupervised learning?**
   (*a*) To predict future outcomes based on past data.
   (*b*) To classify data points into predefined categories.
   (*c*) To discover hidden patterns or structures in data.
   (*d*) To optimize decision-making processes using reinforcement signals.

5. **What is overfitting in machine learning?**
   (*a*) When a model performs well on training data but poorly on unseen data.
   (*b*) When a model performs poorly on both training and test data.
   (*c*) When a model cannot capture the complexity of the data.
   (*d*) When a model converges too quickly during training.

6. **Which evaluation metric is commonly used for classification tasks in machine learning?**
   (*a*) Mean Absolute Error (MAE) (*b*) Root Mean Squared Error (RMSE)
   (*c*) Accuracy (*d*) R-squared (R^2)

7. **What is reinforcement learning?**
   (*a*) Learning from labeled data with predefined input-output pairs.
   (*b*) Learning from unstructured data without any guidance.
   (*c*) Learning from rewards or punishments in a dynamic environment.
   (*d*) Learning from human demonstrations and examples.

8. **Which algorithm is commonly used for sequential data analysis, such as time series forecasting or natural language processing?**
   (*a*) Random Forest (*b*) Recurrent Neural Network (RNN)
   (*c*) K-nearest neighbors (KNN) (*d*) Principal Component Analysis (PCA)

9. What is the purpose of feature engineering in machine learning?

(*a*) To automate the process of data collection.
(*b*) To optimize the learning algorithm's performance.
(*c*) To preprocess raw data into a format suitable for machine learning models.
(*d*) To visualize the relationships between variables in the dataset.

10. Which of the following is NOT a category of machine learning algorithms?

(*a*) Supervised Learning
(*b*) Unsupervised Learning
(*c*) Reinforcement Learning
(*d*) Rule-based Learning

11. Which programming language is widely used for implementing machine learning algorithms and deep learning models?

(*a*) Java (*b*) C++ (*c*) Python (*d*) MATLAB

12. What is TensorFlow?

(*a*) A programming language specifically designed for machine learning.
(*b*) An open-source machine learning framework developed by Google.
(*c*) A cloud-based machine learning platform provided by Amazon Web Services.
(*d*) A statistical computing environment for data analysis.

13. Which of the following is a popular deep learning library built on top of TensorFlow?

(*a*) SciPy (*b*) Theano (*c*) Keras (*d*) Pandas

14. What is PyTorch?

(*a*) A Python library for numerical computation and machine learning.
(*b*) An open-source deep learning platform developed by Facebook.
(*c*) A high-level programming language for machine learning.
(*d*) A cloud-based machine learning service provided by Microsoft Azure.

15. Which of the following is a popular visualization tool used for analyzing and interpreting machine learning models?

(*a*) Jupyter Notebook
(*b*) Matplotlib
(*c*) NumPy
(*d*) TensorFlow Playground

16. What is scikit-learn?

(*a*) A Python library for machine learning built on top of TensorFlow.
(*b*) An open-source machine learning library for numerical computation.
(*c*) A cloud-based machine learning platform provided by Google Cloud.
(*d*) A programming language specifically designed for statistical analysis.

17. What role does Docker play in machine learning development?

(*a*) Docker is a deep learning framework similar to TensorFlow and PyTorch.
(*b*) Docker is a cloud-based machine learning service provided by Microsoft Azure.
(*c*) Docker is a platform for packaging, distributing, and running machine learning applications in isolated environments.
(*d*) Docker is a visualization tool for analyzing machine learning models.

18. What is NVIDIA CUDA used for in machine learning?

(*a*) NVIDIA CUDA is a programming language specifically designed for machine learning.
(*b*) NVIDIA CUDA is a deep learning framework similar to TensorFlow and PyTorch.
(*c*) NVIDIA CUDA is a cloud-based machine learning service provided by NVIDIA.
(*d*) NVIDIA CUDA is a parallel computing platform and programming model used to accelerate deep learning computations on NVIDIA GPUs.

19. What is AutoML?

(*a*) A machine learning technique for automatically generating code from high-level specifications.
(*b*) An open-source machine learning library developed by the Apache Software Foundation.
(*c*) A cloud-based machine learning platform provided by Google Cloud.
(*d*) A set of techniques for automating the process of model selection, hyperparameter tuning, and feature engineering.

20. Which of the following is NOT a cloud platform commonly used for deploying machine learning models?

(*a*) Google Cloud Platform (GCP) (*b*) Amazon Web Services (AWS)
(*c*) Microsoft Excel (*d*) Microsoft Azure

21. What is the primary goal of data preprocessing in machine learning?

(*a*) To increase the complexity of the model (*b*) To decrease the size of the dataset
(*c*) To transform raw data into a format suitable for machine learning algorithms
(*d*) To reduce the dimensionality of the dataset

22. What is feature selection in machine learning?

(*a*) The process of generating new features from existing ones
(*b*) The process of removing irrelevant or redundant features from the dataset
(*c*) The process of scaling numerical features to a similar range
(*d*) The process of encoding categorical variables into numerical format

23. What is model training in machine learning?

(*a*) The process of evaluating the performance of a trained model
(*b*) The process of selecting the appropriate machine learning algorithm
(*c*) The process of adjusting the parameters of a model to minimize error on the training data
(*d*) The process of splitting the dataset into training and testing sets

24. What is hyperparameter tuning in machine learning?

(*a*) The process of selecting the best features for the model
(*b*) The process of optimizing the parameters of the machine learning algorithm
(*c*) The process of preprocessing the data before training the model
(*d*) The process of selecting the best model architecture

25. What is model evaluation in machine learning?

(*a*) The process of training the model on the entire dataset
(*b*) The process of assessing the performance of the trained model on unseen data

(*c*) The process of selecting the best model based on validation metrics
(*d*) The process of visualizing the decision boundaries of the model

26. What is model deployment in machine learning?
(*a*) The process of training the model on new data
(*b*) The process of integrating the trained model into a production environment
(*c*) The process of fine-tuning the model parameters
(*d*) The process of visualizing the model's predictions

27. What is model interpretation in machine learning?
(*a*) The process of explaining the predictions made by the model
(*b*) The process of optimizing the model's hyperparameters
(*c*) The process of visualizing the model's decision boundaries
(*d*) The process of evaluating the model's performance on unseen data

28. What is model monitoring in machine learning?
(*a*) The process of evaluating the performance of the model over time
(*b*) The process of selecting the best model architecture
(*c*) The process of preprocessing the data before training the model
(*d*) The process of training the model on new data

29. What is transfer learning in machine learning?
(*a*) The process of transferring knowledge from one machine learning model to another
(*b*) The process of transferring features learned from one task to another related task
(*c*) The process of transferring data from one dataset to another
(*d*) The process of transferring the trained model to a production environment

30. What is ensemble learning in machine learning?
(*a*) The process of training multiple models independently and combining their predictions
(*b*) The process of training a single model on multiple datasets
(*c*) The process of training a single model with multiple hidden layers
(*d*) The process of training a model using an ensemble of hyperparameters

31. What is categorical data in machine learning?
(*a*) Data that represents numerical values.
(*b*) Data that consists of labels or categories.
(*c*) Data that measures the frequency of occurrences.
(*d*) Data that describes relationships between variables.

32. Which of the following is an example of categorical data?
(*a*) Temperature in degrees Celsius
(*b*) Height in meters
(*c*) Colors (e.g., red, blue, green)
(*d*) Stock prices

33. What is numerical data in machine learning?
(*a*) Data that consists of labels or categories.
(*b*) Data that represents numerical values.
(*c*) Data that measures the frequency of occurrences.
(*d*) Data that describes relationships between variables.

34. Which of the following is an example of numerical data?

(*a*) Gender (e.g., male, female)
(*b*) Age in years
(*c*) Country of residence
(*d*) Product categories (e.g., electronics, clothing)

35. What is ordinal data in machine learning?

(*a*) Data that consists of labels or categories.
(*b*) Data that represents numerical values.
(*c*) Data that measures the frequency of occurrences.
(*d*) Data that has a natural ordering or ranking.

36. Which of the following is an example of ordinal data?

(*a*) Temperature in degrees Celsius
(*b*) Rank of students in a class (e.g., 1st, 2nd, 3rd)
(*c*) Colors (e.g., red, blue, green)
(*d*) Stock prices

37. What is nominal data in machine learning?

(*a*) Data that consists of labels or categories.
(*b*) Data that represents numerical values.
(*c*) Data that measures the frequency of occurrences.
(*d*) Data that has a natural ordering or ranking.

38. Which of the following is an example of nominal data?

(*a*) Age in years
(*b*) Height in meters
(*c*) Gender (e.g., male, female)
(*d*) Income level

39. What is count data in machine learning?

(*a*) Data that consists of labels or categories.
(*b*) Data that represents numerical values.
(*c*) Data that measures the frequency of occurrences.
(*d*) Data that describes relationships between variables.

40. Which of the following is an example of count data?

(*a*) Temperature in degrees Celsius
(*b*) Number of students in a classroom
(*c*) Country of residence
(*d*) Stock prices

41. What is the primary purpose of a histogram?

(*a*) To display the distribution of categorical variables
(*b*) To compare the means of different datasets
(*c*) To show the relationship between two continuous variables
(*d*) To visualize the frequency distribution of a single continuous variable

42. Which of the following best describes a box plot?

(*a*) A graphical representation of the mean and standard deviation of a dataset
(*b*) A visualization of the frequency distribution of a single continuous variable
(*c*) A summary of the five-number summary: minimum, first quartile, median, third quartile, and maximum
(*d*) A plot showing the correlation between two continuous variables

43. In a box plot, what does the length of the box represent?

(*a*) The range of the dataset
(*b*) The interquartile range (IQR)
(*c*) The mean of the dataset
(*d*) The standard deviation of the dataset

44. What does the central line in a box plot represent?
(*a*) The median of the dataset
(*b*) The mean of the dataset
(*c*) The mode of the dataset
(*d*) The first quartile of the dataset

45. In a histogram, what does the height of each bar represent?
(*a*) The frequency of data within each bin or interval
(*b*) The range of the dataset
(*c*) The standard deviation of the dataset
(*d*) The median of the dataset

46. What type of data is most suitable for visualization using a histogram?
(*a*) Categorical data
(*b*) Discrete data
(*c*) Continuous data
(*d*) Ordinal data

47. How many peaks can a histogram have?
(*a*) One
(*b*) Two
(*c*) Three
(*d*) Any number

48. What does the width of each bar in a histogram represent?
(*a*) The range of the dataset
(*b*) The interquartile range (IQR)
(*c*) The bin width or interval size
(*d*) The standard deviation of the dataset

49. Which of the following statements about outliers in box plots is true?
(*a*) Outliers are always displayed as individual data points outside the whiskers.
(*b*) Outliers are data points that fall within the interquartile range (IQR).
(*c*) Outliers can indicate potential errors or unusual observations in the dataset.
(*d*) Outliers have no impact on the interpretation of box plots.

50. How do box plots and histograms differ in terms of their visual representation?
(*a*) Box plots provide summary statistics, while histograms display raw data.
(*b*) Box plots show frequency distributions, while histograms summarize data distributions.
(*c*) Box plots visualize continuous data, while histograms are used for categorical data.
(*d*) Box plots and histograms represent the same type of data in different ways.

51. What is data remediation?
(*a*) The process of collecting raw data from various sources.
(*b*) The process of identifying and resolving issues in existing datasets.
(*c*) The process of transforming raw data into a structured format.
(*d*) The process of analyzing data to extract meaningful insights.

52. Which of the following is NOT a common issue addressed during data remediation?
(*a*) Missing data
(*b*) Duplicate records
(*c*) Data encryption
(*d*) Inconsistent formatting

53. Why is data remediation important in data management?
(*a*) To enhance data security
(*b*) To improve data visualization
(*c*) To ensure data quality and accuracy
(*d*) To increase data storage capacity

54. Which step typically follows data identification in the data remediation process?
(*a*) Data extraction
(*b*) Data cleansing
(*c*) Data validation
(*d*) Data analysis

55. What is the primary goal of data cleansing during data remediation?
(*a*) To collect data from various sources
(*b*) To transform raw data into a structured format
(*c*) To remove errors and inconsistencies from datasets
(*d*) To analyze data for patterns and trends

56. What is dimensionality reduction?
(*a*) The process of increasing the number of features in a dataset.
(*b*) The process of decreasing the number of features in a dataset while preserving its essential information.
(*c*) The process of transforming categorical variables into numerical ones.
(*d*) The process of splitting a dataset into training and testing subsets.

57. Which of the following is a primary reason for using dimensionality reduction techniques?
(*a*) To increase the complexity of machine learning models.
(*b*) To improve the interpretability of the data.
(*c*) To reduce computational costs and storage requirements.
(*d*) To introduce noise into the dataset.

58. Which dimensionality reduction technique aims to find a lower-dimensional representation of the data while maximizing the variance?
(*a*) Principal Component Analysis (PCA) (*b*) Linear Discriminant Analysis (LDA)
(*c*) t-Distributed Stochastic Neighbor Embedding (t-SNE)
(*d*) Autoencoders

59. In PCA, what are the principal components?
(*a*) The features with the highest variance in the dataset.
(*b*) The components that maximize the separation between different classes.
(*c*) The orthogonal vectors that define the directions of maximum variance in the data.
(*d*) The dimensions with the least amount of information.

60. Which of the following is a potential drawback of dimensionality reduction techniques?
(*a*) Increased interpretability of the data. (*b*) Loss of information due to compression.
(*c*) Improved performance of machine learning models.
(*d*) Reduction in computational efficiency.

Answers

1. (*a*)	2. (*a*)	3. (*d*)	4. (*c*)	5. (*a*)	6. (*c*)	7. (*c*)	8. (*b*)	9. (*c*)
10. (*d*)	11. (*c*)	12. (*b*)	13. (*c*)	14. (*b*)	15. (*b*)	16. (*a*)	17. (*c*)	18. (*d*)
19. (*d*)	20. (*c*)	21. (*c*)	22. (*b*)	23. (*c*)	24. (*b*)	25. (*b*)	26. (*b*)	27. (*a*)
28. (*a*)	29. (*b*)	30. (*a*)	31. (*b*)	32. (*c*)	33. (*b*)	34. (*b*)	35. (*d*)	36. (*b*)
37. (*a*)	38. (*c*)	39. (*c*)	40. (*b*)	41. (*d*)	42. (*c*)	43. (*b*)	44. (*a*)	45. (*a*)
46. (*c*)	47. (*d*)	48. (*c*)	49. (*c*)	50. (*a*)	51. (*b*)	52. (*c*)	53. (*c*)	54. (*b*)
55. (*c*)	56. (*b*)	57. (*c*)	58. (*a*)	59. (*c*)	60. (*b*)			

CHAPTER 3

1. **What is the primary objective of linear regression?**
   (a) Minimize the sum of squared errors
   (b) Maximize the correlation coefficient
   (c) Minimize the absolute errors
   (d) Maximize the R-squared value
2. **Which of the following assumptions is NOT required for linear regression?**
   (a) Linearity
   (b) Homoscedasticity
   (c) Multicollinearity
   (d) Normality of residuals
3. **In a simple linear regression model, how many independent variables are there?**
   (a) One (b) Two (c) None (d) Depends on the data
4. **What is the range of values that the coefficient of determination (R-square (d) c a n take?**
   (a) [−1, 1] (b) [0, 1] (c) [0, ∞) (d) (−∞, ∞)
5. **In multiple linear regression, what does the term "multicollinearity" refer to?**
   (a) High correlation between independent variables
   (b) Low correlation between independent variables
   (c) Perfect prediction of the dependent variable
   (d) High variance in the residuals
6. **Which statistical test is used to assess the overall significance of a linear regression model?**
   (a) F-test (b) t-test (c) Chi-square test (d) Z-test
7. **What does the p-value associated with a coefficient in linear regression indicate?**
   (a) The probability of making a Type I error
   (b) The strength of the relationship between variables
   (c) The probability of observing the coefficient given that the null hypothesis is true
   (d) The confidence interval of the coefficient
8. **What is the name of the technique used to handle outliers in linear regression?**
   (a) Z-score normalization
   (b) Cook's distance
   (c) Leverage
   (d) Ridge regression
9. **Which of the following is a disadvantage of linear regression?**
   (a) Susceptible to overfitting
   (b) Cannot handle non-linear relationships
   (c) Requires large amounts of data
   (d) Limited to categorical variables
10. **What is the formula for the equation of a simple linear regression line?**
    (a) y = mx + c (b) y = c + mx (c) y = m/x + c (d) y = c – mx
11. **What does multiple regression analyze?**
    (a) Relationship between one dependent variable and one independent variable
    (b) Relationship between one dependent variable and multiple independent variables
    (c) Relationship between multiple dependent variables and one independent variable
    (d) Relationship between multiple dependent variables and multiple independent variables

12. In multiple regression, what is the dependent variable?
(*a*) Variable used to predict other variables (*b*) Variable being predicted
(*c*) Variable that has the most impact (*d*) Variable that has the least impact

13. What is the main goal of multiple regression analysis?
(*a*) To determine causality between variables
(*b*) To predict the value of the dependent variable based on independent variables
(*c*) To prove correlation between variables
(*d*) To identify outliers in the data

14. What is the term used to describe the difference between the observed value and the predicted value in multiple regression?
(*a*) Residual (*b*) Intercept (*c*) Slope (*d*) Coefficient

15. What is multicollinearity in the context of multiple regression?
(*a*) When there is no relationship between the independent and dependent variables
(*b*) When there is a strong relationship between the independent variables
(*c*) When there is a strong relationship between the dependent variables
(*d*) When there is a strong relationship between the dependent and independent variables

16. How is the goodness of fit of a multiple regression model typically measured?
(*a*) Mean Squared Error (MSE) (*b*) R-squared
(*c*) Standard Deviation (*d*) Coefficient of Determination

17. Which assumption of multiple regression states that the relationship between the independent and dependent variables is linear?
(*a*) Normality (*b*) Independence (*c*) Homoscedasticity (*d*) Linearity

18. What is the purpose of residual analysis in multiple regression?
(*a*) To identify influential data points
(*b*) To determine the strength of the relationship between variables
(*c*) To check for violations of regression assumptions
(*d*) To calculate the standard error of the regression

19. In multiple regression, what does the coefficient of determination (R-squared) measure?
(*a*) The strength of the relationship between the independent variables
(*b*) The percentage of variance in the dependent variable explained by the independent variables
(*c*) The significance of the independent variables
(*d*) The standard error of the regression

20. When conducting multiple regression analysis, what does a p-value indicate?
(*a*) The strength of the relationship between variables
(*b*) The significance of the coefficient (*c*) The accuracy of the prediction
(*d*) The presence of multicollinearity

21. What is the purpose of a likelihood function in statistical inference?
(*a*) To measure the probability of observing the data given a specific parameter value.

(*b*) To measure the probability of observing a specific parameter value given the data.
(*c*) To calculate the cost associated with parameter estimation.
(*d*) To estimate the parameters directly.

22. Which of the following is true regarding the likelihood function?
(*a*) It is used to estimate parameters directly.
(*b*) It is a probability density function of the parameters given the data.
(*c*) It is a measure of the probability of the observed data given the parameters.
(*d*) It is always symmetric around the maximum likelihood estimate.

23. In parameter estimation, what does the cost function represent?
(*a*) The likelihood of observing the data.
(*b*) The probability distribution of the parameters.
(*c*) The measure of accuracy in estimating parameters.
(*d*) The computational complexity of the estimation process.

24. Which optimization technique is commonly used to minimize the cost function in parameter estimation?
(*a*) Gradient Descent
(*b*) Random Search
(*c*) Evolutionary Algorithms
(*d*) None of the above

25. What is the goal of parameter estimation in statistical modeling?
(*a*) To maximize the likelihood function.
(*b*) To minimize the cost function.
(*c*) To find the parameters that best explain the observed data.
(*d*) To achieve a perfect fit between the model and the data.

26. Which of the following statements is true about maximum likelihood estimation (MLE)?
(*a*) MLE aims to maximize the likelihood of observing the data.
(*b*) MLE always guarantees unbiased estimates of parameters.
(*c*) MLE is only applicable to linear models.
(*d*) MLE requires the assumption of a normal distribution.

27. How is the cost function related to the likelihood function in parameter estimation?
(*a*) The cost function is another name for the likelihood function.
(*b*) The cost function is the negative logarithm of the likelihood function.
(*c*) The cost function is the reciprocal of the likelihood function.
(*d*) There is no relationship between the two.

28. Which parameter estimation method is robust to outliers in the data?
(*a*) Maximum Likelihood Estimation (MLE)
(*b*) Ordinary Least Squares (OLS)
(*c*) Maximum A Posteriori (MAP) estimation
(*d*) Regularization techniques

29. In Bayesian parameter estimation, what is the role of the prior distribution?
(*a*) It represents the probability of observing the data given the parameters.
(*b*) It represents the likelihood of the parameters given the data.
(*c*) It represents the prior knowledge or belief about the parameters before observing the data.
(*d*) It measures the cost associated with parameter estimation.

30. Which of the following is a drawback of using maximum likelihood estimation (MLE)?

(*a*) It doesn't provide a measure of uncertainty in parameter estimates.
(*b*) It always requires large amounts of computational resources.
(*c*) It is highly sensitive to outliers in the data.
(*d*) It tends to overfit the data.

31. What is the primary objective of Maximum Likelihood Estimation (MLE) in the context of Gaussian noise?

(*a*) To minimize the mean squared error
(*b*) To maximize the likelihood of observing the given data
(*c*) To minimize the variance of the estimator
(*d*) To maximize the mean of the observed data

32. In the case of Gaussian noise, what is typically assumed about the likelihood function?

(*a*) It follows a uniform distribution
(*b*) It follows a Gaussian distribution
(*c*) It follows a Poisson distribution
(*d*) It follows an exponential distribution

33. Which parameter(s) of a Gaussian distribution is/are typically estimated using MLE?

(*a*) Mean only
(*b*) Variance only
(*c*) Both mean and variance
(*d*) Skewness and kurtosis

34. What is the logarithm of the likelihood function often used for in MLE?

(*a*) To simplify the calculation of likelihood
(*b*) To make the likelihood function Gaussian
(*c*) To maximize the likelihood easily
(*d*) To handle numerical stability issues

35. Which statistical property ensures that maximizing the likelihood function is equivalent to minimizing the mean squared error in the case of Gaussian noise?

(*a*) Unbiasedness
(*b*) Consistency
(*c*) Efficiency
(*d*) Gauss-Markov theorem

36. What is the main advantage of using MLE for estimating parameters in the presence of Gaussian noise?

(*a*) It always provides unbiased estimates
(*b*) It is computationally less expensive than other methods
(*c*) It provides asymptotically efficient estimates
(*d*) It is robust to outliers

37. In the context of MLE with Gaussian noise, what happens to the estimator's distribution as the sample size increases?

(*a*) It becomes skewed
(*b*) It becomes uniform
(*c*) It becomes Gaussian
(*d*) It becomes bimodal

38. Which of the following is a common technique used to estimate the parameters of a Gaussian distribution using MLE?

(*a*) Gradient Descent
(*b*) Expectation-Maximization
(*c*) Principal Component Analysis
(*d*) K-means Clustering

39. What does the term "maximum likelihood" refer to in Maximum Likelihood Estimation?

(*a*) The likelihood of observing the maximum value in the dataset
(*b*) The maximum value of the likelihood function
(*c*) The likelihood of observing the given data under the estimated parameters
(*d*) The likelihood of observing the minimum value in the dataset

Answers

1. (*a*)	2. (*c*)	3. (*a*)	4. (*b*)	5. (*a*)	6. (*a*)	7. (*c*)	8. (*b*)	9. (*b*)
10. (*a*)	11. (*b*)	12. (*b*)	13. (*b*)	14. (*a*)	15. (*b*)	16. (*b*)	17. (*d*)	18. (*c*)
19. (*b*)	20. (*b*)	21. (*a*)	22. (*c*)	23. (*c*)	24. (*a*)	25. (*c*)	26. (*a*)	27. (*b*)
28. (*d*)	29. (*c*)	30. (*a*)	31. (*b*)	32. (*b*)	33. (*c*)	34. (*d*)	35. (*b*)	36. (*c*)
37. (*c*)	38. (*b*)	39. (*c*)						

CHAPTER 4

1. **What is the primary objective of logistic regression?**
   (*a*) To predict continuous outcomes (*b*) To classify data into two or more categories
   (*c*) To estimate the mean of a response variable (*d*) To perform dimensionality reduction

2. **In logistic regression, what type of function is used to model the relationship between the independent variables and the probability of a binary outcome?**
   (*a*) Linear function (*b*) Exponential function
   (*c*) Logistic function (*d*) Polynomial function

3. **What is the name of the logistic function used in logistic regression?**
   (*a*) Sigmoid function (*b*) Step function
   (*c*) Hyperbolic tangent function (*d*) Exponential function

4. **Which technique is commonly used to estimate the parameters (coefficients) of logistic regression?**
   (*a*) Ordinary Least Squares (OLS) (*b*) Maximum Likelihood Estimation (MLE)
   (*c*) Principal Component Analysis (PCA) (*d*) Singular Value Decomposition (SVD)

5. **In logistic regression, what is the name of the equation used to calculate the log-odds of the event occurring?**
   (*a*) Logit function (*b*) Odds ratio (*c*) Logistic equation (*d*) Probability function

6. **What is the range of the predicted probabilities in logistic regression?**
   (*a*) $[-\infty, +\infty]$ (*b*) $[0, 1]$ (*c*) $[0, +\infty]$ (*d*) $[0.5, 1]$

7. **What is the purpose of the link function in logistic regression?**
   (*a*) To link independent variables to dependent variables
   (*b*) To transform the response variable into a binary outcome
   (*c*) To linearly combine the independent variables
   (*d*) To connect the linear combination of predictors to the probability of the outcome

8. **Which algorithm is commonly used to optimize the parameters (coefficients) of logistic regression?**
   (*a*) Gradient Descent (*b*) K-nearest neighbors
   (*c*) Random Forest (*d*) Support Vector Machine

9. **In logistic regression, what is the purpose of the threshold value?**
   (*a*) To determine the number of iterations during optimization
   (*b*) To define the learning rate for the algorithm
   (*c*) To classify predicted probabilities into discrete classes
   (*d*) To control the complexity of the model

10. **Which evaluation metric is commonly used to assess the performance of logistic regression models?**
    (*a*) Mean Absolute Error (MAE) (*b*) Mean Squared Error (MSE)

(*c*) Area Under the Receiver Operating Characteristic (ROc) Curve (AUC-ROC)
(*d*) R-squared (R^2)

11. What is the primary objective of Maximum Likelihood Estimation (MLE) in logistic regression?
(*a*) Minimize the mean squared error
(*b*) Maximize the likelihood of observing the given data
(*c*) Minimize the classification error
(*d*) Maximize the variance of the estimator

12. In logistic regression, what type of function is used to model the relationship between the independent variables and the probability of a binary outcome?
(*a*) Sigmoid function
(*b*) Linear function
(*c*) Exponential function
(*d*) Polynomial function

13. Which algorithm is commonly used to optimize the parameters in logistic regression?
(*a*) Linear Regression
(*b*) Gradient Descent
(*c*) K-nearest Neighbors
(*d*) Decision Trees

14. What role does the learning rate play in the Gradient Descent algorithm?
(*a*) It determines the size of each step in the optimization process
(*b*) It determines the number of iterations required for convergence
(*c*) It controls the bias-variance tradeoff
(*d*) It adjusts the regularization parameter

15. In Gradient Descent, what happens if the learning rate is too small?
(*a*) The algorithm converges slowly
(*b*) The algorithm may fail to converge
(*c*) The algorithm converges quickly
(*d*) The algorithm becomes more prone to overfitting

16. What is overfitting in the context of logistic regression?
(*a*) The model captures noise in the training data
(*b*) The model performs well on the training data but poorly on unseen data
(*c*) The model fails to capture important patterns in the data
(*d*) The model converges too quickly during training

17. Which technique can help prevent overfitting in logistic regression?
(*a*) Decreasing the regularization parameter
(*b*) Increasing the learning rate
(*c*) Adding more features to the model
(*d*) Early stopping during training

18. What does the regularization term in logistic regression aim to penalize?
(*a*) Large coefficients
(*b*) Small coefficients
(*c*) The intercept term
(*d*) The learning rate

19. Which type of regularization technique is commonly used in logistic regression?
(*a*) L1 regularization
(*b*) L2 regularization
(*c*) Dropout regularization
(*d*) Elastic Net regularization

20. How does L1 regularization differ from L2 regularization?
(*a*) L1 regularization penalizes the square of the coefficients
(*b*) L1 regularization shrinks coefficients toward zero more aggressively
(*c*) L1 regularization is computationally more expensive
(*d*) L1 regularization is not suitable for logistic regression

21. Which statement about the cost function in logistic regression is correct?
(*a*) It is convex (*b*) It is linear
(*c*) It is concave (*d*) It has no global minimum

22. What happens to the cost function in logistic regression when overfitting occurs?
(*a*) It decreases (*b*) It increases
(*c*) It remains constant (*d*) It becomes non-convex

23. What is the purpose of adding polynomial features to logistic regression?
(*a*) To reduce model complexity (*b*) To decrease the training time
(*c*) To capture nonlinear relationships between features
(*d*) To increase the bias of the model

24. What effect does increasing the regularization parameter have on the decision boundary in logistic regression?
(*a*) It makes the decision boundary more complex
(*b*) It moves the decision boundary away from the data points
(*c*) It makes the decision boundary less sensitive to outliers
(*d*) It makes the decision boundary more sensitive to outliers

25. Which evaluation metric is commonly used to assess the performance of a logistic regression model?
(*a*) Mean Squared Error (MSE) (*b*) Accuracy
(*c*) R-squared (*d*) F1-score

26. What is the primary disadvantage of using Gradient Descent for optimizing logistic regression parameters?
(*a*) It requires the calculation of second-order derivatives
(*b*) It can get stuck in local minima (*c*) It is computationally expensive
(*d*) It is not suitable for high-dimensional data

27. In logistic regression, what does the decision boundary represent?
(*a*) The line that separates the classes in feature space
(*b*) The line that connects the centroids of the classes
(*c*) The line that minimizes the classification error
(*d*) The line that maximizes the margin between classes

28. Which statement about the log-likelihood function in logistic regression is correct?
(*a*) It is always concave (*b*) It is always convex
(*c*) It has multiple local maxima (*d*) It has a closed-form solution

29. What is the purpose of cross-validation in logistic regression?
(*a*) To estimate the generalization error of the model
(*b*) To increase the variance of the model (*c*) To reduce the bias of the model
(*d*) To optimize the learning rate

30. Which technique can be used to handle class imbalance in logistic regression?
(*a*) Oversampling the minority class (*b*) Undersampling the majority class
(*c*) Adjusting the decision threshold (*d*) Both A and B

31. In multiclass classification, how many classes are there?
(*a*) Two (*b*) More than two
(*c*) Exactly three (*d*) None, it's the same as binary classification

32. What is the primary difference between multiclass and binary classification?
(*a*) Multiclass involves only two classes, while binary involves more than two.
(*b*) Binary classification deals with multiple classes simultaneously, while multiclass focuses on one class at a time.
(*c*) Multiclass deals with more than two classes, while binary deals with only two.
(*d*) There is no difference; they are interchangeable terms.

33. Which algorithm is commonly used for binary classification tasks?
(*a*) K-means (*b*) K-nearest neighbors (KNN)
(*c*) Logistic Regression (*d*) Decision Trees

34. In binary classification, what is the typical output format of a classifier?
(*a*) Probability distribution over multiple classes
(*b*) Decision boundaries
(*c*) Class labels such as "positive" and "negative"
(*d*) None of the above

35. How many decision boundaries are typically present in binary classification?
(*a*) One (*b*) Two (*c*) Three or more (*d*) None

36. Which evaluation metric is commonly used for assessing the performance of binary classifiers?
(*a*) Accuracy (*b*) F1-score (*c*) Confusion Matrix (*d*) ROC-AUC

37. What is one-hot encoding commonly used for in multiclass classification?
(*a*) Representing categorical variables as binary vectors
(*b*) Handling missing data (*c*) Reducing dimensionality
(*d*) Balancing class distributions

38. Which algorithm is commonly used for multiclass classification tasks?
(*a*) Support Vector Machines (SVM) (*b*) Naive Bayes
(*c*) Decision Trees (*d*) Random Forest

39. In multiclass classification, what is the typical output format of a classifier?
(*a*) Probability distribution over multiple classes

(*b*) Decision boundaries (*c*) Class labels for each instance
(*d*) None of the above

40. Which evaluation metric is commonly used for assessing the performance of multiclass classifiers?

(*a*) Area Under the Curve (AUC) (*b*) Precision-Recall Curve
(*c*) Mean Absolute Error (MAE) (*d*) Confusion Matrix

41. In a Bernoulli distribution, what does the parameter p represent?

(*a*) Mean (*b*) Variance
(*c*) Standard deviation (*d*) Probability of success

42. In hypothesis testing, what does the null hypothesis (H0) typically represent?

(*a*) The hypothesis we want to prove (*b*) The hypothesis we want to disprove
(*c*) The absence of an effect or relationship (*d*) The presence of an effect or relationship

43. What is the alternative hypothesis (H1) in hypothesis testing?

(*a*) It's the hypothesis we want to prove (*b*) It's the hypothesis we want to disprove
(*c*) It's the same as the null hypothesis (*d*) It's always true

44. What is the significance level (denoted as α) in hypothesis testing?

(*a*) The probability of rejecting the null hypothesis when it is true
(*b*) The probability of accepting the null hypothesis when it is false
(*c*) The probability of making a Type II error (*d*) The probability of making a Type I error

45. In hypothesis testing, what is Type I error?

(*a*) Rejecting the null hypothesis when it is true
(*b*) Accepting the null hypothesis when it is false
(*c*) Rejecting the alternative hypothesis when it is true
(*d*) Accepting the alternative hypothesis when it is false

46. In hypothesis testing, what is Type II error?

(*a*) Accepting the null hypothesis when it is true
(*b*) Rejecting the null hypothesis when it is false
(*c*) Accepting the alternative hypothesis when it is true
(*d*) Rejecting the alternative hypothesis when it is false

47. What is the critical region in hypothesis testing?

(*a*) The region where the null hypothesis is accepted
(*b*) The region where the null hypothesis is rejected
(*c*) The region where the alternative hypothesis is accepted
(*d*) The region where the alternative hypothesis is rejected

48. What is the test statistic used in hypothesis testing?

(*a*) A parameter of the population
(*b*) A random variable calculated from the sample
(*c*) The p-value (*d*) The significance level

49. What is the test statistic typically compared to in hypothesis testing?
(*a*) The null hypothesis (*b*) The alternative hypothesis
(*c*) The population mean (*d*) The sample mean

50. Which distribution is often used to approximate the distribution of the test statistic under the null hypothesis in hypothesis testing?
(*a*) Normal distribution (*b*) Binomial distribution
(*c*) Poisson distribution (*d*) Exponential distribution

51. How do you make a decision in hypothesis testing based on the p-value?
(*a*) If p-value < 0.05, reject null hypothesis (*b*) If p-value < 0.05, accept null hypothesis
(*c*) If p-value > 0.05, reject null hypothesis (*d*) If p-value > 0.05, accept null hypothesis

52. What does a smaller p-value indicate in hypothesis testing?
(*a*) Stronger evidence against the null hypothesis
(*b*) Weaker evidence against the null hypothesis
(*c*) Stronger evidence for the null hypothesis
(*d*) No evidence against the null hypothesis

53. What is the power of a statistical test?
(*a*) The probability of making a Type I error (*b*) The probability of making a Type II error
(*c*) The probability of correctly rejecting the null hypothesis
(*d*) The probability of incorrectly accepting the null hypothesis

Answers

1. (*b*)	2. (*c*)	3. (*a*)	4. (*b*)	5. (*a*)	6. (*b*)	7. (*d*)	8. (*a*)	9. (*c*)
10. (*c*)	11. (*b*)	12. (*a*)	13. (*b*)	14. (*a*)	15. (*a*)	16. (*b*)	17. (*a*)	18. (*a*)
19. (*b*)	20. (*b*)	21. (*a*)	22. (*b*)	23. (*c*)	24. (*b*)	25. (*d*)	26. (*b*)	27. (*a*)
28. (*a*)	29. (*a*)	30. (*d*)	31. (*b*)	32. (*c*)	33. (*c*)	34. (*c*)	35. (*a*)	36. (*a*)
37. (*a*)	38. (*d*)	39. (*c*)	40. (*d*)	41. (*d*)	42. (*c*)	43. (*a*)	44. (*d*)	45. (*a*)
46. (*c*)	47. (*d*)	48. (*b*)	49. (*a*)	50. (*a*)	51. (*a*)	52. (*a*)	53. (*c*)	

CHAPTER 5

1. What is the primary objective of clustering algorithms?

(*a*) Supervised classification (*b*) Dimensionality reduction
(*c*) Identifying natural groupings in data (*d*) Anomaly detection

2. Which of the following clustering algorithms is a density-based approach?

(*a*) K-means (*b*) Hierarchical clustering
(*c*) DBSCAN (*d*) Expectation-Maximization

3. In K-means clustering, what does the "K" represent?

(*a*) Number of clusters (*b*) Number of dimensions
(*c*) Number of data points (*d*) Number of iterations

4. Which of the following statements about K-means clustering is true?

(*a*) It always converges to the global optimum.
(*b*) It requires the number of clusters (K) to be specified in advance.
(*c*) It is a density-based clustering algorithm.
(*d*) It is robust to outliers.

5. What is the main disadvantage of K-means clustering?

(*a*) Sensitivity to initialization (*b*) Inability to handle non-linear clusters
(*c*) High computational complexity
(*d*) Difficulty in determining the number of clusters

6. Which of the following clustering algorithms is agglomerative?

(*a*) K-means (*b*) DBSCAN
(*c*) Hierarchical clustering (*d*) OPTICS

7. What is the linkage criterion used in hierarchical clustering?

(*a*) Silhouette coefficient (*b*) Dunn index
(*c*) Distance between clusters (*d*) Davies-Bouldin index

8. Which of the following is not a common distance metric used in clustering?

(*a*) Euclidean distance (*b*) Manhattan distance
(*c*) Mahalanobis distance (*d*) Pearson correlation coefficient

9. Which clustering algorithm does not require the user to specify the number of clusters in advance?

(*a*) K-means (*b*) DBSCAN
(*c*) Hierarchical clustering (*d*) Spectral clustering

10. What does DBSCAN stand for?

(*a*) Density-Based Spatial Clustering of Applications with Noise
(*b*) Distance-Based Spatial Clustering of Applications with Noise
(*c*) Density-Based Sampling Clustering Algorithm with Noise
(*d*) Distance-Based Sampling Clustering Algorithm with Noise

11. **In DBSCAN, what are the two parameters that need to be specified?**
    (*a*) Number of clusters and cluster size
    (*b*) Radius of neighborhood and minimum number of points
    (*c*) Number of iterations and convergence threshold
    (*d*) Learning rate and momentum

12. **Which of the following statements about DBSCAN is true?**
    (*a*) It assumes that clusters have a spherical shape.
    (*b*) It is sensitive to the order of data points.
    (*c*) It cannot identify noise points.
    (*d*) It can handle clusters of arbitrary shape.

13. **Which clustering algorithm is known for its ability to discover clusters of varying sizes and shapes?**
    (*a*) K-means (*b*) Hierarchical clustering
    (*c*) DBSCAN (*d*) Spectral clustering

14. **Which of the following statements about hierarchical clustering is true?**
    (*a*) It is computationally efficient for large datasets.
    (*b*) It requires the number of clusters to be specified in advance.
    (*c*) It produces a partition of the dataset into disjoint clusters.
    (*d*) It is sensitive to the initial choice of cluster centroids.

15. **What is the main advantage of hierarchical clustering?**
    (*a*) It is computationally efficient for large datasets.
    (*b*) It does not require the number of clusters to be specified in advance.
    (*c*) It is robust to outliers.
    (*d*) It can handle high-dimensional data.

16. **What is the time complexity of the single linkage hierarchical clustering algorithm?**
    (*a*) O(n) (*b*) O(n log n) (*c*) O(n^2 log n) (*d*) O(n^3)

17. **Which of the following is a drawback of hierarchical clustering?**
    (*a*) It cannot handle noisy data.
    (*b*) It is sensitive to the choice of distance metric.
    (*c*) It requires the number of clusters to be specified in advance.
    (*d*) It cannot handle large datasets.

18. **What is the main limitation of agglomerative hierarchical clustering?**
    (*a*) It cannot handle non-linear clusters.
    (*b*) It is computationally expensive for large datasets.
    (*c*) It requires the number of clusters to be specified in advance.
    (*d*) It is sensitive to the order of data points.

19. **Which of the following is not a step in the K-means clustering algorithm?**
    (*a*) Initialization (*b*) Assignment (*c*) Splitting (*d*) Update

20. What is the objective function optimized by the K-means algorithm?

(*a*) Silhouette coefficient (*b*) Dunn index

(*c*) Within-cluster sum of squares (*d*) Davies-Bouldin index

21. What is the drawback of the K-means algorithm with respect to initialization?

(*a*) It is sensitive to the order of data points.

(*b*) It requires the number of clusters to be specified in advance.

(*c*) It may converge to a local optimum depending on initialization.

(*d*) It cannot handle clusters of varying sizes and shapes.

22. Which of the following statements about the K-means algorithm is true?

(*a*) It is guaranteed to converge to the global optimum.

(*b*) It produces a hierarchical clustering of the dataset.

(*c*) It is robust to outliers.

(*d*) It assumes that clusters have a Gaussian distribution.

Answers

1. (*c*)	2. (*c*)	3. (*a*)	4. (*b*)	5. (*d*)	6. (*c*)	7. (*c*)	8. (*d*)	9. (*b*)
10. (*a*)	11. (*b*)	12. (*d*)	13. (*c*)	14. (*c*)	15. (*b*)	16. (*c*)	17. (*d*)	18. (*b*)
19. (*c*)	20. (*c*)	21. (*c*)	22. (*d*)					